D1145167

# THE GUN, THE SHIP
# AND THE PEN

ALSO BY LINDA COLLEY

*In Defiance of Oligarchy: The Tory Party 1714–1760*

*Namier*

*Britons: Forging the Nation 1707–1837*

*Captives: Britain, Empire and the World, 1600–1850*

*The Ordeal of Elizabeth Marsh: A Woman in World History*

*Acts of Union and Disunion*

# THE GUN, THE SHIP AND THE PEN

### WARFARE, CONSTITUTIONS AND THE MAKING OF THE MODERN WORLD

LINDA COLLEY

P

PROFILE BOOKS

First published in Great Britain in 2021 by
Profile Books Ltd
29 Cloth Fair
London
ECIA 7JQ

www.profilebooks.com

1 3 5 7 9 10 8 6 4 2

Typeset in Dante by MacGuru Ltd
Printed and bound in Great Britain by
Clays Ltd, Elcograf S.p.A.

A CIP catalogue record for this book is available from the British Library.

ISBN 978 1 84668 497 5
eISBN 978 1 84765 926 2

In Memory of my Father
ROY COLLEY
And his Father
HARRY COLLEY
Lives Shaped by War

# CONTENTS

# INTRODUCTION

It was in Istanbul that Kang Youwei witnessed the transformation at work. Sixty years old, a philosopher and a reformer, he had been exiled from his native China on account of his politics, and was persistently on the move. Crossing into the heartland of the Ottoman empire that summer in 1908, he found himself in the midst of turmoil. Rumours had been circulating of a Russian and British takeover of Macedonia, part of Sultan Abdülhamid II's dominions. Viewing this as further proof of the inadequacies of their government, sections of the Ottoman army had rebelled. They wanted a parliament. Even more, they wanted a reinstatement of the empire's first written constitution, which had been implemented in 1876, but then swiftly withdrawn. Kang Youwei arrived in Istanbul on 27 July, the day these army rebels succeeded in getting the constitution formally restored. Pushing his way through the crowds, cut off by language, but not from the excitement, he watched as 'Half-moon flags hung, people drink, hit drums, sung songs together and danced. People were chanting long live, it did not stop day and night, streets, parks and everywhere were the same ... it is astonishing.' Writing later, he set down the essence of the rebel leaders' ultimatum to the sultan: 'They all bent down respectively and told [him] ... "Every country has a constitution, only Turkey first declared and then abolished it, so people are not satisfied. The ideas of soldiers have changed."'[1]

This episode speaks to themes that are central to this book. There is the prominence of military men in this constitutional crisis. There is the fact that it was precipitated by threats and fears of foreign aggression; and there is the behaviour of Kang Youwei himself. Wanting constitutional change in China, he nonetheless saw it as essential to pay close attention as well to political experiments and ideas in other sectors of the world. 'On the run for sixteen years', proclaimed this man's favourite personal seal: 'circling the globe three times, traversing four continents'.[2] Like other activists who feature in these pages, though to an extreme degree, Youwei took it for granted that a viable political constitution could not be the introspective creation of a single polity. Learning and borrowing from others was indispensable, a position that by the early twentieth century had become the norm.

But it is his account of the arguments used by these military rebels to face down the Ottoman sultan that is most striking. As Youwei tells it, these men insisted that – even among the empire's common soldiery – 'ideas' had 'changed'. They made a still more arresting assertion: that, by now – in 1908 – 'every country has a constitution'. To an important degree, these claims were substantially correct. Since the mid eighteenth century, new written constitutions had spread at an increasing rate across countries and continents. This had worked to shape and re-forge multiple political and legal systems. It had also altered and disrupted patterns of thought, cultural practices and mass expectations.

Collections of rules of government were nothing new, of course, but went back a long way. Some city states in ancient Greece had enacted them in the seventh century BCE. Codes of written laws emerged in different societies earlier still. Slabs of stone inscribed with the code of Hammurabi, ruler of Mesopotamia in what is now the Middle East, survive from before 1750 BCE. But such ancient texts were generally the work of single authors and potentates. Most were far more concerned to set out rules of conduct for subjects, and fearsome penalties for defying them, than to establish curbs on those in authority or provide for individual rights. Moreover, most early codes and collections were not produced in large numbers or designed for a wide audience. Even when law codes and charters began to be set down on parchment and paper, and levels of print and literacy expanded in some regions of the world, acute limits on circulation persisted. In 1759, the English jurist William Blackstone would complain of the continuing lack of a 'full and correct copy' of King John's Magna Carta, even though this was a celebrated charter and had emerged five centuries before.[3]

Yet, as this outburst of impatience on Blackstone's part suggests, by this stage, the situation was changing. From the 1750s, and in some particularly war-torn countries such as Sweden even before that, widely distributed iconic texts and single document constitutions aimed at constraining governments, and promising a variety of rights, became more numerous and more prominent. Thereafter, such documents proliferated exponentially and in connected waves across multiple frontiers. The quantum surge in the number of constitutions that followed the First World War, and still more the Second World War, lay in the future. Nonetheless, by 1914, devices of this sort were operating in parts of every continent barring Antarctica. In addition, and as emerges from Kang Youwei's account of the Young Turk revolution in Istanbul, a written constitution had come to be widely regarded as a trademark of a modern state and of the state of being modern. This book investigates these global transformations, and it connects them to shifting patterns of war and violence.

★

This is not how the advance of written constitutions is usually understood. Because they are often looked at through the lens of particular legal systems, and because of patriotic pieties, constitutions are normally analysed only in regard to individual nations. Insofar as they *have* been viewed as a contagious political genre progressively crossing land and sea boundaries,

3

this has generally been put down to the impact of revolutions, not war. In particular, the emergence of written constitutions has been credited to the success of the American Revolution after 1776, and to the impact of those other epic revolutions that swiftly followed: the French Revolution of 1789, what evolved into the Haitian Revolution shortly afterwards, and the revolts that erupted in the 1810s in one-time Spanish and Portuguese colonies in Central and South America. Since their onset is so strongly linked to these famous revolutions, the essential motive power of these new constitutions is often viewed in selective ways. Their genesis and growing popularity are seen as co-extensive with the rise of republicanism and the decline of monarchy, and associated with a relentless growth throughout the world of nation states and the inexorable progress of democracy.[4]

These great Atlantic revolutions and the texts and ideas they generated remain an important part of the interpretation I advance here. But approaching constitutions as being quintessentially to do with certain major revolutions, and with republicanism, nation-building and democracy, is unduly narrowing and misleads. By 1914, written constitutions were already becoming the norm across continents. Yet, outside of the Americas, most states at this time were still monarchies (some of the most liberal still are). Few states anywhere in 1914, including in the Americas, were full democracies (many fail in that respect even today); while the most powerful players across the globe on the eve of the First World War were *not* nation states in fact. They were overland or maritime empires or both.

Looking at constitutions overwhelmingly through the lens of certain classic revolutions misleads in a further respect. We may like to feel that revolutions are inherently more attractive and constructive phenomena than wars. But the divide between these two expressions of mass human violence – revolution on the one hand, and warfare on the other – is often an unstable one, and this was increasingly so after 1750. The American and

French revolutions, along with their successors in Haiti and South America, were all fuelled and precipitated by passages of transcontinental warfare. They were also further revolutionised as regards ideas, scale and consequences by yet more outbreaks of warfare.[5] War became itself revolution. Moreover, even before 1776 and the American Declaration of Independence, war and constitutional creativity were becoming more vitally and visibly intertwined. Why was this?

The primary and most persistent cause was a growth in the geographical range, frequency, intensity and demands of warfare and cross-border violence. Detailed information on some regions remains imperfect, but the broad outlines of what happened seem clear. In some parts of the world, there may have been a decrease in the early 1700s in *the total number* of armed conflicts. But, as Max Roser, Peter Brecke and others have meticulously charted, after 1700, *the regularity* with which large-scale wars erupted across the globe markedly increased. This pattern of a greater regularity of really large-scale warfare continued to obtain into the mid twentieth century.[6]

What have been styled 'umbrella wars' became more frequent. That is, there was a rise in the incidence of conflicts, such as the Seven Years' War (*c.*1756–63), the French Revolutionary and Napoleonic Wars (*c.*1792–1815), and the First World War (1914–18) which were not only hugely expensive in terms of lives and money, but also expanded across water and land into different regions of the world, incorporating and exacerbating multifarious local struggles in the process, and thereby becoming still more dangerous and disruptive.[7] The conventional westernised dates of these 'umbrella wars' – some of which I give above – are deceptive, because, for many of the protagonists involved, conflict began earlier than is suggested by such canonical dates, or lasted longer, or both. The rising pace and scale of armed conflict from the 1700s also helped to make technologies of war progressively more lethal. As far as maritime warfare was

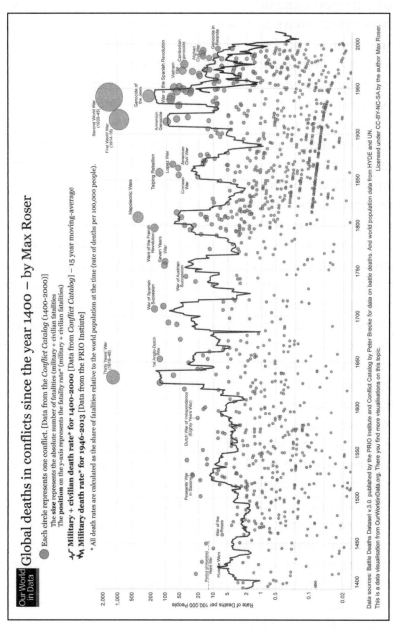

1. Estimated global death rate on account of warfare since 1400. Note the increased recurrence of high levels of combat casualties after 1700.

concerned, this was already becoming more apparent by the 1650s. After 1800, and still more after 1850, overland warfare, too, became rapidly more mechanised and deadlier in its effects. This combination of more recurrent and elastic large-scale wars, and more lethal methods of warfare, continued into the mid twentieth century, by which time possessing or aiming for a written constitution had become the norm almost everywhere.

The impact of these changing patterns of warfare on constitution-making was at one level a structural one. Choosing to engage in, or being dragged into wars that were now, more habitually than before, extremely large, frequently involved substantial navies as well as land forces, often spread across continents, and – even for minor and reluctant players – could be acutely expensive in terms of lives and cash, put states under severe strains, often repeatedly so. As a result, some political regimes were seriously weakened and destabilised. Others fragmented and erupted into civil warfare and revolution. New regimes emerging from these war-bred crises progressively elected to experiment with written constitutions as a means to reorder government, mark out and lay claim to contested boundaries, and publicise and assert their position at home and on the world's stage.

But even states and regimes which proved more successful at war, and avoided collapse or serious fracture, frequently found themselves needing to reorder domestic government and raise their game. Accordingly, even for more resilient states – and not just in the West – the appeal of issuing a new legal and political instrument on paper tended to increase. Drafting and publishing a written constitution supplied governments with a means to legitimise their systems of government anew. It made available a text by which to rally wider support and justify expanding fiscal and manpower demands. This was a vital part of the allure.

The new, more mass-produced constitutions functioned in effect and in part as bargains on paper. Male inhabitants of a state might be offered certain rights, including admission to the franchise, as a quid pro quo for accepting higher taxes and/or military conscription. As the great sociologist and jurist Max Weber recognised, this was increasingly what happened. Himself caught up in constitutional debates in his native Germany in the wake of the First World War, Weber would lecture his students on how the need to expand 'military discipline' over the years had inescapably brought about 'the triumph of democracy'. Different societies, he argued, had 'wished and … [were] compelled to secure the cooperation of the non-aristocratic masses and hence put arms, and along with arms political power, into their hands'.[8] In return for a willingness to fire a gun or serve on a ship – something that, from the 1700s, became increasingly needful across continents – a man might secure the vote and more; and this deal might be outlined, put into law and publicised by means of a written and printed constitution.

Weber's brutal analysis supplies some of the answers. It explains why – especially after 1850 – polities in parts of Asia and Africa, as well as in Euro-America, were issuing constitutions that simultaneously made military service compulsory and enfranchised all, or sectors of, their adult male populations – but *only* men. Because this was a further outcome of the intimate connections between accelerating levels of warfare on the one hand, and the proliferation of constitutions on the other. Women's perceived incapacity for 'military discipline' helped to ensure that, at the outbreak of the First World War, the vast majority of these texts still explicitly excluded them from active citizenship.

There is another major respect in which mounting levels of violence influenced the spread and the quality of constitutions. As levels and scales of conflict accelerated from the 1700s, so, too, did rates of imperial competition and conquest. Every continent – including Europe itself – was exposed to heightened levels and threats of imperial invasion. Written constitutions have traditionally been examined in relation to the rise of nationalism and nation-making: and that is part of the story. Yet empire also played an essential role in their design and proliferation, unavoidably so. Of the twelve most populous political jurisdictions existing in the world by 1913, eleven were *not* nation states. They were empires: Britain, China, Russia, France, Germany, the Netherlands, the Habsburg monarchy, the Ottoman empire, Japan, Italy, and the United States, the last of these with its overland continental empire combined by now with control over the Philippines in South East Asia.[9]

All of these empires – not excluding Britain – experimented with written constitutions, and, in the process and for their own interests, contributed to their spread and diversity. Different empires used these pieces of official, mass-produced paper to legitimise their rule, and to regulate territories seized by their armies and settlers. Some empires deployed new constitutions so as to disadvantage and discriminate against peoples who were in the way of their territorial expansion, especially those who were not white. On occasions, too, imperial actors issued new constitutions to try out political and social projects in subordinate territories they might have been unwilling to risk in their metropolitan core. Empires on the defensive, meanwhile (like many nation states under pressure), were increasingly drawn in the nineteenth century and beyond to adopt a new constitution as a means of reinventing themselves, and in the hope – as Kang Youwei witnessed in the Ottoman capital in 1908 – of keeping their subjects and lands together and intact in a hostile world.

Yet there was always more involved than this. By their very nature, written constitutions are protean and volatile pieces of political technology. They hold out the enticing promise that the words and clauses contained within them will bring into being a new, improved reality. New constitutions offer, or can appear to offer, the prospect of benign and exciting transformations. Consequently, there was far more to their widening circulation and attraction after 1750 than the top-down responses of hard-pressed politicians, states and ambitious empires. Other forces and lobbies were also powerfully attracted to the genre and progressively drawn into its making: and, yet again, changing patterns of war and violence were instrumental in this regard.

At one level, the same burdens, disruptions and dangers caused by expanding levels of conflict and aggression, which caused political elites progressively to turn their minds to new constitutions, could also agitate and sometimes activate those below – the ruled, the subaltern. Recurrent warfare drained away money while demanding more. It cost the lives of rising numbers of soldiers, sailors and civilians, often undermined livelihoods, and repeatedly disrupted trade and the normal workings of communities. All of this could foster more critical scrutiny and discussions of structures of power and authority, and spark anger and resentment. This, in turn, could – and did – prompt demands *from below* for enhanced rights embedded in new or renovated constitutions.

By the same token, the burgeoning scale of mainly Western imperial expansion caused some outside the West who were at risk and exposed to its force to experiment with their own defensive and distinctive constitutions. This trend was already becoming evident in some regions of the world by the 1810s, and it did not necessarily involve a close emulation of Western political and legal ideas and nostrums. Rather, as we shall see, adopting and adapting paper constitutions enabled some polities and Indigenous peoples outside the West, but pressured by rising Western power, to make adjustments and hopefully strengthen their systems of governments and defences. It gave them a chance to proclaim on paper and publicise that they were viable and modern, and therefore not fit targets for imperial takeover. It also provided an opportunity for advancing different and distinguishing interpretations of what was involved in being a state and a people, and what was involved in being modern.

The rising circulation of written constitutions after 1750 should not then be understood only as a simple case of liberal and nationalist ideas and methods spreading inexorably outwards from the Atlantic world. To adapt Sebastian Conrad's interpretation of the Enlightenment (which is also part of this story), this other transformation – the global spread of constitutions – was rather 'the work of many different actors'. More often than not, these actors were people 'influenced by geopolitics and the uneven distribution of power'. Their ideas and actions were also often 'fed by high hopes and utopian promises'. But writers and advocates of constitutions were almost always influenced as well and at some level 'by threat and [by] violence'.[10]

It follows that paying close attention to the provisions and wording of different constitutions drafted across time and in multiple places is vital, because it is only by doing so that we can uncover, identify and unpick the many and various visions and ideas that were involved. Consequently, this book draws heavily throughout on the texts of multifarious constitutions that were written originally in many different languages, and that derive from locations in six continents. I have also been concerned to look at the ideas, personalities and actions of some of the writers and activists involved, those men (and, before 1914, it mainly though not invariably *was* men) who, as well as being often preoccupied with violence, the gun and the ship, also made studied use of the pen.

Since constitution-making was so interwoven with war and violence, these writers and thinkers are not necessarily those whom you might expect. Monarchs, politicians, lawyers and political theorists figure regularly in this book, to be sure. But so, too, do military, naval and imperial officers, along with one-time slaves, bankers, clergymen, medical doctors, intellectuals, journalists, and cultural figures of all kinds. Since my intention is to track and analyse changing attitudes and strategies over time and geographical space, I look not just at official and successful makers of constitutions, but also at some of the many private actors who attempted documents of this sort, out of anxiety, in the hope of advancing particular political, intellectual and social agendas, or because they were simply addicted to writing and to the written word.

I stress this point because constitutions are often compartmentalised: treated as a category that is separate and distinct from other modes of literature and creativity. Yet many of the constitution-drafters, thinkers and advocates who figure in this book were engaged as well in other literary and cultural activities, from Catherine the Great of Russia, through Rammohan Roy of Calcutta, to Andrés Bello of Venezuela and Chile, to Itō Hirobumi in Japan, to Pomare II of Tahiti and Africanus Horton from Sierra Leone. Kang Youwei himself, with whom we began, was fascinated by and adept at the art of calligraphy, as well as being a student and would-be writer of constitutions.[11]

It was not a coincidence moreover that this same post-1750 period, which saw the critical advance in the invention and take-up of written constitutions under heightened pressures of war and imperial violence, also witnessed an accelerating spread in large parts of the world in levels of literacy, an explosion in print and its transmission, a massive increase in the number and locations of newspapers, the invention of myriad new written languages, a greater frequency in the issue of translations, and – too – the rising popularity of the novel. A constitution, after all, like a novel, invents and tells the story of a place and a people. These documents were – and are – always more than themselves, and more too than a matter of law and politics. They stand in need of reappraisal and rediscovery, and of being read across boundaries.

\*

No single book – and certainly no single author – can hope to address the extraordinary range of constitutional creativity, debates and outcomes that occurred across maritime and land frontiers from the eighteenth century to the First World War, and that continues to shape boundaries, politics and patterns of ideas today. There are many different histories of these developments that can and should be written. My own strategy has been to focus on a series of important themes and signal crises that impinge on, and that emerged from, the repeated inter-meshing of new constitutions and varieties of warfare and violence. Each of the following chapters, which are organised in rough chronological order, is built around one of these major themes and flash-points. Each begins with an evocation of a specific location and a particular episode of constitution-writing. Each chapter then moves on to explore the wider ramifications of the theme in question in other parts of the world.

One final point. I came to this subject as an outsider. Along with New Zealand and Israel, the United Kingdom, my place of birth, is one of very few states left in the world still without a codified constitution. Moving in the late twentieth century to live and work in the United States, a country which has made a cult of its own written constitutions, was therefore an arresting experience in political terms, as in other respects. It was also a call to curiosity. Because of where I came from, these documents seemed profoundly exotic. I was detached, but I also wanted to understand them better. I wondered why they were not treated more ambitiously and variously by historians and in global contexts. This book grew out of these early curiosities and questions.

In the course of writing it, I have become not so much a convert to these kinds of constitutions as a candid friend. They are the frail, paper creations of fallible human beings. Wherever they exist, they only function well to the degree that politicians, the law courts and the populations concerned are able and willing to put sustained effort into thinking about them, revising them when necessary, and making them work. These are also emphatically not innocent devices, and never have been. From the outset, as will become apparent, written constitutions have been as much to do with enabling varieties of power as they have been with restricting power.

But I have come to believe nonetheless that they can serve multiple, useful purposes. I also believe that while the manner in which constitutions evolved and spread still continues to influence ideas and polities across the globe, *some* of the forces that once helped these instruments to function and to command attention and attachment are now weakening and coming under rising pressures. But that is a matter for the end of this book. For now, in order to begin, we need to go back to the 1700s, and to the world of the Mediterranean.

# PART ONE

## INTO AND OUT OF EUROPE

2. Pasquale Paoli by a Dutch artist in 1768.

# ONE

# THE MULTIPLE TRAJECTORIES OF WAR

## Corsica

Small places sometimes generate events of wide historical importance. The man disembarking on this Mediterranean island on 16 April 1755, Pasquale Paoli, will briefly become a celebrity. He will figure in books, letters, newspapers, poetry, art, pamphlets and song as an exemplary combination of a 'soldier and a legislator', the sword and the pen. A British journalist will liken him to a 'planet of liberty, warming every soul in his progress'. Admirers on both sides of the Atlantic will compare him to Epaminondas, the legendary general who freed ancient Thebes from subjection to Sparta. In 1768, *An Account of Corsica*, a book by a louche, clever and ambitious Scot named James Boswell, will become a much-translated bestseller, and further propagate the notion that Paoli is 'something above' the normal run of humanity. Even an unflattering depiction by a Dutch artist at this time represents him as a formidable figure: tall and burly, with watchful eyes, a wide jaw and a cleft chin, and with two pistols tucked firmly into his waistband. Yet the hero worship that once surrounded Pasquale Paoli obscures not only the full nature of the man, but also some of the broader significance of what he did.[1]

Just months before taking ship for Corsica, his place of birth, Paoli had written of himself in terms not of strength, mission and certainty, but rather of weakness and doubt. He was too sickly for armed combat, he insisted in a letter, unfit for 'the least service in that capacity'. This, despite his possessing both formal military training and a family background in armed struggle. Back in 1728, his father, Giacinto Paoli, had joined an armed rebellion on Corsica against its long-time but declining imperial hegemon, the republic of Genoa, before ultimately becoming one of the rebel leaders. As a result, in 1739, he was forced into exile in the kingdom of Naples in southern Italy, taking with him his fourteen-year-old son, Pasquale. Like many young Corsicans seeking refuge here, the boy found employment in the Neapolitan army. But duties in dim garrison towns and time spent at an artillery academy seem to have interested Pasquale Paoli less than Freemasonry, avid reading and stray attempts to secure some further education at the city of Naples's pristine university.[2]

His decision to risk returning to Corsica emerged from a mix of motives, of which frustrated ambition was certainly one. By 1755, Paoli had reached the age of thirty, but did not anticipate receiving military promotion in Naples for several years. By contrast, his home island offered prospects. His family name counted for something there. Moreover, for reasons that extended well beyond Corsica itself, resistance to Genoese rule there was reviving again. Paoli did not view himself as temperamentally or physically well-equipped for warfare. But he possessed military and artillery skills, and a partially trained and intelligent mind. There was something else that persuaded him to put aside his doubts and go back. He had devised a 'governmental plan that I would like to establish'.[3]

By July 1755, Paoli had succeeded in being elected *capo generale politico e economico* on Corsica, effectively its rebel commander-in-chief and head of its executive. Four months later, in Corte, a fortified town high in the granite heart of the island, he used his accomplished Italian to draft a ten-page constitution, a term (*costituzione*) he explicitly employed. No printing press seems to have operated on Corsica before 1760, so he was in no position to publish his text. At Corte itself, not even a supplier of stationery was available. To secure the necessary sheets of blank paper on which to set down his draft provisions, Paoli had to reuse pages from some old letters, using a razor to scrape away the inked words. As a result, this original, fragile document has long since disappeared. Only some early, imperfect manuscript copies survive to give us an indication of the audacity of his plans.

The preamble to Paoli's constitution went like this:

The General Diet of the People of Corsica, legitimate masters of themselves, convoked according to the form [established by] the General [Paoli] in the city of Corte, the 16, 17, 18 November 1755. Having reconquered its liberty, wishing to give a durable and permanent form to its government by transforming it into a constitution suited to assure the well-being of the nation [the Diet] has ordained and decrees ...[4]

Contained within these fractured words were some radical political transformations and aspirations. In place of its customary sporadic *consulte* (assemblies), Corsica was now to have a parliament of sorts, the General Diet. This body, Paoli's text decreed, was to meet annually, as it duly did until 1769. The island was to shrug off its centuries-old subordination to Genoa and be restored to independence. As Paoli wrote, Corsicans had 'reconquered' their liberty. They were, he insisted, to regain – not simply lay claim to – their natural rights, and become again 'legitimate masters of themselves'. This new order was moreover to be anchored and celebrated in a written text, a constitution.

It bestowed on Pasquale Paoli a great deal of power. Confirmed as the island's general for life, he also became leader of its council of state, which was to consist of three chambers responsible respectively for political, military and economic affairs. Only Paoli could decide when and where the Corsican diet would assemble each year. Every petition sent to it and the council of state was initially to go to him. The direction of foreign affairs was also his, along with ultimate responsibility for war or peace. The constitution did not, however, give Paoli a seat in the diet. To this degree, and on frail paper at least, Corsica's executive was cordoned off from its legislature. Moreover, every year – and like every other significant Corsican official – Paoli was to give an 'exact account' of his actions to the members of the diet. He was then, the constitution ordered, to 'wait with submissiveness the judgment of the people'.

Because, as well as having responsibility for taxation and enacting legislation, this Corsican diet was to be widely representative. Paoli's constitution said little about electoral arrangements. In practice, though, and from 1766 by law, all of the island's male inhabitants over the age of twenty-five seem to have been eligible both to stand for election to the diet and to vote for its members.[5] Potentially, this provided for a wider level of democracy on Corsica than existed anywhere else in the mid-eighteenth-century world. Even in Britain's American colonies, where the abundance of cheap land made it easy for settlers to qualify for enfranchisement, only about 70 per cent of adult white men could vote at this time, and fewer still bothered to do so. Yet what did it mean that these new initiatives and transformations in political technology should have occurred on a small island in the western Mediterranean? Why Corsica? And why at this point in time?

## The Wider Reasons Why

Answers to these questions have often focused on Pasquale Paoli himself: on the man's undoubted charisma and gifts of leadership, and on his political ideas – though the evidence for these is patchy and blurred. Certainly, he grew to maturity in Naples during a period when its ancient university was a major incubator of Enlightenment political, economic and legal thought.

Yet just how much time this struggling, itinerant and underpaid junior army officer was able to devote to academic study and intellectual exchange is far from clear. Nor, for all the analysis devoted to the subject, do we know the extent of Paoli's indebtedness to the French political philosopher Montesquieu and his masterwork *The Spirit of Laws* (1748). Yes, Paoli is known to have ordered a copy of Montesquieu's book in March 1755, but that was six months *after* he designed his own first scheme of government for Corsica.

As regards Paoli's evolving interest in political constitutions, it seems to have been his early exposure to the Greek and Roman classics that was more influential. He is known to have read works by Livy, Plutarch, Horace and Polybius, as well as volumes on ancient history, encouraged by his father, Giacinto Paoli, who had nurtured his own ambitions to be a lawmaker.[6] In 1735, twenty years before his son drafted *his* first constitution, Giacinto had worked alongside a lawyer, Sébastien Costa, to formulate a set of constitutional proposals for Corsica. They were never implemented. But these early projects by Paoli's father are significant in terms of the emphasis they place on the importance of military men and values, and in their insistence on the supreme virtue and utility of words set down on paper.[7]

Costa and Giacinto had wanted a reforming Office of War to be established on Corsica, staffed by six of 'the bravest soldiers of the kingdom'. They also advocated the appointment of a 'Captain General of the Armies', along with the election in each of the island's provinces of a lieutenant general who would be responsible for selecting the officers of the local militia. In addition, Paoli senior and Costa envisaged a literal bonfire of the island's existing alien political writings and laws. If its governance was ever to be successfully remodelled, they argued, old words of power deriving from Genoa's claims over Corsica since the thirteenth century must be systematically and ritually destroyed, and replaced by new texts:

That all the laws and statutes made by the Genoese ... will be abolished, and that it will be ordered, by the publication of an edict, that all the people of Corsica bring the copies of the laws and statutes that they have in their homes to the Secretary of State, so that a public bonfire can be made of these laws and statutes as a sign of the eternal separation of the Corsicans from the Genoese and of Corsica from Genoa.[8]

As these abortive proposals illustrate, there were precedents for Pasquale Paoli's 1755 constitution. His father, Giacinto, had been sketching out plans for an independent, reorganised Corsica while Pasquale himself was still a child; and there had been other schemes devoted to changing the island's forms of government. Driving the production of these serial paper projects and making them more urgent was not only Corsica's continued subjugation to Genoa, but also the island's vulnerability to other, even harsher pressures from outside.

Corsica was a poor place. It possessed few minerals and only limited arable land, and in the 1750s its largely illiterate population totalled no more than 120,000. Cut across by vertiginous mountains, the island was split into hundreds of semi-autonomous communes and afflicted by competing jurisdictions and clan warfare. These internal divisions go some way to explaining why much of Paoli's 1755 constitution is given over to providing for more centralised control and improving domestic order. Hitting someone on the head with a stick, stipulated Paoli with all seriousness, was to land the guilty party in jail for at least fifteen days. As for committing murder in the course of a blood feud, the offender would:

Not only be declared guilty of willful homicide, but on the site of his house, which shall be immediately destroyed, one will erect a column of infamy on which the name of the guilty one and the crime shall be indicated.[9]

Partly to root out such disorders, and as his father had sought to do earlier, Paoli provided for multiple layers of tough, essentially militarised authority. His 1755 constitution ordered that each Corsican commune was to have a military commissioner, and each parish a captain and a lieutenant at arms. 'Zealous patriots', these officers were to respond to any outbreaks of internal unrest and armed challenge by calling up the local males ('failure to report carries a fine of 20 soldi'), organising them into columns, and crushing opposition 'with armed force'. Paoli saw no contradiction whatsoever between these provisions and his constitution's support for mass male political engagement – very much the reverse. The reasoning he gives is telling. 'Every Corsican must have some political rights', he argued, since otherwise 'if the franchise of which he is so jealous is, in the end, but a laughable fiction, *what interest would he take in defending the country* [my italics]?'[10] War, the persistent threat of armed violence and written provisions for wider male democracy were all necessarily intertwined.

This commitment to forging an armed citizenry owed something to Paoli's love of the ancient classics. But it was also a response to the specific dangers confronting Corsica itself, not simply internally, but also from without. Even at the height of Paoli's power on Corsica, Genoese military and naval forces remained strung out along the island's coastlines. And there were other, larger foreign challenges. Vulnerably small, Corsica was also strategically desirable. Situated in the western Mediterranean, where naval competition between the major European powers was intense, it was barely a hundred sea miles from France. As James Boswell noticed when he visited the island in 1765, grubbing for copy, Corsica possessed a range of useful harbours. But, as he also recorded, it lacked the economic resources and the skilled workforce necessary to construct an effective navy which might be able to repel attacks from the sea.[11]

To a substantial degree, then, Pasquale Paoli's determination in 1755 to remake Corsica's government in a 'durable and permanent form' stemmed from the fact that the island was doubly endangered. It was disorderly and subject to Genoa within, and it faced a potential threat from without of naval invasions by a great power. It was no accident at all that this first attempt at drafting a Corsican constitution on Paoli's part (he would try again in 1793) should have emerged in the early stages of what would later become known as the Seven Years' War (Americans call it the French and Indian War).

This huge, sprawling mid-eighteenth-century conflict, an aggregation of multiple struggles in different continents, worked to focus Paoli's mind. For a while, the scale of the fighting also worked to his advantage.[12] Although resistance to rule by Genoa had been on the rise in Corsica since the 1720s, these local struggles had regularly buckled in the face of French military interventions. France much preferred for a declining Italian republic to be nominally in control of the island than for it to be taken over by another, more formidable foreign power. In 1739, it had been a French army led by the marquis de Maillebois which had crushed Corsican rebels in a matter of weeks, and forced Giacinto Paoli and his young son into exile. French forces intervened again on Corsica in the 1740s. Tellingly, though, France did *not* intervene in 1755 to prevent Pasquale Paoli from landing and renewing the independence campaign. When some French troops did arrive on the island the following year, they confined themselves to keeping guard on its coastlines, while in the main staying studiously away from the political revolutions that were now underway in its interior.

The reasons for this unusual level of French restraint are clear. From the mid 1750s, the rulers of France had to focus the bulk of their attention, and their land and maritime forces, on the business of fighting and monitoring Britain and its allies, not just in continental Europe, but also in parts of Asia, coastal west Africa, the Caribbean and North America. It was this high level of French distraction on account of the Seven Years' War

– the 'first world war', as Winston Churchill aptly styled it – that allowed Pasquale Paoli his brief window of opportunity, his few years of exploratory and momentous political time.[13]

For Paoli and for Corsica – as would be the case later on for many other peoples in many other places – it was in large part the threat of war, and the outbreak of war, that enabled, enforced and influenced innovative written constitutionalism. That outbreaks of armed conflict, and the fear of them, were to be increasingly formative in this respect was due to the fact that the nature and the demands of warfare were shifting. We need to understand why.

## A More Expansive, More Expensive Warfare

War has always been a major contributor to the making of states and empires and their fortunes. As the American sociologist Charles Tilly famously remarked, states make war, and war in turn often works to make and strengthen (and also to unmake) states. But, by the mid eighteenth century, the impact of war in many regions of the world was changing and intensifying. These changes had little to do with the introduction of new technologies, especially as far as conflict on land was concerned. Gunpowder weaponry had long since already altered the quality of large-scale violence, not just in Euro-America, but also in China, Korea, Japan, Vietnam, Java, the Indian subcontinent, the Ottoman empire and west Africa.[14] Nor, although in parts of the world the number of men at arms was rising appreciably, were the signal changes in warfare that were becoming more evident by the mid 1700s *primarily* to do with the size of armies. The more critical shift in the quality of warfare at this stage was of a different sort. The geographical range of many major conflicts – and consequently the demands they posed in terms of men, money and machines – was expanding more dramatically and more rapidly than ever before.

The contest that facilitated Pasquale Paoli's brief constitutional experiment on Corsica was an extreme case in point. The Seven Years' War involved lethal levels of fighting within continental Europe itself. Between 1756 and 1763, the powerful German state of Prussia lost an estimated 500,000 troops and civilians out of a pre-war population of 4.5 million. But well before Europeans themselves began to suffer serious levels of destruction, mortality and ecological damage on account of this conflict, vicious fighting connected with one of its prime dynamics – the rivalry between Britain and France – was already affecting parts of Asia and North America. As early as 1754, areas of what is now Tamil Nadu in south-eastern India had 'been so long the seat of war' between British and French troops and their respective South Asian allies, it was reported, that 'scarce a tree was left standing for several miles'.[15]

As its transcontinental reach makes clear, the Seven Years' War was not fought out overwhelmingly on land. By contrast with most epic contests involving multiple powers during the seventeenth century – the Thirty Years' War, for instance – fighting in *this* mega-conflict embraced multiple seas and oceans. Three of the six biggest naval engagements in the Seven Years' War occurred, not in European waters, but on the Indian Ocean. This umbrella war also witnessed tens of thousands of European troops being shipped expensively across the Atlantic – a far greater number than in previous contests. The actions of these men, along with those of American colonists and indigenous warriors, altered political boundaries in North America from Upper Canada down to present-day Florida. In addition to these North American transformations, and along with its impact on the Indian subcontinent, the Seven Years' War also swept through different parts of the Caribbean and into coastal South America. It touched Senegal in west Africa; and, in its final stages, reached Manila in the Philippines, between the South China Sea and the Pacific Ocean.[16]

The widening geographies and damage levels of warfare becoming more evident by the middle decades of the eighteenth century were not, it should be stressed, only the result of Western aggression and ambitions. Markedly long-distance warfare was also conspicuously practised at this time by some Greater Asian powers. From the late 1720s, the Persian ruler Nādir Shāh Afshār, by origins a working herdsman though from a recognised family, had quickly evolved into both a brilliant recruiter of men and a ruthless tactician. He engaged in a succession of ferocious assaults on the Caucasus region and Mesopotamia, and on what is now Turkey, Afghanistan and northern India. Nādir was assassinated in 1747, on the verge of moving further into eastern Asia, but one of his former generals, Ahmad Shāh Durrānī, continued the onslaught. By 1757, he had already annexed Punjab, Kashmir and Lahore, sacking holy cities in his path and implementing mass killing on a terrible scale. The number of dead as a result of his armies' onslaughts was reputedly so great that barriers made up of rotting human bodies blocked the flow of the Yamuna river, a tributary of the Ganges.[17] And there was another, infinitely more established and mighty Asian power that was also ambitiously on the march at this time.

Ever since its conquest of China in the 1640s, the Qing dynasty had wanted to strengthen its Central Asian frontiers, and move against the Zunghar state of the western Mongols, a loose nomadic empire claiming control over what is now Xinjiang, Inner and Outer Mongolia and parts of Tibet and Kazakhstan. For a long time, as the historian Peter Purdue describes, Qing rulers were held back by the logistical difficulties involved in keeping their huge armies adequately supplied for protracted campaigns over such vast overland distances. But in the mid eighteenth century, under the sixth member of the Qing dynasty, the Qianlong emperor, there was a major breakthrough.[18]

A patron of different styles of art, a writer himself of poetry and political essays, and an unquestionably intelligent and thoughtful man, Qianlong was also a serial and effective war-monger. He ordered the construction of a new supply route into Xinjiang, and built a chain of military magazines. As a result of these preparations, in the 1750s he was able to dispatch three armies, each 50,000 men strong, into Zunghar territory, and keep them there for a protracted campaign. Covering greater overland distances than Napoleon's armies were to do in their march on Moscow in 1812, these Qing forces finally defeated the Zunghars. They wiped out virtually all of their young boys and able-bodied men. The women were taken as booty or killed, and the Zunghar–Mongolian empire was erased from the map. As Qianlong proclaimed in December 1759, it had been eliminated.

In terms of the rise in long-distance aggression, it is possible, then, to identify something of a 'great convergence' occurring by the middle decades of the eighteenth century.[19] Violent incursions into northern India on the part of some south-eastern and Central Asian powers were increasing in ruthlessness and range in this period; and while, in the 1750s, major Western powers were waging war over longer distances than before, the same was true of the Qing empire.

Yet for all these mid-century convergences in long-distance aggression between some Western and some Asian powers, there were also some significant divergences. Most, though not all of the main Western powers conspicuously active at this time pursued variants of hybrid warfare. Today, this phrase – hybrid warfare – normally refers to the synchronised deployment in conflict of multiple instruments of power and destruction: irregular forces alongside regular armies, together with terrorism, cyber-warfare, disinformation campaigns etc.[20] In this book, however, I use the term hybrid warfare more narrowly, to refer to a calculated amalgam of fighting at sea as well as fighting on land. By the 1700s, this mode of hybrid warfare was progressively becoming the favoured style of aggression among many major Western powers. By contrast, most non-Western

3. Conquering by land: Qianlong's cavalry units
in action in central Asia in the 1750s.

powers at this stage still fought disproportionately on land. This had by no means always been the case. In the fifteenth century, the maritime reach and investment of China's Ming dynasty had surpassed those of any Western power; and the Qing dynasty's navies were still winning sea battles in the later seventeenth century.

But, while Qianlong himself continued to keep guard over his own coastlines and pursued overseas commerce in certain directions, *his* power rested overwhelmingly on control of vast agrarian territories and on massive armies and cavalry units that fought and conquered only on land. By 1800, some Chinese scholars have suggested, even the memory of Ming sea power and its workings may have disappeared from Qing government archives and from the knowledge of its senior bureaucrats.[21] Warfare here – in the Qing empire – had become overwhelmingly a matter of armed men, millions of horses and the land.

The fact that, by contrast, most substantial European powers in the eighteenth century fought to a rising degree at sea *as well*

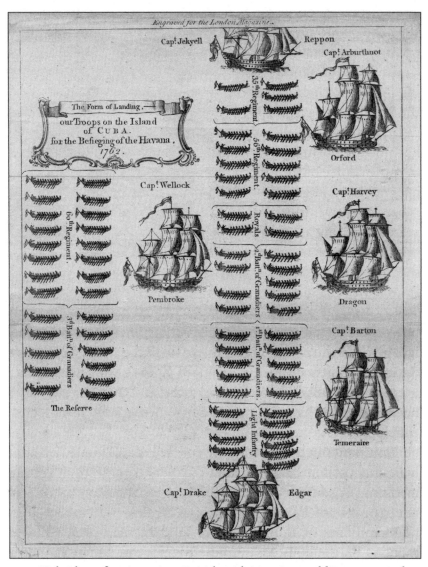

4. Hybrid warfare in action: British and American soldiers protected and transported by warships invade Spanish-controlled Havana in 1762.

*as* on land had wide, protracted but also paradoxical consequences. It was the costs, challenges and imperatives involved in this more hybrid mode of warfare – fighting on a large scale, over large distances, on water as well as on land – that, in multiple ways, helped to precipitate, enforce and shape new attempts at political and constitutional change and invention.

The sheer financial costs involved in providing for repeated indulgences in hybrid warfare were one reason why this proved the case. By 1650, purpose-built, state-financed warships, as distinct from specially adapted merchant vessels, had already become the norm in much of western and eastern Europe. But, over the course of the long eighteenth century, warships became progressively larger, more numerous, more intricate and far more expensive. In 1670, having thirty guns was sufficient for a vessel to qualify as a 'ship of the line', the most formidable and prestigious type of warship in European navies. By the time of the Seven Years' War, though, sixty guns were customary for ships in this category, and some vessels carried more than that.[22] The order for building the *Victory*, the first-rater that Horatio Nelson used as his flagship at the battle of Trafalgar in 1805, was given in the midst of the Seven Years' War. This vessel was designed to carry at least one hundred guns.

Constructing, manning and maintaining these maritime behemoths was hideously expensive. In order to build a 74-gun warship – that is, not even the most lethal ship available – a ship-building yard might require close to 3,000 mature oak trees; and high-quality timber was only one of the necessary raw materials involved. In addition, a big ship like this easily absorbed over twenty miles of flax and hemp rope, acres of canvas for sails, huge amounts of iron for nails and cannon, yards of copper sheeting for the hulls, and – once finished – an unending supply of victuals. Specialised yards and expert craftsmen were also needed to construct such a ship in the first place, along with hundreds more men to sail it and naval bases to maintain it. Yet, in the 1780s alone, France built almost fifty of these monster and monstrously expensive 74-gun warships.[23]

As the scale of this French investment suggests, mega-navies were never the monopoly of a single state. To be sure, for much of the 1700s, and until the second half of the nineteenth century, access to this level of maritime firepower was usually confined to a small clique of mainly European powers. During the same period, it was also generally accepted that Britain's Royal Navy was unlikely to be surpassed in size by that of any other power. But, with the geographical range of warfare expanding so rapidly, *all* states with access to the sea faced growing pressure to acquire some sort of navy. Not to fight set-piece sea battles necessarily, but to defend coastlines and protect merchant fleets. There were periods of time, indeed, when the scale of naval expansion on the part of its competitors overtook the rate at which Britain itself was growing its sea power. By 1790, for instance, Britain's navy was still comfortably bigger than its rivals, but it was only twenty-one vessels larger than in 1750. By contrast, over this same period – 1750–90 – both France and Spain almost doubled the size of their respective fleets while simultaneously maintaining huge armies.[24]

Sea power, though, was never enough. Since the emphasis was now increasingly on hybrid warfare – more ships at sea, but also more troops on the ground – the British in turn were unable to rely only on having a dominant navy. They also had to bulk up their armies, and they did. During the War of the Austrian Succession of 1740–48, some 62,000 men served annually in the British army. During the Seven Years' War, the equivalent figure was 93,000. By the time of the American Revolutionary War of 1775– 83, and as well as running over 220 ships of the line, the British state was needing to employ annually over 108,000 troops.[25]

In broad terms, then, it was not the case that 'naval warfare changed much less than land warfare during this period'. But neither was it ever a case of war at sea coming to subordinate overland warfare in significance.[26] The vital point is that, by the 1750s, ambitious Western powers – and ultimately some outside the West – had come to believe more strongly and actively than before that they needed to run substantial armies and substantial navies in tandem.

The global consequences of these developments were seismic and harsh. They were also, as I say, paradoxical. At one level – and as is widely recognised – the build-up on the part of *some* European powers of far more troops on the ground and far more warships at sea rendered these states ever more dangerous to those parts of the world that lacked the means or the will to respond in kind. 'I can defeat them on land', Haidar Ali, the self-made ruler of Mysore in southern India, is supposed to have remarked in the 1770s of incoming British forces; and he sometimes did exactly that. Haidar's well-armed and well-financed armies, variously estimated at between 100,000 and 200,000 men, forced the encroaching British East India Company to sue for peace in the late 1760s, and later inflicted a humiliating defeat upon the Company's legions at the battle of Pollilur in 1780. Haidar, along with his powerful and brilliant son and successor at Mysore, Tipu Sultan, also made attempts to construct a naval fleet. But, like other Indian rulers at this time, these Mysore sovereigns lacked the fiscal organisation and resources and the fixed plant necessary for staging and sustaining full-scale hybrid warfare. As Haidar Ali himself acknowledged, for all his formidable military strength on land, he could not 'swallow the sea'.[27]

To make these points is not, however, to advance yet another version of a 'rise of the West' thesis. To be sure, the combination of big, state-run navies and swollen, state-run armies allowed – for a while, at least – a small number of Western states to project power, people, information and goods across land and seas insolently and on a rising and terrible scale. But there was another, sometimes overlooked side to all of this. Engaging in and sustaining the business of large-scale hybrid warfare – not just *more* wars, but *changing qualities* of wars – indulging in this mode of conflict repeatedly, and making provision for the large numbers of men and machines that were necessarily involved, put those Western powers most deeply invested in these modes of warfare under extreme levels of stress.[28] These multiple stresses, which were becoming more evident by the mid eighteenth century, played a substantial and recurring role in fostering the emergence of new political ideas, and in provoking a series of major political and constitutional shocks and reconfigurations.

## Hybrid Wars and Revolutions

Most dramatically, the pressures and irritants of increasing levels of hybrid warfare helped to give rise to a series of canonical revolutionary conflicts, each of which expanded the design and spread of written constitutions, and the ideas involved in them. All three of the world's prime practitioners of hybrid warfare in the 1700s and early 1800s – Britain, France and Spain – were mutilated by these serial revolutionary conflicts, but in different ways. As far as Britain was concerned, the biggest crisis occurred not within its own domestic territory, but in one of its oldest and most emotive colonial outposts, mainland North America.

With some cause, historians of Britain tend to wax complacent about its growing capacity from the mid seventeenth century to raise taxes, fund its national debt and deploy its Westminster Parliament to legitimate these exactions. Yet the slide into ever-larger, wider-ranging hybrid warfare still took a heavy toll here. During the War of the Austrian Succession, Britain's annual expenditure was already running at two-thirds higher than in the previous, relatively peaceful decade. Over 40 per cent of this rising outflow of funds went on the Royal Navy. The rest, however, went on the army. Traditionally, this had been the less favoured of Britain's armed services, but it was now swelling in size so as to meet the demands of hybrid warfare. The Seven Years' War proved still more expensive, not just because of the unprecedented levels of transcontinental fighting involved, but also because of the scale of British victories.

Before the Seven Years' War, the British state had felt little need to maintain permanent military bases in any of its overseas colonies (Ireland, as so often, was an exception to the rule). But after sending an unprecedented 20,000 troops to North America to fight in the course of this war, London made the fateful decision at its formal end in 1763 to provide for 10,000 regular troops to be distributed throughout its Atlantic empire as a peacetime force. Of these, about 7,500 men were sent to British America, which now stretched from Hudson's Bay to the Florida Keys, and from the Atlantic coast to the Mississippi River.[29]

This distinctly modest force proved utterly insufficient for the mix of tasks and the vast geographies confronting it. To begin with, its men were expected to monitor Britain's newly won and often unimpressed Francophone subjects in Quebec. In addition, troops were needed to watch over the populous towns on America's eastern seaboard, and to put down smuggling there as well as growing outbursts of what London viewed as sedition. These sparse British army units were also supposed to regulate the rising numbers of settlers and speculators scrambling for a place on North America's western frontiers, and pacify and protect the angry Indigenous peoples whose lands these incomers were invading. Predictably, the overstretched redcoats failed substantially on all three counts. 'What did Britain gain by the most glorious and successful war on which she ever engaged,' remarked a one-time British colonial governor as he looked back on events in North America in the aftermath of the Seven Years' War, but 'an extent of empire we [were] ... equally unable to maintain, defend or govern'.[30]

As whole libraries of books have been devoted to documenting, the post-war British soldiery in North America (some of whom were American-born in fact) were, however, highly effective as agents of political education and imperial division. Many civilian colonists viewed these soldiers, with some cause, as representatives of a more assertive and intrusive style of British imperial authority. Opposition to this, and to the taxes London levied to help pay for these men, forged bonds of sympathy and cooperation between different American colonies that had previously tended to go their own separate ways.

The new imperial soldiery fostered opposition in other ways too. During the Seven Years' War, American colonists had been in a position to witness British redcoats in their localities as never before. Post-war, some colonists encountered yet more men in red uniforms: and they did not always like what they saw. In March 1770, the 'Boston Massacre', as American polemicists immediately and cunningly styled the affair, involved the killing of just five colonial rioters in this major east coast settlement of some 16,000 people. The critical point, however, was that influential American colonists in Boston (like educated Britons on the other side of the Atlantic) were primed by their readings of history and political thought to associate soldiers operating aggressively in civilian spaces with tyranny – and those firing the shots on this occasion were wearing British army uniforms.[31]

In turn, growing American resistance to taxation and questioning of the very limited armed official British presence in their midst provoked mutterings about colonial ingratitude on the other side of the Atlantic. Maintaining these regiments in the American colonies cost Britain itself about £400,000 a year, close to 4 per cent of its national budget. Coming on top of heavy post-Seven Years' War debt repayments, these extra tax burdens help to explain why agitation for political change – and rising interest in constitutional matters – also manifested itself in the 1760s in London and in other British towns and cities, and why politicians at Westminster persisted so stubbornly in trying to extract more money from the American colonists to cover at least some of their costs.[32]

If the American colonies expected 'our fleets' for their protection, thundered a British minister Charles Townshend in 1765 – making clear again the strains of having to combine unparalleled levels of naval power with big land armies – they 'must assist our revenue'.[33] As it was, financial pressures in the wake of the Seven Years' War forced cutbacks in the size and repair levels of the Royal Navy, something that arguably inhibited Britain's early performance when transcontinental war broke out again after 1775, this time with most of its mainland American colonies. Before the end of this contest in 1783, twelve of these one-time American colonies had adopted their own written state constitutions. Eventual American victory in this war also resulted, of course, in the drafting of a seminal constitution for the new United States as a whole in 1787.[34]

For France, too, participation in the Seven Years' War proved a tipping point, though for different reasons. Like their counterparts in London, politicians in Paris and Versailles had to contend with near bankruptcy after 1763. But whereas Britain also faced the challenge of learning how to govern, adjust to and pay for an overabundance of new territorial conquests, France, post-war, had to deal with the shocks and shame of wide-scale defeat and the loss of most of its overseas colonies. The French Crown had invested twice as much money in this conflict as it had in the previous War of the Austrian Succession. As a result, by the 1760s debt repayments were absorbing over half of King Louis XV's annual revenue. Nonetheless, a determination to restore French national prestige led to a spate of expensive new military projects and costly reforms.[35]

There were more French colonial land grabs both outside and inside Europe. Thus, in 1768, 25,000 French troops landed on Corsica, suppressing its frail autonomy and Pasquale Paoli's political experiment by force, and annexing the island. The machinery of French hybrid warfare was also lavishly upgraded after 1763. Over the course of twenty years, France more than doubled the number of its first-rate warships. Simultaneously, thousands of army officers viewed as having been complicit in the failures of the Seven Years' War were dismissed, and fresh ones trained up in their place. Money was sunk into a new military nobility and a string of new training academies.[36] These included a military school at Brienne in the Champagne region of France. It was here in 1779 that a sullen and scrawny Corsican youth who still called himself Napoleone di Buonaparte arrived to learn the art of war.

These investments in the machinery and personnel of hybrid warfare may well have worked to France's advantage when it openly allied with American revolutionary forces in 1778. But while this large-scale military intervention ensured the independence of the United States, the essential precondition for its successful constitutional redesign, the costs to France itself of this further bout of hybrid warfare were enormous – over 1 billion livres. Almost all of this money was raised through short-term loans. Because of the French Crown's reputation for partially defaulting on its debts, the interest rates demanded were punitive, and by 1787 the regime was in financial and political meltdown. The historian Lynn Hunt's summary of what happened next is to the point:

> The threat of bankruptcy forced the [French] Crown to seek new sources of revenue, and when it could not get them from a specially convened Assembly of Notables or the Parlement of Paris, it reluctantly agreed to call the Estates General to consider new taxation. Since the Estates General had not met for 175 years, its convocation in May 1789 opened the door to a constitutional and social revolution.[37]

The subsequent successive violent regime changes in France between 1789 and 1815 would be accompanied by nine official attempts to supply the country with a new, written constitution. In addition, post-revolutionary French governments and their armies worked at exporting this form of political technology – a written constitution – to other parts of continental Europe, durably altering ideas, expectations, boundaries, legal practices and systems of government in the process.

The last of the three main exponents of hybrid warfare in the eighteenth century, Spain, is often perceived as the weakest. Yet had the Spanish joined their substantial navy to France's fleet at the outset of the Seven Years' War, the end results of that conflict and the course of subsequent world history might conceivably have been different. Such an early Franco-Hispanic armed alliance might have emerged victorious, or at least forced the British and other opponents to a speedy truce. In that event, France might have held on to its North American colonies for longer. This, is turn, would have kept Britain's American colonies more dependent on London's protection for longer, and the outbreak of armed opposition on their part might have been substantially delayed. As it was, Spain only entered the Seven Years' War on the side of France in 1761 – a belated step that served little strategic purpose and proved an expensive disaster as far as its own situation was concerned.

Nonetheless, Spain's post-war responses proved more effective in some respects than those of its rivals, Britain and France. Like France's monarchs and ministers, Carlos III of Spain worked hard after the end of the war to refurbish his country's hybrid war machine. By the time of his death in 1788, and in keeping with his soubriquet 'The Sergeant King', his army totalled, on paper, 50,000 men – more than Britain's land forces at that time. The resources that Carlos channelled into Spain's navy were greater still. Two hundred ships strong by 1800, 'it received', grumbled one leading Spanish minister, 'all the treasury could give'.[38]

Much of this money came from Spain's American colonies. To safeguard these streams of revenue and preserve its global reach, Spain, like Britain – but again with greater success in the short term – put in place after 1763 a more systematic, hands-on imperial policy. More fortified outposts were built in Spanish America. There were new Spanish cartographic and fiscal projects, more soldiers and imperial proconsuls, and more treaties with Indigenous peoples. There was also fresh territorial expansion, new Spanish settlements on the Pacific coastline from San Diego to San Francisco, and a stronger presence, too, on the north-west Pacific coast.

As was true for the British in regard to *their* American colonies, this more rigorous imperial policy on the part of Spain provoked resistance. Both the Quito revolt of 1765 in what is now Ecuador, and the Revolt of the Comuneros in New Granada in 1781 were fuelled by increased tax demands and other 'reforms' emanating from Madrid. So – though only in part – was the more dangerous Túpac Amaru insurrection of 1780–83, which for a while threatened Spanish control throughout the entire viceroyalty of Peru, and in parts of the viceroyalty of Río de la Plata as well.[39]

Nonetheless, initially, the Spanish monarchy succeeded in keeping a lid on these colonial outbursts and in keeping itself afloat. In part, this was because it was able to count on huge shipments of American silver, overwhelmingly from Mexico. This inflow of silver into Spain, worth an estimated 250 million pesos fuertes between 1760 and 1810, went to pay for the colonial administration of New Spain. Mexican silver also funded shipyards in Havana that were responsible for much of the refurbishment of the Spanish navy. In addition, Mexican silver served as collateral for loans from Dutch banks, and these in turn helped to finance Spain's successive imperial wars. Not until the outbreak of a further massive bout of hybrid warfare, after 1792, was the position of the Spanish monarchy seriously challenged within the Iberian peninsula, and attachment to it decisively undermined in South America.[40]

In this further extended period of conflict, each part of Spain's expensively overhauled war machine eventually proved inadequate to its task. Its enlarged navy could not match British sea power, as shown most terribly at the battle of Trafalgar in 1805, while Spain's expanded army failed to prevent Napoleon Bonaparte's legions from invading and occupying much of the Iberian peninsula itself three years later. As in the United States from 1776, and in France after 1789 – and as in Corsica in 1755 – one result of these war-related crises was an innovatory turn to pen and ink. In 1812, opposition legislators meeting at Cádiz, a major port on Spain's south-western coast, issued one of the most ambitious and widely influential political constitutions produced in the nineteenth century. Even before this, Spanish colonists in Argentina, Guatemala, Venezuela and Colombia were embarking on their own wars, and drafting their own new constitutions.

## Haiti: The Exception that Broke and Proves Some Rules

Rising levels of hybrid warfare posed severe but different challenges, then, for all three of the powers most expensively and extensively invested in it – Britain, France and Spain. For all three, the costs, adjustments and challenges involved in these changing modes of long-distance warfare acted as catalysts for political and ideological change. The strains of hybrid warfare helped to provoke outbreaks of extreme violence, either on these polities' own soil, or in territories connected to them, or both. In the process, the legitimacy of customary ruling orders was brought into question and undermined, fresh political configurations emerged, and influential new written constitutions were precipitated and enabled.

Claims of this sort may appear problematic. For some, laying stress on the impact of transcontinental warfare – or on any other large-scale and wide-ranging sets of changes – risks flattening out important and essential differences, and detracts from the specific roles and contributions of particular nations, cultural groupings and individuals. There can be a fear, as the anthropologist Arjun Appadurai puts it, that addressing the large-scale will tend 'to marginalise the already marginal' and foster neglect of 'small agencies and local lives'.[41] Yet there is no need, I would argue, to become trapped in such chicken-and-egg type arguments. Drawing attention to the big and the wide and to connections does not mean – and should not mean – ignoring and effacing the specific, the local, the small-scale and finely researched individual details. The last of the four best-known war-related revolutionary explosions breaking out between the mid eighteenth century and the early decades of the nineteenth century makes the point.

What became known as the 'Haitian Revolution' has often been viewed in terms of its singularity, and there are some good reasons for this. Situated on the humid and mountainous western sector of the island of Hispaniola in the Greater Antilles (Spain occupied the other part), Saint-Domingue, as its French invaders named it in the 1650s, grew over the next century into the world's biggest producer of coffee. Its plantations also exported as much sugar as Jamaica, Cuba and Brazil combined. Far and away France's richest overseas colony, the settlement imprisoned within its boundaries close to half a million Black slaves, of whom perhaps seven in every ten adults may have been African-born. But when the strains of its overindulgence in hybrid warfare finally sparked political crisis in France in 1789, the ripples also spread to an already riven Saint-Domingue.

In recent decades, the basic storyline of what happened next has been rehearsed and investigated many times.[42] Initially, some of the colony's 30,000 or so white settlers, fired up by the early stages of the French Revolution, began agitating for their own share of political change. Then, some of Saint-Domingue's relatively prosperous free Blacks staged a small-scale rebellion, demanding their own concessions from Paris, civil rights and

5. Allegory of Toussaint Louverture proclaiming the
first constitution of a future Haiti in July 1801.

political representation. But it was a much larger rebellion on the
part of some 100,000 enslaved people in the northern plains of
the colony in August 1791 that really transformed events. 'Principles, destructive of our property,' as the French president of

Saint-Domingue's General Assembly at Cap Français lamented, 'have kindled a flame amongst us, and armed the hands of our own slaves.'[43]

Slave uprisings were recurrent phenomena in the Caribbean and the Americas, but most were small and quickly extinguished. The 1791 slave rebellion on Saint-Domingue was neither of these things. Soon, all the shifting groupings involved in the fighting were mobilising large numbers of Black enslaved soldiers. Under pressure and in an attempt to calm things down, France abolished slavery throughout its dominions in 1794. Only, on Saint-Domingue, there was no calm.

Some ten years later, after successive waves of extreme violence and starvation had destroyed half of its Black population, after interventions by British, Spanish and French naval and military forces had failed and been defeated, and after the issuing of a first written constitution in 1801 proclaiming that slavery was 'forever abolished', Saint-Domingue succeeded in breaking free of European-dominated armies and controlling actors. On 1 January 1804, its triumphant Black and mixed-race leaders issued a formal Declaration of Independence and inaugurated the sovereign polity of what they initially called Hayti. Before 1820, five more official constitutions would be produced here.[44]

Not just the violence of these changes, but also their innovativeness was widely recognised at the time. As a European abolitionist remarked in 1804, in a tone of surprise that was itself revealing: 'An African people, insubordinated to any European inhabitants of the same territory, and independent of all exterior government, is [now] planted in the centre of the Antilles.'[45] Haiti became the first and only sovereign Black-ruled polity equipped with a constitution to exist in the Caribbean world until decolonisation began to quicken in this region in the 1960s. Events on Haiti after 1790 had a still more profound political significance. They served to demonstrate that, having spread from areas of Europe, evolving as they went, into parts of North America and then into South America, the new constitutions might be deployed and adapted by activists and among a population that were disproportionately Black.

It was this point – the drafting of written political texts on the part of men who in some cases seem to have viewed themselves as entirely or in part African – that a sympathetic witness of Haitian politics chose to stress in 1816. 'All the public documents', he observed, 'are written by those ... whose names they bear, and ... they are all black men, or men of colour.' The preamble to the constitution drafted in 1805 for Haiti's first post-independence leader, Jean-Jacques Dessalines, a ruthless and intelligent soldier and a former slave, made the same fundamental point but in more grandiloquent language:

> In [the] presence of the Supreme Being, before whom all mankind are equal, and who has scattered so many species of creatures on the surface of the earth for the purpose of manifesting his glory and his power by the diversity of his works, in the presence of all nature by whom we have been so unjustly and for so long a time considered as outcast children ...[46]

Rights were now to be formulated, written down, put into print, distributed and laid claim to by those who had formerly been stripped of all rights.

All this was indeed remarkable. Yet what happened on Saint-Domingue / Haiti also confirms the importance of trends and developments that were evident in *other* regions of the world. To begin with, events here further illustrate the rising importance by the 1700s of maritime reach and resources. Only, in this case, it was not naval warships that played the most crucial role, but another fast-growing component of European maritime technology: long-distance slaving ships.

In practice, considerable overlaps existed between these two kinds of violent seagoing vessels. Like naval warships, most slave ships were armed. Even a relatively compact French slaver, the *Diligent*, operating out of the port of Nantes in Brittany in the 1730s and 1740s, carried 'eight four-pound cannons, fifty-five muskets, eighteen pistols, twenty swords, and two swivel guns, all in excellent condition'.[47] Since slave-ship owners and captains wanted crews that were capable of handling such weaponry, they frequently recruited men who had previously seen service in fighting navies.

Accordingly, there are close – and still insufficiently explored – links between the unprecedented expansion of some European navies at this time and the increase in European slave trading. France illustrates this point well. In the first quarter of the eighteenth century, French vessels carried an estimated 100,000 captive human beings out of Africa. But, as the French navy surged in size after 1750, so, too, did the volume of French slaving. Over the last quarter of the eighteenth century, French slave ships transported 400,000 Africans. Around 70 per cent of these people, who were overwhelmingly male, came from suppliers on the Angola coast and the Lower Guinea coastal regions (Benin, Togo and what is now Nigeria). A disproportionate number of these captives who managed to survive the 5,000-mile passage to the Caribbean ended up on the northern, western and southern coasts of Saint-Domingue.[48]

What happened on Saint-Domingue/Haiti also confirms the political impact and disruptiveness of expanding levels of warfare in the 1700s. It underlines, too, the degree to which this was not exclusively a Western phenomenon. In much of west Africa, the middle decades of the eighteenth century also witnessed a busier plurality of conflicts. Take Dahomey, a formidable kingdom in present-day Benin, with its own standing army and gunpowder weaponry. In 1724, its soldiers invaded the once powerful coastal kingdom of Allada, seizing over 8,000 captives. Dahomey itself was invaded seven times between the

1720s and the 1740s, by the armies of the Yoruba Oyo empire. This was based in what is now Nigeria, and sometimes deployed armies of over 50,000 men. There were other conflicts in this huge region. In the declining kingdom of Kongo, a polity which extended into parts of what is now Angola, Gabon and the two republics of Congo, a long-running civil war reached even sharper levels of violence between the 1760s and the 1780s.[49]

Since land in west Africa was abundant, while people were thinly spread, rulers in this vast region usually preferred to take human captives as war booty rather than use their victories to seize additional territory. They also sometimes sold these prisoners of war to European slavers in return for imported goods, guns, Asian textiles, cowrie shells and more. It is possible, therefore, that the rising levels of warfare evident in parts of west Africa by the mid eighteenth century also had the effect of bringing increasing supplies of Black captives to slave markets on its Atlantic coast at exactly the same time that the volume of French slaver activity was also on the rise.

As a result, some Africanists have contended, 'a great many of the slaves' who were shipped by French slavers into Saint-Domingue in the later 1700s may in effect have been military veterans, men who had 'served in African armies prior to their enslavement', and been taken captive by rival African armies before being sold to European slavers. It may have been the presence of these one-time trained African soldiers on Saint-Domingue, speculates the historian John Thornton, that was 'the key element of the early success' of its rebellion in the 1790s against slavery, and that enabled Black insurgents here to endure and fight back when they were 'threatened by reinforced armies from Europe'.[50]

Since the vast majority of Black people who fought on Saint-Domingue in the 1790s and early 1800s left no surviving records of any sort, the degree of their involvement in earlier west African military campaigns, and the influence on them of stories and traditions of African warfare, will never be known.

It is amply clear, however, that the accelerating levels of hybrid warfare that fostered convulsions in so many parts of the world after 1750 also fed into this momentous crisis in Haiti.

As a result of the manpower demands and financial costs it incurred by its participation in the American Revolutionary War, France had to cut back on the size of its army garrisons on Saint-Domingue. This reduction in the number of white regular troops available to maintain Saint-Domingue's plantation economy and slave quiescence meant that more of the burden of keeping order in this colony shifted to its local militias. These groupings included large numbers of free Blacks: precisely the sort of men who opted in many cases to join the rebellion in the early 1790s.[51]

French military and financial overstretch as a result of surging levels of hybrid warfare impacted on events in Haiti in a further, decisive respect. From 1792 to 1801, and again after 1802, successive French regimes were unable to focus their energies and resources on suppressing Black resistance on Saint-Domingue because their armies and navies were engaged in fighting full-scale wars against a range of major powers in multiple continents, countries and oceans. The ratcheting-up of levels of European warfare also fed into events on Haiti at a more individual level. In addition to whatever they may have derived from experience in, and remembered legends of, west African warfare, some of Haiti's most prominent Black commanders were able to acquire military experience and skills from serving in the armies of one or more of the prime European exponents of hybrid warfare.

Toussaint Louverture, the best-known and most charismatic revolutionary war leader on Haiti, who secured his own personal freedom from slavery in 1776, and was the instigator of the country's first constitution in 1801, spent time, for instance, in Spanish army regiments as well as working and fighting alongside French troops. He had received a bullet 'in the right hip which remains there still', Toussaint later recalled of this service with European troops, and had been struck on the head by 'a cannonball, which knocked out the greater part of my teeth'.[52]

Toussaint's principal lieutenant and ultimate nemesis, Jean-Jacques Dessalines, also borrowed from those European legions that in due course became his enemies. Possibly African-born, and certainly a one-time slave, Dessalines served for some eight years before 1802 as an officer in the French republican army.[53] As for Henry Christophe, a free Black who may have been of Grenadian origins, and who signed Haiti's Declaration of Independence and subsequently seized control of a northern sector of the country, he seems to have acted as a cog in France's hybrid war machine even earlier than this, fighting alongside French military forces in 1779 in the American Revolutionary War.

Henry Christophe has never enjoyed the high reputation of some of the other prime Haitian independence leaders. He appears less noble and less tragic than Toussaint, who died in 1803 in the dungeons of a French fort in the Jura Mountains. Nor was he an architect of Haitian independence at the same level of importance as Dessalines, who was himself assassinated. But the relative neglect of Henry Christophe, who still lacks a major and imaginative biography, is chiefly owing to the type of government on Haiti that he ultimately sought to construct. Yet, like much of what happened on Saint-Domingue / Haiti, the projects and ultimate career of this man are important and possess more than just local significance.

Confronted with the challenge of governing an only recently emancipated population that was very poor, overwhelmingly illiterate and substantially trained to violence, with no well-established civilian institutions available to them, and with the threat of a renewed French invasion and re-enslavement present until the 1820s, all early Haitian leaders were of necessity hard men and highly reliant on military force. Like Pasquale Paoli's constitution for a profoundly endangered Corsica in 1755, Haiti's early constitutions bristle nervously with provisions for military organisation and strong rule.

By its first such document, in 1801, Toussaint Louverture became 'General-in-Chief … for the rest of his glorious life'. The constitution promulgated by Dessalines in 1805 in turn made clear that 'no person' (that is, no man) was 'worthy of being a Haitian who is not a … good soldier'. This same constitution stipulated that Haiti was to be split into six military divisions, each commanded by an army general. Well into the 1820s, presidents of Haiti made use of official printed stationery that was headed with engravings of cannon.[54]

To this extent, Henry Christophe's own brand of tough authoritarianism was very much par for the course. The constitution created under his direction in 1807 for the breakaway northern State of Haiti affirmed the 'inalienable rights of man', and the freedom 'in full right' of every resident Haitian. But it also made him general-in-chief, with the right to choose his own successor. Though only, it was stressed, 'from amongst the generals'. By means of another constitution, however, issued in April 1811, and read out in 'all the public places' to 'the sound of warlike music', Henry Christophe went further and in a different direction.[55] He declared himself to be a monarch, King Henry I of Haiti.

The constitution presided over by Dessalines in 1805 had already announced that Haiti was to be an empire. But this text had stipulated that the country's imperial crown was to be 'elective not hereditary'. Henry Christophe, by contrast, aimed at full hereditary rule. 'To convey an idea of the supremacy of power', proclaimed his 1811 constitution, the succession was 'to be vested only … [in] the male legitimate children (to the perpetual exclusion of females) in an illustrious family constantly devoted to the glory and happiness of the country': namely, Henry's own family. His spouse, Marie-Louise, was to become queen of Haiti. His sons were to be princes and his daughters, princesses; while his heir presumptive, Victor, was given the title of Prince Royal.

There was to be a full supporting aristocracy of dukes, counts and barons 'nominated and chosen by His Majesty', with each rank in this new-made Haitian peerage adopting specially designed robes. There was to be a royal court in which formal dress codes were to apply, and new orders of chivalry. There were also, this 1811 constitution stipulated, to be palaces built throughout northern Haiti, wherever King Henry judged 'proper to fix upon'. In the end, there were nine of these, plus a generous sprinkling of 'châteaux', with names like Victoire and Bellevue-le-Roi.[56]

It is tempting to see all this purely as megalomania, or at least as a particularly brazen exercise in inventing traditions. Yet to do so would be to miss too much. Henry Christophe was hardly the only ruthless general turned self-made ruler at this time eager to award himself a crown and perpetuity. As this new Haitian monarch was well aware, his almost exact contemporary, Napoleon Bonaparte, had crowned himself emperor of France in 1804, and subsequently also made himself king of Italy. Like Napoleon, Henry Christophe viewed becoming a hereditary monarch not only as a form of self-aggrandisement, but also as a means of securing wider international recognition and acceptance. He also saw it as part of a strategy for restoring order and stability to a territory long riven by warfare that was still threatened by foreign invasion, 'that abyss in which its most inveterate enemies would extinguish it' as his new constitution put it.[57] Like Napoleon, too, and like many later rulers, Henry saw no inconsistency whatsoever between assuming a crown on the one hand and issuing written constitutions on the other.

In case anyone missed these parallels with Napoleon, one of Henry Christophe's publicists made a point of claiming in print that the Haitian monarch was actually 'a near relation to Bonaparte'.[58] Yet while Henry deliberately borrowed language, ritual, methods and legitimisation techniques from Napoleonic France, this newly self-appointed king was also prudently eclectic in his alliances, just as he was always revolutionary. He

6. Richard Evans, *King Henry Christophe, c.*1816.

developed close links not only with France but also with its prime enemy, Britain, corresponding with politicians and abolitionists in London, and consulting its College of Arms, Britain's official authority on heraldry, on the design of Haiti's chivalric orders and coats of arms.

Henry also commissioned a grand state portrait of himself from the artist Richard Evans, who had been a pupil and assistant of Thomas Lawrence, the premier painter at this time of members of the British royal family and aristocracy. Evans's portrait of Henry shows him wearing a dark green, double-breasted military dress coat, with his newly founded military order of Saint Henry pinned against his heart and his recently manufactured crown on a table beside him. He poses against a background of threatening rolling clouds, a soldier king valiantly engaged in defending a realm whose very independence had been secured by Black warfare.[59]

Again, such self-conscious investment in his royal image has sometimes given Henry a bad name, in part justifiably so. These initiatives and indulgences were funded by means of the still-enforced plantation labour of the mass of impoverished Haitian men and women. More questionable, though, is the often implicit and occasionally explicit assumption that Henry's monarchical experiments were somehow intrinsically counter-revolutionary acts, and essentially at odds therefore with written constitutionalism. Neither interpretation is tenable.

There is little evidence that the mass of free and enslaved men and women who rose up and fought on Haiti after 1790 were themselves committedly republican; it would have been strange if they had been. Most parts of the world at this time, including most of the African continent, were still ruled by individuals who regarded themselves as kings or their equivalents. In most countries and empires outside the Americas – and for all of the surge in transformative written constitutions – monarchy would remain the default mode of formal state leadership until the First World War, and in some regions even longer.

Moreover, there was a sense in which, in seeking so inventively and elaborately to turn himself into a monarch and to create his own dynasty, Henry Christophe was not an exponent of counter-revolution, but rather profoundly revolutionary. Napoleon Bonaparte, that other parvenu monarch, had at least been able to lay claim to a minor noble background and to his formal training as an army officer. But for Henry Christophe, an uneducated Black artisan, turned drummer boy, turned innkeeper, turned butcher, to become a general and finally to proclaim himself a hereditary monarch, was a massively audacious act – and recognised as such by many of his contemporaries. He wanted, Henry declared, to become 'the first crowned monarch of the New World' and the 'Destroyer of Tyranny, Regenerator and Benefactor of the Haitian nation'.[60]

This is one reason why Henry's career merits closer attention. His ideas and actions confirm that this age of rising hybrid warfare, which fed so dramatically into a succession of violent revolutionary explosions, was not necessarily at odds with fresh monarchical experiments, any more than monarchy itself was necessarily at odds with the forging and adoption of important new written constitutions. Henry Christophe's own experiment at royal rule in northern Haiti soon faltered, however. In October 1820, ill, and knowing that he was losing authority, he committed suicide, shooting himself through the heart. His sixteen-year-old son and heir, Prince Victor, who had also been portrayed in oils in the grand manner by Richard Evans, was promptly bayoneted to death and his body tossed on a dung hill.

Yet none of this detracts from the fact that Henry Christophe was an innovator who recognised that written constitutions might be put to adventurous and profitable use by someone who aspired to be a hereditary monarch. A growing acceptance that this was the case – that written constitutions could be made compatible with modes of monarchy and not just with republicanism – would be crucial to the rising success of this new political technology.

Events on Haiti, for all their distinctiveness, confirm what we have seen in other warlike and political crises discussed in this

7. A satirical British print of 1821 both attacks the late Haitian king as a tyrant and associates him with unpopular European monarchs.

chapter, in Corsica, in Britain and its American colonies, in France, and in Spain and its Atlantic empire. For large stretches of the world after 1750, warfare, especially the shocks and ramifications of hybrid warfare, proved systemic, ever harder to avoid and a source and sharpener of revolutions and regime changes of different kinds.[61] It is against this background of volatility and mounting violence on land and on sea that the rising interest in writing, utilising and propagating constitutional texts must partially be understood.

Yet we are still left with critical questions. Rampant warfare, and changes in the nature and scale of warfare, were key precipitants of major political and territorial disturbances and shifts in ideas and practices. But why did responses to these war-related disturbances and shifts increasingly take the form of new written texts? To begin settling on answers to this question, we need to double back in time and look at other regions of the world.

8. Catherine II at work on the *Nakaz*.

# Two

# OLD EUROPE, NEW IDEAS

## St Petersburg

Compared with most of the paintings on view in the galleries of the State Hermitage Museum, it appears at first glance insignificant. Framed in metal, and less than four inches by eight inches in size, it is amateurish in style and overly busy. There is a cluttered royal apartment, complete with pillars, scarlet curtains and a velvet upholstered throne; and there is a bust of Peter the Great, the most titanic of Russian tsars, a reformer and a warmonger. The bust is positioned so that its stone eyes appear to look approvingly across at the woman seated at the centre of the picture, working at a gilded writing desk. She, meanwhile, turns away from her papers to gaze uncompromisingly outwards. Catherine II of Russia was almost forty when this enamel picture was made, and the anonymous artist shows her heavily rouged, already slightly overweight and with a slackening jawline. But her dark blue stare, Roman nose and thin, cunning lips are arresting. So much so that it is easy to be distracted from her hands. Portraits of European royal females at this time occasionally show them gesturing towards emblems of power. But these things generally remain at a physical distance away from them. Here, though, Catherine does not gesture. She grasps. In one substantial hand, there is a quill pen. The other holds the manuscript of the most important of her many written works, the *Nakaz*, or Grand Instruction.

Starting early in 1765, the third year of her reign, Catherine worked on this text most mornings for over eighteen months, rising regularly between 4 and 5 o'clock, and reputedly developing headaches and eye strain as a result. After circulating an initial draft among her advisers, she sent a revised version to the printers in July 1767, adding two further sections the following spring. Altogether, the completed *Nakaz* contained twenty-two chapters and 655 clauses; and, while she worked alongside a secretary, it was Catherine herself who selected and organised the material, and wrote out the finished version. Her avowed reason for investing so much time and effort in this document was to supply a guide and an agenda for a legislative commission she had summoned to Moscow to work on modernising and systematising the laws of the Russian empire. So, for all its aesthetic limitations, this image in the State Hermitage Museum is important and remarkable. It is one of very few depictions from before the twentieth century of a woman actively engaged in drafting a major legal and political text.[1]

Catherine's gender and how she lived her life help to explain why the wider significance of the *Nakaz* has gone underexplored. The place of its making has also played a part in this regard. Works of global history still often marginalise the Russian empire, approaching it as a singular, even exotic set of territories. The risk of this happening becomes even greater where matters of political innovation and modernisation are involved. When Catherine seized the throne in 1762, and for long afterwards, the Russian empire was 'an absolute monarchy, placed at the despotic end of the spectrum'.[2] No institutional limitations existed on the power of its rulers and legislative initiative was lodged entirely in them. There were not even any locally trained lawyers at work in Russia during Catherine's reign. That an innovative constitutional text should have emerged from such a setting, and that it might have an impact beyond the Russian empire's own territorial boundaries, can seem therefore inherently unlikely. Yet while not a written constitution, the *Nakaz* is a significant text that casts light on how this political genre evolved, and how it came to proliferate.

Sharper, wider levels of warfare worked progressively after 1750 to precipitate a series of influential and creative political revolutions. But focusing *only* on these early revolutionary eruptions, in Corsica, the Americas, France, Haiti and elsewhere, risks shrinking the story of how new constitutional initiatives and texts came to spread into a tale of just a few big moments in a few favoured sites of action. Paying attention to how rising levels of warfare also fed into more imaginative modes of constitutional activity in other sectors of the world makes for a more accurate, nuanced and comprehensive picture. Once this wider, more searching lens is adopted, Russia becomes a place that demands close attention, along with many others. In the aftermath of the Seven Years' War, this was one of a range of European monarchies where 'a written document, an endurable objective thing', in the philosopher Hannah Arendt's words, acquired more prominence and traction.[3] How did this come to pass?

## War, Paper and Enlightenments

To understand the rising vogue for more ambitious constitutional texts in the mid eighteenth century, it helps to situate them in the context of other pieces of new, official paperwork prompted by surging warfare and growing state competition. In the wake of the Seven Years' War, there was a feverish rush among victorious powers to accumulate information on freshly acquired territories and publish plans for reordering them in the conquerors' chosen image.

Thus, in the wake of Britain's conquest of what would eventually become Canada, Joseph Des Barres, a Swiss-born military surveyor, assisted at times by a young, adventurous and promising Royal Navy officer named James Cook, embarked on a project to map the coastline between Newfoundland and the colony of New York. Their work resulted in *The Atlantic Neptune* of 1777: four monumental volumes of charts, maps and views that were designed to aid Britain's maritime and imperial reach, and that remain works of art in terms of their fine detail, beauty and precision.[4]

There was also a riot of new paper schemes in the 1760s among wartime losers as well as winners, aimed at raising revenue and rebooting government in the debt-ridden aftermath of extreme, and extremely expensive, conflict. After arriving in the northernmost Spanish American viceroyalty of New Spain in 1765, for instance, José de Gálvez, a one-time shepherd turned lawyer, turned imperial bureaucrat, designed a plan to replace what he and his masters viewed as venal colonial officials with civil servants appointed directly by Madrid. Law codes were also issued in the wake of the Seven Years' War, including King Charles Emmanuel III of Sardinia's *Laws and Constitutions* of 1770.[5] This was a counterpart on paper to the king's simultaneous efforts to build up his fortresses and army; yet another way, as he saw it, of buttressing and reconfiguring his state in the face of rising levels of warfare and pressures from without.

Since surging levels of conflict were afflicting multiple continents at this time, some of this blizzard of new paperwork was generated by regimes beyond Europe. After bringing the Qing empire's genocidal campaigns against the Zunghars to their bleak conclusion in the 1750s, the Qianlong emperor commissioned what became known as the *Comprehensive Treatises of Our August Dynasty*. Some 150 scholars and officials based in Beijing laboured on this compendium for eighteen years. Together, they researched and drafted over 120 chapters on the geography, legal systems, administrative practices, natural resources and languages of a now much extended Chinese realm. The intention was to make available a source book for Qing imperial government, especially in regard to the newly conquered territories in central Asia.[6] Like British expansionists in the 1760s in regard to

Bengal and North America, Qianlong wanted his new Central Asian conquests to be made legible in order that they could be adequately ruled and known.

Like much other post-war official paperwork at this time, the *Comprehensive Treatises* also had a propaganda and celebratory function. The idea in this case was to proclaim Qianlong's firm command over his much-expanded dominions. The completed 2,000-page work – which merits wider and more comparative treatment – was finally put into print in 1787, the same year that a constitution for the United States was drafted in Philadelphia.

As this mammoth Qing production illustrates, the sharper, almost insatiable appetite at this time for accumulating, system-ising and publishing information was not confined to Europe and its colonies. Similar trends can be seen in other parts of the world, especially in locations coping with the aftermath of war. What *was* more distinctive about the surge in Euro-American official paperwork in the decades after 1750 was the degree to which this sometimes took an explicitly constitutional turn. Also significant was the extent of the influence on this paper-work by men who were associated with the Enlightenment with a capital 'E'.

Catherine II's *Nakaz* is an extreme case in point. In com-piling it, the empress selected and edited her borrowings from other authors very carefully, tailoring them in line with her own priorities. Even so, the scale of her Enlightenment larceny is striking. Over 290 of the clauses in the *Nakaz* – almost half of the total – owe something to Montesquieu's *The Spirit of Laws*, the bestselling work that Pasquale Paoli had belatedly purchased. A further hundred or so clauses in the *Nakaz* are lifted from the Italian jurist Cesare Beccaria's seminal work *On Crimes and Pun-ishments* (1764), which Catherine is known to have read in French a year after its publication. The empress also took ideas and phrases from the *Encyclopédie*. This was a multi-volume compil-ation published between 1751 and 1772, and intended by its chief

French promoters both as a work of reference and as a 'war machine' (an indicative phrase) to advance enlightened reform. Catherine's plundering of this work was extensive. Her insistence throughout the *Nakaz* that laws must be plainly written and easily accessible, for instance, echoes advice put forward in the *Encyclopédie*: 'The best possible legislation is that which is the simplest.'[7]

As the nature of Catherine's plagiarism illustrates, many of the authors who exerted a conspicuous influence on official minds at this time were French, or individuals publishing in French. In part, this was because French was still the main language of diplomatic exchange and polite culture in much of Euro-America, as well as in parts of the Ottoman world. But while Frenchness was important, so, too, in practice was geographical range. The Enlightenment figures and texts that exerted most influence on Euro-American monarchs and high-level political actors after 1750 tended to be those which addressed themselves to transcontinental events, and showed an interest in the widening scope of conflict and its consequences. 'We drain ourselves of men and money', wrote Voltaire in 1751, 'to destroy one another in the farther parts of Asia and America.'[8]

The amount of space and analysis Enlightenment luminaries devoted to the widening scope and danger of warfare is telling. It underlines the point that these violent changes were recognised as significant at the time. 'I raise my eyes to gaze afar', wrote the Genevan-born philosopher and novelist Jean-Jacques Rousseau in 1755–6, in the midst of the quickening of what would become known as the Seven Years' War:

> I see fire and flame, deserted fields, towns being pillaged. Cruel men, whither are you dragging those wretches! I hear a frightful din, such commotion and such screams, I approach and perceive a scene of murder, ten thousand men butchered, the dead stacked in heaps, the dying

trampled underfoot by horses, bearing the image of death and its last agony.[9]

Ten years after summoning up this vision of out-of-control warfare, Rousseau – who himself fantasised about becoming a marshal of France – compiled a manuscript, 'Constitutional Proposal for Corsica'. Forlornly, as it turned out, he set out his ideas on how the island might remain decently independent and safe at a time of incessant and burgeoning conflict.[10]

The worldliness of so many stellar Enlightenment figures, the attention they paid to different parts of the globe and to the operation of power and military violence were vital aspects of their appeal to those in high office. In an era of contagious hybrid warfare, with rulers and politicians facing a recurring need to rethink and restructure governance, some of these published works were seen as offering analysis and solutions that might be of practical use. This was very much the intention of the authors concerned. As one historian puts it, many of the Enlightenment's leading proponents deliberately 'struck a balance between intellectual daring and worldly conventions in order to forge an alliance with the educated elites and rulers', and in the hope that by so doing they might nudge them towards improving government, law and society.[11]

It helped in this regard that some of these men (and these Francophone Enlightenment luminaries were overwhelmingly men) possessed their own direct experience of state service and/or of military affairs. The Swiss jurist Emer de Vattel is a case in point. Throughout the War of the Austrian Succession and the Seven Years' War, he worked as a diplomat in Saxony, a German electorate struggling against the armies and ambitions of the neighbouring state of Prussia.[12] Vattel's remarkable *The Law of Nations*, a book that George Washington borrowed from a New York library in 1789, and still had in his possession at his death ten years later, was originally published in 1758. In this work, Vattel dwells on the inevitability of armed conflict. He also discusses how war's ferocity might be better contained, soothing his potential elite readers by suggesting (falsely) that European armies conducted war more humanely than their equivalents elsewhere: 'The humanity with which most nations in Europe carry on wars at present', purrs Vattel, 'cannot be too much commended.' In addition, and critically, he devotes one of his early chapters to the 'constitution of the state'. It is self-evident, he writes, that:

> the nation has the entire right to form its constitution itself, to maintain, perfect, and regulate at will everything that pertains to the government, without anyone being justly able to prevent it.

A political constitution was not a rigid inheritance, something passed on through the ages and to be taken for granted. It was subject to change and reform by those living within the society involved.[13]

Charles-Louis de Secondat, Baron de Montesquieu, was also personally marked by war and its demands. He was the product of a noble family from south-western France, and studied law at the University of Bordeaux. Montesquieu was also, however, the son of an army officer, and went on to choose for his wife the daughter of yet another army officer. His book *The Spirit of Laws*, published anonymously in 1748, and saluted by Catherine II of Russia as 'the prayerbook of all monarchs with any common sense', is threaded through with references to the systemic quality of contemporary conflict. 'A new distemper has spread itself over Europe,' he observes, 'infecting our princes, and inducing them to keep up an exorbitant number of troops.' Moreover, as Montesquieu recognises, the effect of this:

> ... of necessity becomes contagious. For as soon as one prince augments what he calls his troops, the rest, of

course, do the same; so that nothing is gained thereby but the public ruin. Each monarch keeps as many armies on foot as if his people were in danger of being exterminated … The consequence of such a situation is a perpetual augmentation of taxes.

Soon, he warns his readers, 'we shall be all soldiers'.[14]

Montesquieu also took note of how fiercer levels of military upheaval were on the rise outside Euro-America. 'Great revolutions have happened in Asia', he remarks, and his book is scattershot with references to China and Japan, each of which gets a chapter to itself, as well as to India, the Ottoman empire and what is now Indonesia. There was a sense, wrote his occasional collaborator Jean-Baptiste le Rond d'Alembert (himself the illegitimate son of an artillery officer), in which Montesquieu took it for granted that men everywhere, 'from the time they enter society', were driven by the 'mutual desire and hope of conquest'. Hence the vital need for new laws and institutions that might operate as 'chains … to suspend or to restrain their blows'.[15]

This was the lure that many leading Enlightenment figures held out to European sovereigns, and to the politically aspiring and reforming more broadly: that in an age of rampant, expensive and disruptive military violence on land and sea, innovatory and informed legislators might intervene so as to bind up society's wounds, re-establish order, remodel their respective states, *and in the process burnish their own reputations*. 'If I were a prince or a legislator,' urged Rousseau, with calculation, 'I would not waste my time saying what needs doing; I would do it.'[16]

Activist and aspiring rulers, it was frequently suggested, could profitably take as a model the figure of Moses. A revealer and recorder of laws, a leader of his people through the perils of war, a charismatic figure who features in the Old Testament and the Qu'ran, Moses wins approving mention in the volumes of

9. William Blake, *Moses Receiving the Law*, c.1780.

the French *Encyclopédie* close to 650 times. Celebration of Moses, along with other real and legendary legislators such as Lycurgus, the quasi-mythical lawgiver of ancient Sparta, Charlemagne, Muhammad, Confucius and the Anglo-Saxon King Alfred found enhanced expression from the mid eighteenth century not only in political, philosophical and scholarly writing, but also in art and in architectural design and sculpture.[17] The growing cult of messianic lawmakers at this time even surfaces in novels – in Louis-Sébastien Mercier's utopian bestseller *L'An 2440* (1770), for instance.

Mercier had his own links with armed violence. He was the son of a Parisian artisan who earned money for his clever son's education by polishing sword blades. In his novel, Mercier imagines a twenty-fifth-century Mexico that has been cleansed of colonial violence by a Black 'avenger of the New World'. This hero fights successfully against European predators, but Mercier goes on to describe how 'this great man, this renowned legislator, this negro, in whom nature had exerted all her force' subsequently lays 'down the sword' and instead resolves to 'display to the nations the sacred code of the laws', devising a federal constitution, and becoming in the process a model for his fellow rulers.[18]

But evoking heroic lawgivers from the past and imagining them in a distant future was plainly not enough. The only way to secure real and rational reform in the present, argued some Enlightenment spokesmen, was for there to be informed and energetic action on the part of those individuals actually in possession of real power. 'How happy would mankind be,' urged Beccaria in his *On Crimes and Punishments*, 'if laws were now given for the first time; now that we see on the thrones of Europe benevolent monarchs … fathers of their people, crowned citizens; the increase of whose authority augments the happiness of their subjects'.[19]

Those rulers who proved most responsive to this resurgent cult of the legislator, and who made efforts to promote innovative legal and constitutional texts of their own, shared certain characteristics. They were usually individuals who were proud of their personal Enlightenment culture. They were often writers themselves, and interested in the uses and workings of language. More often than not, they were Protestant in at least part of their background. Almost invariably, they also ruled territories that had been swept up in mid-century warfare and left challenged and disordered as a result. And this takes us back to Catherine II of Russia.

## A Woman Writing

All of these things – a deep interest in Enlightenment ideas, a taste for language and writing, a Protestant upbringing, an appreciation of the need to respond to the shocks and trials of escalating levels of war – characterised this woman, along with much else. Warfare indeed surrounded Catherine throughout her life, influencing most of the crucial phases of her career. She was born the Princess Sophie of Anhalst-Zerbst in 1729 in Stettin, present-day Szczecin in Poland. Then, as now, this was a garrison town as well as a major Baltic port, a place of fortifications, parade grounds and men at arms. It was also part of the spoils of war that Prussia wrested from Sweden at the end of the Great Northern War of 1700–1721; and the minor princeling who was Sophie's father, a Lutheran Protestant, was a senior military officer in Prussian service in charge of a regiment here.[20]

Everything began to change for her in 1744. The childless Empress Elizabeth of Russia selected the fourteen-year-old Sophie as a potential bride for her nephew and heir, Peter. The girl was brought to St Petersburg, underwent official conversion to the Orthodox Church, took the name of Catherine Alekseevna and learned competent spoken Russian. The marriage was duly celebrated in 1745. It proved a disaster for her new spouse, and a scandal for both parties. By the time of the

10. Equestrian portrait of Catherine by Vigilius Eriksen, 1764.

Empress Elizabeth's death and her own husband's accession to the Russian throne as Peter III in January 1762, Catherine had produced at least two illegitimate children, seemingly by different fathers. She had also forged her own political networks and projects.

Six months into the new reign, she accompanied over 12,000 troops and artillerymen to her husband's residence at the Peterhof, a complex of palace buildings and formal gardens on the outskirts of St Petersburg. A painting which Catherine subsequently commissioned to commemorate this coup shows her with her long dark hair loose, and riding a white horse pointedly astride. She raises her sword aloft, and is dressed for the occasion in the dark green uniform jacket and breeches of the elite Preobrazhensky Guards.[21] As well as forcing Peter III's abdication by way of this armed intervention, Catherine may have been complicit in some way in his strangling shortly afterwards. At which point, and as many of her powerful backers expected, she could have settled for the role of regent, ruling on behalf of her eldest, probably legitimate, son Paul, until he reached the age of seventeen. Instead, she took the Russian throne for herself.

Understandably, these events have contributed to Catherine's reputation for exceptionality. Yet some of her subsequent behaviour was more widely representative. Like many individuals who played leading roles in the drafting of significant political and legal texts, Catherine operated under acute pressures and in the shadow of war and danger. Her deep commitment to producing the *Nakaz* drew, to be sure, on her own gifts and inclinations, especially her voracious reading of certain Enlightenment authors and her taste for writing. But these were not the critical root of her actions. She invested conspicuous amounts of thought and time in this project because she wanted and needed to shore up and reinvent both her empire and her own position.

Some of the threats Catherine faced were personal. Her coup in 1762, and what came afterwards, were widely reported, not just throughout Europe but in the Americas, the Ottoman world and even in China. As a result, and for all the celebratory cult she orchestrated around herself, there were from the outset more negative veins of commentary, visual as well as written. Outside Russia, the empress featured in hundreds of satirical prints, many of them harsh and gender-focused. Foreign diplomats sometimes inserted rude caricatures of her in official correspondence. At home, she was the subject of

11. A bare-breasted and aggressive Catherine dwarfs her fellow (male) monarchs, but they still peer up her skirts. A French satire of 1792.

obscene graphic images, the work in some cases seemingly of her own courtiers.[22] The fact that Catherine was a female ruler, and nominally single after Peter III's death, but widely known to be sexually active, undoubtedly contributed to and coloured this obsessive attention. Decades after the event, a Russian general was unable to resist recording how, as Catherine lay on her death bed in 1796, he had managed to snatch a glimpse of 'the Empress's bare arse'.[23] It is also depressingly significant that whereas Catherine – like other powerful leaders of her time – frequently had herself depicted riding a horse, only she was rumoured to have had sexual congress with such an animal. Even now, historians are still sometimes distracted from a full consideration of her mind and projects by speculation about what specifically she did with her body.

But it was Catherine's position as a foreign-born, violent usurper with no blood claim whatsoever to the Russian throne that was potentially the sharpest source of her personal and political vulnerability. Catherine was a 'Slay-Czar', accused one foreign critic, a woman guilty of spouse murder whose plotting had brought about 'a Russian revolution'.[24] Throughout her reign, but especially in its early stages, there was always a risk of a further coup, the chance of another usurper looking to replace her on the Russian throne, the lurking prospect of an assassin.

In addition, and like many of her contemporary rulers, Catherine faced macro-challenges on account of war. With fewer than twenty ships in its navy at this time, many of them old, Russia had been in no position in the 1750s and early 1760s to engage in hybrid warfare. Its land forces, though, were heavily engaged in continental Europe, and expensively so. When Catherine seized the throne in 1762, the prospects for any future successful military and expansionist campaigns on her part appeared slight. Her army's pay was running several months in arrears. Russia's population density was the lowest of any European state, which posed obvious problems for the raising of men and taxes, while Catherine's revenue was initially only a fifth of that of the king of France, who ruled over a far smaller territory. By 1771, when she had nonetheless embarked on yet another war – this time against the Ottoman empire – the gulf between her income and expenditure had swollen to 8 million roubles.[25]

Both Catherine and Russia were characterised, then, by a mix of vulnerability and extreme ambition. She was warlike, unusually hard-working, tough and highly able. But she was also a female usurper whose position and behaviour were open to question, while the empire she had appropriated was massive but inadequately supplied, 'mighty but poor', in the words of a later Russian poet.[26] These circumstances influenced the making and the content of the *Nakaz*. Not a written constitution, it nonetheless shared characteristics and techniques with later texts that *were* constitutions. Not least, it was written in the shadow of extreme danger, and in the hope of forging enhanced support and cohesion at home and of fostering positive publicity abroad.

So the *Nakaz* begins with a preamble that is designed both to impress and to sweep aside doubts and opposition. Russia is a 'European Power', Catherine declares, very much in the tradition of Peter the Great, the Russian tsar whom she regularly referenced as though he really were a blood ancestor. But while Russia is undoubtedly European, the vastness of its geographical dimensions means that it can only be understood in terms of the world at large. It contains '32 degrees of latitude and 165 of longitude on the terrestrial globe', she boasts. This huge territorial extent, she goes on, determines Russia's mode of government: 'The sovereign is absolute, for no other than absolute powers vested in one person, can be suitable to the extent of so vast an empire.'[27]

The object of this absolutist government is not, however, to deprive Russia's people of their 'natural liberty'. On the contrary, its essential purpose is their 'happiness', and 'the glory of the Citizens, of the State, and of the Sovereign' (and the order in which Catherine lists these entities, with 'citizens' mentioned first, is surely deliberate). By the end of the second chapter of the *Nakaz*, indeed, references to absolutism, never mind despotism, have been abandoned. It is the capacity of '*monarchical* [my italics] government' to forge in Russia 'a sense of liberty' on which she chooses to dwell.[28]

At the heart of this liberty is a kind of equality: 'The equality of citizens consists in their being all subject to the same laws.' It follows from this that Russia's laws must be rewritten 'in a plain and easy language' so that everyone can understand them. A future legal code must be accessible and cheap, she argues,

available in print 'at as small a price as an Alphabet'. A supporter
– at least in theory – of mass education, Catherine urged that a
copy of the *Nakaz*, and the law code she expected to evolve from
it, be placed in every Russian schoolroom, and that these be read
aloud to the children alongside the Scriptures. (This idea that
texts on government and law might acquire semi-sacred status
by being scrutinised and celebrated alongside the Bible or other
central religious book would be pushed by many later constitutionalists.) It follows, too, Catherine argues in the *Nakaz*,
that there must be an expansion of mass benefits throughout
Russia, since a state is more than an extent of territory. Instead,
she insists, a state is properly a 'community'. 'The political', the
empress proposes, 'embraces the entirety of the people.' It was
a remarkable assertion on her part.[29]

It will not be enough, then, for Russia's people to secure a
uniform set of laws. Other, allied projects need exploring, too.
Improved levels of religious toleration were essential, Catherine
writes, for 'an Empire which extends its dominion over such
a variety of people'. Any future acts of censorship, she insists,
must be implemented only sparingly, so as not to 'destroy the
gifts of the human mind, and damp the inclination to write'.
There is even an implied approval of a welfare system of sorts.
More than a quarter of a century before the authors of the
French constitution of 1793 proclaimed that public relief was a
'sacred debt', and that society owed 'maintenance to unfortunate citizens', Catherine inserted this prescription for addressing
socio-economic inequalities into her *Nakaz*:

> The giving alms [*sic*] to the poor in the streets cannot
> be looked upon as an accomplishment of the duties of
> government, which must supply all citizens with sure
> maintenance, food, proper clothing, and a way of life not
> detrimental to the health of man.[30]

All these reforms, she insists, will go towards the making of a stronger, better Russia. But this goal demands yet further changes. Taxes, 'the tribute which each citizen pays for the preservation of his own well-being', must increase. This will call for a systematic expansion of manufacturing and trade, since these enterprises nourish state revenue: 'wherever there is commerce, there are custom houses'. The population, too, must increase. No machines should ever be introduced into Russia, she insists, that may result in a reduction in 'the number of working people'. Developing agriculture, though, will be vital, since well-fed men and women – or so she assumes – produce larger families. 'There are People', Catherine writes wistfully, 'who having conquered other parts [of territory], intermarry with the conquered people; whereby they attain two great ends, the securing to themselves the conquered people, and an increase of their own.' Enhancing Russia's stock of human resources, its future workers and taxpayers – and its future soldiers – would be part of her rationale for later annexing the Crimea, and for invading and progressively carving up Poland after 1772, acquiring in the process an extra 7 million or so subjects.[31]

As this suggests, there were ruthless limits to Catherine's own enlightenment. As a result, commentators have always disagreed about the significance and meanings of the *Nakaz*, and about where to situate the empress herself on the political spectrum. For one foreign diplomat based in St Petersburg in 1767, her initiative represented nothing less than 'a voluntary transfer of dominion ... by an absolute Prince in favour of the People'.[32] This was an absurdly generous assessment. But those at the time and since who dismiss the *Nakaz* as nothing more than a vain autocrat's parade of her pretensions to enlightenment have also misread and misunderstood its significance.

More to the point was the objection raised by Denis Diderot, one of the most radical exponents of the French Enlightenment and, for a time, an acquaintance and correspondent of

12. Catherine, along with the monarchs of Prussia and Austria, moves in to complete the colonisation and partition of Poland, a print of 1794.

the empress. 'The first line of a well-made code should bind the sovereign', he wrote in his critique of the *Nakaz*.[33] This the document emphatically and deliberately did not do. In drafting and publicising it, Catherine was not out to create a constitutional monarchy. At best, she was setting out ideas for a legal monarchy by which she, the sovereign, would assiduously draft benevolent laws for different orders of her subjects, perhaps obeying them herself, but also remaining free to alter them.

Yet, for all its limits, the *Nakaz* remains a remarkable text that is revealing about far more than just Russia. It was innovative and influential not least in terms of the techniques that Catherine devised in order to advance and promote it. The Legislative Commission that met in Moscow in August 1767 to discuss the *Nakaz* differed from later, seminal constitution-making assemblies but, in some respects, it also anticipated and even exceeded them. Like the convention that met in Philadelphia in 1787 to draft the constitution of the United States, this Moscow commission brought together delegates from an entire, rapidly expanding overland empire. To be sure, the 564 elected Russian deputies who made up this body possessed far less power and initiative than America's Founding Fathers; and, in the end, they accomplished far less. But these Moscow deputies were also markedly more diverse in terms of social, economic, religious and ethnic background than the men of Philadelphia.[34] About 30 per cent of them were nobles, but some came from much lower down the social hierarchy. To qualify for election as a representative of one of Russia's registered towns, for instance, a man needed only to own a house or possess a trade. Women, too, received some recognition in this Moscow commission, something that did not happen in revolutionary America, or revolutionary France, or revolutionary Haiti, or revolutionary Spanish America. Among those selecting the commission's members in 1767 were female landowners who were able to vote by proxy.

Just as the men of Philadelphia in 1787 would do very little for the 700,000 or so inhabitants of the new United States who were slaves, so the deputies assembling in Moscow in 1767 did nothing for Russia's own slave population, the roughly 50 per cent of its peasant class who were serfs. Catherine had initially planned to use the *Nakaz* to ease the condition of these people and provide for their gradual emancipation, thereby converting serfs into 'new citizens'. But these emancipatory projects fell victim to objections from the landowning class, and to her own nervousness about alienating her nobility.[35]

Russia's so-called 'state peasants' were, however, represented in the legislative commission, returning over 10 per cent of its deputies. Moreover, in sharp contrast with the men of Philadelphia in 1787, not all of the Moscow deputies were white, and not all of them were Christian. The empire's non-Russian peoples, many of whom were Muslims, had been drawn on extensively for military service during the Seven Years' War. They reaped some reward in the Legislative Commission, where they were allotted fifty-four deputies. 'Orthodox sits next to heretic and Muslim,' wrote Catherine complacently in December 1767 of the commission's meetings, 'and all three listen calmly to a heathen; and all four often put their heads together to make their opinions mutually acceptable.'[36]

It bears repeating that the commission was a consultative body. It was not, and was never intended to be, a constitutional convention. But it was an elected assembly, drawn conspicuously from an entire multi-ethnic polity, and called into being for discussions around a single, iconic text. Formally, at least, all of its deputies were on a par. Whatever their social rank, religion, ethnicity or region of origin, each of them was styled 'Mr Deputy' and given a salary, in tacit recognition that some of these men were not at all wealthy. Like the members of the Estates General at the outbreak of the French Revolution in 1789, each Russian deputy in 1767 was instructed to present a written account of his locality's particular grievances and demands. And like the American constitution-makers in 1787, these Moscow deputies were encouraged to view their deliberations as a matter for the admiring attention of the entire world and of posterity. A daily record was kept of their proceedings so that 'the future might have a true account of this important event and might judge the cast of mind of this century'. As for the *Nakaz* itself, the document was treated as many later texts that *were* constitutions would be treated: namely, as something sacred that was to be cherished and venerated. On Catherine's instructions, an original copy was encased in a silver *riza*, a kind of elaborate metal cover normally reserved for protecting and enshrining Russian Orthodox religious icons.[37]

In the end, the Legislative Commission and its work faded away. Its proceedings were marginalised by the outbreak of a

Russo-Turkish war in 1768, though some of its subcommittees continued to meet into the following decade. By then, though, the impact of the *Nakaz* had spread outside the borders of the Russian empire – and also beyond Catherine's own initial intentions and calculations.

From the outset, the empress had been careful to send copies of the work to fellow monarchs and to a select number of foreign intellectuals and journalists. In 1770, under pressure once again from war, she began a more systematic campaign to broadcast the fact and the content of the *Nakaz* across territorial boundaries. That year, Catherine commissioned a new, engraved edition which combined versions in Russian and German – that is, her own acquired and cradle tongues – with translations into Latin and French, the established languages of Euro-American scholarship and diplomacy. There were also part-commercial, part-sponsored editions of the *Nakaz*. In 1768, an official attached to the Russian embassy in London, one Michael Tatischeff, produced an English translation, which was reviewed in British magazines and extracted in some colonial American newspapers. There were also further German and French translations, as well as Greek, Italian, Latvian, Romanian, Swiss and Dutch versions. Altogether, by 1800, the *Nakaz* had appeared in at least twenty-six editions and ten different languages, and had been generously extracted in newspapers and magazines in multiple countries.[38]

As well as publicising Catherine's initiative across boundaries, some of these translations fostered an inflated impression of the degree of radicalism involved in it. The *Nakaz* was not a project for wider individual *political* rights. Nor did it propose serious curbs on executive power. But this was how, in translation, the text sometimes appeared and was read – which helps to explain why an early French version was officially banned. Voltaire, who was Catherine's most unctuous admirer among the French *philosophes*, sent her a carefully worded account of what happened:

Here are the facts: a Dutch publisher put out this *Instruction* [the *Nakaz*], which ought to belong to all the kings and tribunals in the world; he sent a consignment of two thousand copies to Paris. The book was submitted for examination to some ill-mannered cur of a literary censor ... he reported it to the chancellery as a dangerous book, an advanced book; it was sent back to Holland without further examination.

Being censored as a dangerous and advanced book in France, western Europe's foremost absolutist state, did wonders, in some quarters, for the *Nakaz's* reputation as a manifesto for dramatic political change. 'The true reason why the sale of this book was suppressed at Paris', reported a British journalist with predictable chauvinist ire, 'seems to have been, lest the true spirit of liberty which breathes so strong in it, might infect the air of France.'[39]

The way in which versions and readings of the *Nakaz* changed as it passed through different languages and geographical boundaries was due in part to the frictions and fluidities that are always involved in the business of translation, but which were particularly acute in this case. Translators working from the original Russian edition had to cope with the language's imprecision at this time, and also with a lack of adequate dictionaries. But, in addition, some of them seized the opportunity to insert into their versions of the *Nakaz* snatches of their own political ideas and aspirations. Eugenios Voulgaris, for instance, who produced the first Greek edition in 1771, was a deeply learned celibate priest. But he was also a significant Enlightenment actor who translated works by John Locke, and this was reflected in his treatment of the *Nakaz*.[40] Tatischeff, too, who was an acquaintance of the young and already questioning political and legal reformer Jeremy Bentham, made generous, surely wilful alterations in his English translation. Take Tatischeff's use of the word 'constitution'. The equivalent term for this in

Russian is *konstitutsya*. This word did not emerge until the early nineteenth century, and its usage remained controversial among Russian conservatives as late as the 1860s. But in Tatischeff's English translation of the *Nakaz*, Catherine is made to use the word 'constitution', and to do so in order to advance claims that she herself seems never to have intended. 'A state may change in two different ways', Tatischeff has her proclaiming: 'Either because the constitution of it *mends*, or because the *same* constitution corrupts.'[41]

The degree to which Catherine's *Nakaz* crossed geographical borders and into other languages, and the ways in which it mutated and was reinterpreted in the process were again anticipations of what was to come. One reason why the new written constitutions would over time achieve an ever-widening political and cultural impact was that they were rarely read and disseminated only within their place of origin. Made up of words, and therefore custom-made for print reproduction, these constitutional texts spread easily into other geographies and into other languages. As they moved across territorial and linguistic boundaries, how readers and political actors understood and made use of them would persistently alter and evolve.

## Male Monarchs and Innovation

In parts of the world, then, rising levels of warfare after 1750 fostered not extreme revolutionary crisis but rather attempts to reconfigure and re-represent the government of states, occasionally by way of the issuing of a significant new text. These initiatives should not be pigeonholed away simply as exercises in enlightened despotism. As Catherine's *Nakaz* demonstrates, they could involve discussions of rights and experiments with new forms of political communication. 'General rule,' Montesquieu had reasoned in *The Spirit of Laws*, 'one can raise higher taxes, in proportion to the liberty of the subjects.'[42] This point

– that making available and announcing improved rights within a state might aid in the raising of revenue and so strengthen the sinews of war – was duly noted by some in possession of power. In an era of increasingly demanding warfare, deploying innovative state texts in order better to engage the mass of subjects and ensure their armed service and taxes, while offering in return some guarantees around liberties and care, seemed to some European monarchs prudent, and a gamble worth taking.

It was often rulers who resembled Catherine II in certain respects – individuals from a Protestant background, who were drawn to Enlightenment ideas and simultaneously predatory and vulnerable – who proved most adventurous in advancing ambitious political and legal paperwork of this sort. Frederick II of Prussia is an example. He inherited the throne of this expanding, northerly German kingdom in 1740, along with a highly disciplined army of 80,000 men built up by his relentless and ruthless father, Frederick William I. Frederick II's own march that year into Silesia, a region of central Europe which is now split between Poland, the Czech Republic and Germany, precipitated the War of the Austrian Succession. Not content with this, he also invaded Saxony in 1756, thereby ramping up levels of fighting in the European theatre of the Seven Years' War.[43]

This conspicuous aggressiveness was primed, however, by an awareness on Frederick's part of the potential weaknesses of his own dominions. Prussia was made up of different, non-contiguous territories, so there was always a risk that its multiple, divided boundaries might be set upon by belligerent rivals – that Russia, Sweden, Austria, Poland or Saxony, or an alliance of all or any of these, might move in and carve up the country in some way. 'I am in the position of a traveller', the king wrote famously at the outset of the Seven Years' War, 'who sees himself surrounded by a bunch of rogues, who are planning to murder him and divide up the spoils among themselves.'[44]

As with Catherine of Russia, this mix of aggression and insecurity led Frederick to explore different initiatives that might
enhance unity and a sense of political community and readiness within his Prussian dominions, especially among males, the
future soldiery and the most prominent taxpayers. As in Catherine's case, too, Frederick's search for new modes of public and
political communication was combined with marked Enlightenment leanings on his part and a relish for the written word.
'He writes as well as he fights', Catherine remarked enviously.[45]
This was not true. But it was the case that, as well as leading
his armies into twenty different battles, the king wrote poetry,
philosophical tracts, essays on government and works of history,
including in 1763 a selective account of the Seven Years' War. He
also set in motion some experimental paperwork.

In the first decade of his reign, Frederick commissioned a
jurist and senior official named Samuel von Cocceji to design
reforms that would render Prussia's laws more efficient and accessible, and that might lead to a new German legal code. A scheme
for the latter was published in 1751 and, as Catherine would do
with the *Nakaz*, Frederick ordered the text to be translated into
multiple languages. Never properly implemented, this scheme
nonetheless served as a basis for a subsequent codification of
Prussian law, which in turn evolved into a written constitution
of sorts. But the *Frederician Code*, as it became known, was not
merely about the workings of the law; and, as with the *Nakaz*,
portions of it lent themselves to multiple readings. 'The first
state which man acquires by nature, is the state of liberty; for
naturally all men are free', begins the English translation of the
*Code*, which was published in Edinburgh in 1761 and snapped up
by Thomas Jefferson for his library at Monticello. 'The second
state of persons', this translation continues, 'is that of a citizen.'[46]

But it is Sweden's monarch Gustaf III who offers perhaps
the more striking example of how, in advance of the American Revolutionary War, some European rulers were already

experimenting creatively with new political texts and techniques. In some respects, Gustaf ran true to form. Like Catherine of Russia and Frederick of Prussia, he was from a Lutheran background. Like them, he participated actively in Enlightenment culture, founding the Swedish Academy in 1786, having earlier visited Paris and its intellectual salons and met Rousseau, Helvétius and other *philosophes*. Gustaf's one-time tutor and close political collaborator, Carl Fredrik Scheffer, was also very much an Enlightenment man. He was well acquainted with Montesquieu's writings, and corresponded with a range of French reformers, including the physiocrat Pierre Samuel du Pont de Nemours, an ancestor of the dynasty that founded America's DuPont corporation, and a future president of France's National Constituent Assembly. As for Gustaf himself, he also resembled Catherine and Frederick in being at once aggressively ambitious and conscious of operating under severe challenges, not least those posed by escalating levels of war. In the case of Sweden and Gustaf, however, the challenges of war took a particularly protracted and insidious form.[47]

Justifiably regarded today as a distinctively peaceful and civilised country, Sweden possessed a very different reputation in the early modern era. From the 1550s, its rulers had embarked on a succession of major conflicts. Initially, these sequential armed struggles allowed Sweden to develop into one of Europe's major overland empires, with a reach extending over much of the Baltic region, and with colonies and settlements in west Africa and the Americas. But in the course of the Great Northern War of 1700–1721, in which Sweden took on Russia, Poland, Denmark–Norway, some German states and at times the Ottoman empire, the country suffered debilitating casualty rates, debts and defeats. It was forced to surrender substantial amounts of its territory. It also lost its king, Karl XII, who was killed in 1718 by an enemy bullet – or possibly by a shot from one of his own exhausted soldiers – and died without leaving an heir.[48]

This emergency forced the Swedish monarchy into making substantial political concessions. As one contemporary chronicler put it: 'The Swedes, being tired out, and their treasure almost exhausted, by the continual wars ... were determined to shake off the yoke of absolute sovereignty.'[49] Sweden thus exemplifies in a precocious way extreme warfare's rising tendency in the eighteenth century to foster and enforce enhanced levels of political change. In 1719, and again in 1720, its monarchy was obliged to accept terms set out in new 'Instruments of Government', documents that were in effect written constitutions. These dismantled much of the machinery of absolutism that had grown up in Sweden since the 1680s. These Instruments of Government also required the country's monarchs to share power, as they had done back in the early seventeenth century, with the Council of the Realm, and with the Swedish diet or Riksdag.

This was a considerable and momentous shift, not least because the Riksdag consisted of four different estates. There were estates of the nobility, the clergy, and the burghers. In addition, and uniquely among parliaments in large European polities, there was an estate of the peasantry. When decisions were taken in the Riksdag, each of these four estates had one vote, and the principle of simple majority applied. This meant that if the three elected non-aristocratic estates – those of the peasantry, clergy and burghers – joined forces, Sweden's nobility could be outvoted. All this helps to explain why some foreign observers in the mid eighteenth century viewed the 'love of democracy' as an 'epidemic disease' in this country, especially as rising levels of education and print availability made the non-aristocratic estates in the Riksdag and Sweden's general population increasingly politically aware and demanding.[50] All this also helps to explain why Gustaf III was determined to make a change.

Gustaf was, and remains, a hard man to pin down. He belonged to a younger generation than the two other monarchs we have looked at so far. In 1771, when he began his reign, he was still in his mid twenties, whereas Frederick of Prussia (his uncle) was close to sixty, while Catherine II of Russia (his cousin) was in her early forties. Genuinely clever, personally elegant and volatile, Gustaf was also ambivalent in his spoken and written language, and in some of his actions. Unhappily married to a Danish princess, and accused by some political opponents of homosexuality, he may rather have been fundamentally asexual: interested less in any kind of intimate human contact than in devising new political and cultural projects, and in making an impression and exploring ideas. His relaxed and quizzical reaction on hearing news of the American Declaration of Independence in 1776 was typical of the man. 'It is such an interesting drama', he is said to have remarked, 'to see a nation create itself.'[51] The stress on theatre and performance is suggestive. Politically, Gustaf also aspired to create and to make a show.

His bid in August 1772 to reassert the monarchy's authority in Sweden was a military coup of sorts. Yet his actions involved minimal violence, and seem at the time to have been widely popular. They were also accompanied by radical, even democratic language and initiatives. Gustaf used his coup to introduce a new Swedish constitution, the Form of Government, which he had drafted hurriedly with the aid of Carl Fredrik Scheffer. This text retained some of the language and provisions of the 1719 and 1720 Instruments of Government, but shifted the balance of power more in the direction of royal initiative. The Riksdag was to retain most of its taxation powers, and laws could only be made by it and the king acting together. But the enforcement of laws was now given to Gustaf alone, ruling with the help of the Council of the Realm. Moreover, only the king could appoint the members of this council, and they could not take decisions in defiance of him, except if they unanimously agreed to oppose him on matters to do with treaties and alliances.[52]

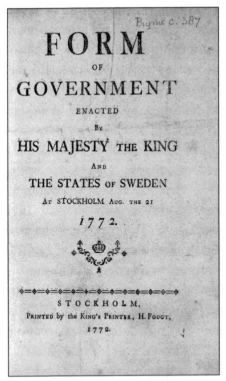

*Pryme c. 387*

# FORM
OF
# GOVERNMENT
ENACTED
By
## HIS MAJESTY THE KING
AND
### THE STATES OF SWEDEN
AT STOCKHOLM AUG. THE 21
*1772.*

STOCKHOLM,
PRINTED by the KING's PRINTER, H. FOUGT,
1772.

13. Gustaf III's Swedish constitution of 1772,
in one of its published translations.

As this provision suggests, the Form of Government of 1772 devoted substantial attention to foreign relations and war. This was deliberate. Gustaf's public justification of his coup was that he wanted to rescue Sweden from an old, corrupt noble elite that had damaged the country at home, and that had also failed it in the Seven Years' War. Sweden's involvement in that conflict had cost it 30,000 men, and racked up fresh war expenses equivalent in size to the country's existing national debt. These military and financial failures, coming on top of Sweden's earlier experiences of large-scale, catastrophic warfare, help to explain why Gustaf's promise of a fresh political and national start initially proved attractive.[53]

Yet, privately, Gustaf hungered for yet more wars, albeit this time successful hybrid warfare. He wanted to build up the Swedish navy, something he had achieved by the early 1780s. He also wanted to reverse Sweden's territorial contraction: to move into Norway, and into Russia, where, towards the end of his reign, he was planning to capture St Petersburg. This city had been built in part in the early 1700s by some of the 25,000 Swedes taken prisoner in the course of the Great Northern War, and seemed therefore an ideal target for a revenge attack.

None of these expansionist and warlike schemes were touched on in the 1772 constitution. Gustaf did, however, insert provisions underlining his military powers, albeit carefully. He retained clauses from previous Instruments of Government forbidding the monarch to raise men and money without the 'free will and consent' of the Riksdag. He also, though, inserted a new provision that, were Sweden to come under attack, 'His Majesty has power to take such measures as are in conformity with the security of the realm and the good of his subjects'. He added a further clause. 'The supreme command of his whole military power, by land and sea', Gustaf insisted, belonged only to him, 'as it has been the custom in the ancient and happy times, when the kingdom was most glorious'.[54]

Some of this constitution's most dramatic innovations, however, lay in the language surrounding it. References to 'citizens' had come easily enough to Catherine II of Russia, though she seems to have used the term more with rhetorical intent than to imply any political and legal rights. Frederick the Great of Prussia at times went further. In his private writings, he was sometimes prepared to refer to his Prussian subjects as *'fellow citizens'*. But, coming from a younger generation, Gustaf went further still, using his new constitution to declare himself a citizen openly and in print. His 'greatest glory', he wrote into the text, was 'to be *the first citizen* among a truly free people [my italics]' – and he made sure that this claim was widely reported.[55]

In the aftermath of his coup, on 21 August 1772, Gustaf addressed the members of the Riksdag in the Hall of State of the royal palace in Stockholm, boasting that, having 'saved my parent country, and myself, without injury to one single citizen … I have promised to govern a free people'. Copies of this speech were subsequently printed in blackletter, the typeface commonly used for Sweden's elementary school books and religious publications, which meant that it was familiar to most of the country's largely literate population. In a further effort to ensure mass awareness of his words, the king ordered copies of the speech to be posted up and read aloud in Sweden's churches, where attendance at public worship was compulsory. Subsequently, Gustaf would often refer to himself in speeches 'as a king, as a citizen', deliberately linking these two terms – king and citizen – together. Nor was this emphasis, or the king's relish for invoking equality and liberty ('the noblest of the rights of men', as his constitution put it), simply gesture politics on his part.[56]

The text of the Form of Government of 1772 stipulated that it was to be regarded as 'a fixed and sacred fundamental law', an 'unalterable law' in the original Swedish. All adult males in Sweden were to take an oath of allegiance to this written and printed constitution as well as to the king, as distinct from swearing allegiance only to the latter. Crucially, too, Gustaf himself was to swear allegiance to the new constitution. It was, he declared in his speech at the royal palace on 21 August, to be 'a law, as binding to myself as you'. The constitution also made clear that the same was to apply to the king's officials and to his descendants on the throne:

We now, by this, do declare and establish, this Form of Government to be a fixed and sacred fundamental law; which We, for us, and our posterity, as well born as unborn, bind ourselves to fulfil, to follow its literal contents, and look on him or them as enemies to our country who should attempt to lead us to deviate from it.[57]

Potentially, these provisions represented a significant political and legal leap. It was in the years 1776–87, and in the new United States, it has been argued, that the notion of a written constitution as a 'supreme fundamental law … simultaneously empowering but also limiting the institutions of government it establishes' began to be articulated.[58] In fact, ideas of this sort had been circulating and experimented with earlier than this, and within certain Europe monarchies. What happened in Sweden in 1772 offers a prime example.

These paper initiatives on the part of some European monarchs in the aftermath of the Seven Years' War help to explain indeed why uses and understandings of the word 'constitution' were already in flux *before* the American Revolution. In several European languages, the word 'constitution' and its equivalents had traditionally been used both for the organisation and government of a state, and to describe the intrinsic make-up of something, including the human body. By the late 1760s, however, this kind of usage was coming under pressure, not just in learned texts intended for the few but also in more popular writings. In 1771, even a workaday English journalist felt able to dismiss analogies 'between a political frame, and the system of the human body' as a stale and obsolete commonplace that plainly made no sense. A 'human body … consists of the same stamina from its birth to its dissolution', this writer reasoned. By contrast, 'a form of government is subject to a sudden, and total change'. Political communities, this anonymous journalist had decided, were 'not established by nature, but by human art'. They were therefore eligible for making, and for remaking.[59]

Post-Seven Years' War royal political paperwork was deeply significant, then. Its limitations, though, are also important. Neither Frederick of Prussia nor Catherine of Russia ever

produced a written constitution, although both monarchs
– especially Catherine – developed techniques for political
communication and publicity that later exponents of written
constitutionalism were to borrow and build on. Moreover,
monarchical actors at this pre-1776 stage were rarely interested in
devising and publicising texts that might seriously restrict their
own authority. As Diderot remarked of Catherine the Great and
her *Nakaz*: 'You come across lines [in it] in which, without her
being aware of the fact, she takes up again the sceptre she had
put down at the beginning.'[60]

Gustaf III's Form of Government, with its provision that
both king and people were 'bound to the law, and both of us
tied together and protected by the law', came closer to establishing restrictions on executive power. But although some of
this Swedish king's language and actions were radical and even
quasi-democratic, his 1772 constitution did not prevent him in
practice from arrogating more power in the later stages of his
reign. This helps to explain why, twenty years after the issue of
his constitution, in 1792, Gustaf would be mortally wounded
at a masked ball in Stockholm's Royal Opera House. His assas-
sins, who shot at him with a mix of bullets and bent nails, were
mainly Swedish nobles and army men angry at his war with
Russia, but some of them were also disturbed by his constitutional tampering. 'Good day, fine masked man', they said to
him, before moving in for the kill.[61]

Even apart from their other limitations, these royal ventures
– while important – were also very much top-down initiatives.
Yet, on both sides of the Atlantic after 1750, growing interest in
exploring new forms of political paperwork was also evident
among broader social groupings – and understandably so. Rising
levels of warfare, along with Enlightenment ideas, tempted and
obliged some European rulers and their officials to devise and
publish new written texts to reorder their states and reach out to
their respective populations. In addition, though, more systemic

warfare also fostered an increase in critiques and claim-making from below, and wider political awareness.

Those paying taxes to fund increasingly expensive wars, those seeing their lives, work, property and businesses disrupted by more recurrent armed conflicts, those forced into fighting themselves, or into sending off family members to fight and perhaps never seeing them return: these men and women, too, could be attracted by the prospect of new political laws and texts which might increase their leverage in some way, and impose curbs on their political masters. For a dramatic instance of this kind of more demotic constitutional activism in advance of the American Revolutionary War, we can turn to another European Protestant state that was impacted on early by Enlightenment ideas and heavily invested in warfare, namely Britain.

## Enter the Charter Man, Enter Tom Paine

He was utterly unlike the individuals we have been looking at in so many ways: increasingly alienated from the kind of political systems and social hierarchies they embodied and represented. Nonetheless, although they – and he – would have been outraged at the suggestion, there were points in common between these crowned players and Thomas Paine. Warfare forced some mid-eighteenth-century European monarchs into more creative political writing. Accelerating levels of hybrid warfare also shaped the course of this very different man's life and career, influencing what he did and what he came to write about and argue.

Keeping Tom Paine's close connections with war firmly in mind is important, because he has always posed challenges for biographers.[62] Born in 1737 in the English market town of Thetford in Norfolk, he came from a background that was modest, provincial and riven. He was the son of a mixed marriage between a Quaker tenant farmer and maker of stays (the whalebone

14. Thomas Paine: an engraving based on a lost portrait of 1779.

stiffeners in women's corsets) and an Anglican woman of somewhat higher social status. Paine himself was taken out of school
at the age of twelve, and the nature and extent of his subsequent
reading and intellectual influences remain unclear. The man was
also repeatedly on the move, from jobs, from wives, from different towns and countries, from former allies quarrelled with
and turned into enemies. Along the way, many of his personal

and family papers were lost, especially from the early phases of his life. As a result, the years he spent in his country of birth are easily telescoped into relative insignificance. Yet when Paine embarked for America in October 1774, he was thirty-seven years old. More than half of his life was already over, and some of his most vital responses, insights and obsessions had already been forged: forged in part and critically by Britain's rising involvement in hybrid warfare.[63]

Paine's first temporary physical absence from its shores, 'a kind of emigration', as he later described it, was as a fighting seaman. In the early stages of the Seven Years' War, he had joined a privateer, the *King of Prussia* (named after Frederick the Great, who was allied with the British), harrying French merchant ships. But his direct contacts with the costs and consequences of war went on for longer than this. Paine's most protracted paid employment was working as an excise officer, a position he occupied from 1761 to 1765, and again from 1768 to 1774. Excise taxes were the British state's prime fiscal resource for paying for its successive conflicts. They were levied on articles of common consumption – soap, salt, beer, paper, coal, leather, candles and the like – and they were enforced by an expanding army of excise men. Back in 1690, there had been some 1,200 excise officers. By 1770, when Paine was labouring as an excise officer in the strongly Protestant market town of Lewes in Sussex, the rising incidence, geographical range and costs of hybrid warfare had driven up the number of these tax gatherers to over 4,000.[64]

Having to earn his living administering a tax that 'hit the pockets of most consumers rather than just the purses of the prosperous' was vital in shaping Paine's evolving politics. The experience stoked and focused an argument that would figure in most of his major writings: namely, that monarchies were congenitally addicted to warmongering, while it was the great mass of ordinary men and women who paid the price. As had been true of Montesquieu and Vattel, but at a different, far more modest level, the circumstances of Paine's own life and career quickened his understanding of how warfare was becoming more endemic: 'Europe is too thickly populated with kingdoms to be long at peace', he complained.[65]

Having once been a fighting mariner himself, Paine also understood that it was rising naval competition between the major European states, operating in tandem with sharper levels of overland conflict, that was largely responsible for driving up both the geographical range of conflict and its expense. 'Navies now in existence' should be cut back tenfold, he would propose in the 1790s:

> If men will permit themselves to think, as rational beings ought to think, nothing can appear more ridiculous and absurd, exclusive of all moral reflections, than to be at the expense of building navies, filling them with men, and then hauling them into the ocean, to try which can sink each other fastest.

The only beneficiaries of this 'perpetual system of war and expense', he believed, were monarchs and their political and social accomplices. Yet, for all this, Paine came gradually to recognise, the burdens caused by rising levels of hybrid warfare might themselves become a useful source of disruption and change, inciting healthy anger and political activism and heating up radical ideas. 'The enormous expense of Government has provoked people to think, by making them feel,' he would write, 'and when once the veil begins to rend, it admits not of repair.'[66]

Paine's critique of warfare has sometimes been linked to the influence of his Quaker father. Yet Paine seems to have been infuriated less by armed aggression in general than by war-making on the part of hereditary European monarchies in particular. 'Monarchy and succession', he declared, 'have laid (not this or that kingdom only) but the world in blood and ashes.'[67] Most especially, he early on came to despise the warlike British state, which paid him little and gave him few breaks while obliging him to grub away for years as a lowly excise man, dealing with irate traders and reluctant, sometimes impoverished taxpayers.

In terms of the evolution of Paine's politics, it may indeed have been less his Quaker father than his mother, Frances, who influenced him more. Her background was significant. She was the daughter of one Thomas Cocke, an attorney who worked as the town clerk of Thetford. As such, one of his duties was to administer Thetford's various charters, many of which went back to medieval times: charters ordering the town's local government and boundaries; and charters to do with its schools, churches, charities, land rights and more. And so, from childhood, Paine would have grown up with an appreciation of the utility of political paperwork, in this case, charters.

'A charter', he would write later, 'is to be understood as a bond of solemn obligation, which the whole enters into, to support the right of every separate part.' It was this same family background in charters that helped to inform Paine's later profound interest in and advocacy of written constitutions. When he insisted in Part One of his great polemic, *The Rights of Man* (1791), that 'A constitution is not a thing in name only, but in fact', that such an entity possesses 'not an ideal, but a real existence; and wherever it cannot be produced in a visible form, there is none', Paine was undoubtedly writing in part out of his direct experience of American revolutionary constitutions, and out of excitement at what was happening in revolutionary France. But his insistence that constitutions required a real, visible and tangible form stemmed too from his early familiarity with charters. These documents gave him a sense, almost from the outset, of the necessary materiality of instruments of government.[68]

This interest in charters, in paper and parchment outlines of power and rights and law, also marks Paine out as a man very much of his time – and of his country of birth. Increasingly alienated from Britain, he was nonetheless shaped by some of the political ideas that were developing there during his youth and early adulthood. In Britain, as in some other European monarchies, the widening demands of warfare fostered and renewed interest in iconic texts of identity and rights. But British monarchs lacked the absolutist capabilities and freedom of manoeuvre possessed by many of their European counterparts. There was simply no prospect of George II, who ruled Britain from 1727 to 1760, or his young successor, George III, initiating and publicising a signal political and legal text in the manner of Catherine II of Russia with her *Nakaz* or Gustaf III of Sweden with his 1772 constitution. Instead, growing interest in iconic paperwork here often focused on a document that had long been in existence, namely Magna Carta, originally drafted in 1215.

The reviving cult around this liberty text (as some imagined it to be) was less a celebration of ancient constitutionalism, however, than something newer and more volatile. One sees an expression of this rediscovery and reimagining of Magna Carta during the early years of the British Museum, which was founded in London in 1753. Most of the museum's historical manuscripts were kept locked away in cupboards. But, during the Seven Years' War, one of its original copies of Magna Carta was put on ostentatious display. A special glass case was made for it, bearing the label 'The Bulwark of our Liberties'. The significance of these actions becomes even more apparent when you remember that the founders of the British Museum intended it to function as a kind of national university, a place open – at least in theory – to any self-improving Briton who was eager to look and learn.[69]

William Blackstone, a University of Oxford jurist still with his name to make at this point, also contributed to this revival

15. Celebratory print of Arthur Beardmore, a London radical, instructing his son on Magna Carta before being arrested for seditious libel in 1762.

of interest in Magna Carta. His book, *The Great Charter*, published in 1759, at the height of the Seven Years' War, was a close investigation of the various manuscript versions of this text. Yet Blackstone chose to write his book in a style that might conceivably make it attractive and accessible to more than just antiquarians and fellow scholars. At the end of the first edition, his publisher inserted an engraving showing a sylvan British landscape resting safe and secure beneath a celestially placed copy of Magna Carta. There are no references in this image to the Westminster Parliament or the British Crown. There is only a celebration of paperwork, of an overarching, vital constitutional text.[70]

In other words, an argument was re-emerging in Britain by the 1750s that Magna Carta was more than a relic of history and part of a 'canon of great documents' from the distant past. Instead, it was increasingly represented as *the* great document, the foundational text that sustained and was coterminous with Britain's constitution. Such claims were sometimes explicit. The frontispiece of an anonymous tract, *Account of the constitution and present state of Great Britain*, published in London in 1759, the same year as Blackstone's *Great Charter*, shows the figure of Britannia giving out advice to some attentive 'young persons'. Positioned in front of her, the reader is informed, is an 'altar of liberty, on which lies Magna Carta, *denoting the British Constitution* [my italics]'.[71]

In Britain, then, as in Russia, Prussia, Sweden and some other European states, the experience and strains of accelerating levels of warfare were accompanied by a rising interest in constitutional and legal texts. But there was a critical difference. In continental Europe, this evolving cult of paperwork sometimes involved new initiatives on the part of the responsible monarchs. In Britain, an increase in attention to constitutional texts was also evident after 1750. But here, because of the limits on royal power, such developments were less top-down and more diverse.

To be sure, George III and some of his fellow aristocrats chose to have themselves painted in the 1760s in close proximity to copies of Magna Carta, thereby symbolically laying claim to it as a support of the existing political and social order. But, in this same decade and after, Magna Carta was also widely referenced by British and Irish radicals and reformers wanting to legitimise

16. Magna Carta represented as Britain's Constitution in 1759.

and advance demands for change, a trend that was recognised at the time. In 1766, a Scottish conservative complained of 'the rashness of those who venture to affirm, that whatever is contained in this great charter, is of so sacred and fundamental a nature as not to be repealable, not even by Parliament'. As this man perceived, Magna Carta was being reconfigured in some quarters as a fundamental law: as a text that might even operate as a brake on decisions made by the Westminster Parliament. Britain's 'common people', grumbled the Scotsman, were being encouraged 'to discover in the Magna Carta ... liberties which these ancient patriots never dreamed of'.[72]

So, as well as inheriting an interest in charters courtesy of his mother's family, Paine's mind was also turned in this direction by the shifting nature of political debate in the Britain in which he grew up. We know that in the 1760s and early 1770s, he was an active and vociferous attendee at radical political clubs and debates in both London and Lewes, a place with a big and rowdy electorate. This helps to explain why Paine's position on charters was very much a forward-looking one. 'I am not fond of quoting these old remains of former arrogance,' he would write in 1780 in regard to the colonial charters of the state of Virginia, 'but ... we must begin somewhere ... and any rule which can be agreed on is better than none.'[73] Antiquarianism and fusty documents for their own sake were not Paine's business. But he had early come to believe that out of ancient liberty texts might be crafted ideas and reinforcement for a new and better future of reform.

These evolving perspectives, these arguments to do with charters and their importance, would shape Paine's first formidable bestseller, *Common Sense*. Published in Philadelphia on 10 January 1776, less than eighteen months after his arrival in America, it quickly passed through multiple editions, selling perhaps up to 75,000 copies in the future United States alone, and possibly many more. Famously, *Common Sense* appealed to

American colonists to make an outright break with Britain and its king, George III, and to pursue independence as a republic. The pamphlet also made the case for a written constitution. Or, more precisely and predictably, Paine recommended that an American congress of twenty-six members, two from each of the Thirteen Colonies, should immediately set to work on devising a new 'charter of government':

> The conferring members being met, let their business be to frame a CONTINENTAL CHARTER, or Charter of the United Colonies; (answering to what is called the Magna Carta of England) fixing the number and manner of choosing members of Congress, members of Assembly, with their date of sitting, and drawing the line of business and jurisdiction between them.[74]

On this side of the Atlantic, there was to be no single, monarch-like figure grandly bestowing laws and modes of government from above. Instead (white) Americans, Paine predicted, would forge their own modes and rules of government, together. Although the scale of the readership and the impact of *Common Sense* in the short term have been questioned, it is clear that its audacious, driving optimism, along with its spare and lucid language, brilliant polemic and evident fiery anger worked to melt away the imperial and monarchical allegiance of many of its American readers. This was exactly what Paine, and Philadelphia allies of his, such as Benjamin Rush, had hoped for.

Yet, for all this, there were limits at this stage to Paine's own iconoclasm. The title page of early editions of *Common Sense* – which were issued anonymously – made clear that the polemic was 'written by an ENGLISHMAN'. This insertion was more than a tactical ploy. In some ways, Tom Paine *was* still thinking and reacting like an Englishman when he wrote this pamphlet. But he was thinking like an Englishman who had been actively caught up in the Seven Years' War and its costs, in post-war radical politics, and in the business of studying and reimagining ancient charters. An anonymous pamphlet published later in 1776, which also seems to have been the work of Paine, illustrates this continuing obsession on his part. The word 'constitution' was often 'bandied about', but rarely defined, the author of this piece complains. Yet, he insists, the meaning is straightforward enough. A constitution, he writes, needs to be viewed essentially as a 'written charter'.[75]

At this point in his career, in 1776, Tom Paine was still Charter Man, which is why he belongs in this chapter. He was one of many mid-eighteenth-century Europeans, from different levels of society, who were drawn to look more closely, urgently and creatively at political and legal paperwork, in part because of the pressures and penalties of unprecedented levels of war. Moving between continents, Paine took ideas and political technologies from one side of the Atlantic to the other. Entranced and emancipated by coming to America, he nonetheless also drew on and recycled arguments and positions from his time in Britain.

Some of the ideas and techniques to be found in the post-war paperwork generated by European monarchs also crossed the Atlantic. Catherine II of Russia had been ruthlessly enterprising in ensuring that her *Nakaz* would be read in multiple countries and languages, hoping thereby to strengthen the position of her controversial regime. Benjamin Franklin, the self-made Massachusetts-born Founding Father, was a very different human being from Catherine, the self-made Russian empress. But, like her, he was an Enlightenment figure who was addicted to the printed word and, like her, Franklin was also adept at publicity and understood its political value.

During the Revolutionary War, Franklin would be inventive in arranging for American constitutional documents to be translated into different languages and distributed across borders, so that – as with Catherine and her *Nakaz* – these texts might summon up foreign support and respect for a still controversial polity. Other American Revolutionaries adapted language and imagery that had been applied to earlier reforming European monarchs. Like some of the latter, George Washington would be compared by admirers and publicists to Moses, a leader of his people in war, a deliverer of them from bondage and a maker of signal laws.[76]

Thomas Paine's own more radical views on politics and paperwork also travelled further afield. But, not being a monarch tied down to a single territory and to the business of rule, Paine was free to migrate and communicate his ideas directly. It was on 30 November 1774 that he landed in Philadelphia, the biggest, richest city in British America. Six months later, another bloody period of hybrid warfare erupted, this time between Britain and most of its American mainland colonies. Rejoicing at the news, Paine quickly recognised its significance. 'By referring the matter from argument to arms,' he cheered, 'a new era for politics is struck; a new method of thinking hath arisen.'[77] In constitutional terms, this would not prove an entirely new era in fact. But it would make dramatic changes on what had gone before.

# PART TWO

# OUT OF WAR, INTO REVOLUTIONS

# Three

# THE FORCE OF PRINT

## Philadelphia

Reaching a quorum on 25 May 1787, they embraced seclusion. Armed guards surrounded their meeting place, the red-brick Pennsylvania state house on the city's Chestnut Street. That summer was typically humid; and most of the delegates wore close-fitting, multi-layered army uniform or formal dress. Nonetheless, the windows of the state house were kept shut, and were covered over on the inside with heavy curtains. As for the green-painted meeting room itself, with its multiple small tables fronting a low stage, no spectators were allowed in, and no journalists were admitted to issue regular reports on what was unfolding here. The delegates themselves, a fluctuating group of fifty-five men, were under instructions not to pass on information to outsiders. 'Nothing spoken in the house', it was ordered, was to be 'printed, or otherwise published or communicated without leave'. Even private note-taking was sometimes frowned on. James Madison, intensely clever, barely five foot four, and one of the representatives for Virginia, had to be discreet when jotting down his entries on each day's business and speeches. His heavily revised account of the Philadelphia Constitutional Convention would remain unpublished until 1840, four years after his death.[1]

This extreme and calculated secrecy allowed the Philadelphia delegates to move far beyond their original brief. Tasked with amending the Articles of Confederation, the formal document that had provided for cooperation among the thirteen American states during and after the Revolutionary War, they went much further, and in a different direction. But only after sharp and protracted debates. Not until 8 September 1787 were they ready to forward a finished text of their work to the 'committee of style' (its very name proclaiming that this convention was essentially to do with words set down on paper). Nine days later, on 17 September, the completed draft of a *c*.4,500-word constitution for the United States was formally inscribed in red and black ink on four sheets of parchment, each about two feet wide and two feet high.

Generally hidden away before the Second World War, and on occasions mislaid entirely, this manuscript has belatedly become an icon.[2] Its shrine in the Rotunda of the National Archives Museum in Washington DC now attracts millions of visitors every year. Yet, in terms both of the immediate domestic impact of this constitution and its influence outside the United States, something more critical occurred in Philadelphia on 17 September 1787 than its formal communication to parchment. That same day, a copy of the draft constitution was handed over to two printers, John Dunlap, by birth an Irishman, and David C. Claypoole, a native of the city.

Revolutionary army veterans both, these men were the joint proprietors of the first successful American daily, *The Pennsylvania Packet, and Daily Advertiser*. On Wednesday 19 September, having trailed its appearance in advance, Dunlap and Claypoole published the draft constitution in full on their paper's front page. By late October, the text had featured in over seventy other American newspapers. At least 200 different printings had appeared by the end of the year.[3] Well before this, extracts from this constitution had also filtered into newsprint, pamphlets, books, magazines and broadsheets in countries and colonies far outside the United States.

These events at Philadelphia, and their aftermath, are among the best-known episodes in the rise of the new constitutions.

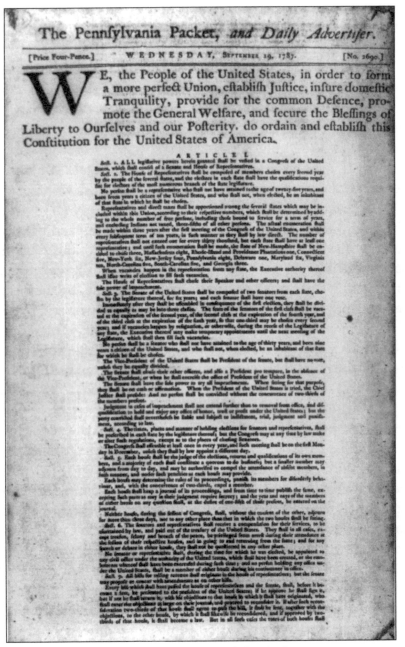

17. The first newspaper printing of the draft constitution
of the United States, 19 September 1787.

Yet establishing the broad significance of these same events is challenging. This is not just because of the enormous amount of analysis and interpretation that has grown up around the American constitution, but also because it is so entangled in narratives of national distinctiveness and exceptionality. The making, content and influence of this constitution have become an essential part of the story of how the United States has been 'useful', as an elderly James Madison put it in the 1830s, 'in proving things before held impossible', part of a tale of quintessential American *difference*.[4]

Important local differences there undoubtedly were, from the very outset. Long before 1775, the autonomy and political aspirations of colonial Americans had been encouraged by the fact of their living 3,000 or more miles away from their titular monarch in Britain. They had been fostered, too, by the rising assertiveness of these peoples' colonial assemblies, and by the unusually wide distribution among them of both voting rights and literacy. Yet the constitution drafted at Philadelphia was a product of more than a unique set of purely domestic developments and characteristics.

To begin with, constitutional thinking and responses here drew on a pre-independence tradition of *British* charters which had outlined the boundaries of the American colonies, and set out the basics of their government. The majority of these colonial charters were issued in the name of the monarch of the day, though a few, such as the Charter of Delaware of 1701 and the Frame of Government of Pennsylvania of 1682, were initiated by incoming Britons, in both these cases by the Anglo-Dutch Quaker colonialist William Penn. But *all* American colonial charters were put into print and served as persistent reminders of transatlantic connections and influences. They also served as reminders and examples of how systems and principles of government might conveniently be set down in writing in a single document. As a historian pointed out long

18. Samuel Adams and the charter of
Massachusetts by John Singleton Copley.

ago: 'It took no wrench of mind, no daring leap' for Americans to move on from these colonial charters to 'the concept
of a fixed, written constitution limiting the ordinary actions of
government'.[5]

Indeed, just as radicals in Britain had worked at reimagining and weaponising Magna Carta in the 1760s, some American dissidents were already busy this same decade in retooling colonial charters to serve oppositionist purposes. John Singleton Copley's portrait of Samuel Adams, the Boston brewer's son turned political activist, makes the point. His intransigent zeal evident in his plain woollen suit and dour expression, Adams, as painted by Copley, jabs with his forefinger towards the charter of Massachusetts. This had been granted and sealed in 1691 by the British dual monarchs, William III and Queen Mary II. But Copley's painting is not a tribute to an old piece of parchment. Its purpose is rather to commemorate Adams's use of this colonial charter to advance a novel and dissident purpose: to back up his demand that soldiers of yet another British monarch, George III, be expelled from Boston in the wake of the 'massacre' there of local protesters by British troops in 1770.

As illustrated by these new twists on old charters happening in the 1760s on both sides of the Atlantic, constitutional changes in America sometimes mirrored political developments in Europe, and not just Anglophone Europe. The constitution drafted at Philadelphia in 1787 was not the first to formalise a new polity and provide for a republic in the wake of a military struggle against a colonising power. As we have seen, Pasquale Paoli had tried this in Corsica in 1755, rebelling against rule by Genoa, and drafting in the process what he explicitly termed a constitution. After 1776, as the historian Gordon S. Wood writes, Americans made a 'unique use of constitutional conventions'.[6] But some of the techniques used in these American conventions, and some of their functions, had already been rehearsed by Catherine the Great of Russia in her Moscow Commission of 1767–8, held to advance another iconic text, the *Nakaz*. By the same token, the idea of a written constitution as a supreme fundamental law, restricting as well as empowering government, was not an invention of a self-made United States.

Gustaf III of Sweden had experimented with such notions in regard to *his* written constitution, the Form of Government of 1772.

I am not arguing that these and other post-1750 European initiatives directly influenced American constitutional projects (though there was certainly wide knowledge in the colonies of Paoli's actions on Corsica). The vital point is that in constitutional terms – as in many other respects – the Atlantic was never in practice all that wide. On both sides of this ocean, political experiments and writings accelerated in number and creativity from the middle of the eighteenth century, because on each side there were some broadly similar stimuli and challenges. In America, as in much of Europe, intellectuals and activists were attracted by Enlightenment notions of systematising and reforming government, law and rights; and in America, as in much of Europe, acting on these ideas was made more urgent by the rising impress and demands of war.

As is true of virtually all revolutionary conflicts, the warfare that erupted in the one-time Thirteen Colonies after 1775 was in part a civil war, with local separatists battling loyalists. This particular revolutionary war also involved slave rebellions, with tens of thousands of Black slaves escaping from their owners, and in some cases attaching themselves to the British. In addition, this was a war for empire in several guises, with Britain seeking to subdue its one-time colonists, and American revolutionary troops invading Canada, with the aim of incorporating it by force into their new republic. This same war also involved frequent, vicious struggles between multiple Indigenous peoples and white-led armies and marauders.[7]

Most importantly as regards its immediate outcome, this American conflict was the largest outbreak in world history up to this point of hybrid warfare, in the sense of fighting at sea as well as on land. The British expeditionary force that landed in New York in July 1776 ultimately involved half of the Royal Navy and two-thirds of the British army. When the British were effectively finished off at Yorktown in 1781, it was again by means of hybrid warfare, by the combined efforts of a Franco-American land army of 16,000 and a French fleet manned by 19,000 sailors.

From the outset, this multi-stranded American war had signal constitutional repercussions. The Declaration of Independence of 1776 itself functioned in part as a declaration of war, and designedly so. The intention of its authors was to show that, like other 'powers of the earth', Americans now possessed the right to issue ultimatums of this sort. In their text, King George III becomes a particularly malign exponent of hybrid warfare. He had, they claimed:

> plundered our seas, ravaged our coasts, burnt our towns, and destroyed the lives of our people. He is at this time transporting large armies of foreign mercenaries to complete the works of death.[8]

The new American state constitutions that emerged from 1776 were also intimately bound up with war. In the case of states particularly devastated by fighting, this was sometimes made explicit. The language of New York's constitution of 1777, for instance, groans under the weight of glum allusions to the strains and uncertainties of conflict: 'as soon as may be after the termination of the present war'; 'during the continuance of the present war', and so on.[9]

But warfare also shaped these American state constitutions in a more profound sense. The limits which these texts imposed on the powers of the respective state governors, along with the emphasis of many of them on bills of rights, secret ballots and reduced property qualifications for voting took fire from many ideas and many different local circumstances. Always, though, these widenings of American political life from 1776 were designed to attract and cement local popular support for the revolutionary project in the face of extreme military and ideological pressures from without.

State constitutions were also deployed to advance and publicise the revolutionary cause outside of the United States. After 1776, and like the Declaration of Independence, these texts were regularly reprinted and circulated overseas, especially in France, whose financial and armed assistance the new United States desperately needed if it were to have any chance of withstanding protracted hybrid warfare on the part of the British.[10]

The centrality of print in this American struggle makes it an invaluable lens through which to examine more searchingly the constitution drafted at Philadelphia in 1787, and indeed at the constitutions that came after. Looking at the Philadelphia delegates' sustained exploitation of print in 1787–8 helps us to excavate how fraught with risk many of these men felt their work to be. Looking at its close connections with print also helps to explain why, unlike analogous texts drafted in earlier periods, this American constitution was able to take root and endure. Looking hard and widely at the operation of print is revealing in a further, more long-term respect. Doing so casts light on the influence of this particular political text on other regions of the world. It also illuminates some of the limits of that impact.

## Arms and the Men and the Printed Word

The fierceness and scale of the American Revolutionary War shaped the debates at the Philadelphia Convention in 1787, and help to explain why early reactions to its work were divided and unsure. At one level, there was evident pride, ideological conviction and exultation among supporters of the United States at what was being attempted here and the future prospects it offered. But there was also anxiety and a depth of insecurity that account for the extreme secrecy adopted by the men attending this Convention.

Take the famous initial seventy-seven essays written in support of ratifying the constitution by two of its most formidable delegates, James Madison and the Caribbean-born Alexander Hamilton, along with the American diplomat John Jay (later first Chief Justice of the United States). Published under the joint pseudonym 'Publius' in the New York press between October 1787 and May 1788, and only retrospectively collected with others as *The Federalist Papers*, these essays are probably best known now for Hamilton's initial euphoric boast:

> It seems to have been reserved to the people of this country [the United States] … to decide the important question, whether societies of men are really capable or not of estab-lishing good government from reflection and choice, or whether they are forever destined to depend for their polit-ical constitutions on accident and force.[11]

Claims of this sort proved highly compelling and attractive, and not just in the United States. Alone in a dangerous Paris in the 1790s, except for her unreliable American lover Gilbert Imlay, the English radical and feminist Mary Wollstonecraft was still able to feel cheered when she thought about the new constitutional politics of the United States. That country had demonstrated, she rejoiced, that 'constitutions formed by chance and continu-ally patched up' were not inescapable. Americans had shown that systems of government might rather be forged afresh 'on the basis of reason'.[12]

Yet for all this celebratory stress on new beginnings and free political choice, nine of the first ten *Federalist* essays by Ham-ilton and his allies focus in fact on the threats and constraints posed by armed force. Four of the opening essays are entitled 'Dangers from Foreign Force and Influence'. Three others are devoted to 'Dangers from Dissensions between the States'; while a further two wrestle with the issue of 'domestic faction and insurrection'. Similar fears and insecurities recur later in the series. Essays 21–36, for instance, worry over how the United States can possibly afford the army and navy necessary to parry future outbreaks of hybrid warfare, now that 'improvements in the art of navigation have … rendered distant nations, in a great measure, neighbours'.[13]

Hamilton and his collaborators wrote in this fashion in part as a deliberate tactic. They wanted to frighten their American readers into putting pressure on their local delegates to ratify the draft constitution. But more was involved than this. Even in his private correspondence at the time, Hamilton regularly admitted to deep nervousness, to being 'in the habit of considering the state of this country as replete with difficulties and surrounded with danger'.[14] He was not alone among the Philadelphia delegates in this respect.

Once the United States and its constitution appeared safely rooted, the men of 1787 could be widely reimagined as an 'assembly of demi-gods', in the words of Thomas Jefferson; as a gathering of enlightened men possessed of legal training, making calm, sage and exemplary decisions for a privileged American posterity and an attentive world. Many of the delegates at Philadelphia in 1787 were indeed attached to Enlightenment ideas, and many of them also possessed some background in the law. It was equally to the point, however, that an even higher proportion had been trained for war and/or were experienced in making provision for war.[15]

On average, these men were in their forties. This meant that they had lived through the Seven Years' War (a few of them had even fought in it) before committing themselves to an armed struggle for independence in the Revolutionary War. Thirty of the Philadelphia delegates had seen active military service in this latter conflict, including Alexander Hamilton, who served as a lieutenant colonel in the artillery. This contact with military hardware and dangerous combat may indeed help to explain why – even before his last fatal encounter with his political rival Aaron Burr in 1804 – Hamilton allowed himself to become involved in several duels.[16]

Hamilton was one of five delegates at Philadelphia to have served as a military aide-de-camp to George Washington. Some less well known delegates, who attended the convention more regularly than he did, were even more unabashedly caught up in the war and the culture of war. The influential pro-slavery representative for South Carolina, Charles Cotesworth Pinckney, and the English-born William Richardson Davie of North Carolina, for instance, both commissioned portraits of themselves, not as sober legislators but in proud and flamboyant army uniforms.

Even those delegates who had remained in a civilian capacity after 1776 frequently possessed administrative acquaintance with military affairs and war finance, either at state level or as former members of the Continental Congress, or both. This was the case with the formidable and essentially self-educated Connecticut representative Roger Sherman, and the rich, clever and lecherous New York merchant and lawyer Gouverneur Morris, who served as one of Pennsylvania's delegates. And all of the delegates at Philadelphia in 1787 were presided over by an army general, *the* army general. Initially, George Washington had been reluctant to take part in the convention, and not just because of the demands of his estate at Mount Vernon in Virginia. He had a prior engagement with the Society of Cincinnati, an elite organisation for officers who had served at least three years in the American Continental Army or Navy.

Their high and wide levels of military experience influenced the Philadelphia delegates' priorities and perceptions. It shaped how they thought and acted. It also had an impact on what they wrote and put into print. War, after all, might not be over. Ostensibly now an independent, coherent nation, the United States remained a confederation of quasi-autonomous, often uncooperative states. Hence the separate tables set out in the

19. Army General and Legislator: Antonio Canova's
model for a statue of George Washington in 1818.

green room of the state house in Philadelphia: to give delegates from the different American states their own particular places to plot and confer. These continuing domestic fractures made the prospect of future attacks by an outside power appear even more ominous. It seemed very possible in 1787, and long after, that an expansionist European state – Britain, obviously, with its continuing base in Upper and Lower Canada, or Spain, with its hold on Florida and Louisiana, or even Russia, moving south-wards from its evolving settlements in Alaska – might launch a future invasion of the United States, detaching or destabilising restive American states along the way.

For all their excitement at the prospect of constructing their own overland republican empire, some Philadelphia delegates also worried – just as British imperialists had done before 1776 – about how to regulate and rein in the settler communities that were spreading rapidly in the trans-Appalachian west. 'Settlements are forming to the westwards of us,' warned Gouverneur Morris darkly, 'whose inhabitants acknowledge no authority but their own, and of consequence no umpire but the sword.'[17] What if these restless frontier peoples, whose land claims on the map comprised half of the territory of the United States, sought in the future to forge their own separate nations?

To a degree, then, these men of Philadelphia faced similar challenges to those confronting many European and Asian regimes by the mid eighteenth century. Like the latter, the delegates at Philadelphia and their supporters had to plan how to recover from the strains and damage of massive warfare. Simultaneously, they had to work out how to provide for sufficient levels of citizen solidarity and fiscal–military preparedness in the event of future armed conflicts which they might not choose, but which might happen anyway. 'Nations in general', warned John Jay, 'will make war wherever they have a prospect of getting anything by it.' What 'fleets could they ever hope to have', he worried, acknowledging the rising currency of hybrid warfare on the world's oceans, if the United States remained fractured and internally at odds. And how could such things possibly be afforded?[18]

In the immediate aftermath of the Revolutionary War, under the Articles of Confederation, Congress had possessed no power to levy taxes to pay off war loans or guarantee fresh loans. It had relied instead on individual states implementing their own fiscal levies. This system proved woefully inadequate. In 1785, the United States was obliged to stop paying interest on a loan from France, and subsequently had to default. The following year, 1786, its leaders failed to extract sufficient funds from the states adequately to finance troops tasked with putting down tax and secession revolts in Massachusetts and Vermont. America was 'making an experiment without a real military force', warned a former revolutionary army general turned Philadelphia delegate in 1787. It was at risk, he thought, of 'rapid approaches towards anarchy'.[19]

As historians have increasingly argued, these pressures and anxieties meant that the constitution drafted at Philadelphia, by men overwhelmingly marked by war, was often approached at the time less as a 'blueprint of a liberal democratic society', and an exercise in confident nation-building, than as a grimly necessary plan for a more effective and defendable union. 'The objects of the Union, he thought were few', a blunt Roger Sherman told his fellow delegates in June 1787:

1. Defence against foreign danger. 2. [Defence] against internal disputes & a resort to force. 3. Treaties with foreign nations. 4. Regulating foreign commerce, & drawing revenue from it ... These & perhaps a few lesser objects alone rendered a confederation of the States necessary.[20]

Yet, like most political actors most of the time, most of the men of Philadelphia combined prudential initiatives and lurking anxieties with a measure of hope and idealism. Hence the last-minute changes made to the preamble of the draft American constitution, chiefly, it seems, by the New Yorker Gouverneur Morris, who, at twenty-five years of age, was one of the convention's youngest delegates. Initially, the draft constitution was to begin: 'We the people of the states of New Hampshire, Massachusetts, Rhode Island ...', and so on, with each and every American state listed in turn down the Atlantic coast. At the last minute, however, Morris altered this, of course, to: 'We, the People of the United States', for reasons that were in part aspirational, but also tactical and rooted in unease.

Instead of drawing attention to the separate, all-too discordant states, this word-change summoned up a united American nation which in reality did not as yet exist. As the wording of political constitutions frequently does, it conveyed a beguiling and triumphant impression of unanimity and order. Morris's alteration also served to balance the preamble's otherwise more pragmatic character. It helped to offset its stern emphasis on the need to form 'a more perfect union, establish justice, insure domestic tranquility [and] provide for the common defence': priorities indicatively listed in advance of the wish to 'secure the blessings of liberty'.[21]

And, crucially, Morris's new, inspiring wording deflected attention away from the secretive Philadelphia delegates themselves. Instead, it became 'We, the People' who were foregrounded, represented by means of this adjusted, powerful fiction as the essential owners, even instigators of the American constitution. Publishing the draft on the front page of the *Pennsylvania Packet*, John Dunlap and David Claypoole consciously encouraged such an interpretation by printing the 'W' of 'We' in super-large bold type, thereby drawing readers' attention to this arresting opening assertion and promise.

As this typographical ploy illustrates, to a greater degree than in any previous written constitution, print, and the techniques and possibilities of print, functioned in this American case not just to record and communicate what was happening, but as a vital agent and engine in that happening. To be sure, exploiting print to advance a constitutional initiative was nothing new. In the 1760s, Catherine the Great had understood full well the power and advantages of print when she commissioned multiple editions and translations of her *Nakaz*. But there were no newspapers or provincial presses available in Russia at this time to help her, and the empress had anyway to deal with a domestic population which was less than 10 per cent literate.

By contrast, most whites and some free Blacks in the United States were already familiar with a wide spectrum of print. American newspapers alone had doubled in number between 1760 and 1775, and would double again by 1790. In addition, by this point in the eighteenth century, 80 per cent of adult white American men were able to read – a higher level of literacy than in any other large territory in the world, except perhaps for parts of Scandinavia.[22] The degree to which the Philadelphia delegates and their supporters were able to take literacy and print for granted shaped the strategies that they adopted. It may also have influenced the shaping of the constitution itself.

One reason why the Western novel was able to overtake the much older Chinese novel in popularity and transcontinental impact, the literary scholar Franco Moretti has suggested, is that by the 1700s the former tended to be much shorter in length, and was more tailored therefore for easy print reproduction and relatively wide consumption.[23] True or no, it seems likely that the striking brevity of the draft American constitution – in its final form it contains just seven articles – *was* both an element of its success and wide distribution and a product of its writers' familiarity with commercial print. The men of Philadelphia used print enthusiastically in multiple ways. But many of them also *thought* in terms of print and were alert to its possibilities for different forms of communication.

In this respect, they acted true to revolutionary American precedents. The earlier Declaration of Independence had also been a notably short document, just 1,337 words in length. This made it easy for it to be reproduced in cheap broadsheets that could be nailed to the walls of houses, shops and taverns; and made it possible, too, for the text to be printed on just one side of a newspaper page. The declaration's brevity also allowed it to be read out aloud in full to audiences without too much effort, as it was on occasions to George Washington's troops, lined up specially to listen 'in hollow squares on their respective parades'.[24]

And for the Philadelphia delegates, as for the authors of the Declaration, a turn to print was not just instinctive, it was also indispensable. The last article of the final draft constitution in September 1787 stipulated that, in order to come into operation, it needed the approval of at least nine of the thirteen American states, all of them holding ratification conventions for this purpose. This challenge, of getting a controversial and secretive draft ratified by a majority of states, was made easier by the geography of America's printing industry. Most of the country's white working population was made up of farmers living in rural areas, with limited access to information. But its newspapers were concentrated in the towns, which conveniently was where the ratification conventions were also set to take place. Moreover, most of those running American newspapers and post and printing offices at this time appear, like Dunlap and Claypoole in Philadelphia, to have been supporters of the proposed constitution, and to have acted and intrigued accordingly. Even so, as is now well established, ratification was a close-run thing.[25]

In Massachusetts, in many ways the ideological heartland of resistance to the British empire, the local ratification convention approved the draft constitution by just 187 votes to 168. Virginia and New York, two big, rich and vital states, ratified by even narrower margins. The protracted uncertainty over the result – the constitution was not conclusively ratified until September 1788 – meant that for months on end activists and advocates invested energy, thought and cash in circulating copies of the draft constitution, and in generating polemical print on its validity and meanings. The impact of this spread far outside the United States, which was always the intention.

It bears repeating that, during the Revolutionary War, the new republic's most significant political documents had been circulated overseas. These careful distributions abroad of printed copies and translations of the Declaration of Independence, the state constitutions and other exploratory and ambitious documents, had been designed to convince European governments of the seriousness of this emerging American polity, the enlightenment of its political experiments, its determination to resist the British, and consequently its claims to be taken seriously as regards war loans, continuing trade and military aid. From 1787, very similar print strategies were put into practice to publicise the United States constitution abroad.[26]

American diplomats and consuls arriving in foreign capitals would routinely distribute copies to local rulers and other major players. Many American overseas merchants and patriotic travellers did the same. John Paul Jones, the Scottish-born one-time slaver turned successful revolutionary privateer, made sure, for instance, to present a copy to Catherine the Great in 1788, when he paid court to her at St Petersburg while seeking a job. Copies of the text were also enfolded into American diplomatic correspondence. Writing to inform the formidable sultan of Morocco, Sidi Muhammad, of the constitution's final ratification, George Washington was careful to add: 'of which I have the honour of, herewith, enclosing a copy'.[27]

The official thinking behind these efforts was that powerful and wealthy players in select foreign spaces would be at once impressed by the language and ideas of the new constitution, and persuaded by its provisions that the United States now possessed a far more effectual central government than before. Publicising this fact would, it was hoped, help deter armed invasions from abroad, and also reassure and entice overseas merchants and potential investors. These official and quasi-official distributions of the American constitution abroad were aided – and swamped in volume – by more informal coverage in foreign-based print media.

In this regard, the United States benefited from the very empire that it had so violently rejected. There were naturally old and close links between American printers and publishers and their counterparts in Ireland and Britain. Because of these long-established trade and professional relationships – and because of the commonalities in language – newsprint, pamphlets and books issued in the United States regularly crossed the Atlantic. The text of the draft American constitution was published in London newspapers only five weeks after its first appearance in the *Pennsylvania Packet*. Moreover, because London was the world's biggest port, with the largest mercantile marine, some of this incoming American material was promptly shipped onwards from there, not only to other parts of Europe, but to south and east Asia, west Africa, South America, the Caribbean and ultimately to sectors of the Pacific world. Even Canadians seem to have learned about the details of the new United States constitution less by way of overland communications than by means of published accounts shipped back across the Atlantic from London.[28]

But what about those on the receiving end of this relentless blizzard of print? What were the effects on men and women in different regions of the world of being exposed to so much published material on American constitutionalism?

## Reading and Borrowing

At some levels, and in some places, the effects were substantial, rapid and formative. Among certain radicals and reformers, especially, and in multiple continents, what happened in the United States, its revolution, the ideas of its protagonists, its victory against a greedy empire and the political and legal innovations on paper that followed – plus, critically, the fact that this hard-won polity survived – nurtured an exciting sense of possibility.

The new American political texts also confirmed and accelerated those changes in understandings of the term 'constitution' that were already emerging before 1776. It became more common now to argue that political constitutions might – perhaps even should – be set down in a single, easy-to-print document. One sign of this shift is the response of opponents. From the 1780s, conservatives in some of the disparate German lands and in Britain began to refer derisively but suggestively to 'paper constitutions'. Paper, of course, being the essential fuel of a printing press.[29]

Americans' busy use of print to promote and embed their constitutions also became a tactic that others were eager to explore. This helps to explain why provisions for an enhanced availability of print feature so prominently in constitutions crafted in the late eighteenth century and after. A breakdown of those issued across the world between 1776 and 1850 helps to make the point:

### Rights Mentioned in Constitutions between 1776 and 1850[30]

Freedom of the press 560

Freedom of religion 534

Habeas Corpus 492

Popular sovereignty 477

Freedom to petition 408

Freedom of speech 196

Freedom of assembly 172

Freedom of trade 169

Freedom of movement 68

In the many hundreds of constitutional texts crafted in different countries and continents between the issuing of the American Declaration of Independence in 1776 and the middle of the nineteenth century, provisions concerning print were thus more numerous than clauses providing for freedom of religion or popular sovereignty. They easily exceeded, too, the number of provisions concerning freedom of speech and freedom of assembly. On the basis of the texts they issued, constitution-makers in this era judged access to print to be more immediately vital than almost any other right. This was not just because some of these actors believed devoutly in the intrinsic value of a well-instructed citizenry. Print was deemed indispensable if this new political technology was to function effectively and do its work, both at home and abroad.

Toussaint Louverture, the prime fighter responsible for a future Black-ruled Haiti, seems instinctively to have appreciated this point. In late 1799, Napoleon Bonaparte issued a new constitution for France (which was, of course, printed), stipulating that its colonies were henceforward to be governed by 'special laws'. This was interpreted in the Caribbean as a threat to reinstate slavery in French colonies there, as duly occurred in Martinique and Guadeloupe. But on what was still officially Saint-Domingue, Toussaint responded by issuing his own constitution in 1801. Defying his French advisers, he also very deliberately put this text into print. By not simply issuing a constitution, but also printing it, he publicised its stipulation that all former Black slaves on Saint-Domingue were now citizens *and therefore by definition would remain free*. It was this action on his part that persuaded Napoleon to launch a major naval and army assault against Saint-Domingue, destroying Toussaint in the process, but also in the end accelerating the demolition of French power in the region and the emergence of an independent Haiti.[31]

Toussaint's political successors on Haiti also understood the value of print. They drew, too, on other devices employed by American revolutionaries, issuing their own Declaration of Independence, for instance, on 1 January 1804.[32] These borrowings were not, however, combined with a deep political and institutional emulation of the United States. The new Haiti was, as we have seen, very much an authoritarian and militaristic state. Conscious and explicit emulation *both* of American techniques for advancing constitutions *and* of elements of the United States' own political system were more evident in parts of South America – and for good reasons.

After the revolutionary wars in this continent in the 1810s and 1820s, considerations of geographical proximity made some South Americans view the United States as the best and most obvious political model. So did other factors. Apart from Brazil, which remained a monarchy until 1889, each of the ten independent states which eventually emerged in South America selected – with some hiccups along the way – to become republics, like the United States. And, like the United States, these emerging South American polities were the products of successful revolutionary warfare against European empires, and self-consciously recent creations. So, whereas a French constitution-maker in 1789 had positively shuddered at the idea of his own 'ancient people' emulating in any way the political design of the United States, 'a new people recently born to the universe', this very newness, for some South Americans, only added to the appeal of the political projects generated by their northerly neighbours.[33]

As a result, some South American states cheerfully borrowed provisions as well as methods from the 1787 American constitution. They took ideas from it about presidential systems. Above all, they often copied American federalism. Gran Colombia, for instance, which for a while after 1819 encompassed much of present-day Colombia, Panama, Venezuela and Ecuador, promptly declared itself a federal republic. Even Brazil copied American federalism when it finally ditched its monarchy and issued a fresh constitution in 1891.

South American states also borrowed some of the print and publicity techniques that Americans had deployed so effectively. The authors of Chile's first provisional constitution in 1818 promptly took pains to have this document ratified, and stipulated that: 'Once the draft is printed, it will be published by order in all of the cities, villages and towns of the state.'[34] Other South American activists appropriated the tactic deployed so effectively after 1776 by the US Congress. They compiled portfolios of their own constitutional documents, and then dispatched these compendia overseas so as to influence and woo foreign opinion, and entice future investments, alliances and loans.

This was what Venezuela did in 1811, after becoming the first South American state to declare independence from Spain. Together with other revolutionary texts, a copy of the new Venezuelan constitution drafted in its capital, Caracas, was quickly shipped to London. Here, bound editions were published in 1812, with Spanish and English-language versions made available on alternate pages, ready to be dispatched to multiple locations overseas.[35]

Substantial and sometimes moving, this Venezuelan portfolio is still well worth examining because it reveals so much. It shows, to begin with, the extent to which Venezuelan revolutionaries, working under immense military and political pressures, chose to borrow from the United States. After invoking God, their constitution begins: '*We* the people of the states of Venezuela'. It goes on, as well, to provide for a federal republic, the carefully named *United* Provinces of Venezuela. It also makes provision for a house of representatives and a senate, whose members – as in the United States – were to be over twenty-five and thirty years respectively. This Venezuelan portfolio includes yet another tribute to America's example, a Declaration of Independence. But, whereas the American declaration had focused repeatedly on George III's real and reputed failings, this Venezuelan version keeps reverting to the number 300 to make its

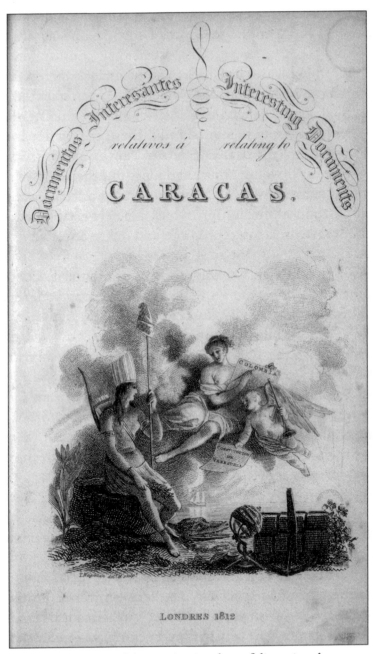

20. Venezuela's constitutional portfolio, printed
in Spanish and English in 1812.

anti-imperial case: '300 years of captivity, hardship and injustice', courtesy of the Spanish; '300 years of submission and sacrifice', and so on.[36]

Like United States legislators and politicians, those compiling this Venezuelan portfolio understood that constitutional texts could do more than serve as instruments for domestic law and government. By means of print, these critical documents could be used to communicate information on a new polity and the nature of its ruling orders and ideas to others, across territorial and maritime borders. A written and printed constitution could be an ideal medium by which a newly established state or political regime could promote and define itself across the globe.

As the compilers of this portfolio themselves declared, without the print export of their constitution, Venezuelans 'could not have solemnly declared [their] … intention to the world'.[37] And while they apologised for any typographical errors due to 'the hurry of publication', it is clear that the makers actually devoted careful thought to the physical appearance of their volume and how it might strike future foreign readers. Scattered among its pages are engravings of shields, helmets and spears so as to remind those viewing them of how the new Venezuela was gallantly emerging into the light by way of war and sacrifice. There are also recurring graphic images in the book of a large galleon at full sail, visual alerts to a foreign audience of the commercial opportunities that would become available once Venezuela had successfully achieved its independence.

For all this effort and ingenuity, by mid 1812 this first Venezuelan republic had succumbed to Spanish armed forces and civil warfare. Its lavish portfolio of constitutional texts endured, however, forming part of what was becoming a rapidly expanding print archive of different countries' constitutional plans and projects. The existence in print of a constantly expanding stock of constitutions from multiple parts of the world serves to make an important point. The scale and skill of the United States' constitutional and print initiatives fostered emulation of some of its political ideas and methods elsewhere: yes, indeed. Quite as significant, however, was the way in which such enterprise on the part of the Americans also helped to bring into being *other*, sometimes competing political systems in different parts of the world, and rival written and printed constitutional texts. Writing constitutions, putting them in print, and then publicising them across continents was a game that many – though not all – could play.

## Revising the Script across Continents

Without doubt, then, America's Revolutionary War and the written constitutions emerging from it played significant and durable roles in altering and shaping ideas, and in advancing that new political technology which was already emerging in some European locations before 1776. Because of its content and circumstances, but also because of its propagation by means of print, the United States constitution, especially, exercised a broad influence during the long nineteenth century, a far broader influence than the American Declaration of Independence. The latter text was certainly widely read and reprinted in some regions of the world but, in advance of the First World War, it never exerted the same degree and depth of impact as the American constitution.

For all its ideological verve, the Declaration was something of a niche document. After 1776, it was chiefly attractive to those inhabiting territories where there was a desire and the capacity to break away from the rule of another state or empire. Before 1914, such breakaway situations remained sparse. To be sure, the South American republics that emerged from Spanish rule in the 1810s and 1820s, along with Haiti, found this device

– a declaration of independence – a useful one, and copied it. Outside the Americas, though, it was a different matter. Here, only ten countries between 1790 and 1914 seem to have chosen to issue their own declaration of independence.[38]

How could it be otherwise? Most of the world's empires and composite monarchies remained intact throughout this period. Only after the First World War – and, still more, after 1945 and the collapse of the remaining European maritime empires, followed by the fall of the Soviet Union – was this type of constitutional text, a declaration of independence, able to acquire greater allure and traction.

By contrast, American constitutions appealed broadly much earlier than this. Alexis de Tocqueville's *Democracy in America* (1835–40), probably the most widely read foreign analysis of the United States produced in the nineteenth century, significantly leaves out mention of the Declaration of Independence altogether. But Tocqueville does devote a large chapter and many references to the constitution of 1787.[39] This allocation of space was understandable, given his own interests and priorities and those of many of his readers. During the nineteenth century – as increasingly after – activists in all sorts of polities became attracted to the business of experimenting with constitutions: not just in republics, but also in monarchies; in old countries as well as in new ones; and in some empires as well as in would-be nations rebelling against empire. For most people outside the United States, it was its constitution that appeared its most pertinent and arresting text, the one that most merited close attention.

However, a caveat is in order here. For all the widening interest it commanded, the constitution drafted in Philadelphia in 1787 was never the sole influence on foreign activists and enthusiasts seeking to devise their own equivalent document. Instead, as more and more countries adopted written constitutions, and as more and more of these texts were put into print and published across borders, men and women who were interested in this form of political technology were increasingly presented with a choice. Not only could they study and plunder the United States' own much reproduced and translated texts. Progressively, they were also in a position to secure information about, and read and rifle the constitutions of other places.

Already, by the 1790s, savvy publishers had recognised and were beginning to capitalise on this trend. Instead of simply publishing the constitution of a single country separately, they also began to issue omnibus collections of constitutions produced by several different countries.[40] This way, curious readers – and aspiring constitution-makers – could compare and contrast rival models of how to organise a state on paper, and also garner ideas on how to formulate rights and rules. By the early twentieth century, indeed, some newly emerging states and regimes were themselves sponsoring and publishing these kinds of collections of multiple constitutions.

This was what happened in 1922 in the new Irish Free State, precariously established after six years of civil warfare against the British. The Free State government in Dublin commissioned and issued a hefty volume entitled *Select Constitutions of the World*. With the text of its own new Irish constitution printed prominently in first place, the book also contained the texts of eighteen other countries' current constitutions. Like the United States' busy promotion of *its* constitutional texts abroad after 1776, this print initiative on the part of politicians in Dublin was an act of deliberate official calculation. By printing their own new and still insecure constitution in this book, side by side with other, more established countries' constitutions, and then dispatching copies of this omnibus volume to multiple foreign capitals, the politicians of the Irish Free State were proclaiming that their brand new republic was now to be viewed as being on a par with every other independent nation of the world.[41]

State-sponsored publications of this sort, which brought together multiple examples of constitutions from different parts of the world for an international readership, still lay in the future. But the roots of such official printed compendia were set much earlier. Increasingly emerging after 1787 – though pre-figured in parts of Europe before then – was a new form of knowledge assemblage and distribution. Courtesy of fast multi-plying print technologies, the new constitutions were being put into wide circulation in ways that would not have been imag-inable earlier. This in turn resulted in a changing politics of extraction, appropriation, comparison and selection. Politicians, lawyers, intellectuals and soldiers engaged in drafting a new constitution, along with private individuals wanting to imagine one, were increasingly in a position to pick and mix. They could study and select between ideas, institutions and laws set out in an expanding print array of different countries' constitutions. They could then meld and combine the borrowings of their choice with their own ideas, aspirations and legal and political conventions.

We can see this sort of mixing of local and foreign influences at work in the making of Norway's constitution in 1814.[42] Next to that of the United States, this is the oldest such document still enduring today; and, once again, this was a constitution precipitated and shaped by military conflict. By 1814, Norway's long-time union with Denmark had been shattered by struggles and pressures connected to the Napoleonic Wars. These led the Danish king to cede his rights in Norway to the king of Sweden. The 112 men who assembled in April 1814 in a room on the second floor of Eidsvoll Manor, an elegant neoclassical mansion some thirty miles outside Oslo, were obliged, therefore, to work at great speed. Desperate to craft some guarantee of national sovereignty in advance of their country being seized by Sweden, they completed their task of drafting a new Norwegian con-stitution in five weeks, surrounded by 'heaps of newspapers', many of them reporting on the marches of Sweden's troops and the likelihood of an invasion.

21. Oscar Wergeland's late nineteenth-century painting
of the founding fathers of the Norwegian constitution
in 1814. It now hangs in Norway's parliament.

This threat of an imminent foreign takeover – Swedish forces
duly arrived in Norway that July – did not prevent these Eidsvoll delegates from scanning multiple foreign texts in order to
help them construct their own constitution. It made them even
more eager to do so. As the global historian William McNeill
remarked, it is easier to borrow than it is to invent: and, under
intense pressure, the men of Eidsvoll borrowed furiously.[43]
Divided among themselves, and with their own conflicting
ideas, they were determined nonetheless to work out a viable
text and have it available in print before alterations in government could be imposed on them from without. So they worked
hard. They read omnivorously and promiscuously, and they
sifted and sometimes copied.

Traditionally, Norway had received much of its political

information from abroad by way of the Danish capital, Copen-hagen, an important print and university centre with close links to Paris. Most Norwegians seem first to have learned about the American constitution in 1787, for instance, by way of this over-land route. Norway also, however, received regular supplies of foreign news and print by sea, especially from English, Scottish, Irish, Dutch, Swedish and German coastal traders. These mixed information networks help to explain why the Norwegian constitution drafted in 1814 exhibits such an array of different bloodlines.

This point was recognised very early. The 1814 text crafted at Eidsvoll was painstakingly investigated by a Victorian scholar, the Swedish jurist Nils Höjer. Despite working without the computer analysis that aids investigators of this sort today, he was able to uncover and identify influences on the Norwegian constitution:

> And in some cases verbatim translations – from the French revolutionary constitutions of 1791, 1793 and 1795, the American Federal Constitution and several state constitu-tions, the Polish Constitution of 1791, the Batavian [that is, Dutch constitution] of 1798, the Swedish of 1809 and the Spanish of 1812.[44]

In addition to taking material from these different printed foreign sources, plus position papers drawn up by Norwegian intellectuals, clerics and royal officials, the delegates at Eidsvoll also drew on published British political writings for ideas about constructing a constitutional monarchy in their own country.

In other words, what these men stoically hammered out, as they waited for Swedish armed forces to arrive in their country, was emphatically not a pure, domestic invention. But neither was it derived in the main from the United States constitu-tion (one of the most repeated words in this Norwegian text is 'king'), nor from any other single foreign source. Instead, like most constitutions, Norway's 1814 constitution resembled rather a patchwork quilt. In its final form, it was a brand new creation, but it had been put together, in part, from a multitude of different, older materials that had originated elsewhere.

Like most constitution-makers, the promoters of this Norwegian text also made extensive use of print. They did so in ways that demonstrate how the possibilities for using print in this way expanded in tandem with developments in communications more broadly. Taking advantage of the country's burgeoning postal system, printed copies of the new constitution were put on sale in 1814 in Norway's twenty-five major post offices and close to 100 sub-post offices. Men and women dropping in to post or pick up letters or parcels were thus able to study a copy while they waited, or purchase one for themselves, or send one off to relations and friends living in more remote regions of the country. Norwegians were also encouraged to paste pages from these print versions of the constitution on the inside walls of their houses, thereby – quite literally – domesticating the country's new politics and making it part of their everyday lives. In addition, when the Norwegian postal service invested in steamships to deliver mail at stops along the country's huge, twisting coastline, it chose to name one of these vessels *Constitution*. As people waited on the shore to receive their mail, they would see this word inscribed on the side of the ship, and be reminded.[45]

As well as catering to official constitution-makers in different locations, the ever-expanding print archive of constitutional texts and commentaries also lent itself to study and exploitation by dissident and opposition groupings, not least by those confronting imperial invasions from without. Take the way in which Mexico's Plan de Iguala was disseminated and repurposed by different groupings contending against modes of empire and exclusion.

This plan was originally issued in February 1821 by the Mexican warlord and subsequent would-be emperor, Colonel Agustín de Iturbide, and was intended as a blueprint for the government of a more independent, though possibly still royalist Mexico. However, the twelfth clause of the plan, especially, proved eminently attractive to those pursuing different political causes in other regions of the world: 'All the inhabitants of New Spain, *without any distinction between Europeans, Africans, or Indians* [my italics], are citizens of this monarchy, and have access to all employments according to their merit and virtues.'[46] Once translated and set in motion across frontiers by way of print, this passage in the Plan de Iguala came sometimes to be interpreted as an example of how generous political rights might, in a reformed future, be accorded to all males, irrespective of religion, skin colour or ethnicity. (Women remained another matter.)

By the autumn of 1821, an English-language version of the Plan de Iguala was already circulating in the United States. By the end of that year, this version had reached Ireland, where understandings and uses of it promptly shifted. It was published in the *Connaught Journal*, a liberal Catholic newspaper which offered a reading of the plan's lessons for Ireland itself. Although Ireland had been formally absorbed into the United Kingdom in 1801 by way of a parliamentary Act of Union, the bulk of the country's Catholic majority population remained excluded from direct representation in the London-based parliament. Only a minority of Irish Catholics were able to vote at this point; and none, under legislation disqualifying men of their religion, could stand for election to the Westminster Parliament until 1829.

Hence some of the allure of Mexico's Plan de Iguala for the proprietors of the *Connaught Journal* and its mainly Catholic readership. 'How profitable a moral might our own country derive from the example of a nation just emerging from abject slavery and almost hopeless barbarism!' declared the paper's editor, at once a reformer and a xenophobe:

> Ireland would not now exhibit a scene of wretchedness and despair – of deadly feuds, and nightly murders, if that conciliatory spirit which dictated the twelfth article of the Mexican constitution pervaded the councils of our statesmen and legislators.[47]

By 1822, this kind of gloss on the wider significance and implications of the Plan de Iguala – the sense that the Mexican constitutional text offered a model for the better recognition and empowerment of males across different cultures, classes and races – had reached India and the great city port of Calcutta.

This was the headquarters of Britain's East India Company which, by now, laid claim to hegemony over much of the Indian subcontinent. Calcutta was also very much a composite city. Fine, white mansions were set alongside dirt tracks. Most of the half a million or so civilian inhabitants were very poor, though a minority – and this applied across racial divides – were moneylenders, speculators and rich merchants. Only a couple of thousand residents of the city could be said to be 'English', and most of these mingled – or not – with other Europeans and demi-Europeans. But, most importantly, Calcutta was already one of the world's centres of print, a base for Indian and British-owned printing houses that together published more material than many European capitals.[48]

Perhaps a third of Calcutta's total print output was linked in some way to the East India Company and its machinery of rule. But the city's print resources were also utilised by disgruntled Europeans, as well as Indian activists, in order to criticise the Company and its impositions, and agitate for political, religious, economic and social change. A prime early example of this print resistance was the *Calcutta Journal*, the subcontinent's first daily newspaper. Flourishing erratically between 1818 and its final suppression in 1823, it was the joint work of two transgressors of borders, an Englishman named James Silk Buckingham, who sometimes affected versions of Arab and Indian dress, and Rammohan Roy, a high-status Kulin Brahman from Bengal, who enjoyed wearing European shoes.

Utterly different in terms of their origins, wealth, social class and education, both were remarkable men. Buckingham was entirely self-made and an adventurous traveller, familiar – as he boasted – with parts of 'Europe, Asia, and Africa, and ... the Mediterranean, the Atlantic, the Red Sea, the Persian Gulf, and the Indian Ocean'.[49] At different times he worked as a preacher, a seaman, a journalist and writer and, of course, as a printer. Buckingham was also a more principled individual than he sometimes allowed himself to appear, a vociferous opponent of the colour bar, and a fervent anti-slavery activist who established close links with leading abolitionists in the United States.

Rammohan Roy was a far more educated, affluent and intellectually formidable figure who has attracted rising attention in recent years. Six foot tall, he possessed striking black hair, a source, like his high-caste origins and appeal to women, of considerable vanity on his part. A controversial man then, as now, on account of his efforts to 'reform' Hinduism, Roy was also a critic of the East India Company, while nonetheless sometimes doing work for it and investing in its stock. Our understanding of his evolving ideas is limited by the disappearance of most of his Persian and Bengali papers, but it is clear that he was fascinated by the workings and diversity of languages. An adept linguist fluent in Persian, Sanskrit and Arabic as well as in several European languages, Roy also published, along with many other works, a book on English and Bengali grammar.[50]

He and Buckingham first met in 1818, and for a while seem to have got together on an almost daily basis, sometimes driving in a carriage slowly of an evening around Calcutta's recently

22. James Silk Buckingham and his wife in Baghdad in 1816.

completed Circular Road, so as to discuss political and journal-
istic projects in privacy; sometimes meeting over protracted
working breakfasts (which Roy, for reasons of caste, would not
eat) with a mix of other Indian and European intellectuals and

writers. The two men also exchanged copy. Roy contributed pieces in English to the *Calcutta Journal*, and advised on its format and campaigns, while Buckingham fed occasional material for translation and insertion in the Persian and Bengali newspapers run by his friend and ally.[51]

Both men were interested in the progress and politics of the new constitutions, though to differing degrees. Even after becoming a Member of Parliament at Westminster in his more conventional late middle age, Buckingham remained convinced of the superior merits of written constitutionalism. 'Having no written constitution for our guide,' he wrote accurately enough of Britain in 1841, '... there is nothing fixed or tangible for us to refer to.'[52] As for Roy, as well as looking overseas for ideas, he also gradually developed his own theories about the ancient constitutionalism of India itself, insisting that there had once been indigenous variants there of charters and political rights.

Roy's intention in so arguing was to push back against claims that it was only the dominion of the East India Company that had rescued India from its ancestral despotism. But his status as an enlightened intellectual and patrician liberal, along with the movements of print, ensured that some of his ideas about an ancient, pristine Indian constitutionalism ultimately reached Britain itself. One can see their influence in some early Victorian editions of William Blackstone's classic *Commentaries on the Laws of England*, which had originally been published between 1765 and 1770. By the mid nineteenth century, readers of these volumes were being assured that the name of the legendary Anglo-Saxon parliament, the Witenagemot, actually echoed words to be found in north Indian languages. Ancient English freedoms, it was implied, might well possess ancient Indian counterparts.[53]

Both Buckingham and Roy were admirers of the political achievements of the United States. Buckingham had travelled there, and Roy was still hoping to do so when he died during a visit to England in 1833. Yet, for all this, and for all their

23. A drawing of Rammohan Roy in 1826, possibly completed in India.

enthusiastic embracing of 'this age of creating, changing [and] remodelling ... constitutions', the two allies devoted limited space to North American constitutionalism in the pages of the *Calcutta Journal*. Instead, the newspaper's focus was more on political changes in the Iberian peninsula and South America. Thus, in 1822, Roy and Buckingham published a translation of the first draft constitution of an independent Peru. They also published part of the founding constitution of Gran Colombia. And, of course, they published the text of the Mexican Plan de Iguala of 1821, including a version of the clause that Catholic Irish journalists had earlier found so compelling:

All the inhabitants of New Spain, without any distinction of Europeans, Africans, *or Indians* [my italics], are citizens of this monarchy, and eligible in every office, according to their merit and virtue.[54]

The word 'Indians' naturally signified something different in Calcutta than it did in Mexico; and this was the essential point. Both Buckingham and Roy wanted to secure improved liberties and legal rights for India's Indigenous populations. In this connection, United States written constitutionalism was – for all its other qualities – of limited use, and becoming progressively less so. By the 1810s and 1820s, a growing number of American states were issuing new constitutions which explicitly excluded men who were not white from exercising political rights.

By contrast, South American constitutionalists paid close attention to the vitally important Cádiz Constitution of 1812. Reissued in Spain in 1820, and dedicated in this version to Rammohan Roy, this offered, as we shall see, a measure of political emancipation and hope across racial divides. Like the Plan de Iguala – though not to the same degree – it could be read as relatively open, meritocratic and colour blind. These Hispanic texts, in South America and in Spain itself, therefore possessed an appeal to Roy and Buckingham as models for what they hoped to achieve within the Indian subcontinent itself: not an end to rule by the British East India Company, since, to most early nineteenth-century Asian and European radicals, this seemed beyond the realms of possibility, but rather reforms in the company's governance and legal practices, and an altered British empire in which, 'without any distinction of Europeans … or Indians', all groupings might be treated 'according to their merit and virtue'.

## Power and the Limits of Print

These events in Calcutta help to explain why, by the 1820s, some optimistic observers felt able already to envisage a world in which written and reforming constitutions were universal. 'Revolutions hitherto have been solitary,' wrote one European radical early that decade, 'but now, one feeling seems to pervade all nations. We shall see the Asiatic states demanding the representative system in a few years – aye, and the African too.'[55] The degree to which advocacy of the new constitutions was by this stage crossing borders and oceans was indeed striking. But while print was vital for this spread, and always would be, matters to do with print and language also worked to put a brake on the development of constitutions in some parts of the world.

The limits on the diffusion of written constitutions at this early stage were not primarily the result of the widespread illiteracy still existing in most regions of the world. As American revolutionaries had understood in regard to their own Declaration of Independence in 1776, one did not need to be able to read in order to obtain some sense of what was contained in a constitutional text. Men and women who were illiterate but who lived in a society where there *was* literacy could normally find someone who was literate – a priest, a lawyer, a politician or a military man, say, or simply a better educated neighbour – to explain to them the rough contents and significance of a new constitution. But the growing vogue for these kinds of political constitutions did tend to work against peoples who lacked a written language. It could also pose challenges for regions of the world where there were long, illustrious traditions of bureaucratic, religious and scholarly script, but where printing presses and an easy commercial dissemination of their products emerged only slowly and unevenly. This was the case, for instance, in parts of the Ottoman empire, and in regions of central Asia and the Middle East.

Here, the relative paucity of print and printing presses in the early 1800s by no means prevented the emergence of new, written law codes. Nor did it prevent the exchange of ideas and the introduction of important reforming political texts.[56] But, in societies lacking widespread print machinery, it could be harder to diffuse information about domestic political changes. It could also be harder to broadcast copious amounts of information about these changes to foreign states.

Benegal Shiva Rao, an Indian nationalist and a future key player in the making of his country's independence constitution, discovered this on a visit to London in 1933. While there, he came across a copy of the Dublin-produced *Select Constitutions of the World* of 1922, and immediately recognised that a version of this compendium might be useful 'to those who are actively interested in the constitutional changes which are taking place in India'. Rao quickly secured permission from the Irish Free State to produce an Indian edition of the work. But, as he later remarked, he had initially hoped to offset the Western bias of the original Dublin version of this compendium by also including the Persian constitution of 1906 and the Afghanistan constitution of 1923. But Rao found that he could not easily track down published copies of these texts in London. Consequently, when his new edition of the *Select Constitutions of the World* appeared in Madras in 1934, it was selective indeed, containing no examples of such texts from predominantly Islamic states.[57]

Yet, in both non-Western and Western regions of the world, access to print was by no means the main controlling issue in regard to the spread of constitutions. More than anything else, it was prevailing structures of power – and the attitudes of the powerful – that tended to impose the most critical limits.

Consider events in Japan and China, where print had long been widely available. Even before the sea changes in print culture that came about in the late nineteenth century, traditional woodblock technology in China allowed for cheap printed material to reach as far as some of the more prosperous peasantry. In this vast region of the world, there were no insurmountable technological or skill barriers, then, to the introduction of written and printed constitutions. An American merchant based in Macao made precisely this point in 1831. 'Constitution manufactories' were now hard at work in Spain and Portugal and even in 'minor states' like Hanover and Saxony, he wrote accurately enough in an essay published in the *Canton Miscellany* that year. Since 'the paper manufactories in China' were 'surely equal' to these European outlets, he went on, why were no new written and printed constitutions being produced in the Qing empire?[58]

As this writer will have been aware, these queries were provocative fantasies, nothing more. There would be no sustained attempts among Chinese rulers, politicians or bureaucrats to engage in serious political refashioning until the last third of the nineteenth century. This was in part because, until that point, the disruptions of major warfare in this region of the world were kept – just about – under control.

To be sure, a few Chinese bureaucrats and intellectuals did show some interest in the widening spread of constitutionalism in the wake of the First Opium War of 1839–42, a conflict in which Britain's Royal Navy devastated the Qing empire's maritime defences and forced the cession of Hong Kong. But until the Chinese authorities were put under more sustained warlike pressure, first by the Taiping Rebellion in the 1850s and early 1860s, and then – still more – by defeats in the Sino-French War of 1884–5 and the Chinese–Japanese War of 1894–5, and until they seriously accepted the need to raise taxes and reorder their state so as to make provision for the demands of modern hybrid warfare, calls for constitutional changes, and official responsiveness to such calls, remained limited here.[59]

By the same token, there would be minimal high-level discussion of written constitutionalism in print-laden Japan until after the political and military convulsions there in 1868. This was not in the main because of obstacles in terms of printing technology or literacy levels, but rather because of limited interest on the part of Japan's ruling orders in the new political technology and in what it might achieve. Print, in other words, played a vital role across continents in the advancement and shaping of the new constitutions. But by itself, print was never enough.

Considerations of power sometimes constrained print's ability to foster constitutional initiatives even within the United States itself, as an ultimately brutal chain of events in the 1820s and 1830s serves to illustrate. By this stage, the original thirteen American states which the men of Philadelphia had taken for granted had expanded to twenty-four and, over this same period – 1787 to the 1820s – the registered American population had tripled. Left out of these official United States census calculations, however, were Native Americans, or Indians as they were termed. Not in the main liable for tax, these peoples were not included among the citizenry of the United States. Neither were most of them slaves. So what were they? In 1827, leading activists among the 15,000 or so Cherokees, who were based largely in the emerging state of Georgia, decided to make clear that what they were in fact was an independent nation, and consequently that they required a written constitution.

As these men saw it, the preconditions were in place. By this time, Cherokee lands and numbers had been seriously eroded by white invaders. But rising numbers of Cherokees were now partially literate, and many were working farmers. Moreover, and critically, they had acquired access to print. One of their number, Sequoyah – about whose origins and ideas we still know far too little – had invented a writing system which allowed the Cherokee language to be set down on paper, put into print and read.[60] One result of this was the *Cherokee Phoenix*, the first ever Indian-owned and edited newspaper in the United States. Another outcome of Sequoyah's work was that, when

24. Sequoyah and his syllabary of the Cherokee language.

some leading Cherokee held a convention in 1827, and adopted 'a Constitution for [their] future government', this text was issued in print, with Cherokee and English-language versions of the provisions laid out in parallel columns on each page.

Like other constitution-makers, these Cherokee legislators cut and pasted, quite deliberately replicating parts of the United

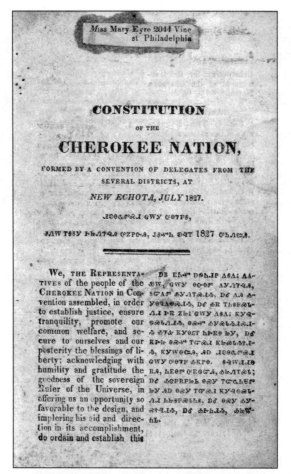

25. The constitution of the Cherokee nation, 1827,
printed in both Cherokee and English.

States constitution. 'We, the representatives of the people of
the Cherokee Nation in Convention assembled' is how their
constitution begins. But these men also set down in close geographical detail the territorial 'boundaries of this nation', which
were 'hereafter [to] remain unalterably the same':

Beginning on the North Bank of Tennessee River at the
upper part of the Chickasaw old fields: then following the

main channel of said river, including all the islands therein, to the mouth of the Hiwassee river, then up the main channel of the said river including islands, to the first hill which closes in on said river, about two miles above Hiwassee old town ...[61]

But neither this particular vision of the land, nor the Cherokees' claim to be a 'free and distinct nation' with the right to govern itself achieved any traction. The US federal government in Washington, along with Georgia's all-white legislature, rejected the legality of this constitution and the validity of Cherokee national aspirations. In the 1830s, most Cherokee were driven out of their lands in Georgia and forced to migrate into what is now Oklahoma, some 4,000 of them dying in transit. This is usually represented as a distinctively American frontier tragedy. But it was more than that.

At one level, this episode underlines again just how closely access to print could be linked to active involvement in constitution-making. At another level, this same series of events in Georgia in the 1820s and 1830s confirms how the opportunities and ideas made available by print in this regard might be pushed to one side by those in possession of superior levels of power. After 1776, white Americans progressively used a web of written and printed constitutions to help forge, knit together, legitimise and broadcast to the world a vast transcontinental empire. Rival attempts to use these devices to advance separate legislative and national projects within United States territory were not permitted and often brutally repressed.

Yet, for all that, this Cherokee initiative in 1827, which other Native American groupings subsequently emulated, is a reminder that constitutions – like print itself – were inherently volatile, and that no one could have absolute ownership of them.[62] Later in the nineteenth century, other peoples threatened by Western imperial advances would also endeavour to use written and printed constitutions to assert their separate, autonomous political identities, sometimes with more success than the Cherokee.

There is a final respect in which these peoples' efforts in the 1820s, and the suppression of those efforts, serve to make an important wider point about written constitutions in general. Often viewed only as essential auxiliaries of nation-building, in practice such texts could also function as aids in the construction and legitimisation of empires. Well before the crushing of the Cherokee by way of American expansionism, other powers, in other regions of the world, had taken notice of this fact.

FOUR

# ARMIES OF LEGISLATORS

## Paris

Barely a year after finalising a draft constitution for the United
States, Gouverneur Morris of New York encountered this new
political technology again, but in another place. In December
1788, he had crossed the Atlantic, hoping to recruit European
investors in American land and tobacco. But he arrived in Paris
just days after the formal summoning of the Estates General on
24 January 1789. This was France's long-dormant consultative
assembly, and its revival was expected to resolve the financial
crisis brought about by that country's overindulgence in hybrid
warfare, and to advance work on restructuring its administration and taxation systems. Wealthy, clever, personable and
possessed of good French, essentially a confident man, Morris
quickly involved himself in these developments. He gained easy
access to the French court and some of the city's political salons,
and he attended the opening of the Estates General in May 1789,
taking notes on the delegates' speeches. He made contact with
events in other ways. An unabashed rake ('I know it to be wrong,
but cannot help it'), he tangled with prostitutes who passed on
rumours from the streets. He also wooed more affluent women.
Along with other things, some of these gave him political gossip
and confidences picked up from their husbands.[1]

Initially, Morris was both optimistic and proprietorial,
confident that France was beginning to emulate the political
advances of his own United States. 'I find on this side of the

Atlantic a strong resemblance to what I left on the other', he wrote. 'Existing forms' had been 'shaken to the very foundation', and a 'new order of things' was fast emerging. Such early euphoria was widespread among genteel reformers across the Atlantic world. If, in Morris's case, it faded unusually fast, this was partly because – unlike many former delegates from the Philadelphia convention – he possessed little direct experience of extreme physical violence. Witnessing it now on the streets of Paris – the killings, the riots and the random cruelties – left him disoriented and frightened.[2] He was also unsettled by how quickly French constitutional projects were diverging from his own Anglo-American norms.

Even the terminology was different. Members of the Estates General, and its successor body, the National Assembly, spoke not of writing or drafting a constitution, but of *fixing* one.[3] Back in 1787, the men of Philadelphia had chosen to omit a bill of rights from their draft constitution, and steered well clear of anything approaching social revolution. Morris himself had argued for a new American Senate to be stocked 'by men of great and established property – an aristocracy' who would enjoy their seats for life. But the Declaration of the Rights of Man and the Citizen adopted by the National Assembly in August 1789 proclaimed that, in the new France, 'social distinctions' would be based 'only on common utility'.[4]

Other differences alarmed him. The United States constitution had provided for a bicameral legislature, as did most early American state constitutions. But France's first constitution, published in September 1791, adopted a more radical, unicameral model. It also hollowed out executive power, hobbling the monarch, Louis XVI – now barely sixteen months away from his appointment with the guillotine – and creating a national legislative assembly of over 740 mainly young and politically inexperienced members. A firm believer in a robust executive, Morris was appalled and contemptuous. 'The Almighty himself', he denounced, would be hard-pressed to make this proposed system of French government function 'without creating a new species of men'.[5]

But his most significant epiphany occurred shortly afterwards, on 8 December 1791. Convinced by now that the French were 'going headlong to destruction', but still resolved to 'stop them if I could', Morris had decided to spend that day in his lodgings on the rue de Richelieu, then one of the most fashionable streets in central Paris. He resolved to draw on his own experience and draft 'the form of a constitution for this country', something that would surely be an improvement on the efforts of the National Assembly. He had just started work when a stranger burst into the room. The intruder was French and, by his own eager admission, had never visited the United States in his life. Nonetheless, he assured the bewildered Morris, he was confident that he understood the country 'perfectly well'. So much so, that, having studied 'such objects ... for above fifty years', he had recently drawn up 'the form of a constitution for America' and posted it off for the immediate attention of George Washington himself.[6]

Morris coaxed the man (whose name we never learn) out of his lodgings as soon as he could, but not before recognising that there were parallels between the intruder's naïve and presumptuous zeal and his own. 'I cannot help being struck', he confided ruefully in his diary, 'with the similitude of a Frenchman who makes constitutions for America and an American who performs the same good offices for France.'[7]

Morris stayed on in Paris until 1794, becoming progressively more alarmed and disillusioned. But this was perhaps his most penetrating insight during his time there. The comments he scribbled down the day of the stranger's interruption, and the events leading up to this encounter, are revealing about how the new constitutions were evolving in two respects. Morris's experience is an example, first of all, of how the business of imagining and writing these devices was, by now, attracting not just official players but also amateur and informal practitioners. Today, we usually think of constitution-making as the province of lawyers, politicians and civil servants. Yet, as the efforts of Morris himself and of his unknown French visitor demonstrate, by the end of the eighteenth century – and for long afterwards – constitution-writing was frequently also a private pursuit, as much a mode of literary and cultural creativity as writing a poem, a play, a newspaper article or, indeed, a novel.

Like writing a novel, attempting to formulate a constitution was, after all, something you could do almost anywhere. Jane Austen, who died a year after Morris in 1817, wrote sections of some of her major novels at Chawton Cottage, in a village close to Winchester in Hampshire, in a small interior space that doubled up as a hallway, and that had a squeaking door to alert her to impending intruders. By the same token, individuals wanting to try their hand at writing a political constitution required no great investment in money or space. Any literate person with sufficient time, blank paper, enthusiasm and confidence at their disposal could sit down at home, or – like Morris – in lodgings, or in a tavern or coffee house, or even on the deck of a ship, and set to work planning and penning a constitution.

Increasingly, this was what happened. As more and more information circulated about these devices, and as the rate of political change quickened, so the appeal to individuals of making their own attempt at this genre blossomed. In the 1790s, one newspaper in Strasbourg, a hotbed of French revolutionary activism and violence, even printed a template for do-it-yourself constitution-writers, suggesting suitable headings, and leaving blank spaces for enthusiasts to fill up with their own reforming ideas.[8]

Gouverneur Morris's Parisian encounter illustrates something else. Those attempting to draw up constitutions – whether in an official or a private capacity – did not always confine themselves to redesigning the government of their own particular homeland. Like Morris, and like his French intruder, some wrote and planned for territories and peoples other than their own.

But writing for others in this fashion involved severe challenges. If you wanted to attempt a political constitution for a foreign country, and have some chance of gaining wider notice for your efforts, it helped if you could demonstrate some evidence of direct experience of the country concerned. Yet, especially before the spread of railroads and steamships, long-distance travel – unless dictated by work, commerce, religion or family emergencies – was too expensive and arduous for most private individuals even to contemplate. The elderly Frenchman who interrupted Gouverneur Morris in his lodgings in December 1791 was clearly obsessed with the United States, and desperately eager to leave his mark on its government. But Paris was over 3,500 miles and an ocean away from America, so this man, whoever he was, is unlikely ever to have seen that country except in his imagination.

An even more fundamental obstacle, though, was lack of leverage. How could a private individual possibly hope to shape the political workings of a foreign country? Gouverneur Morris was rich, worldly and clever. He enjoyed a transatlantic reputation as the man responsible, in James Madison's words, for 'the finish given to the style and arrangement' of the American constitution. Yet, once in France, this pristine legislative background in the United States counted for little. Morris was able to submit some of his ideas to various revolutionary politicians and to Louis XVI himself, but to no effect. 'Perhaps he does have the vain insolence to place his work under the eyes of the king', sneered one Parisian journalist. 'But it would be absurd', this man went on, to imagine that Morris's schemes 'received any more attention than a hundred others of the same nature which other individuals have published in secret': a comment which also underlines how much the writing of constitutional blueprints on the part of enthusiastic amateurs was now a proliferating trend.[9]

But, for one broad category of men, these obstacles to writing constitutions for foreign spaces – the costs of travel, and a lack of obvious leverage – were less formidable and could sometimes be overcome. Before 1850, only limited numbers of human beings anywhere in the world were in a position to undertake long-distance travel. Among soldiers and navy men, however, the case was sometimes otherwise. Overwhelmingly young and relatively fit, these men frequently undertook transnational and transcontinental journeys as an integral part of their jobs. Moreover, for men in uniform, the expenses involved in long-distance travel were generally borne by others; paid for out of taxation, or funded in transit by pillage and forced requisitioning.

Those commanding armed forces might possess even greater advantages. Both at home and abroad, they could be in a position to use military force to dislodge existing political regimes. They could then use yet more force, or the threat of force, to impose a changed constitutional order. Establishing new constitutions by way of armed power in such ways has proved an enduring phenomenon to this day. Since 1958, for instance, Pakistan's government and constitution have repeatedly been retooled by interventions on the part of its military, and that country is hardly unique in this respect.[10] No less notable has been the way in which armed invasions on the part of a single country, or set of countries – usually from the West – have been instrumental in imposing their own versions of constitutions on other countries. Thus, allied soldiers, lawyers and officials used their victory in the Second World War to create new constitutions in a defeated Germany and Japan. The United States and its allies would try, far less effectively, to do the same in Iraq after the invasion of 2003.

The use of military power and aggression to enforce new constitutions in domestic sites – and sometimes in foreign spaces

– has been a recurring factor in the spread of these devices. This trend became more apparent from the 1790s. Deploying military force to push and shape written constitutions became more prominent at this time because of changes, but also continuities in warfare, power structures and ideas. Using force to implement new constitutions also grew in prominence in the wake of the French Revolution because of the relentless rise of the man who had begun to style himself Napoleon Bonaparte.

## Hybrid Warfare Repeated and Extended

How far and how rapidly the geographical range and scale of the new constitutional technology shifted in the three decades after 1790 is easily demonstrated:

### New Constitutions, 1776–1820[11]

|           | USA | Europe | South America and Haiti | Africa |
|-----------|-----|--------|-------------------------|--------|
| 1776–91   | 20  | 2      | –                       | –      |
| 1792–1800 | 7   | 20     | –                       | –      |
| 1801–10   | 2   | 59     | 5                       | –      |
| 1811–15   | 1   | 38     | 16                      | –      |
| 1816–20   | 7   | 24     | 7                       | 1 (Liberia) |
| **Totals** | 37 | 143    | 28                      | 1      |

Like most sets of figures, these do not tell the whole story. Left out of this table are the many amendments that were made to *existing* constitutions during this period. Some of these – conspicuously the American Bill of Rights of 1791 – were of signal importance. In addition, the totals given above for European and South American constitutions include many that lasted only a brief time. Conversely, however, these European and South American totals would be much higher if *all* constitutions drafted in these regions – but then not implemented – were to be included. In 1808, a long-running armed rising in Serbia led to a flurry of attempts at writing constitutions, the first to emerge from the Balkans. But these were never put into practice, and were soon obliterated by Ottoman and Russian power.[12]

Yet, for all this, the overall pattern revealed by these figures is incontestable and dramatic. Before 1776, some European leaders had responded to accelerating levels of warfare and the stimulus of Enlightenment ideas by issuing innovative constitutional texts. But, from then on, it was the United States that experimented with constitutions most adventurously and successfully. That this pattern subsequently changed was not only due to the outbreak of the French Revolution. It was the subsequent prolonged period of warfare and its repercussions that most caused new constitutions to fan out rapidly into other regions of the world. The year 1791 saw both the implementation of France's first written constitution – the document which so exasperated that American in Paris, Gouverneur Morris – and the National Assembly's decision to make members of the National Guard subject to military service. In June that year alone, this led to the recruitment of a further 100,000 troops into the French army. With the fall of the French monarchy in 1792, and the outbreak of conflict between the new revolutionary regime and a series of European powers – Austria, Prussia, Spain, Britain, Holland and more – the spread of these texts through continental Europe began conspicuously to gather pace.

This trend became still more pronounced with the rise of Napoleon Bonaparte. In the Italian peninsula, there had been a few earlier written constitutional experiments, but these rarely advanced beyond preliminary plans on paper. Napoleon's first military campaigns in Italy in 1796–7, while still a general for the French Republic, resulted, by contrast, in the issuing of four new constitutions there, plus two declarations of rights. Once he was established as ruler of France, levels of military aggression and transregional constitutional activism accelerated further; and the resulting disruptions to traditional ruling orders were not confined to Europe. Nor, as the table shows, were the effects of all this cancelled out by Napoleon's eventual destruction at the battle of Waterloo in 1815. Immunity to the new constitutional technology never recovered from the French Revolutionary and Napoleonic wars. Taking different forms, the technology continued to spread into rising numbers of locations at an ever more rapid rate.

Why was the political and constitutional impact of these wars so great, and what manner of warfare was this? The answers to these questions depend very much on where you look and on what you choose to look at. Focus on land conflicts, and on revolutionary France, and the fierce struggles beginning in 1792 can appear to be a new species of warfare: new, in terms of the ideological fervour and extremism often involved, and new in the sense of mission sometimes exhibited – especially in the early stages of these conflicts – by even very ordinary French soldiers.[13]

The common soldiery of Ancien Régime Europe (and elsewhere) were rarely the downtrodden automata of legend. Many were committed and motivated actors, not mere sullen and damaged victims of coercion. Nonetheless, it is clear that *some* French Revolutionary troops were politicised to a quite different level, in part because widely distributed written and printed constitutions now existed to serve as instructional and inspiring scripts. Take Joseph-Louis-Gabriel Noël, a yeoman farmer and quiet family man from the still quieter village of Ubexy in north-eastern France. When he signed up as an infantryman in a local battalion of volunteers in August 1791, he quickly came to represent himself, even in the privacy of his letters home, as a 'soldier of the constitution', a child of destiny. 'We must be put to the test', he wrote to his family sternly. What he read, saw, heard and was told by his officers convinced him, however, that triumph was assured, and not just for France. 'It is we', he rejoiced, 'who must attack to send shivers down the tyrants' spines and free enslaved peoples.'[14]

Because of the stimulus this sort of zeal occasionally gave to volunteering, but much more because of the introduction in France and elsewhere of conscription, these wars drew in an unprecedentedly high number and mix of men. Over the course of her long reign, Catherine the Great had raised 1 million troops. But her grandson, Alexander I, who succeeded to the Russian throne in 1801, would require 2 million soldiers merely to defeat the French and their allies. His greatest challenge came, of course, in 1812. The army that Napoleon let loose on Russia in the summer of that year consisted of about 680,000 men, over half of whom were not French by birth.[15]

Few of these foreign soldiers fighting in the name of a trans-figured France travelled as far as one Abdel-Talut. Originally captured in Ethiopia and sold as a slave in Cairo, he was plucked from captivity there by Napoleon's invading soldiery, and sub-sequently exposed to different forms of hardship and duress, taking part in several French military campaigns before dying in frozen agony on the retreat from Moscow.[16] But while the nature of Abdel-Talut's personal military progress was excep-tional, the border crossing he was obliged to undertake in the course of it was a more widespread experience. Because fight-ing in these French Revolutionary and Napoleonic Wars went on for so long – from 1792 to 1815 – and because these conflicts reached into so many parts of the globe, very large numbers of men were repeatedly set in motion across seas, countries and continents. These high and protracted levels of military mobil-ity had significant political consequences.

Yet – as the degree to which the Revolutionary and Napo-leonic Wars were fought out on a transcontinental scale makes clear – viewed in their entirety, these conflicts did *not* in fact represent a wholly new form of warfare. Rather, they marked a continuation, on a notably bigger scale, of that combined fighting on land and sea which had been escalating in expense and reach since the early 1700s. Yet again, this was a case of large-scale hybrid warfare: and Napoleon was not particularly good at it.

This point is easily obscured by the gorgeous and grotesque plurality of this man's victories on land. Some fifty of them, they have understandably exerted a mesmerising effect both on his admirers and on historians (there has sometimes between an overlap between these constituencies). Yet, for all the trumpets and drums on land, events at sea were actually crucial in determining the overall course and direction of this long and wide conflict. The marked maritime component of the Napoleonic Wars also helps to account for the growing recourse from the 1790s to new written constitutions.

Napoleon is reputed initially to have yearned to be a fighting sailor, and some of the most decisive episodes of his warlike career involved navies as well as armies.[17] When he invaded Egypt in 1798, it was with 330 warships and transports, and over 50,000 soldiers, scientists and workmen: numbers of men and seagoing machines that easily eclipsed the French investment in the American Revolutionary War. The aim of this Egyptian invasion was to secure for France a permanent strategic position at the juncture of Africa and Asia. This, it was hoped, would compensate for its earlier loss of colonies to the British, and possibly also provide a gateway to India. Both these long-term strategic ambitions and the expedition itself failed. But carefully massaged reports of Napoleon landing in Egypt, taking Alexandria and Cairo, doing battle in the shadow of the Pyramids and marching into Syria allowed him to return to Paris in October 1799 even more of a public hero than before.[18] This considerably eased the political coup he staged there shortly afterwards.

There were other significant, long-distance maritime and naval ventures on Napoleon's part. In 1800, he approved an expedition led by a sea officer, naturalist and former French East India Company man, Nicolas Baudin, to map the coastlines of what would soon come to be called Australia. Baudin and his crewmen reached what is today called Tasmania two years later, and the surviving members of the expedition eventually returned to France with some 200,000 rare and stolen objects, including plants for the Empress Joséphine's gardens. In addition, Baudin sent back reports and charts that were intended to facilitate a future French naval descent on New South Wales, the first British settlement to be established in this vast Pacific territory.[19] Again, nothing came of these overseas projects, and Napoleon's next transoceanic venture was a far more comprehensive and damaging failure.

In December 1801, Napoleon dispatched over fifty ships and 22,000 men to the Caribbean to restore French rule over its one-time plantation colony, Saint-Domingue, later shipping in a further 55,000 troops. Napoleon's ambitions for this expedition extended beyond regaining Saint-Domingue. He envisaged its reconquest, along with the vast Louisiana Territory ceded to him by Spain in 1800, as wedges that might open up a revived French imperial presence in North America and the Caribbean. 'With an army of twenty-five to thirty thousand Blacks' recruited in Saint-Domingue, mused Napoleon towards the end of his life, 'what might I not [have undertaken] against Jamaica, the Antilles, Canada, the United States itself'. He also relished the prospect of securing access to the Mississippi. Regular supplies of timber floated down this mighty river would, he thought, be invaluable for the construction of a renewed French fighting fleet.[20]

Again, these projects failed, with enduring repercussions, not least as regards the spread of constitutions. The final surrender of the French invasion force in Saint-Domingue in 1803 ensured the creation of a free, Black-ruled Haiti. Over the next fifteen years, five significant constitutions emerged here. French defeat in Haiti and the collapse of Napoleon's North American and Caribbean schemes (though he was still contemplating a comeback as late as 1810) precipitated further transformations.[21] He decided to sell the still-unmapped Louisiana Territory to the United States for 15 million dollars, a mammoth transfer of land that had profound and lasting results.

As it turned out, obtaining control of this vast, uncharted territory served to double the size of the United States, expanding its boundaries from the Mississippi River into the Rocky Mountains, a transformation in geographical scale and resources that allowed it – and its modes of government – to gain a far higher profile in the world at large. The Louisiana Purchase, as it came to be called, also allowed American settlers and soldiers to swarm into lands where a wide spectrum of Indigenous peoples had previously remained relatively secure and intact. In time, this influx of settlers and American troops would provide for the emergence of eleven new US states, each of them equipped with its own written constitution.

Napoleon had planned to use the profits from selling the Louisiana Territory to the United States to finance a huge invasion fleet against Britain. With the battle of Trafalgar in late 1805, which destroyed nineteen large, hugely expensive ships out of a combined Franco-Spanish fleet of thirty-three, this further maritime project also miscarried. We do not usually think of Napoleon before the march on Moscow and the battle of Waterloo in terms of failure. Nor do we usually think of him in relation to the sea. Yet, even more than his previous maritime setbacks, this last reverse – Trafalgar – proved significant for the overall fortunes of his wars.

Since he was unable to stage a successful invasion of Britain, Napoleon could neither knock out nor win control over its Royal Navy. By 1805, this contained 136 ships of the line, as against the forty-one big warships of the French navy, or what was left of it.[22] The fact that this vast, fighting British navy remained intact and was able to operate freely on the world's oceans meant that not only had Napoleon's previous attempts to forge a transcontinental empire proved abortive, but any future long-distance maritime ventures on his part were likely also to be in jeopardy. Napoleon was at once formidable and for a long time unbeatable within continental Europe, and simultaneously and progressively landlocked there.

It is wrong, then, to see Napoleon's expansionist ambitions as being consistently and voluntarily only to do with Europe. He fought hard on this 'molehill', as he suggestively styled continental Europe, because this turned out to be the only region of the world where for a while he was able to construct and retain an empire. These circumstances, his construction of an overland European empire which encompassed at its peak some 290,000 square miles and 40 million people – at once impressive and, in his own eyes, not enough – drove much of Napoleon's interest in written constitutions.

He repeatedly turned to these devices in order to stabilise, embellish and legitimise his European possessions, the only ones that he was able to win and for a while retain. Napoleon imposed political constitutions on some of these continental territories with the aim of anchoring them as sources of manpower and taxation, and thus of maintaining and extending his own power and his family's position. He also experimented with constitutions as instruments of change, and as a means to foster certain modernities.

## The Napoleon of Constitutions

Unsurprisingly, given the number of his military invasions and the millions of deaths and massive destruction of infrastructure, cultural property and livelihoods for which he was directly and indirectly responsible, Napoleon's investment in the new constitutional technology has frequently aroused scepticism. An early, brilliant expression of the case for the prosecution is a work by the most significant and original graphic artist of the French Revolutionary and Napoleonic era, James Gillray. His print, *The French-Consular-Triumvirate Settling the New Constitution*, was published in London on the first day of 1800. This was less than two months after Napoleon's successful coup d'état in Paris, and just weeks after he supervised the production of a new constitution for France, the fourth to be implemented in that country in less than ten years. Gillray's image is powerful because of its design and execution, but also because he makes it do so much work.

His print shows four real-life characters in a dark and oppressively over-furnished Parisian room. Two of them are lawyers, the porcine Jean-Jacques-Régis Cambacérès, who later played a major role in the working out of Napoleon's Civil Code, and Charles-François Lebrun, a future governor of a conquered Holland and creator of the Banque de France. The third figure, hugging the background, is Emmanuel Joseph Sieyès, a Catholic clergyman and political theorist who had been the leading intellectual progenitor of the French constitution of 1791. But it is Gillray's fourth character, Napoleon himself, who naturally dominates. Leaner and hungrier-looking than Lebrun, never mind the podgy Cambacérès, his viciously pointed army boots contrasting with the latter's shapeless ankles, only he wears a sword. And only he is shown actually writing the document on the table that is labelled '*nouvelle constitution*'. Napoleon is filling every line of it with the same word: 'Bonaparte'.

Gillray was an unstable, often impoverished artist of genius who wanted above all to sell his work, and whose politics were never straightforward. But in this particular image, he draws on the ideas and imagery of Edmund Burke, the Irish polemicist, philosopher and Member of Parliament who quickly came to fear both the French Revolution and its modes of constitutional writing and proselytising.

Gillray takes from Burke, first of all, an element of ridicule: mockery of the very notion that a state can somehow be

26. James Gillray, *The French-Consular-Triumvirate
Settling the New Constitution*, 1800.

remodelled on paper in accordance with new-minted ideologies. The point is made in this print through the figure of Sieyès, who had helped to stage-manage Napoleon's coup, believing that its success would enable him to design yet another French constitution. Here, he is portrayed as an arid, cadaverous intellectual with a quill pen between his emaciated lips, already being pushed to the back by more worldly conspirators. Sieyès is also shown drawing apart a curtain to reveal rows of wooden pigeonholes that are crammed full with drafts of different constitutions. The reference is to a passage in Burke's pamphlet *A Letter to a Noble Lord* (1796), itself one of the most caustic indictments of the advance of the new political technology:

> Abbé Sieyès has whole nests of pigeon-holes full of constitutions readymade, ticketed, sorted, and numbered; suited to every season and every fancy ... Some with councils of elders and councils of youngsters; some without any council at all. Some where the electors choose their representatives; others, where the representatives choose the electors ... So that no constitution fancier may go unsuited from his shop, provided he loves a pattern of pillage, oppression, arbitrary imprisonment, confiscation, exile, revolutionary judgment, and legalized premeditated murder.[23]

Like Burke, too, who had deliberately othered the new revolutionary French regime by likening it to the 'system of Mahomet ... with Koran in one hand, and a sword in the other', Gillray connects Napoleon's constitution-making with rampant armed aggression.[24] Look closely and you can see that the tricoloured ribbon at the top of the print, flaunting the motto '*Vive le constitution* [*sic*]', is entwined around two blunderbusses, short-barrelled ancestors of the modern shotgun. Napoleon's hat is festooned with the laurels of his military victories. But his army boot is grinding into the floor a copy of the radical, egalitarian, although never properly implemented, French constitution of 1793 (one sign that Gillray did not always shadow Edmund Burke in his politics). The only place for the word *liberté* in this sinister, cynical interior is as an inscription on Napoleon's sword; while beneath the table around which these French powerbrokers are gathering is a parallel scene of industry, this time taking place in Hell. Devils are shown busily at work in forging chains. So, too, Gillray wants us to understand, are Napoleon and his fellow constitution-manufacturers.

This is hostile British propaganda aimed at the enemy across the Channel. But, like all good propaganda, it contains an element of truth. As some French observers also pointed out at this time, Napoleon *did* knowingly employ and shape con-stitutions in order to advance and legitimise his own power.[25] This happened in France itself. Unlike its predecessors, the brief constitution he issued there on 15 December 1799, which Gillray satirises in this print, contained no declaration of rights. Instead, it vested executive authority in three consuls, with actual power being exercised by the First Consul, Napoleon himself. This arrangement was pushed through, moreover, by a rigged pleb-iscite, with the French army brought in to ensure a majority. In 1802, Napoleon issued a further French constitution, proclaim-ing himself First Consul for Life, with the right to nominate his successor. By means of yet another constitution in 1804, he declared himself Emperor of the French, with the succes-sion now to be 'hereditary in the direct, natural and legitimate lineage of Napoleon Bonaparte, from male to male'.[26]

Yet while Napoleon undoubtedly sought to make the new political technology work for him, there were respects in which he also took it seriously. Like so many promoters of these texts over time, he possessed a deep attachment to words and print. At different stages of his career, he hired journalists, publicists and tame memorialists to chronicle and celebrate his achievements, set up newspapers for his soldiers, and took printing presses along with him on his military campaigns. He was also personally addicted to the written word, both as a reader and as an author. As a young man, he had experimented with writing novels, poems, short stories and history; and, like many self-made, self-fashioning people, he compiled careful lists of any unfamiliar words he came across so as to expand the range of his personal vocabulary.[27]

This belief in the utility and transformative power of the written word never left him. One sees this even in his invasion of Egypt in 1798–9. Napoleon never set up a commission to frame a constitution here. But, along with establishing a fourteen-man national *diwan* (governing council) and regional *diwans*, he did issue proclamations that were translated into Arabic which made reference to liberty and equality. He also at least played with the notion of writing and issuing some kind of dirigiste, improving text. He had wanted to free Egypt 'from the obstacles of an irksome civilisation', he claimed later, orientalism ablaze, and envisaged himself 'founding a religion [there] ... riding an elephant ... *and in my hand a new Koran that I would have composed to suit my need* [my italics]'. He would be the new Muhammad, he fantasised: a warrior, yes, but also a dealer in inspiring words and an instigator of wise laws.[28]

Napoleon's interest in constitutions was also fuelled by his origins and, from the outset, by war. He had been born in Ajaccio on the western coast of Corsica in 1769, when France was consolidating its military annexation of the island. 'I was born when the French were vomited upon our coasts', he would later recall: 'the cries of the dying, the groans of the oppressed, tears of despair surrounded my cradle at my birth'. This was largely posturing and legend-making on his part. But it does seem to have been the case that, initially, Napoleon viewed himself less as a willing subject and citizen of France than as a victim of French conquest and colonisation.[29]

'Corsica's history', he wrote in his teens, 'is nothing but a perpetual struggle between a small nation ... and its neighbours who want to dominate it.' For a time, indeed, Napoleon hero-worshipped and worked at impressing Pasquale Paoli, the soldier-patriot who had designed a Corsican constitution in 1755.[30] It required intense ambition and considerable adroitness on Napoleon's part, plus the enormously enhanced opportunities for military advancement made available by the French Revolution, with its ruthless winnowing of royalist army officers, to turn the alienated and awkward Corsican christened Napoleone di Buonaparte into a committed, armed Frenchman with a modified name.

Napoleon's shifting self-identification was aided by a ruling of the French National Assembly in November 1790. This stipulated that, while retaining a measure of self-government, Corsica was in the future to be fully incorporated into France and governed by the same laws. From his early life on his home island, Napoleon thus took two lessons that influenced his later constitutional activity. At one level, his Corsican origins gave him some understanding of the humiliations and resentments felt by those who are conquered and occupied by alien armies. At another level, he also acquired a sense of how military invasions might sometimes be smoothed over, and those exposed to them mollified, by legislative initiatives on the part of the conquerors. 'Conquered provinces must be kept obedient to the victor by psychological methods', he would write, by changes in 'the mode of organisation of the administration'.[31]

Napoleon was, after all, the son of a lawyer, aware from early on of the significance and utility of the law. He was also for a while a devotee of the works of Jean-Jacques Rousseau, and of other Enlightenment writers on the cult of the legislator. To be sure, he possessed limited patience with 'long-winded' theorists and project-makers – men like Sieyès – and could be crudely reductionist in his attitude to written constitutions inside France itself. But, outside of France, Napoleon's responses were sometimes more creative. As with many empire-builders, there was a degree to which, for him, imperial outposts functioned as laboratories of sorts: sites where he could try out political experiments that he would never have been willing to risk in the imperial heartland of France itself.

This point emerges even from one of his earliest creations, the Cisalpine Republic. Napoleon established this in July 1797 when he was almost twenty-eight, still a mere general and forcing his way through the Italian peninsula. At its height, the Cisalpine Republic consisted of parts of Lombardy, Piedmont, Switzerland, Venice, Modena and the so-called Papal Legations, Romagna, Ferrara and Bologna. Napoleon appointed two committees to work on crafting its constitution, supervising them himself. Since he was under intense pressure from military events, and his primary aim was assimilation and French republican empire, many of this document's provisions were taken from France's own 1795 constitution, though he went beyond it in some respects. The Cisalpine population was provided with a declaration of rights and a bicameral legislature supervised by a five-man directory. It also gained – on paper – freedom of the press and provisions for primary education. Simultaneously, its menfolk were made ready for fighting.[32]

As in France since 1791, only males who entered their names on the rolls of the national guard, thereby making themselves easily identifiable for future conscription, were declared eligible to vote. Active citizenship was thus explicitly gendered, and tied to military service. Cisalpine citizen-soldiers, the new constitution stipulated, were to learn 'the military exercise', and each man was to equip himself with a gun and a leather cartouche box for carrying ammunition. Napoleon imposed a similar constitution on another of his manufactured Italian states, Liguria (based around the former republic of Genoa), which he divided into ten military districts, and undertook to supply with an army institute and a network of military schools.[33]

As this suggests, a main driver of Napoleon's constitutional design was his ceaseless need for additional supplies of men and money. There was to be reform, yes; there was to be wider democracy for males; and, at times, there was to be greater modernity in the sense of a reduction of traditional social and religious hierarchies. But there was also always control and the provision of machinery to ease military mobilisation and taxation.

These different aspirations jostle awkwardly in the wording of the Cisalpine constitution. Napoleon used a section of it explicitly to renounce France's right of conquest. This newly invented Italian republic was, according to its constitution, to be 'free and independent'. Nonetheless, it would be Napoleon himself who would name the members of its government, though 'for this time only'. No foreign troops were to come within the borders of this new creation, the constitution stipulated, except those of 'the republic friendly and allied to the Cisalpine Republic', that is, the huge encroaching armies of France itself.

These sorts of contortions have always fed into arguments over whether Napoleon was a 'cruel despot or a wise reformer', as one recent commentator put it.[34] As well as being futile (at different times, and in different places, he was sometimes both of these things, and more), this kind of debate obscures something important. There was nothing new or startling in Europe, or in any other continent, about a military conqueror attempting to win territory by means of armed violence, or wanting to concentrate power in himself. What was striking in Napoleon's case were some of the methods by which he sought to do this: the scale on which he resorted to constitutional and legal initiatives as a component part of his warmongering and imperial ambitions.

'We sought to make them over to move them into our column', an American academic lawyer would write in 2004, anguishing over the ethics of his country's post-invasion exercise in constitution-writing in Iraq, while also recalling its constitution-making for Germany and Japan in the wake of the Second World War. In writing and legislating for others, he went on, the United States had wanted to make these defeated countries: 'take our side in a global war and be useful to us in it'.[35] Making countries over in order to move them firmly into his column and make them useful in the context of a global war was also very much Napoleon's purpose with the foreign constitutions that he engineered. But his actions in this regard were far more numerous than later American ventures, and there was less agonising along the way.

Insofar as Napoleon did seek to rationalise his actions either in public or to himself, it was often – as with earlier French Revolutionary leaders – with a dual language of degeneracy (to describe the regimes he was overthrowing) and regeneration (to evoke how their newly liberated peoples would now, as a result of these fierce transformations, be able to flourish). 'It belongs to the Cisalpine Republic', he declared in 1797, 'to show to the world … that modern Italy has not degenerated.'[36] Describing old regimes as degenerate in this fashion allowed Napoleon to represent their forcible takeover as acts of virtue and necessity. Towards the end of his life, in his last exile on Saint Helena, a small volcanic island lost in the midst of the south Atlantic, he even likened himself to 'Providence, which … applies remedies to the wretchedness of mankind, by means occasionally violent, but for which it is unaccountable to human judgment'.[37]

Again, this was legend-making on his part. But it is clear that the language of degeneracy and regeneration became steadily more indispensable to him. After invading and occupying much of Spain, and in advance of issuing its first draft constitution in 1808, Napoleon ordered his officials to send him information on the country's current 'disorder and confusion'. These reports were 'necessary', he insisted, 'for me to publish one day to show the state of decadence that Spain has sunk to', and thus to legitimise what he had done there. 'I come to bring a remedy,' he declared shortly afterwards in a proclamation addressed to the

Spanish people: 'Your monarchy is old: my mission is to rejuvenate it.'[38]

Even on Elba, the tiny Mediterranean island off the coast of Tuscany which was the location of his first exile in 1814–15, Napoleon found it essential to cultivate an image of himself as a rescuer of multiple peoples from ancient blights and inefficiencies. A hostile witness noted his efforts to make 'an impression on the minds of the people'. How 'all classes' on Elba became, for a while, convinced that Napoleon's mere presence among them would somehow of itself provide 'extraordinary resources and advantages'. Elba's minuscule capital, Portoferraio, he promised its inhabitants, would in the future become known as 'Cosmopolis', the city of the world.[39]

This appetite for acclaim and reaffirmation, this image that Napoleon cherished of himself as a legislator, rescuer and improver – not simply a warrior – meant that he was sometimes prepared to concede to his imperial outposts more than was strictly demanded by military and strategic considerations. This was the case in Westphalia, a client state of some 2 million inhabitants that he created west of the river Elbe, after his victories over Prussia at the battles of Jena and Auerstädt in 1806. Westphalia's constitution was drafted by three senior jurists, possibly edited by Napoleon himself, and issued late in 1807. It was in part and unmistakably a document for empire and exploitation. Its first publication in *Le Moniteur Universel*, one of Napoleon's print vehicles in France, was not in the newspaper's columns given over to foreign news. Instead, it was pointedly inserted in the section of the paper headed '*Interieur*'.[40]

The constitution required Westphalia to fund a constant supply of 25,000 troops. Half of these were to be raised through local conscription and the rest were to be Frenchmen, paid for by the Westphalians, while the ruler of this manufactured kingdom was to be Napoleon's youngest brother, Jérôme Bonaparte. He was, however, to be a 'constitutional king' of sorts, governing in tandem with a new representative body, the first time that a German monarch had formally been bound and regulated on paper in this fashion. Those of Jérôme's new subjects who had been serfs under Prussian rule were now, according to this new constitution, to become legally free. There was also to be equality before the law, which meant among other things that Jews in Westphalia were declared emancipated in the same manner as their French brethren, and that Westphalians possessing noble status would no longer be allowed to claim immunity from taxation.[41]

A similar mix of modernising and liberal change, on the one hand, alongside provisions, on the other, to ease control and continued conquests characterised the constitution that Napoleon drafted in 1807 for the Duchy of Warsaw, a 104,000 square mile territory carved out of Prussian Poland. Reputedly, the emperor dashed off its main contents in less than an hour, 'only from time to time', one Polish witness recorded, bothering to 'turn to us and ask if we were content, certain the answer would be in accordance with his will'.[42]

Nonetheless, Napoleon viewed his new Polish creation, as he did Westphalia, as more than usually valuable, and therefore worth taking trouble over. But whereas Westphalia's prime value, apart from its men and its tax revenues, was as a model state advertising the benefits of his rule to other German lands, the Duchy of Warsaw's chief attraction was as a frontier post. Napoleon envisaged it as operating as a check on surrounding powers: on Austria; on what remained of Prussia; and, potentially – if things went wrong – on Russia. The duchy's usefulness in this regard was assisted by the fact that it contained an ample supply of singularly motivated manpower.

Humiliated by the successive violent partitions inflicted on them by these adjacent powers, and the final erasure of their country from the map in 1795, some Poles – like some Italians conscripted into Napoleon's wars – seem positively to have welcomed the chance to fight for France. This was not neces-sarily out of sympathy with its revolutionary ideals, or because of the lure of regular pay, but because they hoped that acquir-ing military skills courtesy of service in French-led legions might equip them in future struggles for the independence of their own homelands. Initially, 30,000 Poles from the Duchy of Warsaw entered French military service. By 1812, their numbers had swollen to 75,000 men. In return, the duchy secured notable concessions. Under its new constitution, there was to be an end to serfdom and there would also be a measure of equality before the law. A new representative system was implemented that may have enfranchised 40,000 men among the peasantry alone. On top of this, for some Poles, there was a brief expe-rience of renewed hope, and the prospect of armed revenge against Russia, Austria and Prussia, the powers that had previ-ously carved up their commonwealth.[43]

This point – the ways in which Poles and the inhabitants of some of Napoleon's other imperial provinces forged their *own* rationales for living under the constitutions he imposed on them – is an important one. It can be easy to look at these Napoleonic constitutions (indeed, at all constitutions) only in terms of the ideas and aims of their prime makers. Yet, more even than is usually the case, constitutions imposed by foreign invaders are susceptible to a wide range of interpretations on the part of those men and women who are expected to live under them.

The *ideal* of Napoleon as omniscient and omnipotent legisla-tor is captured in Jacques-Louis David's famous 1812 painting of the emperor at work in his study at the Tuileries Palace in Paris. Not commissioned by Napoleon, but possibly created with some input on his part, this canvas by David, a staunch admirer of Napoleon, depicts the great man in military uniform. But he is changed. Napoleon was still in his early fifties at this time. Nonetheless, his grip on detail and his judgement, along with

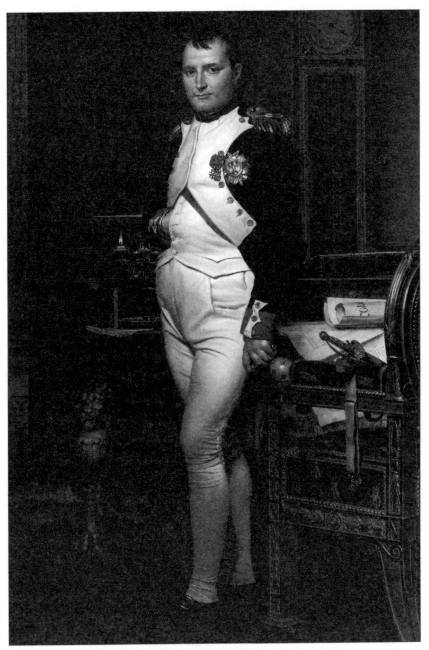

27. Jacques-Louis David, *The Emperor Napoleon
in his Study at the Tuileries*, 1812.

his health and resilience were already in decline. Cold weather, and even reputedly the smell of paint, could quickly make him ill.[44] Even this portrait by a committed supporter hints at the emperor's physical deterioration. He appears crumpled, portly and balding. His face is sheened with perspiration; and he is without a sword strapped to his side (though it remains within reach).

Yet, for all that, David shows Napoleon still standing devotedly at his desk. He is surrounded by paperwork, a quill pen to one side of him and, on the other, a rolled manuscript of part of his greatest legal achievement, the *Code Napoléon*. As the standing clock in this image makes clear, it is almost 4.15 in the morning. The candles are guttering out. But Napoleon, we are meant to understand – for all his advancing age and encroaching frailties – is continuing to labour hard and productively into the small hours on behalf of his multifarious European subjects, while they sleep their way safely into a reformed and better-regulated future. This was the legend of Napoleonic lawfare.

In reality, and as with his warfare (David's great painting dates, after all, from 1812, the year of the calamitous French advance on Moscow), Napoleon's legal and constitutional initiatives for others did not always work out well. Imposed from without, and relying for their continuance on the presence or threat of French armies, most of his constitutions proved short-lived. His constitution for the Cisalpine Republic was overthrown by foreign forces in 1799. Even that for his model German kingdom, Westphalia, survived only four years. Like all empire-makers, Napoleon was always dependent on underlings and local collaborators. Such men often chose to disregard his constitutional texts, or implemented them only selectively.[45] And, as in the Duchy of Warsaw, those below frequently interpreted these texts in their own distinctive and discordant fashions.

None of this makes Napoleon's constitutional initiatives insignificant. In all sorts of ways, they proved highly important.

But they were always potentially fragile. They were also unpredictable, sometimes setting in motion developments that he had not foreseen. What happened in Spain and Spanish America offers an extreme example.

## Invading the Spanish World, Encountering God

In October 1807, some 50,000 French troops poured into the Iberian peninsula. Initially, they focused their energies on Portugal, driving its royal family into exile in Brazil, along with many of its supporters. By March 1808, this invading French army had swollen to 100,000 troops and moved into much of Spain, occupying major cities including Madrid and Barcelona. This armed presence was used to force the abdication of the reigning Spanish monarch, Carlos IV. Shortly afterwards, his singularly unpleasant successor, Fernando VII – whose combination of vacuousness and stubborn ruthlessness are brilliantly conveyed in Goya's portraits of the man – also went into exile in France. In place of these Bourbon princes, Napoleon inserted his own elder brother, Joseph Bonaparte, who now became King José I of Spain.[46]

Joseph had trained in the law in Corsica, and had already done useful service for his brother as a moderately popular king of Sicily and Naples. However, assuming the Spanish Crown was a qualitatively different challenge, because *this* monarchy presided over an empire extending into four continents. Up to a point, and for his own purposes, Napoleon recognised and welcomed the vast geographical range of his new Spanish dominions and responded creatively to it.

In June 1808, he ordered the implementation of what became the Bayonne Statute, effectively Spain's first modern written constitution.[47] This was drafted by Jean-Baptiste d'Esménard, a French journalist and one-time army officer, but was substantially planned and revised by Napoleon himself. Ratified by a small assembly of francophile Spaniards, the constitution's provisions were designed at one level to give a gloss of continuity to the new Bonapartist political order. Spain was to remain an unlimited monarchy; the customary privileges of its noble and clerical orders were to be preserved; and Catholicism was to continue as its only official religion. But the Bayonne Statute also provided for transformations. Under its terms, there was to be a new parliament in Madrid made up of delegates from both peninsular Spain and its territories in America and Asia. The 'Spanish kingdoms and provinces of America and Asia', the statute declared, were now to enjoy 'the same rights as the metropole'.

The idea of a mega-parliament that might encompass representatives from across the expanse of a maritime empire was not new. Before 1776, various schemes had been scouted to offer Britain's American colonists their own direct representation at the Westminster Parliament in London. But these projects had never come remotely close to implementation. To this extent, Napoleon's formal offer to Spain's overseas peoples of 'the same rights as the metropole', and direct representation in a legislature for a Greater Spain, was unprecedented, and yet another example of his willingness sometimes to consider radical political experiments in the frontier zones of his empire. This Spanish initiative also further underlines Napoleon's abiding interest in acquiring a global empire. What seemed for a while a real prospect of acquiring control, through his brother Joseph, over Spain's vast extra-European possessions was sharply attractive to him. He was soon making plans for better and more regular transoceanic communications.[48]

Yet while the Statute of Bayonne is an example of Napoleon's sometimes wide and exploratory vision, it is also the most dramatic instance of how his constitutional ventures could have unforeseen and drastic consequences. Since its provisions were widely publicised in the press and through proclamations, the issue of this Bayonne Statute virtually compelled Spanish political groupings opposed to the new Bonapartist regime to respond in kind. If they wanted to rally support in peninsular Spain and secure backing from Creole elites in South America, these oppositionists had little choice but to come up with a rival and better constitution on paper that would also be imperially inclusive.

Accordingly, the parliament or *cortes* that met in September 1810, in the opposition stronghold of Cádiz on Spain's Atlantic coast, protected offshore by the guns of Britain's Royal Navy, contained not just metropolitan Spaniards, but also from the outset twenty-seven delegates from South America, and two more from the Philippines, the most easterly outpost of the Spanish empire. By the time the debates and business of this *cortes* had ended, over 20 per cent of its 300 representatives hailed from Spanish America. In terms of population, this did not give the latter anything like parity of representation with metropolitan Spain. Nonetheless, the new constitution hammered out at Cádiz, and finally issued in March 1812, was explicitly a document for a reformed, more inclusive Spanish empire. 'My compatriots, inhabitants of the four quarters of the world,' announced the president of the *cortes*, the Bishop of Mallorca, 'we have now recovered our dignity and our rights.'[49]

Predictably, the makers of this Cádiz constitution took their ideas from multiple locations and sources, in particular from the 1791 French constitution, the United States constitution and printed works on Britain's political system. But, as with all constitutions, the finished text also catered to distinctive local imperatives, perceptions and conventions. It provided for a hereditary monarchy, while cutting back on the power of future Spanish kings to interfere in the legislature, and giving the latter sole control over taxation. Like Napoleon's Bayonne Statute, this Cádiz constitution also provided for freedom of the press and the abolition of the Spanish Inquisition, the bodies traditionally tasked with maintaining Catholic orthodoxy.

28. The text of the constitution of Cádiz, a reissue in 1822.

But chiefly because of the rising levels of rebellion in parts of South America by this stage, the men of Cádiz also pushed the more inclusive provisions of the Bayonne Statute still further. The discriminatory fiscal and labour exactions formerly imposed on South America's Indigenous peoples were now abolished. The majority of free adult males of good standing were promised voting rights, and this was to apply throughout the Spanish world:

The Peninsula with its possessions and adjacent islands ... the Canaries with the other possessions of Africa. In Northern America: New Spain and New Galicia and the peninsula of Yucatán, Guatemala ... the Island of Cuba with the Two Floridas, the Spanish part of the Island of Santo Domingo, and the Island of Puerto Rico ... In Southern America: New Granada, Venezuela, Perú, Chile, the provinces of the Río de la Plata, and all adjacent islands in the Pacific and Atlantic Ocean. In Asia, the Philippine Islands and those that depend on its government.[50]

As the governor-general of Manila in the Philippines announced to its inhabitants, when a copy of this Cádiz constitution finally arrived there early in 1813, all of the empire's (male) inhabitants – or something much closer to all – were now to be accounted 'Spanish, equals, and capable of obtaining any work and distinctions that they garnered through their merits and conduct'.[51] Chinese, Indigenous, Creole and *mestizo* populations of the empire were to be gathered into a common Spanish citizenship; their treatment, at least on paper, dependent not on race or place of birth, but rather on their shared connections and devotion to the Spanish Crown.

As far as most free men in the Spanish world were concerned, moreover, no property or educational qualifications for political participation were to be insisted upon until 1830. This, it was argued, would allow poorer males the necessary time in which to educate and better themselves, and thus have a chance of continuing to enjoy full citizenship rights, even after these stricter qualifications finally came into force.

Men of African ancestry, however, along with all women, were to remain excluded from active citizenship. But even in this regard, some loopholes were provided, though only for males. In the future, promised the Constitution of Cádiz, 'the door to the virtue and merit of being citizens' would be left ajar for those African or part-African men who demonstrated a record of 'proven services'.[52] Chief among these services was, naturally, participation in the Spanish military.

In terms of the range of men of whatever ethnicity explicitly invited into active citizenship, this was the most capacious written constitution formally produced anywhere in the world up to this point in time. Hence this text's subsequent appeal

PROYECTO

DE CONSTITUCION POLÍTICA

DE LA MONARQUÍA ESPAÑOLA

PRESENTADO A LAS CÓRTES GENERALES

Y EXTRAORDINARIAS

POR SU COMISION DE CONSTITUCION.

CADIZ: IMPRENTA REAL: 1811.

CON SUPERIOR PERMISO.

*MÉXICO:*

Por D. Manuel Antonio Valdes, Impresor de Cámara de S. M.
calle de zuleta, el mismo año.

29. The draft constitution of Cádiz, as published in Mexico in 1811.

to Rammohan Roy and his radical British and Bengali allies in Calcutta. The essential problem with this remarkable constitution of Cádiz, however, was well summed up by Arthur Wellesley, the Anglo-Irish commander of the mixed forces fighting in Spain against Napoleon, and future Duke of Wellington. Tough, adroit, politically conservative and a relentless and strikingly mobile man at arms, Wellington was blunt. The *cortes* of Cádiz, he judged, had 'formed a Constitution very much on the principle that a painter paints a picture, viz. to be looked at'.[53] It was a dazzling piece of work. But it was not, and could not be, a substantial reality.

When the constitution of Cádiz was proclaimed in 1812, the bulk of peninsular Spain was still under French military occupation. In addition, much of Spanish America, including modern-day Venezuela, Argentina, Colombia, Chile, Bolivia, Paraguay and Uruguay, was by now in open revolt. One of the 'what ifs' of history is whether this process of Spanish imperial disintegration might have been contained or delayed by imaginative efforts at reform on the part of Madrid. But, as it turned out, there was no chance of that. While the constitution of Cádiz was briefly and unevenly implemented in 1813, it was promptly disavowed the following year by the returning Bourbon monarch, Fernando VII. Reinstated by liberal revolutionaries in 1820, the constitution itself, along with many of the individuals who had backed its return, was brutally put down three years later, and it was only fleetingly and finally revived in 1836–7.

Yet, despite such repeated failures, this proved to be a massively influential, even game-changing constitution. As a result of its never being properly implemented, its idealism and ambition remained uncontaminated in retrospect by the squabbles and compromises of regular politics. It continued to function as a beacon of enlightened possibilities – an alluring promise of what might have been, and of what might still be in the future – and not just for Spain. The constitution of Cádiz became one of the most translated documents of its kind. Between 1814 and 1836, there were eleven German translations, while twelve different Italian translations were published between 1813 and 1821 alone. There were English, Russian and French translations, too; and possibly Arabic, Bengali and Mandarin versions as well.[54]

Its transnational and transcontinental impact was aided by the fact that this Cádiz constitution could be viewed *both* as a liberationist document, drafted by men who had resisted Napoleon and struggled for wider colonial rights, *and* as a political blueprint that made room for some traditional hierarchies and values. The constitution specifically provided for a monarchy.

It also gave pre-eminent status to Roman Catholicism, and this had profound consequences.

Up to this point, the 1810s, most major exploratory constitutional texts had emerged out of predominantly Protestant societies, such as the United States, Sweden and the Batavian (Dutch) republic. Or, they had been the work of rulers with a Protestant background, such as Catherine the Great with her *Nakaz*; or their instigators, while Catholic in name, had possessed an uneven relationship with Rome, as was the case with Napoleon himself. Those few overwhelmingly Catholic polities that issued important new political constitutions early on, such as Poland Lithuania in 1791, had generally come to grief. The circumstances of the men of Cádiz, however, were different. So was the fate of the text they produced.

Almost 30 per cent of the delegates at Cádiz in 1810–12 were Catholic clergyman, which made them the biggest occupational group in the *cortes*. Catholic clerics also made up close to half of the committee members drafting the constitution.[55] Clerical delegates in general exercised a disproportionate influence in this episode of constitution-making because, along with Spain's legitimate royal dynasty, Catholicism was widely viewed as the most potent force still capable of holding together an increasingly contentious and divided Hispanic world. All this helped to ensure that the Catholic Church and its agents were foregrounded in the provisions and ritual of this new constitution. Enacted on St Joseph's Day (19 March), and therefore on a date already sacred in the religious calendar, the constitution of Cádiz both stipulated that Catholicism was 'and ever shall be' the sole Spanish religion, and prohibited the exercise of any other.

Some Protestant commentators (Thomas Jefferson, for one) who otherwise admired this new Spanish constitution, dismissed these provisions for the primacy of the Catholic Church as an aberrant lapse into reactionary intolerance.[56] Yet, in terms of fostering the spread of written constitutions, these religious clauses of the constitution of Cádiz were of enormous importance. By issuing such an unapologetically Catholic text, the men of Cádiz substantially altered and expanded the brand. Because of their work, and the many subsequent translations of their text, what had previously appeared a mainly Protestant, revolutionary or irreligious genre – a written constitution – underwent a partial makeover. It now became something that predominantly Catholic societies could embrace without having to feel so concerned that doing so might compromise traditional religious affiliations and cultures.

Soothing Catholic interests in this fashion brought other advantages in its wake. Catholic priests were powerfully situated to deal with the challenges posed to the new political technology in many regions by continuing mass illiteracy. Like clerics in other denominations and faiths, priests could read out passages from a constitution to their flocks, and expound on their virtues and meanings. Moreover, by *speaking* to these texts, priests – if they felt so inclined – could lend them emotional colour and even spiritual power, and appeal to their listeners' imaginations.[57] This kind of advocacy on the part of some (although by no means all) Catholic priests was not a phenomenon that was confined to Europe.

Take the case of the first constitution proclaimed in an independent Mexico in 1824, a document which borrowed heavily from the constitution of Cádiz. Like the latter, it was issued on a saint's day, in this case on the feast of Saint Francis of Assisi. Like the men of Cádiz, too, those responsible for drafting this Mexican text were careful to affirm the unique status of the Catholic religion, and prohibit the operation of any other. Reassured on these points, Catholic clergymen in this newly independent Central American state swung concertedly into action. On 24 October 1824, all men, women and children attending worship in Mexico City's fourteen Catholic parish churches took an oath of allegiance to the new constitution. They also listened as their priests read out and explained to them the rights and duties contained in this document.[58]

The fact that in 1824 a constitution was being adopted by an independent Mexico points to the most conspicuous failure of the Cádiz constitution and its makers. When they assembled in 1810, many of the men of Cádiz had hoped that, by incorporating delegates from across the Spanish imperial world, and advancing provisions for a more transracial, transcontinental Spanish citizenship, they might be able to resolve some of the empire's internal frictions and fractures. But the concessions they offered in the end proved insufficient. Moreover, because French armies were still entrenched in Spain when it was first issued in 1812, and because of the subsequent stupidity of Fernando VII, the constitution of Cádiz was never systematically implemented in Spain's overseas empire any more than it was in Spain itself.

Even before these difficulties, Napoleon's invasion of the Iberian peninsula had put fresh strains on the ties that bound together Spain's vast overseas empire. The bulk of Spanish America's Creole, Indian, *mestizo* and slave populations had retained an attachment to a distant imperial monarchy, however much they might resent the empire's local administrators and tax collectors. By engineering the abdications of the Bourbon monarchs, Carlos IV and Fernando VII, and by making his brother Joseph Bonaparte king in their place, Napoleon did not immediately undermine these reserves of Spanish American loyalism. But his actions complicated issues of allegiance, and provoked discussion about where sovereignty in the Spanish empire should properly reside, especially since, as a result of the French occupation of much of Spain, the traditional machinery of press censorship in the Hispanic world began to wind down. This resulted in a sharp rise in the number of printing presses in Spanish America, and in the volume of political publishing there, a surge in the number of new manifestos, tracts, papers and projects for future constitutions.

The ensuing rebellions and wars of independence in Spanish America would ultimately draw in almost 50,000 troops from Spain itself. But, by the mid 1820s, Spain's Atlantic empire had shrunk to just Cuba and Puerto Rico. The new independence constitutions crafted in Argentina in 1826, in Chile and Peru in 1828, and in New Granada, Uruguay and Venezuela in 1830 still retained, however, strong traces of the original Cádiz model.

In this fashion, because of his invasion of the Iberian peninsula, and because of the complex repercussions of his Bayonne Statute, Napoleon helped to foster the spread of written constitutions into the length and breadth of South America, and the spread of knowledge of them into parts of south-east Asia. 'Napoleon Bonaparte,' testified a Mexican patriot in the 1820s, 'to you Spanish America owes the liberty and independence it now enjoys. Your sword struck the first blow at the chain which bound the two worlds.'[59]

## Assessing the Monster and His Works

Yet note that this had never been Napoleon's intention. His forces had not entered Spain in 1808 with the aim of freeing and detaching its South American colonies. One of the attractions of invading the Iberian peninsula as far as the emperor himself was concerned was indeed the prospect this seemed to offer of securing access to, and influence over, Spain's massive overseas empire. A more accurate and nuanced assessment of Napoleon himself, and of the mixed and wide repercussions of his actions, was offered by a very different revolutionary, Mary Wollstone-craft Shelley.

Embarrassingly rich in activist and radical relatives – her mother, the feminist Mary Wollstonecraft, died after giving birth to her in 1797, the philosopher and anarchist William Godwin was her father, while the republican poet Percy Bysshe Shelley was ultimately her husband – Mary Shelley herself is often passed over in regard to her political interests. Yet, even as an adolescent, in 1812, she had composed a lecture on 'The Influence of Governments on the Character of a People'. Among the first to hear it, when it was read out aloud in London for propriety's sake by her half-brother, was the one-time American vice president Aaron Burr, a supporter, whatever his other failings, of women's rights.[60]

Of necessity, Mary Shelley was also attuned to the centrality of war. Born in the year of Napoleon's first constitution for the Cisalpine Republic, she eloped with Shelley in 1814, setting out with him on a walking tour through a ravaged continental Europe in the lull before the battle of Waterloo. The couple made sure to stay in a French hotel 'in the same room and beds in which Napoleon and some of his generals had rested'.[61] Two years later, they were in Geneva, the birthplace of Napoleon's early philosophical hero, Jean-Jacques Rousseau, and the locus of her own most famous literary creation.

French revolutionary armies had invaded Geneva and supplied it with a written constitution even before Napoleon came to power. By 1816, when Mary Shelley was living there, the province formed part of Switzerland, a country which was itself a target of military invasion and multiple constitutional rewritings by others. The seminal novel she wrote here, *Frankenstein; or, the Modern Prometheus*, published – initially anonymously – in 1818, is far from being simply what we would now style science fiction or fantasy. It can be interpreted and, before the gender of its author became known, *was* interpreted by some reviewers and readers as a work with political content, and as a meditation on the multiple meanings of Napoleon Bonaparte.

At one level, Napoleon is clearly an inspiration for the monster of her story, an unnatural, increasingly violent creature who nonetheless possesses 'powers of eloquence and persuasion', and who develops a passion for reading, especially 'histories of the first founders of the ancient republics', and tales of 'men concerned in public affairs governing or massacring their species'. At another level, Napoleon's career colours Mary Shelley's descriptions of her central character, the scientist Frankenstein himself. In the novel, he is presented as a furiously ambitious individual who believes himself to be above the 'herd of common projectors' and 'destined for some great enterprise'. Rather like Napoleon with his military invasions and paper experiments, Frankenstein's aim is to bestow 'animation upon lifeless matter'. He reanimates bones from a charnel house in order to create a new, superior kind of man. But this venture into the unknown only succeeds in letting 'loose into the world a depraved wretch, whose delight was in carnage and misery', and from whose actions nowhere on the face of the globe, not even the North Pole, is safe.[62]

Almost Burkean in her insistence that artificial, non-organic creations are dangerous, Mary Shelley was too much the radical, however, simply to write an indictment of any experimental action. The subtitle she chooses for her novel, 'Or, the Modern Prometheus', links Frankenstein/Napoleon to the titanic figure from Greek mythology who broke the laws of the gods in order to give men the gift of fire, thereby enabling them to progress. Linking Napoleon to Prometheus was a common (and generally approving) trope during the last years of the former emperor's life and after his death in 1821 because to admirers, and even to those merely dazzled by his career, it appeared so apt. Napoleon could also be viewed as having bestowed perilous, but ultimately improving gifts upon mankind. And, like the classical Prometheus, he had ended up punished and chained to a rock – in Napoleon's case, the rocky island of Saint Helena.

But, in her novel, Mary Shelley is careful to make clear that the violence and destruction he lets loose will not end with Frankenstein himself. The monster he creates is not conclusively destroyed. Moreover, as she makes one of her characters, the naval officer whose letters frame her story, remark, too few

30. Napoleon as Prometheus: a French etching of 1815.

human beings are content any more merely to 'seek happiness in tranquility'. The scale of modern warfare anyway will not let them. In her next major book, *The Last Man* (1826), which is set in the twenty-first century, Mary Shelley imagines 'fire, and war, and plague' engulfing the entire globe, along with a continuing militarisation of society. 'I have learnt,' she has a character say:

> that one man, more or less, is of small import, while human bodies remain to fill up the thinned ranks of the soldiery, and that the identity of an individual may be overlooked, so that the muster roll contain its full numbers.[63]

Still sometimes approached primarily as a member of a singularly Romantic literary coterie, Mary Shelley can thus be read as a witness and an imaginative commentator on the incessant warfare and political disruptions of her time; and some of the points she inserts into her novels are acute and perceptive. As with Frankenstein, it *was* the case that many of Napoleon's experiments did not end with him, and were not cancelled out by his demise. In many of the territories Napoleon had invaded, occupied and dominated, the violence and shocks he and his armies and auxiliaries inflicted on pre-existing local elites, legal systems, governing practices and economies were simply too extensive for the status quo ante ever to be properly restored.

This was manifestly true of France itself. Elderly, overweight, conservative and understandably on edge, that country's return-ing monarch, Louis XVIII, nonetheless had little choice but to act out the role of *roi législateur* in new ways, issuing his Charter of 1814, a written constitution in all but name. Some of Napoleon's former imperial provinces, too, were changed beyond recovery, and not always for the better. It is arguable, for instance, that the scale and violence of Napoleon's military rampages in Prussia actually worked to set back previous movements there towards governmental and legal reform. But, in some other German lands exposed to his influence and invasions – Württemberg, Frankfurt, Baden, Bavaria, Brunswick and Saxony – the years immediately after Waterloo saw a series of new constitutions. Most were con-servative, monarch-focused texts rather like the French charter. Nonetheless, these were single documents outlining structures and rules of government, which were often put into print, and so made available to be read, judged and discussed.[64]

As this suggests, in large parts of continental Europe, there had by the 1820s been an irreversible shift in ideas about the necessary and desirable furniture and trappings of states, and about what was owed to their populations. Rising numbers of Europeans – though not remotely yet a majority – had, in the words of a former Italian army officer, come to believe that 'a written constitution is sufficient to change a political system and remedy all a nation's woes', or at least that this was something that should be explored and attempted.[65]

31. Monarchs come to terms with the new written politics: Dom Pedro, emperor, king, and a prime author of both the Brazilian constitution of 1824 and, here, the Portuguese constitution of 1826.

However, as Mary Shelley recognised and wrote into *Frankenstein*, these and other alterations were not to be attributed merely to the ideas and actions of a single, titanic individual. More vital were two connected and combustible forces: the ideas fostered by revolution in France, and – still more – unparalleled levels of war and military mobilisation. During the French Revolutionary and Napoleonic wars, some of the very large numbers of people set in military motion had operated as transmitters and promoters of new political ideas and techniques; and, in some cases, their activism and commitment continued and even expanded after Napoleon's defeat.

In the wake of his fall, about 20,000 officers judged overly loyal to the deposed emperor were dismissed from the French army. Some of these men promptly took their swords and political ideas into different countries and continents, into Persia, into Egypt and other parts of the Ottoman world, as well as into Central and South America. Some of Napoleon's non-French military supporters pursued similar post-war routes, the Italian Carlo Luigi Castelli among them. Left disconsolate after the battle of Waterloo, Castelli immediately took his ambitions and military skills off to Haiti. When this proved unprofitable, he moved on again, attaching himself to Simón Bolívar's independence campaigns in South America.[66]

As Mary Shelley recognised, some of those who had fought and worked *against* Napoleon were also driven – both before and after 1815 – in the direction of political change and new constitutions. This had been true of the Cádiz *cortes* as a body. It was also true of individuals. It was a British army officer fighting alongside irregular forces in the Iberian peninsula against the French, for instance, who published the first English-language translation of the Cádiz constitution, thereby enormously expanding its circulation and impact.[67] Some armed opponents of Napoleon went further. The Russian guards officer Nikita Muravyov already had multiple languages under his belt when he took part in his country's military occupation of Paris in 1814. However, living for a while in the French capital allowed him to expand his political education. He attended its university, and got to know the liberal philosopher Benjamin Constant, the man who drafted Napoleon's final constitution. Ten years later, having accumulated his own library of different published constitutions, Muravyov became one of several Russian army veterans to lead the Decembrist revolt against the reactionary Tsar Nicholas I in 1825.[68]

Yet, as Mary Shelley wrote into *Frankenstein*, the mass militarisation and political shocks fostered by the French Revolutionary and Napoleonic Wars had mixed consequences. Protracted, transregional violence had helped to promote and perpetuate new ideas and initiatives and modes of communication to do with rights and political reforms. It also, however, fostered new ideas and methods to do with control. Other regimes and later individual actors took careful note of Napoleon's demonstration that the new political technology – written and printed constitutions – could be systematically employed to service and embed imperial projects. Consider the case of Thomas Stamford Raffles, the man who purchased and sought to redesign the island in south-east Asia named Singapore.

Raffles is rarely examined outside the frameworks of south-east Asian and British histories. Yet, like Mary Shelley, he rewards being looked at in wider contexts. Like other architects of new states in the early nineteenth century – Simón Bolívar in South America, Mehmed Ali in Egypt, Henry Christophe in Haiti, and a lesser-known innovator whom we will encounter later, the Tahitian ruler Pomare II – Raffles was fascinated by Napoleon's achievements, and also by some of his methods. In 1816 he even took the trouble to visit the exiled French emperor on Saint Helena. At a personal level, the encounter was not a success. Yet, as Raffles wrote, Napoleon's talents had 'always demanded my admiration'.[69] Understandably so, given what he himself hoped to accomplish in a very different geographical space.

Raffles was a committed and inventive imperialist, eager to see the extension of British power in due course into Borneo, Siam and Cambodia. He was also a self-made man, a deliberate moderniser and, as one Dutch observer put it, very much a 'word-peddler' – multilingual and addicted (as Napoleon had been) to the written word. The constitution that Raffles drafted for Singapore's 20,000 or so inhabitants in 1823 was not a finished, discrete document, and it would never be fully implemented. But he was quite clear that this document *was* a 'constitution', created by a self-conscious process of writing. 'I have taken upon myself to widen the base, and to look to a more important superstructure', he remarked: 'I have given the place something like a constitution [and] a representative body.' Singapore's new text, he boasted, would be 'as free a constitution as possible'.[70]

The British had frequently bestowed charters on their colonial spaces. But Raffles' ambitions for his own text were coloured in addition by Napoleon's example. Like the conquered territories in continental Europe to which the French emperor had awarded constitutions, Singapore, in Raffles' vision, was to be engineered, controlled and written into improvement and modernity, while simultaneously operating as a productive part of an empire. There was to be unstinting free trade. All religions and ethnicities here were to be tolerated. Slavery and slave trading were to vanish. Singapore's inhabitants would also, Raffles envisaged, become morally cleansed and improved human beings, weaned off vices such as drinking, gambling and cock-fighting.

The debt to some of the messianic thinking that had flourished in France after 1789 and to Napoleon's own controlling but sometimes reforming politics is clear. Also clear is Raffles' conviction that someone coming in from one part of the world, equipped with force, ideals and determination, could devise a constitutional text as a means to reconfigure, improve and regulate another sector of the world and a different population.

Raffles' ideas and actions, the initiatives of a *British* transcontinental actor, illustrate something else as well. Both intentionally and unintentionally, Napoleon Bonaparte had made a marked contribution to the spread and diversification of the new written constitutions. Paradoxically, one might think, but indisputably, the same was sometimes true of that power across the Channel which had operated as Napoleon's prime and most persistent enemy.

# FIVE

# EXCEPTION AND ENGINE

## London

Shifting ideas, revolutionary outbreaks, burgeoning print, men in arms and in motion, and – relentlessly – the trajectories of war: all these quickened the spread of the new political technology. So, at certain times, did particular places. In October 1831, Eduard Gans made contact with one of these sites of more than usual global significance. In his early thirties and Jewish by heritage, he had converted to Christianity in part so as to be able to advance in German academic life. Successfully established as a professor of law in Berlin, Gans was on a visit to London when he was granted an audience with the eighty-three-year-old Jeremy Bentham at his house in Queen's Square Place, less than ten minutes' walk from the Houses of Parliament. An envious friend briefed him in advance. 'You must never contradict him', Gans was advised. He should rather listen to Bentham 'like an oracle'. Whatever opinions and ideas the great man chose in his wisdom to express, Gans should repeat back approvingly, so as to prod him into offering 'further insights'.[1]

But Gans was a pupil and associate of G. W. F. Hegel, the great philosopher who wrote so uncompromisingly on logic and the mind, and therefore relaxed about dealing with formidable intellects. Like many Germans who had lived through Napoleon Bonaparte's brutal invasions, he was also instinctively attracted to local continuities, and convinced that lawmakers and politicians must pay attention to a society's history before embarking on major alterations in its government. He was also perhaps mischievous.

Strolling with Bentham, white-haired, trim and restless, around the gardens of his substantial house, Gans raised this issue of the relationship between history, local cultures and the making of laws, knowing that it was likely to provoke. 'Do you actually value history?' his host duly exploded: 'This upholder of mindlessness, this page on to which intellect and stupidity are equally written.' There was no need for legal codes or plans of government to be constructed in accordance with a society's specific history and customs. Written constitutions, like other sets of laws, Bentham stormed, should embody rational principles of liberal justice and rights that were of universal application.

Gans was quietly amused by Bentham's tirade, but hardly surprised. This, after all, was the man who in 1823 had issued a manifesto boldly entitled *Leading Principles of a Constitutional Code for Any State*. In another publication the previous year, Bentham had been equally insistent that, for the lawgiver, 'The great outlines which require to be drawn, will be found to be the same for every *territory*, for every *race*, and for every *time* [his italics]'. Which meant, among other things, that he, Jeremy Bentham, was qualified to advise on and draft constitutions and legal codes for any society anywhere in the world. 'The globe', as the Englishman modestly put it, was 'the field of dominion to which the author aspires'.[2]

When finally admitted inside the house in Queen's Square Place, its steam central heating system signalling both its owner's wealth and his eager identification with the modern, Gans saw further evidence of the geographical range of Bentham's interests and ambitions. Affluent Euro-American males at this time habitually stocked their private libraries with fine editions of the Greek and Roman classics, which they might or might not read. But Bentham's library shelves were crowded with contemporary

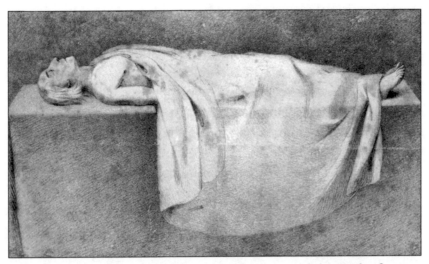

32. Jeremy Bentham readied for public dissection: a lithograph of 1832.

works 'in all languages', especially, Gans noticed, books written in Spanish and Portuguese.[3]

Nine months after this meeting, which lasted over three hours, during which the octogenarian ran 'up and down the stairs to the library multiple times with the agility of a young man', Jeremy Bentham was dead. In advance of dissecting his corpse – a procedure that Bentham had insisted on in his will – the surgeon in charge offered a tribute to the dead man. He reminded the eminent invitees assembled queasily in the chill south London anatomy theatre of how, in life, Bentham had been essentially a warrior. Only *his* weapons had been words – 'personal communication or confidential correspondence' – while his enemies were 'ignorance, error, prejudice, imposture, selfishness, vice, misery'. Bentham had warred against these, continued the surgeon before inserting his knife, not just for his country of origin, but for 'all countries of both hemispheres'.[4]

This was an exaggeration, but Jeremy Bentham had tried. Born in 1748, the son and grandson of successful London attorneys, and precociously brilliant, he himself had been trained in the law. Inheriting a comfortable income and the large house at Queen's Square Place saved him, however, from having to work at a profession. Instead, he used his freedom and life-long bachelordom to write, completing ten to twenty pages of script daily, and keeping himself going with hot spiced gingerbread and black coffee, his own version of jogging, and a select stream of politically and intellectually engaged visitors and correspondents from multiple countries and continents. Attacking with his pen a panoply of topics – economics, education, crime and punishment, the ethics and iniquities of empire, the rights of animals and, secretly, the legalisation of homosexuality – Bentham, like so many other politically obsessed men by this stage, also applied himself to studying and drafting constitutional projects. But he did so on a uniquely impressive and promiscuous scale.[5]

He persistently championed the United States, closely monitoring its plethora of written constitutions. This did not prevent him, however, from also forming a close friendship with Aaron Burr, whose reputation had been damaged in his home country by his fatal duel with Alexander Hamilton, and subsequent accusations of treason. Despite this, when a disgraced Burr arrived in England some years later, Bentham immediately invited the American to stay, receiving in return, with some irony, a gift of a New York edition of Hamilton's *Federalist Papers*. One of Burr's attractions for Bentham was that he held out the prospect of his becoming actively involved in a new constitutional enterprise. Eager to carve out an independent territory for himself in Mexico, Burr promised to send over a warship in due course to transport the Englishman across the Atlantic, so that he could design this private statelet's laws and government.[6]

As this episode suggests, Bentham held himself free to apply his expertise anywhere in the world and for all regimes. 'I accept of no remuneration', he told the Venezuelan revolutionary Simón Bolívar grandly when making him an offer of his constitutional services in 1820: 'I serve no one party at the expense of any other.' He would be an expert free agent, attached only to 'the good of mankind in general'.[7] The vanity involved in this self-characterisation is clear. Eduard Gans noted this quality in Bentham as soon as they met. For all that, the fact remains that over several decades a wide spectrum of powerful and enquiring men chose to take Bentham at his word, meeting and corresponding with the 'hermit of Queen's Square' in order to seek his political and legal insights and advice.

Great emperors made contact. In the 1810s, Alexander I of Russia and some of his ministers wrote to Bentham about the constitutions the tsar was planning for his subordinate territories, Poland and Finland. Men engaged in struggling against empire also consulted him. After the outbreak of Greece's war for independence from Ottoman rule in 1821, some of its political deputies on a visit to London made sure to call on Bentham. The following year, he reciprocated by sending them comments on Greece's first draft constitution. Moreover, Bentham's contacts were not confined to European and American actors. Indeed, the range of his consultancy work illustrates how quickly thinking about the new constitutions was penetrating into other regions of the world.[8]

Naturally, Bentham was in communication with Haiti, the first Black-ruled republic in the Caribbean. 'Whatever may be the difference in [skin] colour', he wrote in 1822 to its president, Jean-Pierre Boyer, a mixed-race veteran of Haiti's wars of independence, it was in the 'true interest of all parties' that these superficial human variations not obstruct the global progress of a common 'identity – in respect of Laws and Institutions'. Bentham enclosed with this message, of course, a scheme for a new Haitian constitution.[9]

He also made contact with Islamic north Africa, especially by way of his 'adopted son', Hassuna D'Ghies. Madrasa-educated, multilingual and a devout Muslim, D'Ghies came from a wealthy family in Tripoli. Visiting London in the early 1820s, he quickly made himself known to Bentham, and for over a year the two men worked on plans for an Arabic language constitution for Tripoli, and for a wider political revolution that might range across northern Africa. One result of their meetings was Bentham's 1822 essay 'Securities Against Misrule', the first full-length discussion by a Western author of how the new constitutional ideas and apparatus might be adapted to an Islamic polity.[10]

As this suggests, Bentham became if anything more radical and enterprising as he aged, though not invariably so. Back in 1789, when drafting a proposal for a constitution for Revolutionary France, he had argued for the extension of its franchise to all citizens, 'male or female', so long as the recipients were 'of full age, of sound mind, and able to read'. Aware that even most of his fellow reformers would likely question 'Why admit women to the right of suffrage?', Bentham pushed the counter-question: 'Why exclude them?'[11]

By the 1820s, however, while the claims of women remained a private interest for Bentham, this cause had dropped out of his major public statements and writings. Time was short for him now, and there seemed so much that he could do. At the start of this decade, he had busied himself corresponding with Spanish liberals working to reintroduce the Constitution of Cádiz, and he forged even closer contacts with the makers of Portugal's first written constitution in 1822. But, while assisting reformist projects in the Iberian peninsula, Bentham worked still harder at aiding some of the most prominent figures who were attempting to dismantle Portuguese and Spanish imperial rule in South America.

He corresponded with Bernardino Rivadavia, the independence fighter who was to become the first president of Argentina. He wrote to and met with Francisco de Paula Santander, an army general who became vice president of Gran Colombia, and later president of New Granada. He was in regular contact with the jurist and philosopher José del Valle, who worked on Guatemala's first civil code, and who heralded the Englishman as '*legislador del mundo*', 'legislator of the world'. He also had a protracted, uneven relationship with the great liberator himself, Simón Bolívar, the extraordinary Venezuelan soldier and political thinker whose campaigns helped to free six South American countries from Spanish control, and who subsequently moved into constitution-writing himself. Bolívar had established contact with Bentham during a visit to London in 1810, strolling – as Eduard Gans would do later – in his gardens. 'Sir,' he would write to Bentham with calculated flattery twelve years later, 'could you have conceived, that the name of the Preceptor of Legislators is never pronounced in these savage regions of America, without veneration, nor without gratitude?'[12]

These and other transnational and transcontinental connections on Bentham's part have attracted wide attention in recent years, and rightly so. Yet there is a risk of becoming so caught up in the abundant evidence of this man's formidable mind and super-energetic networking that one passes over the wider context. The Bentham phenomenon is a vital part of this story of the connections between the rising incidence of warfare and aggression, on the one hand, and the progressive spread, on the other, of new, written constitutions. But the Bentham phenomenon also raises questions and issues that extend far beyond the man himself.

How, to begin with, are we to make sense of the fact that Jeremy Bentham emerged from and spent most of his life *in Britain*, that is, in precisely that part of the world that seemingly rejected the lure of the new political technology? Since the United Kingdom remains to this day one of the very few states in existence without a codified constitution, what does it mean that it was this self-same location which gave rise to an individual who aspired to write constitutions for all the world?

There is also the matter of London. Since most of the foreign reformers and busy constitutionalists who met Jeremy Bentham there had not come to the metropolis primarily in order to see him, why exactly were such individuals drawn to this huge city? Why did the British capital attract so many men of this sort from diverse countries and continents; and what did London offer to individuals and groupings engaged in adventurous, often dangerous political and constitutional projects elsewhere in the world?

There is a further question. After the battle of Waterloo in 1815, Britain was the richest and most widely influential polity on the globe. It retained that status, with increasing difficulty, until the early 1900s. Yet, while the impress of this state empire sprawls across most histories of the long nineteenth century, Britain is normally left out of accounts of the rise and spread of the new constitutional technology, which is one of the big themes of this self-same period. How is this anomaly to be corrected? How exactly do we insert Britain into the story of the rising spread of new written constitutions? And how does that story look different when we do?

## War and the Limits of Exceptionalism

In reality, Britain was not an exception to the rule that the onset and design of innovative, single constitutional texts were more often than not interwoven with rising levels of warfare and military mobilisation. Like some other parts of northern Europe, it actually participated in these trends at a markedly early stage. In Britain's case, this happened during the 1640s and 1650s, when civil wars broke out in England, Wales, Scotland and Ireland, a critical period of violence which led to the brief establishment of a republic.

The actions and ideas of members of the New Model Army, the formidable fighting force that emerged for a while victorious from these struggles and defeated the monarch, Charles I, go to make the point. In 1647, some of this army's grandees drafted the so-called Heads of Proposals, a set of propositions intended as a basis for a new constitutional settlement. More radical and democratic, though, was the Agreement of the People, which was set down between 1647 and 1649 in several versions by New Model Army soldiers as well as their officers. This was intended by its sponsors to be 'signed by every Englishman', and to bring about the subordination of the Westminster Parliament to the will of the people. 'That which is done by one Parliament ... may be undone by the next Parliament', argued its writers: 'but an Agreement of the People begun and ended amongst the People can never come justly within the Parliaments cognizance to destroy.' Such a text would operate as a kind of fundamental law, immune from any future parliamentary tinkering.[13]

The Agreement and its makers failed. But, in 1653, Oliver Cromwell, the leading republican general turned Lord Protector, championed an Instrument of Government which was to apply to England, Wales, Scotland and Ireland, and potentially to Britain's overseas colonies. This text, which was issued in print, was intended to regulate government and elections. It included emancipatory reforms such as toleration for Jews, and it came close – again – to being envisaged as a fundamental law. 'In every government', Cromwell lectured Parliament in 1654, 'there must be somewhat fundamental, somewhat like a Magna Carta, that should be standing and unalterable.'[14]

These and other republican projects ended with the restoration of the monarchy in 1660. But the writing of new, adventurous codes of government in these islands continued. In 1669, the political philosopher John Locke, along with various English aristocrats, drafted the *Fundamental Constitutions of Carolina*, an 'unalterable' form of government intended for a projected colonial province between present-day Virginia and Florida.[15] Although this initiative also failed, it is an early illustration of a recurrent British practice.

During the centuries in which they invested in overseas empire, powerful and exploratory Britons regularly drafted constitutions for different groups of settlers and colonised peoples, a habit that continued until the 1970s, when there seemed to be no one left to write for. This British tendency repeatedly to write constitutions *for others* is explored briefly in the sequel to one of the most famous English-language novels, Daniel Defoe's *Robinson Crusoe*, which was first published in London in 1719 and passed through hundreds of subsequent editions and translations. Towards the end of his spin-off book, Defoe, a fierce Whig in politics, has his hero produce – at the request of the inhabitants – 'one general writing under my hand' for his no longer deserted island. Crusoe causes 'to be drawn up, and signed and sealed' a document which sets out 'the bounds and situation of every man's plantation'. 'As to the government and laws among them', Crusoe tells them, he is 'not capable of giving them better rules than they were able to give themselves'. But he insists on the foundational conditions of 'love and good neighbourhood', and on their never having 'differences or disputes one with another, about religion'.[16]

In the late seventeenth century, though, when Defoe was still establishing his writing career, varieties of Britons did not simply design paper projects for other peoples and places, they also continued to experiment with them at home, among themselves. In 1688, a massive Dutch naval and military invasion of southern England destroyed another monarch, James II, sending him into exile. As a result, the crown was bestowed instead on the incoming Dutch ruler, William of Orange, and his Anglo-Scottish consort, Mary. An important Bill of Rights (in Scotland, the Claim of Right) was subsequently issued, which aimed at banning torture and ensuring free elections and the right to petition, as well as curbing royal power and strengthening the position and autonomy of Parliament and of the judiciary.[17]

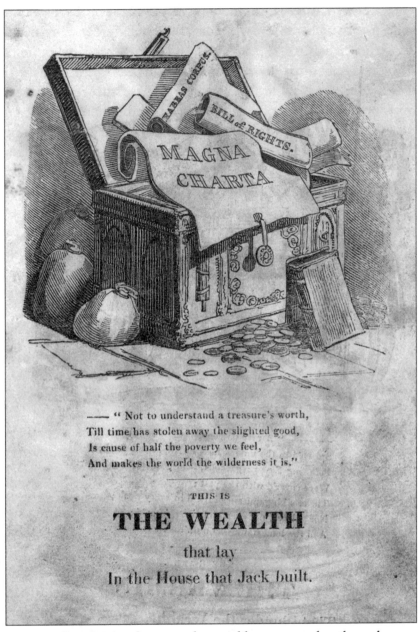

——— " Not to understand a treasure's worth,
Till time has stolen away the slighted good,
Is cause of half the poverty we feel,
And makes the world the wilderness it is."

THIS IS

# THE WEALTH

## that lay

### In the House that Jack built.

33. Constitutional texts, and not gold, represented as the real
treasure of Great Britain: an illustration in William Hone's
radical pamphlet, *The Political House that Jack Built*, 1819.

So far, so impressive, you might think. Yet there was a degree to which these early, constitutionally creative upheavals – the civil wars of the 1640s and the Revolution of 1688 – worked paradoxically to constrain further *written* political remodelling in Britain. As a result of these successive crises, royal power in this polity was reduced and increasingly regulated by Parliament, while individual rights such as freedom of the press and religious toleration became better protected than in much of Europe. Simultaneously, though, the machinery of the British state was made stronger. From the mid seventeenth century, and to a greater degree after 1688, London became more adept at raising soldiers and at building up an increasingly powerful navy. It also became more rigorous, as Tom Paine complained, at raising taxes and loans to pay for these things. And it became more energetic, too, at invading other peoples' territories.

In part because of these increases in governmental efficiency, control and force, when levels of transcontinental hybrid warfare began to escalate in the eighteenth century, this did not involve the British state in financial crisis and *domestic* political upheaval to the same degree as proved the case in its prime European competitors. True, the thirteen American colonies were lost after 1776. But there were no comparable domestic fractures and explosions. Not until the Easter Rising in Ireland in 1916, a crisis enabled by the First World War, did armed conflict in these islands lead to an irrevocable territorial splintering and – though only in the new Irish republic – to more successful ventures in constitution-writing.

This capacity of the British state after 1700 to engage repeatedly in war without experiencing extreme financial meltdown or – outside of Ireland – undergoing severe domestic fractures, was aided by something more than its own formidable capacity to tax, borrow and generate wealth. By 1800, Britain's paramilitary East India Company had been able to build up an army in the subcontinent of over 200,000 men, most of them South Asian troops, and all of them paid for out of Indian taxes.[18]

British governments thus became able to focus most of their domestic defence spending on maintaining a massive navy, while supplementing their own land forces with a huge foreign army that was increasingly employed in multiple continents – a foreign army, moreover, that was not paid for by Britons at home but rather by their captive Indian subjects.

All of these circumstances – an early curbing of royal power, a setting out in law of certain religious and civil rights, a precocious entrenchment of the powers and position of the Westminster Parliament, plus a strong financial system, a large navy and an additional and subsidised army in India – worked to create in Britain not just considerable political stability, but also a degree of constitutional quiescence and complacency. For many (never all) of its inhabitants, this country's substantial immunity after 1700 from major civil wars and successful invasions, plus its generally high level of warlike success, served to validate the existing political and constitutional system. 'Our sword has prevailed on land', declared one euphoric British writer in 1817:

> We are masters of the ocean from pole to pole; revered
> for knowledge, unrivalled for ingenuity; and … the wealth
> of every country rolls into our ports. To what then, under
> Divine Providence, are we to attribute all these advantages,
> if not to the spirit of our free constitution.

Self-congratulatory claims of this sort became very common, especially in the first two-thirds of the nineteenth century.[19]

In 1848, for example, when much of continental Europe was once again convulsed by revolution and war, the Scottish historian and politician Lord Macaulay happily contrasted the 'grievous storm, the thunder and the fire' breaking out abroad with the relative tranquillity of Britain itself, and suggested that

34. The British constitution as a providential blessing:
John Doyle, *The (Modern) Deluge*, 1848.

the essential reason for the latter's good fortune was clear. 'We owe this singular happiness, under the blessing of God,' Macaulay declared, 'to a wise and noble constitution.'[20] The caricaturist John Doyle – for all that he was Dublin-born and Catholic – adopted a similarly smug position in a political sketch published in 1848. In it, the 'British Constitution' appears as a mighty ark floating serenely on a rough sea through torrential rain. Around this vessel (and Bible readers would have known that the purpose of the original ark was to preserve the virtuous) Doyle depicts various unlucky European rulers up to their necks in water and struggling to stay afloat. Like Macaulay's prose, this visual image plays on the idea that Britain is peculiarly blessed, *and that its existing constitutional order is at the very apex of these blessings.*

Yet the enthusiasm with which some Britons talked up their uncodified constitution can be deceptive. Such triumphalism concealed a marked lack of agreement over what exactly the British constitution was. Was it really unwritten, for instance? There was rarely any agreement on this point.

For some, the British constitution's essential beauty was indeed that it was substantially internalised, and therefore – like the common law itself – something that was perpetually in flux. This, argued supporters, made it superior to any code rigidly set down on mere paper. 'What is the British Constitution?' enquired a conservative journalist in 1832, just months before the death of Jeremy Bentham:

> Our constitution is the air we breathe, the restless blood that circulates in our veins, the food that we eat, the soil that nourishes us, the waves that beat upon our shores, the beauty of our women, the strength of our men, the skill of our artisans, the science of our philosophers, the adventurousness of our merchants, the busy activity and civil ambition that keeps us in a constant state of effervescence, progressing in the arts and advancing in the comforts of civilized life ... Constitutions are not made of paper, nor are they to be destroyed by paper.[21]

But this sort of celebratory rejection of written constitutions was never a unanimously held position. For some leading radicals, notably Tom Paine and – increasingly – Jeremy Bentham himself, the fact that Britain's constitution was not set down in a single, supreme and identifiable text was proof not of its unique virtues, but rather of the fact that it barely existed. Other commentators, however, argued that the British constitution *was* in fact to some degree written down.[22] They cited as proof of this the existence of momentous constitutional texts such as the Bill of Rights of 1689. Some even went so far as to argue that it was actually in Britain that written constitutionalism had first commenced.

Thus, in 1917, James Bryce, a highly regarded Scottish jurist and politician, and a one-time ambassador to the United States, claimed that it was Magna Carta, sealed at Runnymede by King John in 1215, that lay at the root of all subsequent written efforts at constitutionalism. 'It seems not too fanciful', wrote Bryce, seeking cheer in the midst of the First World War, 'to say that the prelates and barons of Runnymede, building better than they knew, laid the foundations of that plan of written or rigid constitutions which has now covered the world from Peru to China.' Bryce's acceptance that, by this point in time – 1917 – the new political technology had penetrated much of the globe should be noted.[23]

I stress this variety of views because Britain is sometimes viewed as unambiguously different to the rest of the world in constitutional terms. The doctrine of parliamentary sovereignty – the notion that no new law passed by an omnicompetent parliament at Westminster can restrict what this same parliament may subsequently determine to do – has often been cited as proof that the spread of the new constitutional technology after 1750 was bound, from the outset, to appear alien in Britain: that, here, the idea of a written constitution was always predestined to fail.

Yet, in the past – as now – there seems to have been no more agreement over the meanings and full implications of parliamentary sovereignty than there was over the written-ness or otherwise of the British constitution.[24] There is a need, then, to approach these subjects in a more questioning fashion, and for reasons that extend beyond ideas and events within Britain itself. The scale of this society's power, wealth, reach and industrial evolution by the early 1800s, and its ultimate success (with the aid of other states) against Napoleon, meant that it attracted wide and growing attention in the nineteenth century from observers from other parts of the globe. Individuals and groupings looking to advance ambitious constitutional programmes in their own countries of origin and in search of ideas, were – for a time – particularly attracted by Britain's apparent capacity to combine extreme modernity, the rule of law and relative political stability. There was also a more specific reason why politically engaged people from multiple regions were drawn to make contact with this society. There was London.

## World City, City of Words and Exiles

Especially in the wake of E. P. Thompson's classic work *The Making of the English Working Class* (1963), the prevailing image of London in the initial decades of the nineteenth century has often been as a place of division and rampant disorder. Stark, sometimes violent divisions and outbreaks of political unrest there certainly were. The year 1820, which witnessed major revolts in Spain, Portugal, Greece and parts of Italy, also saw a significant plot in London to assassinate the members of the British governing cabinet. Yet, for all this, compared to many other big urban spaces at this time in different societies, London was still relatively stable, and it was also physically intact.

In contrast with the experience of Paris, Berlin, Madrid, Rome, Venice and many other European cities, no destructive foreign army had occupied London either during or immediately after the Napoleonic Wars. Unlike some cities outside Europe – Washington, for instance, where British troops set fire to the Capitol and the White House in 1814, or Cairo, where Napoleon's soldiers caused extensive damage after 1797 – London had not been sacked and looted. Unlike the Portuguese prince regent, John VI, who was forced to flee Lisbon for Rio de Janeiro in 1807, Britain's royal family had not been driven out of its capital and obliged to seek refuge overseas on account of the wars. Nor did Londoners in general have to evacuate their city. By contrast, in 1812, Moscow had emptied in the face of Napoleon's advancing armies. The city was then, or so Leo Tolstoy claimed in *War and Peace* (1869), 'set on fire by the soldiers' pipes, kitchens, and campfires, and by the carelessness of enemy soldiers occupying houses they did not own'. It seems likely that Moscow was actually set alight by the Russians themselves, but the end result was just as disastrous – the substantial destruction of an ancient, still mainly wooden city.[25]

London's immunity from warfare's sharper penalties helped to ensure that it was even more populous by the time of the battle of Waterloo than at the outbreak of the French Revolution. Even in the late seventeenth century, this had arguably been Europe's largest city. By 1800, London was the world's second biggest city after Beijing; and by the 1820s, it probably was the prime global metropolis, with an estimated 1.6 million inhabitants. London's enormous size, post-war intactness, wealth and global clout together go some way to explaining why so many political reformers and activists from different continents and countries were drawn into its orbit.[26]

Take the case of Ramón Alesón Alonso de Tejada. He came from a wealthy family in Valladolid in north-western Spain, where he was a successful judge. Yet, for all this affluent urban background, when his support for a restoration of the Cádiz constitution drove Alesón to seek refuge in London in 1823, all that he was initially able to see through the daze of culture shock and loneliness was the capital's 'multitude of men [and] piled-up riches'. This, he wrote to his wife sadly and wonderingly, was truly 'the country of gold'.[27] It was not, of course. But Alesón's reactions suggest how vast London could appear even to relatively sophisticated new arrivals at this time; and how rich and untouched it seemed to individuals whose own home societies had been ravaged by invasion, protracted fighting and civil war. Visiting London after the Napoleonic Wars was rather like visiting big cities in the United States in the wake of the Second World War: an exhilarating experience of abundant butter, by contrast with other locations' devastation by the gun.

London also attracted incomers on a conspicuous scale because it possessed a set of attributes that individually were not unique, but that were combined within this vast metropolis to an exceptional degree. London was the home of Britain's royal court, its parliament, government and foreign and diplomatic agents. Many of the major players from abroad who called on Jeremy Bentham came to this capital city primarily because they wanted its politicians' support for the transformations they were attempting in their respective homelands. London was also a financial centre, *the* financial centre, made still more dominant by war's disruption of some of its competitors, such as Amsterdam, Frankfurt and Hamburg. This financial pre-eminence also drew in serial foreign political activists. The Greek independence fighters who sought Bentham's constitutional advice in the early 1820s were in London hoping to raise loans from its banking houses and merchant capitalists, as well as donations from affluent philhellene liberals.

Greek applications for London's money were as nothing, however, compared to those of emerging South American states. Seeking to establish themselves having thrown off Spanish or Portuguese rule, these new-made polities issued government bonds on a terrific scale. In 1822, Colombia, Chile and Peru all issued bonds. Colombia and Peru did so again two years later, along with Mexico, Brazil and Buenos Aires; and there were many more such bond issues. London was easily the biggest arena for these enterprises. An agent would arrive from a South American state. He would make contact with one of the city's myriad banks or merchant houses. He would then offer it a commission to sell the bonds to investors from Britain and elsewhere. Many of these people with money to spare were greedy and gullible; but some were idealistic men and women who believed that their investment would go to advance the cause of liberty across continents.[28]

These close links between the London money market and

a changing South America possess a significance that extends beyond finance and economics. To begin with, the scale of British investment in South America was one reason why newspapers in the United Kingdom devoted so much coverage to that continent's emerging new constitutions. Investors anxious about the security of their money were naturally hungry for information about the quality of governments that were being set up there. British and Irish newspapers responded voluminously to this interest. Thus, in December 1824, the London *Times* printed a leading article on the 'Completion and Publication of the Constitution ...[of] the Mexican Nation'. 'As the whole of these proceedings and documents cannot fail to interest a portion of the English public,' wrote the author of the piece, 'we shall present them at length' – which he duly did.[29]

There was a close correlation indeed between mounting levels of British investment overseas and the coverage that British newspapers allocated to foreign constitutions. During the warlike 1790s, when capital was sometimes sparse and the risks were high, British and Irish newspapers seem – on the basis of one count – to have devoted only about sixty-five major articles specifically to the subject of 'new constitutions'. By the 1810s, with peace returning, money more flush, and the new political technology spreading fast, the number of articles on the subject had risen to almost 2,000, while during the 1830s close to 5,500 substantial newspaper articles were published in the British and Irish press concerning 'new constitutions', as well as thousands of shorter articles, readers' letters and brief reports. We can safely assume that it was UK investors who often scrutinised this kind of reportage. But so, too, did readers who were interested in political change, texts and ideas, and not just those who were based in the United Kingdom itself, but also some in the many other parts of the world to which its newsprint was regularly exported.[30]

It was also the case that money funnelled into South America by way of London proved an asset to many of that continent's revolutionary governments. In the wake of the sword and the gun, copious inflows of British capital could offer new-made regimes here some respite and provide time for the penning of constitutions and the putting down of roots. London offered other resources too that helped to advance constitutional enterprises elsewhere. Like other cities which drew in conspicuous numbers of visitors and political activists from other countries and continents, it was a port. To this extent, London resembled Marseilles on the south coast of France, which regularly attracted Spanish, Italian and Arab intellectuals and dissidents; or Baltimore, Philadelphia, New York and New Orleans in the United States, which sucked in political enthusiasts and exiles from South America, Cuba and Haiti; or Ottoman-ruled Jeddah on the Red Sea. A transit point annually for tens of thousands of Muslim pilgrims engaged in completing the Hajj, Jeddah would become steadily more important over the course of the nineteenth century, especially with the advent of the steamship, and later with the opening of the Suez Canal. Rising numbers of politically active, sometimes anti-colonial Muslims from India, Indonesia, Russia and parts of Africa and the Ottoman empire would take ship to this city, confident that, even before reaching Mecca, they were likely to find ideological and spiritual reinforcement on their journey, and even perhaps fellow fighters.[31]

Like these other coastal and riverine cities, London persistently drew in the politically engaged, enquiring and rebellious. Only it did so on a quite unique scale. In 1815, and for well over a century after that, London was the world's biggest port, with the biggest mercantile marine. By way of Britain's elastic maritime empire, London also enjoyed privileged access to a multiplicity of other ports in every continent. Among many other imperial ports, there was Liverpool, Glasgow, Cardiff and Cork in the home islands. Outside them, by 1840, there was Valetta in Malta, Bridgetown in Barbados, Singapore, Penang, Hong Kong, and Cape Town in South Africa. In due course, there would also be Melbourne and Sydney in Australia, Aden in what is now Yemen, Mombasa and Zanzibar in east Africa, and Surat, Mangalore, Bombay, Madras and Calcutta in India, to list only some of the better-known centres. All of these bustling places were in turn nodal points for networks of other, smaller ports and trading posts. On top of its dealings with ports caught up in Britain's imperial web, London also traded extensively with a dizzying variety of locations in continental Europe, the United States and, increasingly, a transformed South America.[32]

London's uniquely extensive network of ports at this time has long been the stuff of *economic* history. As such, it can seem to give substance to the view – famously sketched out by the great historian Eric Hobsbawm – that while after 1789 France on one side of the Channel was a pioneer of modern *political* revolution, Britain, on the other side, was the prime exponent of modern *economic* revolution.[33] Yet, as well as being overly Eurocentric, this sort of contrast between a politically innovative and creative France and an economically transformative Britain is too simple and insufficiently exploratory. Economic developments regularly feed into wide political changes. As far as London was concerned, they did exactly that, and on a transcontinental scale.

This river city's multiple maritime networks worked incessantly to bring not just commodities but also new political ideas, writings and activists into Britain. These same networks also worked to transport ideas, writings and activists outwards and onwards. Between 1817 and 1822, for instance, the Venezuelan representative in London, the diplomat and lawyer Luis López Méndez, secured berths on over fifty ships operating out of the city's dockyards. He used these to dispatch some 6,000 men, many of them Irish, to South America to serve as recruits for Bolívar's army and naval forces; and while the military contributions of these men were modest, the propaganda value of foreign fighters flooding in to join the armed struggle for South American independence was substantial.[34]

Then there was seaborne and riverine correspondence. It is unlikely that Jeremy Bentham would have acquired anything like the transcontinental reputation he ultimately enjoyed had he not been able to exploit the easy access to mail facilities afforded him by ships coming in and out of London. As it was, and as one hostile but perceptive journalist wrote in 1819, Bentham was able to send off 'constitutional charters or legal codes to any nation in Europe or America' – and in practice to locations in other continents – 'who may apply to him for that purpose by letters post-paid'.[35] What was true of Bentham applied to differing degrees to other London-based activists. Whether it was a case of transporting information, texts and political actors outwards across sea and land frontiers, or receiving communications or sympathisers or political refugees from elsewhere in the world, all of these activities were facilitated by the array of maritime networks radiating out of this vast global city.

Especially important as regards the new constitutional politics was the scale, speed and range with which London produced and distributed print. This was due both to the reach of its maritime sector and to the changing nature of its printing industry. One result of Britain's precocious industrialisation was to transform print productivity. By 1800, printing presses with iron rather than wooden frames were operating in London, and this led to an exponential increase in output. By the 1810s, steam power, too, was being applied to printing. This allowed some London presses to turn out over 1,000 printed pages per hour, four times the eighteenth-century average. By the 1830s, Britain's steam-driven presses were producing 4,000 imprints an hour.[36]

Again, these developments in the business of print frequently get filed away under the heading of economic and business history. Yet their impact could be profoundly political. Groups and individuals operating in parts of the world where printing technology and skills were sparse, or censored, or disrupted by war – like the Venezuelan constitution writers of 1811 whom

35. John Orlando Parry's vision of the diversity and demotic vigour
of print available in London in 1835, even in a dingy backstreet.

we have already encountered – frequently arranged for important political writings and manifestos to be dispatched by ship
to London. Once there, such papers could be put rapidly into
copious print, and copies then shipped out to chosen locations
across the globe. In addition, rising numbers of politically active
campaigners from other regions set up their own print outlets
in London.

In the early 1800s, displaced Spanish liberals established a
clutch of papers here, many of them with evocative names like
*Ocios de Españoles Emigrados*, which appeared from 1824 to 1827.
Then there were the presses and papers run by South Americans,
including *El Repertorio Americano*. In its first incarnation, this
publication was supervised by the Venezuelan turned Chilean
intellectual and diplomat Andrés Bello.[37] Arriving in London on
a mission in 1810, along with Bolívar and another Venezuelan
activist, he had found himself marooned there by the flux of

wars and politics. Bello spent nineteen, often tough, years in the British capital, acquiring and losing wives and children in the process, and writing hard, before being able finally to leave for Chile, and going on to draft its civil code and contribute to its 1833 constitution. There were Portuguese-language journals based in London, too, including the *Correio Braziliense*, the first newspaper ever to refer to Brazil in its title. By the 1810s, as Portugal's imperial authority dwindled, issues of this paper were circulating openly in Brazil, brought into its ports more often than not by British merchant vessels.[38]

As these foreign-language newspaper titles suggest – and their number would expand exponentially over the long nineteenth century – London contained substantial communities of activists from abroad, individuals who were sometimes in transit, but sometimes self-consciously and protractedly in exile. The city was 'peopled with exiles of every kind and every country', wrote one low-level Italian reformer moored in London in the 1820s: 'constitutionalists ... generals, dismissed presidents of republics, presidents of parliaments dissolved at the point of the bayonet'. London, he went on, half-jokingly but with some point, was 'the Elysium (a satirist would say, the Botany Bay) of illustrious men and would-be heroes'.[39]

London was not unique in this respect. Indeed, some places at this time absorbed higher numbers of political activists and exiles on the run. Thus, although the exodus of liberals from Spain in 1823 after the failure of attempts to resurrect the Constitution of Cádiz was substantial – among this country's civil servants close to 10 per cent fled that year – this did not result in a mass movement of Spaniards to the British capital. Far larger numbers sought refuge instead in France, like the master artist Francisco de Goya, who left Madrid for Bordeaux. Other escaping Spaniards chose to settle elsewhere in continental Europe, or the Americas, or north Africa. Only about 10 per cent went to the UK, mostly to London.[40]

What was striking about the exile community in *this* city was not its numerical size so much as the prominence of so many of its members. This was true in spades of London's South American incomers. 'Between the years 1808 and 1830', writes the historian Karen Racine of this South American presence:

> Over 70 independence era leaders of the first rank lived and worked together in London, including Francisco de Miranda, Bernardo O'Higgins, Simón Bolívar, Andrés Bello, José de San Martín, Fray Servando Teresa de Mier, Lucas Alamán, Agustín de Iturbide, Bernardino Rivadavia, Manuel Belgrano, Vicente Rocafuerte, Juan Germán Roscio, Mariano Montilla, Francisco de Paula Santander, Antonio José de Irisarri, youthful members of the Aycinena and García Granados families of Guatemala, José de la Riva Agüero, Bernardo Monteagudo, José Joaquín de Olmedo, and Mariano Egaña.[41]

What this roll call signifies is that some of the most important figures involved in drafting constitutions and state-making in newly independent Argentina, Bolivia, Chile, Ecuador, Guatemala, Mexico, Peru and Venezuela in the 1810s and 1820s all spent time in the same city, namely London.

Racine's list includes heads of state, such as José Joaquín de Olmedo, a president of Ecuador. It includes multiple generals (O'Higgins, San Martín and Montilla) as well as diplomats such as Egaña, and intellectuals, journalists and propagandists such as Miranda, Bello and Alamán. A full catalogue of top South American activists operating out of London at this time would also need to take in financial and commercial figures such as Francisco Montoya and Manuel Antonio Arrubla, active in 1824 in securing a major loan for Colombia from the London money market, and munitions and weaponry men like José Antonio

Álvarez Condarco, who came to London in 1820 to purchase warships for the first Chilean navy.

As well as its practical assets – its mechanised print industry, its dense and expert financial machinery, its array of manufacturers, its vast port networks and shipping facilities, and its resident governing elites and the global clout they exerted – London offered politically embattled and aspiring incomers more intangible benefits, of which relative physical safety was one. Many of these people were engaged in political, ideological and military enterprises for which the price of failure, defeat or betrayal could be very high. As the English essayist Leigh Hunt wrote of radicals in Portugal struggling to support its first ever constitutional regime in 1822–3: 'They hold up a paper constitution as their shield, which the sword pierces through, and drinks their hearts blood.'[42]

London, by contrast, was relatively peaceful. It possessed at this time only a minimal police force that seems rarely to have pounced on foreign exiles unless they involved themselves in dissident British politics. Moreover, the experience of exile here (as elsewhere) could – with luck and sufficient funds – provide individuals with time to think, time to write, and time to develop and work through complex ideas. The value of this for constitutional creativity could be considerable.

Take the case of the jurist and politician Agustín Argüelles, a brilliant orator who was to be one of Spain's leading liberal figures for close to four decades. Born in the year of the American Declaration of Independence, his first stay in London from 1806 and 1809 was as a diplomat. Subsequently a delegate at the *cortes* of Cádiz, serving on its constitutional commission, Argüelles tried, unsuccessfully, to incorporate into the constitution of Cádiz some of the abolitionist ideas to which he had been introduced in London, listening to debates on the ending of Britain's slave trade at Westminster. It was during his second, more extended residence in London as a political exile from 1823 to 1834 that he worked on his influential two-volume history of the constitution-making at Cádiz, labouring away in that temple of political exiles, the British Museum, and arranging for his *magnum opus* to be published by a London-based Spanish-language press in 1835. He did this in advance of helping draft a new Spanish constitution two years later.[43]

The case of Argüelles is a reminder that the intellectual and ideological gains of foreign exile, if one were lucky and so minded, could take different forms. At one level, exiles were in a position to pick up information and fresh perceptions and ideas from their host community, as Argüelles did from making contact with London's abolitionists. But an enforced or voluntary stay away from one's home country could also provide for extended periods of solitude and deracination; and this relative isolation might allow for the working out of new ideas and writings.

For Argüelles, as for Andrés Bello, as, later on, for Karl Marx and for the Russian socialist Alexander Herzen, as, later still, for Sun Yat-sen, a founding father of China's first republic and a main influence on several of its constitutions, some of this re-evaluation and lonely writing down of ideas happened while working day after day in the British Museum. Living as an outsider in a foreign land, to be sure, but securely cocooned within the museum's great domed reading room, where the very printed regulations (drafted by an Italian liberal refugee) stipulated that 'the fact of a man's being a political exile' was not to exclude him from admission to this lettered space.[44]

## Remaking South America, Imagining Britain

For all its lack after the 1650s of anything resembling a codified constitution, Britain functioned, then, as an engine assisting the pace and variety of such devices elsewhere. Especially, but not uniquely, in the decades after the Napoleonic Wars, its combination of rising wealth and power, relative stability, vast networks of print, ports and ships, plus the assets of its swarming capital city catered to a range of constitutional causes in both practical and more intangible ways.

In addition to all this, *ideas* about Britain itself also played a shaping role. There was a degree to which this polity's very lack of a definitive codified constitution allowed its systems of government and laws to be reimagined and drawn on in multiple ways by those pursuing constitutional change in other parts of the globe.

A conspicuous example of this sort of foreign imagining of Britain and its government is a speech delivered some 5,000 miles from London, in a small town on the lower Orinoco river in south-eastern Venezuela, named at this point Angostura. It was here, in a modest, colonial-style two-storey building that Simón Bolívar addressed a congress of twenty-six delegates on 15 February 1819, on the principles that he believed should inform the constitution of the new country that he and they were seeking to create.

Thirty-five years old at this point, slender, with a long nose, dark, penetrating eyes and an angular face, and still mentally and physically fit for all his intensely dangerous existence, Bolívar was emphatically, as he described himself, a 'son of war'. Born in 1783, he was the son of a Creole landowner and militia colonel, and had himself initially held a commission in Spain's colonial militia. But in 1805, having lost his wife, and following two momentous visits to Europe, Bolívar committed himself to the liberation of Spanish America, a determination he increasingly translated after 1811 into armed action.[45]

Although by 1819 Bolívar had a string of victories to his name, and some 14,000 men under his command, including growing numbers of British and Irish volunteers, his progress at this point had temporarily stalled. Spanish troops and their Creole, Black and Indigenous supporters retained control of New Granada, the adjacent province to Venezuela, and were

36. The military Bolívar: an anonymous portrait of *c.*1823.

currently occupying Caracas, his own place of birth. Bolívar's speech to the delegates at Angostura – which was swiftly put into print and distributed from London – was designed therefore to rally and revive support. It also set out his vision of a free Venezuela and a renovated South America.

Bolívar began by assuring the Angostura delegates of his willingness, once the fighting was over, to deliver up power to the Venezuelan people's chosen representatives. He wanted, he told them, to avoid 'the terrible and dreadful office of dictator', retaining only 'the sublime title of good citizen'. In the future, he promised, there would be free and regular elections, since only 'a just zeal' on the part of the people could 'guarantee ... republican freedom'. Such language would have sounded easily in place in Philadelphia in 1776, or in Paris in 1789. Bolívar's evocation of a future, liberated Venezuela also echoed the kind of exultant optimism indulged in by many earlier revolutionaries. 'I see her seated on the throne of liberty,' he declared, 'grasping the scepter of justice, crowned by glory, and revealing to the old world the majesty of the modern world.'[46]

But Bolívar's identification of the best modern system of government for the Angostura delegates to keep in mind when drafting a constitution for this future Venezuela may seem more surprising. 'Representatives,' he told them, 'I suggest that you study the British constitution, which is the one that seems destined to bring the greatest good to the peoples who adopt it.' He was not, Bolívar rightly insisted, advocating a 'servile imitation' of the British system, only close attention to its more 'republican features'. For, properly looked at, he went on, Britain could scarcely be called a monarchy at all:

How can we use the term *monarchy* to describe a system that recognizes popular sovereignty, the division and balance of powers, civil liberty, freedom of conscience, freedom of the press, and all that is sublime in politics? Can there be greater freedom in any other form of republic? Can we expect more of any social order? I recommend this popular constitution to you, its division and balance of powers, its civil liberties, as the worthiest model for anyone aspiring to the enjoyment of the rights of man and to all the political happiness compatible with our fragile nature.

Bolívar also advised the Angostura delegates to make room in their constitution for a senate whose members would retain their seats for life. He did not want, he assured them, 'to establish a noble class' in Venezuela. But 'the Lords in London', like 'the senators in Rome', had shown themselves to be 'the solidest of pillars supporting the edifice of political and civil liberties'. A new, and possibly hereditary Venezuelan senate, taking in men who had proved their worth in the wars of independence, might therefore, he proposed, likewise function as 'a bulwark for freedom ... a nucleus to perpetuate the republic'.[47]

By the same token, Bolívar went on, and for all that they were rebelling against a Spanish king, a modified variant of monarchy might still be useful for ensuring 'solidity' in the new Venezuela:

> The veneration professed by the people for their monarch is a prestige that works powerfully to augment the superstitious respect given to that authority. The splendor of the throne, the crown, and the purple; the formidable support provided by the nobility; the immense wealth accumulated in a single dynasty over generations; the fraternal protection that all kings provide to each other – these are enormous advantages that militate in favor of royal authority, making it almost limitless.

Thought should therefore be given as to how to secure and enhance the strength of the executive. 'No matter how exorbitant the authority of the executive power in England may seem', Bolívar warned, it would likely prove insufficient for an independent Venezuela. A new republic was intrinsically volatile. Its elected president resembled 'a single athlete striving against a multitude of athletes'. The only prudent path to adopt was for constitution writers to accord far 'greater authority to a republican president than to a constitutional monarch'.[48]

Bolívar would set out similar, even stronger arguments in later speeches and writings on the uses of monarchy and aristocratic government, 'provided they be under the necessary restraints'.[49] This has sometimes given rise to claims that this son of a Creole planter, who for a while himself held slaves, was instinctively authoritarian and essentially a conservative. By the time of his death in December 1830, probably from tuberculosis, critics on both sides of the Atlantic (including Jeremy Bentham) were accusing him of despotic, even imperialistic tendencies. Yet Bolívar's ideas and instincts were more protean than this, and at times almost Jacobin in their uncompromising extremism. In a decree issued in 1813, he had threatened South Americans who persisted in accounting themselves as loyal Spaniards with 'death without appeal', unless they joined him in shaking off 'the yoke of tyranny'.[50]

Nor can Bolívar's endorsement of aspects of Britain's constitution, as he perceived it, be put down to sentimental Anglophilia on his part. To be sure, and like many revolutionaries and advanced reformers at this stage, he was assiduous in exploiting some of the resources made available by the British state and its outworks. His *Jamaica Letter*, one of the great founding South American independence texts, was written in the autumn of 1815 while he was living in downtown Kingston in this then British plantation colony. An English-language version was published in a Jamaican newspaper and in the British press, and copies were shipped on from London to other locations. By contrast, no Spanish-language version of the *Jamaica Letter* seems to have appeared in print until the early 1830s. It was a friendly British army officer, moreover, who translated Bolívar's original manuscript of the *Letter* into English; just as it was a merchant ship owned by other sympathetic Britons that had allowed Bolívar to escape Venezuela and reach Jamaica in the first place.[51]

As this suggests, Bolívar had good cause to be aware of the inroads that British commerce, capital and shipping were making in South America at this time, intimately so in fact. His last serious sexual companion, the beautiful, politically engaged Manuela Sáenz, was herself the estranged wife of an English merchant, a man named James Thorne. Over twice her age, Thorne was based in Peru, where more than thirty-six British commercial houses were doing business by the early 1820s. Understandably, the merchant proved no match for the Liberator's glamour, power and charisma. 'You are boring,' Sáenz told Thorne, with a flash of resentment aimed perhaps not simply at him, but also at Britain's tentacular reach, 'like your nation'.[52]

Yet, for all of Bolívar's many connections with British money, British communication and commercial networks, British sympathisers and British and British-linked individuals, he had little direct experience of Britain itself, a country he visited only once in his life. He was more familiar with other European states – Spain obviously, but also France. Like many constitutionalists, moreover, Bolívar made a deliberate point of taking inspiration from multiple locations.

Thus, he derived important ideas in regard to self-presentation and leadership from time spent in France in 1804, studying Napoleon and his cult and attending the emperor's sumptuous coronation at Notre Dame. Similarly, Bolívar gleaned ideas about liberating South America's Black slaves from visiting southern Haiti in 1816, and holding discussions with its then president, Alexandre Pétion. In rather the same way – to the degree that Bolívar was attracted by aspects of the British political system, and sought at times to recommend it in South America – this was partly a case of calculated opportunism and deliberate choice on his part, a product of the kinds of wars he was obliged to fight, and of the enormous challenges that came after.

All successful revolutionary leaders have to worry about how to stabilise the new regimes that they create. After the American Revolutionary War, the likes of Alexander Hamilton and Gouverneur Morris had argued for the establishment of a hereditary senate in a still insecure United States quite as fervently as Bolívar did in Venezuela; while the idea of experimenting with forms of monarchy as a mechanism for fostering mass allegiance in the wake of imperial withdrawal would prove attractive for some nationalists and constitutionalists in India as late as the 1940s. But in one-time Spanish America, the strains involved in fighting for independence and eventually winning it took a particularly acute and protracted form.

Independence struggles here proved very different from those that had taken place in Britain's American colonies after 1775. Much of what became the United States had been made up of a line of one-time British colonies running neatly down its east coast. Even in 1790, these territories contained fewer than 4 million inhabitants, excluding Native Americans. By contrast, New Spain/Mexico *alone* at this time had a bigger population than this; and New Spain was only one of four vast Spanish viceroyalties in central and South America. Along with Portuguese Brazil, these territories covered in total more than 7 million square miles. By 1830, the wars of independence had splintered this huge continent into ten ill-defined and contested polities: Bolivia, Chile, Gran Colombia, Mexico, Paraguay, Peru, the United Provinces of Central America, the United Provinces of the River Plate (later Argentina), Uruguay and – the only monarchy among them – Brazil.[53]

Moreover, how this division of the spoils came about differed sharply from the unfolding of the War of American Independence. In the latter, local fighters had been able to secure vital support on land and sea from major foreign powers, notably France. These formidable alliances had obliged the attacking British to give way after less than eight years. But no such heavily armed *deus ex machina* was available to intervene in the wars of independence in South America, quickly to force things to a crisis and so shorten the violence.

From 1810, when serious disorder began to erupt in parts of South America, to the battle of Waterloo in 1815, the European powers were too preoccupied with their own hybrid wars to engage in full strength in any other continent. After Waterloo, there was too much post-war exhaustion in Europe, and too much accumulated post-war debt, for any of its powers – other than Spain and Portugal – to interest themselves in further extensive fighting in South America. In these circumstances lay its own independence fighters' opportunity, but also sources of danger and long-term damage.

In the absence of major armed interventions from without, small-scale but often fierce and fratricidal fighting among different local forces persisted in South America for a very long time, in some areas from 1810 until after 1825. As a result of these prolonged bloody skirmishes, the continent became both a heaven and a hell for new constitutional projects and initiatives.

It became a heaven, to the extent that – in the absence of large-scale military aid from the outside – South American independence leaders had to make repeated efforts to mobilise from within, among the very poor, among Indigenous peoples, and increasingly among slaves and men of African ancestry. From 1816, Bolívar himself issued a series of decrees against slavery, swayed both by his recent visit to Haiti and his own rising aversion to slavery, and by his recognition that 'The Republic needs the services of all her children'. It needed them to fight. Once summoned into armed service in this fashion, on whatever side, Black and Indigenous South American males, along with poor whites, easily became involved in the business of political claim-making and constitutional debate. In this way, as the Argentinian historian Hilda Sábato puts it, protracted warfare worked here to force-feed political and social modernisation.[54]

The demands of war and mass mobilisation fostered wider civic participation and awareness in South and Central America in a further respect. After 1810, printing presses, which had previously been restricted to large cities, fanned out into smaller towns and pueblos. In Mexico, in 1813 alone, new presses sprang up in Yucatán, Acapulco and in the small mining village of Tlalpujahua.[55] Some of the material these and other presses issued were printed in Indigenous as well as European languages, so as to reach as many people as possible. Even before full independence was achieved, prolonged mass fighting, along with this ever-widening provision of print, fostered the production of multiple, exploratory written constitutions. According to one estimate, at least seventy-seven national and regional constitutions were implemented in South America between 1810 and the early 1830s. But very many more than this were planned and discussed, while failing in the end to materialise.[56]

In terms of voting rights for males, some of these documents were strikingly democratic. Again, Mexico serves to make the point. In the years immediately before independence, what became this territory had officially been governed in accordance with the constitution of Cádiz, which, as we have seen, excluded most Blacks from active citizenship. But, in 1821, the Mexican warlord General Agustín de Iturbide eliminated these racial restrictions and expanded the local franchise. He 'effectively enfranchised every man over eighteen who had employment of any kind'.[57]

In some ways, though, it is Mexico's impromptu provincial constitutions that best illustrate mass interest in the new political projects: how excited some white and non-white activists became at the idea of using a printed document, not simply to outline government, but hopefully to reorder their own mundane lives and local circumstances. In 1825 in Chihuahua, in the north-west of Mexico, activists wanted to use a new constitution to firm up the family, and so included clauses threatening

239

children who were ungrateful to their parents with the loss of citizenship. The makers of Yucatán's new constitution that same year inserted provisions aimed at making its inhabitants better human beings, requiring them in writing to be just and charitable. Two years later, the constitution of Coahuila y Tejas in the east of Mexico was written so as to penalise both those of its inhabitants who tried to sell their votes and those indulging in electoral bribery.[58]

This was the innovating constitutional heaven brought into being by Spanish American independence struggles; and, in some regions, the impact was dramatic and long-lasting. By the mid nineteenth century, the political life of large stretches of South America was more inclusive in terms of social class and race – though not gender – than in the United States or much of Europe. But, alongside this comparative constitutional heaven, there was a countervailing constitutional hell.

As the sheer number of constitutions issued in this continent suggests, their initial survival rate was generally low. Venezuela ran through six between 1810 and the 1830s. Creative and experimental Mexico experienced over twenty constitutions across its territory during the same period. The provinces of New Granada adopted at least ten constitutions between 1811 and 1815 alone. Hardly any constitution devised in former Spanish America during the last decade of Bolívar's life, the 1820s, lasted longer than a year or so. 'Our treaties are scraps of paper,' the Liberator lamented, 'our constitutions empty texts.'[59] The gun and the sword might eventually, and with huge costs, have triumphed. But the pen, apparently, had failed to create stability. It was his growing sense that this was the case which reinforced Bolívar's turn towards the British system as he imagined it.

Several other prominent South American independence leaders shared his growing frustration and disillusionment: the Catholic priest and republican activist Servando Teresa de Mier in Mexico, for instance, and Bernardo O'Higgins, the

37. An older, thin and tired Bolívar, sketched in Bogotá, Colombia, in 1828.

Irish-Hispanic liberator of Chile. If Bolívar's increasing melancholy by the 1820s appears particularly marked ('the only thing one can do in America', he wrote morosely towards the end of the decade, 'is emigrate'), this was in part because he had fought too hard for too long, and because he was a man who luxuriated in words. But it was also the case that, from the outset, Bolívar – who was as much a voracious reader as Napoleon – had devoted serious thought to the question of what kinds of political systems might effectually replace Spanish imperial rule in South America while also guaranteeing order and stability.[60]

Although he did not formally break with Jeremy Bentham until the later 1820s, Bolívar had long been sceptical about what he regarded as idealistic, purely rational schemes of government. Bentham was comfortably distanced for the most part from people who were very poor, or uneducated, or violent, and he had the luxury of writing from the security of his study in the centre of an affluent London undamaged by the ravages of war. Bolívar's own experience was necessarily very different. 'The cries of the human race on battlefields or in angry demonstrations', he warned the delegates at Angostura firmly:

> rail against insensitive or blind legislators who mistakenly believed they could try out whimsical institutions with impunity. Every country on earth has sought freedom … only a few were willing to temper their ambitions, establishing a mode of government appropriate to their means, their spirit, and their circumstances.[61]

These perceptions pushed Bolivár increasingly towards an advocacy of sections of the British system. So, too, did his close readings of Montesquieu's *The Spirit of Laws*, a work to which he had been introduced by his childhood tutor Simón Rodríguez, and which underwent a revival of popularity in the wake of the Napoleonic Wars.[62] Montesquieu had argued that a country's laws and institutions should be crafted in accordance with its specific culture, manners and geography. He had also devoted parts of Book XI of his work to a selective celebration of the British constitution, its mixed government of monarch, aristocracy and (very constrained) democracy, each of these acting, or so he claimed, as a check upon the others. Montesquieu's private views of Britain were sometimes scathing. But he viewed the balance which he detected in its central government as the essence of a successful state. So, too, did Bolívar and – even more than Montesquieu – he found support for his ideas from a selective vision of Britain.

A formal monarchy was hardly feasible in the new South America, he accepted. But there could and should be, he believed, strong presidents who were appointed for life, perhaps with the power to nominate their successors. This was the arrangement he proposed in the constitution he designed for Bolivia in 1826, which he envisaged also operating as a blueprint for neighbouring republics. Formal South American aristocracies, too, Bolívar understood, were probably impracticable. But, as he urged at Angostura and on later occasions, there might usefully be hereditary senates, or at least ones where the members sat for life. As for 'the unrestrained multitudes', those across his continent who had risen up and fought, they desperately needed to be managed, and their myriad voices and aspirations offset through the 'stewardship of paternalistic governments to cure the wounds and ravages of despotism and war'. There would have to be a pacifying middle way. There needed, as he had written in British-ruled Jamaica, to be a search for a 'proper balance'.[63]

## Crossings

Other prominent South American politicians, military men and intellectuals were also drawn to such positions. In Chile, for instance, the makers of its 1833 constitution, which endured with amendments until the 1920s, deliberately broke with earlier attempts to create a federal system in the new republic. Instead, these legislators made provision for a stronger executive, and incorporated aspects of what was styled 'the English pattern' of government.[64] In parts of continental Europe, too, the decades immediately after Waterloo witnessed an emphasis on pragmatic, middle of the road constitutional design that was often explicitly linked by supporters with the British example. One sees this not just in conservative documents like the French Charter of 1814, but also in Belgium's more liberal and widely influential constitution of 1831.

The latter was crafted as a result of a revolution which detached what became the independent state of Belgium from the northern sector of the previous United Kingdom of the Netherlands. Despite these violent beginnings, most Belgian legislators hungered for balance, and kept an eye on the seemingly successful stability of the British system. They rejected federalism. They also rejected republicanism by a large majority, opting instead for a hereditary but constitutional monarchy on the British pattern. As the formal head of the executive, this new Belgian king was to be hedged in by a bicameral legislature, again on the British model. Like other constitution-makers, members of the Belgian National Congress were careful to adopt a policy of pick and mix. They rejected anything resembling Britain's then entirely hereditary House of Lords. Nonetheless, they were clear that there was to be no 'brilliant utopia' in the new Belgium. 'We have to close our hearts and listen only to reason', declared one of them: 'we have to beware of abstractions and theories and measure coolly the realities of our times.' Debates on this Belgian constitution were peppered with approving allusions to Montesquieu's *The Spirit of Laws*.[65]

Nor was any of this surprising. Brussels, where this constitution was drafted, was only twelve miles from the battlefield at Waterloo. Too much had been lost and damaged, too many people and places violently destroyed for too long. For most Belgian politicians and thinkers, as for many supporters of post-Napoleonic France's restored monarchy, as for Bolívar and some of his fellow weary revolutionary victors in South America, this was the vital point. In the wake of decades of warfare and extreme ideological ferment, stability, gradualism and compromise often exerted a greater appeal than grand experimental projects and leaps into the unknown. These priorities could – and sometimes did – turn minds and pens towards real and imagined aspects of the British political system.

But what of Britain itself? Yes, its systems of government and perceived values, and its own infrastructure, were drawn upon during this era, in multiple ways, by constitutionalists and reformers from different parts of the world. The obverse of this, though, is also important. Not only did Britain contribute to political and constitutional shifts in other countries and continents, it was itself also affected by some of these shifts.

I come back to the geographical range of Jeremy Bentham's interventions, and to Eduard Gans seeing books in Portuguese and Spanish and other languages lined up on his library shelves in the house at Queen's Square Place. I come back to the exponential coverage devoted to foreign constitutions in the British and Irish press. I come back to the political exiles, revolutionaries and regime-changers crowding so persistently into the British capital; as well as to this country's unsurpassed maritime links with different sectors of the globe, and its long indigenous tradition of significant and innovative political texts. Given all this, and given that Britain itself was repeatedly and protractedly at war in this era, it was unlikely that people here would remain stoutly impervious to the spread of the new political technology and the ideas swirling around it. Nor were they.

Some individual examples of Britons who were caught up, post-Waterloo, in the contagion of constitutions are well

38. Major Cartwright holding one of his constitutional schemes.

known. In the spring of 1822, Percy Shelley and Lord Byron purchased vessels from the same Genoese shipbuilder and then staged races against each other in the Bay of La Spezia, off the north-west coast of Italy. Like their inexpert poet captains, both of these boats were marked by revolution, war and constitution-making. Shelley's was poorly designed. His death that year, when it capsized in a storm, put an end to his plans for an epic poem on England's struggle against Charles I for the sake of a republic. This, after the poet, a reader of Jeremy Bentham, had also devoted thought and words to supporting the Neapolitan revolution of 1820 and the constitution that briefly emerged from it. As for Byron, who was a considerably richer man, he chose to name his own more substantial schooner *The Bolivar*.

Two years later, though, he too was dead, perishing from a fever caught in Greece, where he had journeyed to join the struggle for that country's political liberation from the Ottoman empire, and for its right to implement its own written constitution.[66]

Since these two men were so hugely gifted, their chosen politics can appear merely exceptional. They were not. But a more revealing and rewarding example of how multifarious Britons at this time were caught up in wider political and constitutional events is perhaps offered by a more mundane figure, the one-time naval commander and later military officer John Cartwright, a veteran reformer and political associate of Jeremy Bentham. Far less intellectually gifted and original than the latter – whose favourite, damning description of him was 'worthy' – Cartwright is still sometimes discussed, if at all, in condescending and purely insular terms, as a man stolidly attached to traditional forms of protest and addicted to quaint antiquarian pursuits. But he was more than that.

Unlike Bentham, who tended to ignore the existence of Indigenous peoples in his grand political projects for South America and elsewhere, Cartwright was already advocating the protection – and, hesitatingly, the political identity – of native peoples in North America in the 1760s and 1770s.[67] He also supported the introduction of a written constitution for Britain itself, and did so repeatedly in print and in speeches from at least the 1790s.

Once this constitution was drafted, Cartwright wanted it 'printed, circulated, and submitted to a three-years national discussion'. Once agreed on, the provisions of this new written British constitution should, he insisted, be inscribed in letters of gold on the interior walls of the Westminster Parliament, as a permanent reminder to its legislators that they were answerable to a fundamental law endorsed by the (male) population.[68] A busy oppositionist throughout the French Revolutionary and Napoleonic Wars, Cartwright, like Bentham, was also re-energised and in some ways redirected by the influx into London of foreign constitutionalists and their ideas.

Courtesy of his friendship with the exiled Spanish liberal Agustín Argüelles, some of Cartwright's reform writings were published in translation in Spain. Indeed, his final book, in 1825, an imaginary dialogue between a Spaniard, a Frenchman, an Italian, a German and an Englishman on the nature of constitutional reform, was published only in Spanish, and dedicated to the brother of Rafael del Riego, the prime military martyr of Spain's constitutional revolution of 1820–23.[69] Cartwright also made connections by way of London's émigré community with South American independence activists, especially in Mexico, a country for which he designed his own constitutional project. Almost his last words on his death bed, or so his niece and devoted biographer claimed, were to give thanks for the fact that the Mexican generalissimo Agustín de Iturbide had failed in his attempt to restore an imperial monarchy, and that Mexico would therefore remain a republic. 'I am glad, I am very glad', a dying Cartwright is supposed to have exclaimed.[70]

As this suggests, Jeremy Bentham's busy constitutional writing and contacts with foreign political and reforming activists in this era were hardly unique. Other, less distinguished and less well-known British actors at this time were also involved in such practices. Cartwright's career widens our understanding of the range and variety of British constitutional thought and language at this time in a further respect. In sharp contrast to Bentham, Cartwright was supremely an itinerant activist; not just a man with a mission, but also a man who was persistently on the move. During the late 1810s and early 1820s, he embarked on a series of epic tours throughout Great Britain, preaching the gospel of political change to large audiences at open-air hustings and holding meetings with local groups of reformers. These activities have generally been examined only in regard to the domestic British campaign to reform the Westminster Parliament.[71] But,

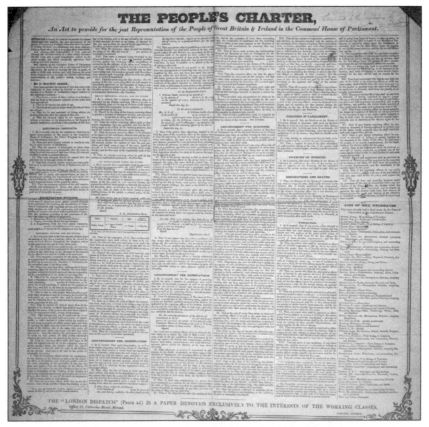

39. A cheap, one-page printing of *The People's Charter*, c.1839.

while in motion around Britain, Cartwright seems regularly also to have pushed the cause of written constitutionalism, and to have energised wider interest and enthusiasm for this project.

Some of the supporters of Chartism, the British and Irish mass movement of the 1830s and 1840s which captured the avid attention of Friedrich Engels and Karl Marx, for instance, are known to have taken inspiration and ideas from Cartwright. Chartism derived its very name from a written text, the People's Charter. This was drawn up in London in 1838 and outlined a set of democratic demands: universal male suffrage; a secret ballot; payment for Members of Parliament, so that poorer men could take positions there; and more. Massively and repeatedly issued in print, 'every principle laid down in the Charter', claimed a sympathiser, 'was recognized by Major Cartwright'.[72]

There were other Chartist paper projects. Some participants in this diffuse movement experimented with writing declarations of independence and declarations of rights. Others pushed for a National Convention, chosen by 'universal suffrage', that would 'establish a new constitution upon the basis of the People's Charter', and then eventually replace the Westminster Parliament.[73] 'The truth', declared one perfectly ordinary Chartist speaker in northern England in 1838, 'is we have no constitution, and it is high time the people set about making a constitution for themselves [cheers].' To 'a well-defined and written constitution' toasted another Chartist assembly that same year.[74]

The career, writings and connections of John Cartwright, like some of the language and initiatives involved in this later Chartist movement, underline the point that Britain and Ireland did not remain untouched by the rise of the new political technology. Individuals, organisations and initiatives in these countries were rather caught up in this widening transformation, just as they helped at times to shape and accelerate it. But, in the end, it proved possible for successive British governments to disregard movements and demands for extensive written constitutional change *at home*, because, after the seventeenth century, this polity remained so unusually immune to invasion, shattering military defeats overseas and – outside of Ireland – serious episodes of civil warfare and domestic armed revolution.

As happened so often elsewhere, the quality and incidence of warfare proved here to be key, though in a distinctive fashion. The patterns of war and violence in this polity made homegrown written constitutional initiatives *less* likely, not more so. Individuals from Britain who felt drawn towards designing and creating a brand new political world on paper had therefore to look for expression and opportunities in other regions of the globe.

PART THREE

**NEW WORLDS**

40. Marine Lieutenant John Shillibeer's drawing of
Pitcairn island approached from the sea, 1814.

# Six

# THOSE NOT MEANT TO WIN, THOSE UNWILLING TO LOSE

## Pitcairn

We need to broaden and diversify our gaze. It was on 29 November 1838 that Captain Russell Elliott and the crew of the sloop HMS *Fly* made landfall here, and found a people in need of written government. In 1790, Pitcairn, a tiny island in the South Pacific, midway between New Zealand and Peru, had become the last, empty place of refuge for nine mutineers from HMS *Bounty*, including Fletcher Christian, and their eighteen Tahitian companions, most of them young women. Violence within the group, disease, accidents and hardship quickly winnowed these already fragile numbers. Within ten years, all but one of the white males was dead. Accordingly, it was the Polynesian women and their children who initially shaped much of Pitcairn's culture. When Western ships began to make sporadic contact with the place in the 1810s and 1820s, their sailors saw – and drew – the island's inhabitants overwhelmingly as dark-skinned. Most went bare foot and wore brief clothing made out of tree bark, though the two sexes retained some of the separate customs of their hybrid origins. In navy fashion, sewing was the business of the men, while the island's women ate apart from them and together with each other in accordance with Tahitian folkways. By 1838, there were close to a hundred of these predominantly non-white, mixed-culture people clinging to Pitcairn's two square miles of volcanic rock, and they were no longer protected by distance.[1]

A missionary had landed, bringing in bibles and other books, and overseeing the building of a school. There were more predatory visitors. Rising numbers of whaling ships from Nantucket, Salem and Newport were mooring offshore, and some of their disembarking crewmen posed questions about the Pitcairners' legal and political status: 'taunting them that they had no laws, no country, no authority, that *they* were to respect'. These were American mariners, after all, and New Englanders. They took it for granted that political identity was signified by the possession of a distinctive flag and some kind of written charter. Yet, as the whalers pointed out, Pitcairners 'had neither colors, or written authority'. Might not their island therefore be going spare? Might it not be ripe for others' taking? Arriving in 1838, and listening to these concerns, Captain Elliott reacted swiftly. He gave the islanders (of course) a spare Union Jack from his ship. He also drew up what he later described as 'a few hasty regulations to be observed'. The document stuck, and quickly came to be regarded as a written constitution.[2]

It was path-breaking at multiple levels. Elliott's is one of the first texts subsequently styled a constitution to devote serious attention to the environment, an indispensable step given that Pitcairn's natural resources were sparse and animals outnumbered people. Accordingly, Elliott set down laws for the regulation of dogs, pigs, cats and goats, for the preservation and responsible cutting down of trees, and for the protection of a local endangered white bird. He also made enlightened provisions for the island's human inhabitants. Attendance at Pitcairn's only school was declared mandatory for all children between the ages of six and sixteen; and parents were to ensure that their offspring could 'repeat the alphabet' before they commenced formal schooling.

Elliott may have drawn inspiration for these educational measures from his own Scottish background. But his most daring innovation appears to have been substantially his own.

Elections for Pitcairn's 'magistrate and chief ruler', his text stipulated, were to take place annually at the island's school house on the first day of January. Once elected, this official was prohibited from assuming 'any power or authority ... without the consent of the majority of the people'. Pitcairn was to be a working democracy. A democracy, indeed, like nowhere else.

To vote in elections for Pitcairn's 'chief ruler', you had to be an adult, and either 'native born on the islands' or a resident of at least five years' standing. These were the only qualifications Elliott set down. All islanders meeting them, whether 'male or female, who shall have attained the age of eighteen', were to have access to 'free votes'.[3] For the first time in world history, a written constitution – which remained in force on Pitcairn with minor alterations until the 1930s – proclaimed that *all* adult men and *all* adult women were to be enfranchised in elections for the acting head of their executive on equal terms.

Insofar as Elliott's revolutionary act has been noticed by historians of the wider world, it has generally been treated as a stray act of imperial utopianism, a picaresque episode on a tiny island lost in a vast ocean. Such marginalising of what happened on Pitcairn in 1838 has been encouraged by the fact that – even now – the Pacific region tends to receive less scrutiny from historians than the Atlantic or Mediterranean worlds, or indeed the Indian Ocean. This is partly attributable to the sheer magnitude of the space. The Pacific Ocean is 60 million square miles in extent, which makes it larger than all of the land surfaces of the globe added together. Contained within this vast expanse of water are treasuries of very different kinds and sizes of islands. Some of these, such as Australia, the South and North Islands of New Zealand and the four main islands of the Japanese archipelago, range from the substantial to the huge. Others, like Pitcairn and its adjacent islets, are diminutive.

At once massive and diffuse – 'so much ocean, too many islands', as one ethnographer put it – the Pacific world can

41. A Europeanised depiction of two mixed-race
Pitcairners, published in London in 1831.

repel and elude close attention, not only on account of its over-whelming size but also because of its myriad complexity.[4] Small Pacific islands, especially, frequently get passed over. For all their physical beauty and traditional anthropological interest, they are easily dismissed as cut off from the 'real' world and from the pasts that matter. Yet, as regards constitutional change and innovation, developments across the Pacific in general – including on some of its smaller islands – possess a wide significance. Moreover, these places were rarely cut off in fact, and became progressively less so after 1800.

As the levels and sophistication of maritime traffic improved, the 'limitless ocean', as Mark Twain styled the Pacific, provided in practice for increasingly broad and diverse sets of connections.[5] It is the steam train which is often viewed as the prime emblem of advancing modernity in the nineteenth century, and as the chief agent for the enhanced conquest of physical space. Yet, as far as really long-distance journeys were concerned, rail transport was a relative latecomer, while the areas in which it could operate were necessarily restricted. By contrast, ships could cover most of the surface of the world; and, by the 1800s, their size, speed and capacity for distance were all on the rise. Growing numbers of faster and bigger sailing ships, and then steamships, became available for traversing the Pacific's huge distances. This made it easier for its multitudinous islands to be in regular contact with each other, and also to develop links with other continents. Faster, tougher, bigger and more abundant and reliable ships also allowed more traders, migrants, explorers, diplomats, missionaries and empire-makers from the outside to move into this vast oceanic world. Russell Elliott's passage to Pitcairn was a case in point.

At present, too little is known of this man and the nature of his reading and ideas. It *is* known that he was a well-educated, well-connected and socially concerned Scot. It is also clear that his foray into constitution-writing on Pitcairn was something of an over-determined act. Back in the 1790s, one of his distant relations, a Gilbert Elliot (the spelling of the surname shifted), had helped to design a new constitution for the island of Corsica.[6] In addition, Russell Elliott's ship, HMS *Fly*, normally operated out of the port of Valparaiso on the coast of Chile, a country that had passed through no fewer than five constitutions between 1822 and 1833. There was something else that influenced Elliott. He was accompanied for part of his voyage to Pitcairn by a geologist and mountaineer named Pawel Strzelecki.

Of Polish stock, Strzelecki, like Elliott himself, was a highly mobile idealist who seems to have been particularly drawn to small or struggling countries and peoples. Strzelecki may have taken part in the Polish rising of 1830 against Russia. In the 1840s, he would certainly speak out against the dispossession of Aboriginal peoples in Australia; and he subsequently carried out impressive humanitarian work on behalf of victims of the Irish famine, spending 1847 and much of 1848 distributing aid in Donegal, Sligo and Mayo. His friend Russell Elliott, meanwhile, was simultaneously helping starving men and women in those areas of the Scottish Highlands affected by the same potato blight that was devastating so many parts of Ireland.[7]

Sailing together in 1838, Strzelecki and Elliott, a Pole and a Scot, were able to exchange information, enthusiasms and ideas from July, when the *Fly* left Valparaiso, until early September when it anchored off Hawaii. There, both men disembarked for a while and busied themselves meeting various Hawaiian chiefs, local leaders who would be closely involved in implementing their own constitutional projects in 1839 and 1840.[8] So, when Captain Elliott arrived at Pitcairn, he came equipped with connections to constitutional changes and debates in the Mediterranean and continental Europe, in South America and also in another set of Pacific islands.

Elliott's voyage to Pitcairn on a Royal Navy ship was connected with wider developments in a further respect. It was an example of the sharply rising levels by this stage of great power intervention and competition in the Pacific. The rate of Spanish, British, French and Russian naval, scientific and colonising ventures in this oceanic space had been increasing since the Seven Years' War. By the 1830s, Spain had largely dropped out of the race, but only to be replaced by another, fast-emerging power. The year of Elliott's landfall at Pitcairn, 1838, saw the launch of a federally funded United States expedition to explore and survey the Pacific Ocean. The Americans were coming.[9]

So, too, were rising numbers of land-hungry Euro-American settlers. The battle of Waterloo in 1815 did not mark an end to the hybrid warfare that had characterised the long eighteenth century. It rather facilitated the onset of different, and differently directed episodes of violence on land and sea. The temporary cessation of extreme conflicts within Europe itself, along with the ending of the War of 1812 between the United States and Britain, made it easier for various Europeans and Americans to embark on other modes of assertion and aggression, in other parts of the world. The Pacific was one such target area.

Between 1820 and 1860, some 5 million people, mainly from Britain, Ireland, Scandinavia, Holland and the German states, took ship to the United States. On arrival, many of them – along with substantial numbers of men and women previously based in America's eastern states – began moving westwards, some of them ultimately ending up in California and even Hawaii. At the same time, smaller numbers of migrants from much the same regions of Europe migrated to Australia and New Zealand.[10]

The constitutional repercussions of these settler invasions were mixed. On arrival, white incomers to this wide Pacific region frequently campaigned for and introduced their own new and ambitious schemes of government. They often did so, however, at the expense of those Indigenous peoples whose lands and resources they were appropriating. It is telling that even on tiny, volcanic Pitcairn, which offered few material enticements to would-be invaders, New England whaler men in the 1830s instinctively adopted an aggressive, acquisitive stance when confronted by people with brown skin whom they would have seen as semi-naked.

On this occasion, there was a moderately happy ending. The Pitcairners secured their own written constitution, and their own acting chief executive and democratic process. And while the rescuing agent and collaborator this time was an idealistic outsider, Russell Elliott, this course of events – vulnerable Pacific island peoples resorting to a constitutional text in the hope of repelling white invaders – would be repeated elsewhere by other people who were indigenous to the Pacific. Elliott brought ideas into Pitcairn from elsewhere. But there were also individuals from *within* this Pacific world, in Tahiti, Hawaii and some other small islands, who looked to new writings on government and law in the 1800s and later as a means to reorder their home societies and forge their own strategies for survival and resistance.

Pitcairn, then, is a case of *multum in parvo*, a very small territorial space set in the midst of a vast ocean that nonetheless casts light on much more than itself. Pitcairn is revealing about the scale and pace of changes taking place across these vast oceanic distances. It illustrates as well the rising levels of imperial and settler invasions occurring by this stage, and how these could result in fresh and varied constitutional thought and writings. What happened on Pitcairn illumines something else. It raises piquantly an issue that we have not as yet confronted: the connections and disconnections between the onset of new, written constitutions and the position and rights of women. The Pacific world is often pushed aside, or left out in constitutional histories. It belongs right at their centre.

## Why Were Women Left Out?

Russell Elliott's willingness to extend political rights to female Pitcairners in 1838 – positively to incorporate them within the terms of his constitution – inevitably raises the question of why it was that the vast majority of other constitutions drafted before the early twentieth century confined active citizenship only to men. The answers may seem already abundantly clear and straightforward.

In multiple – though not all – cultures, a woman's legal identity had traditionally been subsumed in that of her husband and/or other close male relations. The position set out in the ancient Hindu law code, the *Manusmriti*, that a woman should ideally pass from the authority of a father to that of a husband, or if necessary to that of a son or brother, was broadly echoed by commentators from many other legal and cultural backgrounds, including most practitioners of the European Enlightenment. Marriage, conceded the German philosopher Christian Wolff in the 1750s, was an 'association based on equality'. Nonetheless, he went on, it represented a 'pact of submission', by which a woman effectively accepted subjugation to her husband.[11] Defined in this fashion as dependent beings, it was difficult for women to lay claim to, or even to imagine, an autonomous political identity for themselves. Unless, that is, they happened to be reigning monarchs or chieftains in polities which allowed females to assume these roles; or if they derived some political heft from possession of extensive property, or through close proximity to a powerful man.

All that said, the spread of the new political technology made a difference to the treatment of women and, in some ways and in many places, it made things worse. In the 1790s, barely a decade after Massachusetts had issued an ambitious state constitution enfranchising every modestly incomed 'male inhabitant of twenty-one years of age and upwards', its leading masonic lodge published a version of one of this period's most popular

Freemasons' songs, both a skit on and an affirmation of a vital episode in the Book of Genesis:

> But Satan met Eve when she was a gadding
> And set her, as since, all her daughters, a madding;
> To find out the secrets of Free Masonry
> She ate of the fruit of the forbidden tree ...
> But Adam astonish'd like one struck with thunder,
> Beheld her from head to foot over with wonder;
> *Now you have done this thing, Madam, said he,*
> *For your sake no women Free Masons shall be.*[12]

This masonic validation of an ancient, religiously backed argument – that women were not only physically weak but frivolous and morally fragile, and consequently doubly in need of close regulation – is significant, since there were undoubted links between the appearance and organisation of Freemasonry and the emergence of the new written constitutions.

From the 1710s, lodges of Freemasons – fraternal organisations that met regularly to talk, argue and carouse – spread rapidly throughout Europe and the Americas. From early on, many masonic lodges drafted and published what they explicitly termed constitutions.[13] Becoming a Freemason, participating in the writing and publication of a lodge text of this sort, was one way in which a man could familiarise himself with the idea and uses of paper constitutions more broadly. It is suggestive just how many prominent constitutionalists, be it Pasquale Paoli in Corsica, or George Washington and Benjamin Franklin in the United States, or Jean-Jacques-Régis de Cambacérès in France, or Agustín Argüelles in Spain, or Simón Bolívar and José de San Martín in South America, or later political activists from outside the West such as Motilal Nehru in India or the Young Turk leader Mehmet Talat, were also avid members of masonic lodges. But, in this regard, too, in Freemasonry, with its close connections with the new political technology, women were overwhelmingly shut out. As the Massachusetts song put it: 'No women Free Masons shall be'.

In recent decades, historians (including myself) have been keen to emphasise how, beneath this seemingly frozen surface of legal, political, religious, ideological and customary constraints, there were by the later eighteenth century in some regions of the world some significant currents of change.[14] On both sides of the Atlantic, there was increasing, albeit patchy, provision for female education. A faster growth of towns gave some women wider access to information, cultural involvement and economic opportunities. The self-same sharp rise in print that proved so vital for the diffusion of political constitutions also provided expanded scope for female reading, authorship and publishing. As a result of these changes, notions of women occupying a distinct, intrinsically private sphere came, for some, to appear more problematic and even untenable.

One sign of this was a limited admission of women in some Western states to art, cultural and even scientific academies and exhibitions. In 1787, an ambitious, clever and elegant twenty-nine-year-old French lawyer by the name of Maximilien de Robespierre, the future designer of his country's Constitution of the Year II (1793) and a great deal more, would argue for the admission of women to France's royal academies, insisting that, while the two sexes were inherently different, the contributions of both were essential if enlightenment were to advance.[15] At around the same time, a few individuals, both male and female, began to argue more adventurously than before that the involvement of both sexes was also indispensable for the successful evolution of a reformed mode of politics.

'Consider, I address you as a legislator,' appealed the English radical Mary Wollstonecraft to Charles Maurice de Talleyrand-Périgord, one of the authors of France's 1791 constitution:

whether, when men contend for their freedom, and to be allowed to judge for themselves respecting their own happiness, it be not inconsistent and unjust to subjugate women ... Who made man the exclusive judge, if woman partake with him the gift of reason?

Wollstonecraft inserted this rhetorical (and fruitless) appeal in the dedication to her best-known work, *A Vindication of the Rights of Woman*, published in 1792. However, it was in another, unfairly neglected book of hers, *An Historical and Moral View of the Origin and Progress of the French Revolution* (1794), written while she was in France, in which she offered a definition of the ideal written constitution:

A constitution is a standard for the people to rally round. It is the pillar of a government, the bond of all social unity and order. The investigation of its principles make it a fountain of light; from which issue the rays of reason, that gradually bring forward the mental powers of the whole community.[16]

*The whole community*: for Wollstonecraft, evidently, the new written politics potentially carried within it rich promise for women alongside men.

These limited but important changes and challenges apparent in some places by the late eighteenth century need bearing in mind, because otherwise the position on women adopted by most constitution-writers before 1900 can seem simply preordained. In reality, attitudes were occasionally more fluid, especially at the start. During the Philadelphia Convention's debates in 1787, the Pennsylvanian delegate James Wilson proposed that seats in the lower house of the United States Congress be allocated to American states 'in proportion to the whole number of white & other free Citizens & inhabitants *of every age sex & condition* [my italics]', and this recommendation was allowed to stand. When it came to setting out some of the basic political organisation of the new American republic, therefore, white women, along with free Black women, were treated on a par with free men. This was what one United States senator meant when he wrote in 1804 that 'in the theory of our constitution women are calculated as political beings' – a potentially significant admission.[17] The earliest American state constitutions, too, occasionally sent out mixed messages. Most explicitly excluded women from active local citizenship from the start; others made no mention of women at all; while New Jersey's first state constitution initially allowed some of its female inhabitants to vote.

The fact that New Jersey rescinded this provision in 1807 makes, however, an important point that applies beyond the United States itself. As the new constitutions became more entrenched, previously loose or equivocal phrasing was generally tightened up and the exclusion of women made more unambiguous. One sees this in American state constitutions drafted or revised during the 1810s. By this stage, provisions for white male democracy were becoming more generous. Simultaneously, however, legislators were careful to spell out that women and (usually) Black males were not to share in this expanding democratic bounty. So, while the word 'men' was still sometimes used in the more general sense of also including women, when it came to setting out franchise provisions, specificity reigned. In the new and amended state constitutions for West Florida (1810), Louisiana (1812), Indiana (1816), Mississippi (1817) and Connecticut and Illinois in 1818, lawmakers made studied use of phrases such as 'every free white male person', or 'every white male citizen', or 'all white male inhabitants'.[18]

The trajectory was much the same in parts of Europe. More than had been the case in revolutionary America, the French Revolution of 1789 sparked discussion of the claims of

42. Symbol but not substance: Woman as an allegory of liberty, with the French Declaration of the Rights of Man and of the Citizen in her hand, and painted by a female artist in Paris, Nanine Vallain, in 1793–94.

the second sex. Nonetheless, France's first constitution in 1791 classed females as mere passive citizens. Some countries caught up in French Revolutionary and Napoleonic invasions were even more uncompromising. The meetings of the French Estates General and National Assembly had at least been open to female spectators. But when the *cortes* of Cádiz began to craft its ambitious constitution for the Spanish empire in 1810, women were kept out, not only from its provisions for active citizenship but even from attending the debates. 'Men of all classes' were invited in 'without distinction' to bear witness. Women, by contrast, were not permitted to 'enter any of the galleries of the assembly hall'.[19]

This tendency for the treatment of women in constitutional texts to become more restrictive over time was not confined to Euro-America. In Hawaii, the powerful House of Nobles created by its first written constitution in 1840 initially included a sizeable number of female chiefs. By 1846, such women made up almost a third of its membership. But, outside of the monarchy, formal female participation in Hawaiian politics was progressively cut back. In 1850, for the first time, a law specifically restricted voting to Hawaiian men. By 1855, only a single female chief remained in the unelected House of Nobles. In 1892, women were barred from its membership altogether.[20]

There was a degree, indeed, to which – as the new constitutions spread and became increasingly identified as desirable markers of modernity – states adopting them tended to duplicate the exclusionary tendencies that had been typical of most of these devices from the outset. Thus, the canonical beginning of Japan's systematic political modernisation, the Meiji Restoration of 1868, was promptly followed by a dismantling of the previously powerful female sector of the palace bureaucracy in Edo (Tokyo). And whereas a small number of Japanese women seem, in earlier periods, to have participated at least occasionally in local political matters, the Meiji constitution of 1889 denied all women voting rights. A year later, Japanese women were even banned from attending political meetings, in a measure based on earlier laws in Germany and Austria.[21]

This barrage of formal, exclusionary provisions conceals, of course, as well as reveals. It obscures the ways in which some women, in all continents, devised for themselves alternative modes of public and political engagement. It can also distract attention from the degree to which women, like low-status men, sometimes secured benefits from the introduction of new written constitutions, even when these devices denied them the vote: better educational provision, for instance, or more reliable access to a free press. It is always wrong to reduce political rights merely to access to the franchise.

Nonetheless, the degree to which written constitutions tended almost everywhere to cut women out of the voting process needs explaining. It is not enough to say that these formal texts merely put into words and print patterns of behaviour and assumptions that had always prevailed. As events in Hawaii and in Japan illustrate, this was not always straightforwardly the case. The new constitutions often *amplified*, as opposed to merely reaffirming in words, constraints on female political involvement. Moreover, it was precisely the way in which these devices converted women's earlier, not invariable, exclusion into law, and into official, mass-produced script that proved so serious.

Once written into law and put into print, female disadvantages became harder to change. The experiences of the women of Pitcairn offer an indirect illustration of this. In the 1850s, with the meagre resources of their original rocky refuge almost exhausted, the by now nearly 200 or so Pitcairners moved for a time to Norfolk Island, which is about 700 miles north-west of Auckland in New Zealand. To the annoyance of the local bureaucrats, Pitcairn women refused to give up their voting rights in this new location, and their refusal was allowed to stand.[22] Why? Because in 1838 a recognised state agent, namely Captain Russell Elliott of the Royal Navy, had set down these women's political rights on paper; and this proved sufficient to cement those rights in another territory claimed by Britain. The Pitcairn women had it in writing. For most women across the world, though, the case was otherwise. Overwhelmingly, the new constitutions put into unyielding words on paper, into print and into law the harsh fact that the machinery and political life of states were overwhelmingly masculine preserves.

A resulting sense that, at some levels, written constitutions were alien texts helps to explain, I suspect, why – despite levels of female authorship being on the rise by 1750, including on political matters – women seem rarely to have tried their hand, as men often did, at drafting their own unofficial constitutions. A few prominent radicals, the Parisian revolutionary and playwright Marie Gouze (alias Olympe de Gouges) in the early 1790s and Elizabeth Cady Stanton, the daughter of a successful lawyer, and her auxiliaries at the Seneca Falls Convention in Upstate New York in 1848, did indeed publish declarations of rights demanding equal political treatment for women.[23] But this was not the same.

A declaration is an assertion, a protest and a set of claims. It is thus an essentially different exercise from a political constitution, which outlines how a state is to be organised and run. As regards this latter type of document, a *political* constitution, even some otherwise ambitious and powerful nineteenth-century women seem to have viewed it as a 'shape', in Virginia Woolf's words, that had been 'made by men out of their own needs for their own uses'.[24] That this was something that could not be for women to the same degree as it was for men, and certainly something that could not feasibly be crafted by a woman, even as a cultural and literary exercise in the privacy of her own home.

The responses of Queen Victoria, by some criteria the most

powerful woman in the nineteenth-century world, help to make the point. In April 1848, in the midst of Europe's multiple revolutions, and when the Frankfurt Parliament was assembling in the optimistic hope of crafting a constitution for a united and more democratic Germany, the queen noted in her diary how her husband, Prince Albert, had embarked on his own amateur constitutional exercise. He 'wrote down excellent proposals for a constitution for Germany', she recorded proudly, which 'if adopted might be of great and lasting use'. The following month, she described how, 'during breakfast', Albert read out to her the text of the actual (ephemeral) constitution that the Frankfurt Parliament was planning to adopt.[25]

What is striking here is the queen's passivity – not a quality normally associated with her in any area of her life. Victoria's written and spoken German was fluent. Her family's bloodlines were as German as Albert's own. She knew some of the German states well and was deeply interested in their fate. True, like all women everywhere before the late 1800s, Victoria lacked a professional legal education, but then so, too, did Albert. Yet, unlike him, the queen seems never to have contemplated privately drafting an informal constitution for Germany or anywhere else. In this regard, at least, she was typical of the vast majority of nineteenth-century women.

In the later eighteenth century, before the vogue for written constitutions had fully set in, a very few women had been less diffident. As we saw earlier, another female monarch, Catherine the Great, had been unabashed about writing her *Nakaz*, and about blazoning the fact and her text in print as widely as possible. In the same decade, the 1760s, the English intellectual Catharine Macaulay thought nothing of publishing hints to Pasquale Paoli on how to draft a 'democratical' form of government for Corsica.[26] But once written constitutions became better established and more ingrained, a successful and multiplying genre, even such very limited female involvement seems to have receded. Why?

43. A mezzotint of Catharine Macaulay, with a scroll of
Magna Carta in her hand, and a pen in readiness.

War was the primary, though not the only reason. The
widening scale and demands of armed conflict substantially
account both for the masculinist bias of most late eighteenth-
and nineteenth-century constitutions, and the sense of rising
female detachment from them. Since these devices were so
frequently deployed to offer recompense for adequate supplies of manpower, they tended to lay stress on what was

generally viewed as a uniquely masculine contribution to the state, namely, armed service. In constitutions officially drafted across the globe between 1776 and 1870, there are by one count close to 3,400 provisions concerning armies, navies, militias and conscription.[27] Examples of more generalised warlike language ('every citizen is a soldier' and such like) are also abundant. Since women could not openly serve in armies, navies or militias, and since they were not conscripted or expected to fight, language and provisions of this sort immediately had the effect of marginalising them.

Warlike allusions tended to be especially prominent in texts generated as a result of armed struggles, or by states that felt themselves to be under particular threat. When Peru issued a new constitution in 1828, seven years after its successful struggle against Spanish rule, the first three categories of people it declared eligible for citizenship were as follows (my italics):

1. All free *men* born in the territory of the republic.
2. The *sons* of a Peruvian father or mother ...
3. Foreigners who have *served, or shall serve, in the army and navy of the republic*.

As Venezuela had done in 1819 and Bolivia in 1826, Peru also used the opportunity offered by a new constitution to exempt its military veterans from the property qualifications otherwise demanded of its exclusively male voters. Sacrifice on the battlefield was to be enough. Other South American republics forged out of war – Chile, Argentina and Colombia, for instance – made a point of giving local militiamen and national guard members a conspicuous place in patriotic ceremonies, including anniversary celebrations for their constitutions.[28]

Linking men's obligation to fight with an exclusive fitness for active citizenship was nothing new.[29] Nonetheless, the fact that so many constitutions after 1750 made such a point of genuflecting to ideas of this sort was, in one sense, perverse. Perverse, because in some regions of the world female contributions to war efforts were by now conspicuously on the rise. In France, the German lands, the United States, Britain and the Hispanic and Lusitanian worlds (and I suspect in some non-Western locations), there is increasing evidence from the 1750s of women from different social backgrounds forming groups to sew uniforms and flags, stepping in to care for or raise subscriptions on behalf of the war-wounded, publishing patriotic propaganda, and even making speeches in support of war efforts.[30]

A few women in the late eighteenth century and early nineteenth century even openly engaged in armed conflict. Much to the disquiet of Simón Bolívar, his partner Manuela Sáenz insisted on joining in some of his battles. By the same token, and as immortalised by Francisco de Goya in his harsh but brilliant engravings, *The Disasters of War*, created between 1810 and 1820, a woman named Agustina de Aragón joined in the frontline fighting when French forces besieged Zarogoza in northern Spain in 1808. Subsequently decorated for valour and given the honorary rank of lieutenant, she went on to take part in further military engagements.

Yet Goya's haunting image of Agustina, defiantly firing a cannon and standing on a mound of bloodied male bodies, shows her wearing delicate, feminine and surely inauthentic costume. Even when women plunging into active combat assumed quasi-military uniform, as Sáenz occasionally seems to have done, their actions were often explained away as gestures of support for their menfolk (as in her case). Or, as with many of the women who threw themselves into fighting during the European revolutions of 1848, female armed exertions were explained away merely as pleasing confirmation that patriotic and/or radical zeal was so all-consuming that it was even sweeping up members of the weaker sex.[31]

Because the crucial point was that, in advance of the First

44. Goya's image of Agustina de Aragón.

World War – and with only very rare exceptions such as the 6,000 or so all-female, professionally celibate palace guards of Dahomey in west Africa – women could not openly serve as fully fledged members of regular armed forces.[32] They could not become a part of a state's *formal* military machinery. Whatever the quality of women's occasional, voluntary warlike contributions, therefore, these endeavours could not serve to prise open, or validate, a claim to a greater share in a state's official political life.

In a few parts of the world, however, patterns of development were rather different. And this is where events on tiny Pitcairn again illuminate much more than themselves. When Russell Elliott landed here in 1838, he was undoubtedly concerned by its inhabitants' reports about pushy American whalers, and by what this might portend about the ambitions of the United States in the region. Nonetheless, as Elliott recognised, there was no point in his trying to provide for the formation of a Pitcairn

militia in the constitution he drafted here, still less for the introduction of a regular army. Not only was the island distant from
major centres of potential aggression, but its total population
was less than a hundred souls. In these circumstances, preparing
for possible future wars by offering the resident males exclusive
access to active citizenship in return for a willingness to fight
was neither necessary nor viable. Instead, Elliott was left free
to follow his chosen and idealistic path of including Pitcairn's
women among its voting citizenry.

This pattern – of places situated far away from centres of
power sometimes also proving more congenial at an earlier
stage to women's political rights – can be observed elsewhere.
Before 1914, a disproportionate number of the few parts of the
world allowing women to vote were either, like Pitcairn, Pacific
islands geographically distant from London or any other imperial centre, such as the Cook Islands, New Zealand and Australia.
Or they were territories in the wide midwest of the United States
(Wyoming, Utah, Colorado and Idaho), remote from the grand-
eur and easy reach of Washington DC. Or, like the modestly sized
Isle of Man in the northern Irish Sea, which offered some women
the vote in elections for its local parliament, the Tynwald, in 1881,
or Finland, which allowed women to vote and stand for election in 1906, they were quasi-autonomous and peripheral parts
of much larger political units, the United Kingdom in the first
instance and the Russian empire in the second.

In all of these locations, whether in the Pacific world, the
United States or within Europe, there were additional, local
factors at play. But *all* of these places possessed a characteristic
in common: they were not at the centre of things. Before 1914,
a certain geographical and / or cultural distance from big capital
cities and their machinery of rule, especially their warmaking
powers, was usually necessary for women to have any chance
at all of securing a measure of formal, active citizenship and a
glimpse of a more capacious democracy.

## Settler Warfare

At odds with, yet simultaneously revealing about the constitutional treatment generally accorded to women, what happened on Pitcairn in 1838 is arresting in a further respect. Russell Elliott chose to make written provision for the political rights of people who were perceived at that time overwhelmingly as dark-skinned, and who were substantially indigenous to the Pacific. This behaviour stands in some contrast to how, in many territories in this region – as beyond it – white incomers were arrogating territory at a furious rate, and using constitutional texts to vaunt and consolidate their position, almost invariably at the expense of Indigenous populations.[33]

Settler invasions at the expense of Indigenous people were nothing new, of course, and those occurring in the nineteenth century were not confined to the Pacific world, or carried out only by Anglophones. From the late 1850s, Alexander II of Russia adopted a more aggressive policy of 'cleansing' the western Caucasus so as to open up lands for Russian settlers. By the 1870s, some 2 million tribal people had been driven out of this region, sometimes to the accompaniment of large-scale massacres.[34] What was more distinctive about settler inroads in the Pacific was their variety. That, and the degree to which many of the white invaders involved also pushed enterprising constitutional projects.

Between 1820 and 1860, it bears repeating, 5 million Europeans emigrated to the United States. On arrival, many of these men and women relocated to the American West along with, by 1850, some 1.5 million people born in the easterly regions of the USA. The number of Europeans emigrating to Australia and New Zealand was far smaller, but their impact was severe. In 1810, roughly 12,000 or so settlers lived in what is now Australia, most of them transported convicts from Britain and Ireland and the soldiers and sailors guarding them. By 1840, this immigrant population had risen to 200,000 in number and had also become more diverse. It was successive gold rushes, though, in Australia,

as along the Pacific coast of North America, that radically transformed the number of incomers. Between 1851 and 1861, over
570,000 people flooded into the golden heartland of Victoria in
south-eastern Australia. In all its '100,000 square miles', reported
one journalist in 1863, there was 'scarcely a spot on which the
Aborigine can rest'.[35]

One way of understanding these settler invasions is to see
them as a further manifestation of hybrid warfare, as yet another
phase of aggression taking place by way of the sea as well as
over land. Regular armed forces were indeed sometimes actively
involved. During the 1860s, 18,000 British troops were engaged
in fighting the Māori over lands in the North Island of New
Zealand. More often, though, what happened was closer to long-
running guerilla warfare, with settlers using their own weapons,
or hiring vigilantes, or putting down food laced with arsenic,
or simply seizing land and thus forcing its original inhabitants
to starve or move out. It was this kind of more ad hoc violence
that was chiefly responsible for cutting California's Indigenous
population from about 150,000 in 1848, when Mexico was made
to cede the region to the United States, to 30,000 by 1870.[36]

White settlers throughout the Pacific zone (and beyond)
made use of another weapon. They deployed written constitutions as a means to advance, legitimise and entrench their
actions. This point needs underlining because, while historians
in recent years have reconstructed some of the ways in which
empires employed a broad repertoire of laws to order their
captured territories and subjugate the native populations, the
degree to which the new political technology could itself function in this fashion has been neglected or glossed over.[37] In part, I
suspect, this is because of a lingering notion that written constitutionalism has been invariably benevolent and normally acted
as a liberating force. Yet, in regard to Indigenous peoples, as less
lethally with women, constitutions frequently worked – and
were designed to work – as a means to exclude and marginalise.

45. Thomas Crawford, *The Indian: The Dying Chief Contemplating the Progress of Civilisation*, 1856. A version of this was included in the pediment frieze of the senate wing of the US Capitol building in Washington DC.

From the outset, the United States constitution gave import-ant support to whites hungry for Indigenous lands. But it was the American state constitutions that did much of the spadework in this regard. First, because these texts often set down in writing and detailed the territorial boundaries of the particular state involved. The result was to make such boundaries appear rooted in the law and – over time – as something natural and automatic. Yet territorial clauses in state constitutions were often calculated inventions: arbitrary lines drawn on a map in defiance of, or in ignorance of, Indigenous or other rival land claims. Second, both the American constitution and the state constitutions generally treated Indians as peoples apart: as groupings that were not invariably to be taxed, to be sure, but also as people who were therefore not eligible to vote or run for office in the wider polity. As a result, when subjected to violence and ruthless land confiscation, Indians found themselves debarred from the prescribed modes of political expression and policy influence.

California's original constitution, ratified in November 1849, offers a telling example.[38] Telling, because at the start of that year there were only 25,000 whites in this territory, a considerably smaller number than its Indian population. Telling, too, because by some criteria this 1849 document was impressively enlightened. Issued in an initial print run of 10,000 copies (the average for a successful novel at this time), it began with a declaration of rights providing for trial by jury, freedom of the press, religious liberty and habeas corpus. It also banned slavery and enfranchised all of the state's adult white males. But even though some of the delegates attending California's constitutional convention had argued for general Indian rights, these were not allowed. Local (male) Indians could only secure political citizenship in 'special cases', and only if the applicant obtained the support of two-thirds of the members of California's legislature. Like other constitutions catering to settlers, this one also set out to order the land. Its twelfth article fixed the boundaries of the future state of California, extending its reach as far as 'all the islands, harbors and bays, along and adjacent to the Pacific coast'.

One year later, in 1850, this same Californian constitution was being referenced and celebrated in Sydney, Australia. 'Look for example at what has recently been going on in California', a man named John Dunmore Lang told a noisy, appreciative crowd gathered in one of the city's theatres:

A large portion of the floating population of these Australian colonies, including not a few families and individuals who were notoriously bankrupt both in character and purse, have recently crossed the Pacific to settle in that country … But these men have notwithstanding framed a constitution for themselves, that might serve as a model for any nation upon the face of the earth (*great and continued cheering*).[39]

As the historian James Belich has shown, for all their separation by vast stretches of water and different political allegiances, settler societies in nineteenth-century Australia and the United States were in many respects identical twins: and this salute to the Californian constitution in Sydney is just one example of the regular interchange of ideas and personnel that took place between these two vast regions.[40] In Australia, as in much of the United States, raucous attachment to uninhibited white male democracy and new constitutional initiatives tended to evolve in tandem with relentless land hunger and often, though not always, support for the dispossession, and sometimes eradication, of Indigenous peoples.

It was not only radicals and demagogues like Dunmore Lang in Australia who derived ideological ammunition from the United States in this fashion. Consider some of the arguments deployed by Sir George Gipps, who was a very different sort of individual. An Englishman from a military background, he was a reflective and capable man who combined, for a time, the governorships of both New South Wales and New Zealand, and tried to curb the worst of settlers' atrocities in both places.[41] Yet when he addressed the New South Wales Legislative Council in Sydney in the summer of 1840, Gipps drew heavily on American writings on the necessary subordination of native peoples.

Gipps, it was reported:

read a number of passages from works of standard authority to prove, that by the law and practice, not only of

England, but of all the colonizing powers of Europe, as well as of the United States of America, the uncivilized aboriginal inhabitants of any country have always been held to have but a qualified dominion over it, or a right of occupancy only ... until they establish amongst themselves a settled form of government. The first passages read by His Excellency were extracts from [Joseph] Story's *Commentaries on the Constitution of the United States* ... His Excellency then read ... extracts from [James] Kent's *Commentaries on American Law.* [42]

What is striking here is Gipps's knowledge of, and resort to, recent texts by American jurists. The Supreme Court judge Joseph Story's *Commentaries on the Constitution of the United States* had only been published in Cambridge, Massachusetts, in 1833, but by 1840 it was already being treated as a classic and widely cited in American courts. The four-volume work by James Kent, a one-time lecturer at Columbia Law School in New York, published in 1826, had also passed through multiple influential editions.

In other words, when Gipps addressed his lawmakers in Sydney, Australia, in 1840, he did not rest his case purely on British legal and political theories and precedents. Nor did he directly reference ancient classical sources. Instead – demonstrating how sectors of the Pacific world were connected by ideas, not just by trade, migration, imperial violence and ships – Gipps looked to the United States. He took for granted that its white settlers' rapid westwards advance provided parallels and useful supporting arguments for settler encroachments in Australia and New Zealand.

'The peculiar character and habits of the Indian nations', Gipps quoted approvingly from Kent's *Commentaries*, rendered them 'incapable of sustaining any other relation with the whites than that of dependence and pupillage'. There was 'no other way of dealing with them', Kent had written in his massive work, and Gipps agreed. Only the acquisition of 'civilisation', concluded the Englishman, as he drew together these learned American borrowings for the benefit of his Australian audience, could confer upon a people 'the right of ... disposing of the soil they occupy': this, together with the 'establishment of a government' and, above all, 'the establishment of law'.[43]

John Dunmore Lang, a frequent political opponent of Gipps – and of a great many other people – also borrowed from the United States, but in his own way. Scottish, self-made, incurably pugnacious and energetic, Lang migrated to Australia in the early 1820s. Once there, he became a Presbyterian minister, a politician, a litigious demagogue, a newspaperman and an addict of polemical writing, ultimately laying claim to the authorship of 300 works. Lang was also an incessant traveller, doing much of his writing while on board ship. He knew the United States well, visiting President Van Buren there in 1840, studying the country's politics and history, and cultivating a range of American correspondents, especially fellow Presbyterians. He also made a point of visiting Brazil after it declared independence in 1822, along with other emerging South American states. As he aged, Lang's trans-Pacific vistas broadened still further. He dreamed of a future republican Australian federation that might embrace New Zealand, New Guinea and Fiji; and, by the end of his life, he had begun to appreciate his country's Asian dimensions, belatedly recognising the importance of China.[44]

Lang's progress exhibits, then, to a spectacular degree, the range of connections it was possible to construct both within this vast Pacific world and by voyaging beyond it. But Lang's activist career also illustrates how even exceptional exposure to transregional journeying, and fierce attachment to democratic struggles, could prove fully compatible in practice with an adherence to exclusionist positions and racist ideologies.

Of Lang's fervent attachment to certain reforming causes there can be no doubt. He was an abolitionist. He cultivated fellow democrats in Europe, visiting the German lands in the midst of the 1848 revolutions, addressing the Frankfurt Parliament and urging that any local revolutionaries forced into exile should be given refuge on an island in the Pacific. Unusually for an Australian radical of his generation, Lang was also openly a republican. The constitutional future he envisaged for his adopted homeland called both for the establishment of a 'great federal republic', and for a president, a vice president, a senate and a house of representatives, 'as in the United States'.[45]

This future federal and democratic Australian republic was, however, to be configured by white men. Like many Presbyterian ministers, Lang drew heavily on the Old Testament, in which he believed he had uncovered evidence both for the ancient Israelites' attachment to universal male suffrage and of divine disapproval of female voting. As for Indigenous non-whites, Lang protested (too much) against any imputation that he viewed them as intrinsically inferior. Instead, and like other ardent champions of white settlement, he sometimes drew on a kind of early variant of social Darwinism to argue that Aboriginal Australians, like the 'red race' in the United States and Polynesian islanders, were all victims, not necessarily of violence but rather of 'natural decay' and decline. Even 'when actual collision does not take place between the white and black races,' Lang insisted, 'the latter, like the leaves in autumn, uniformly disappear before the progress of European colonization'.[46] This, to his mind, was the unfortunate but irremediable shadow side of the spread of democratic politics.

Along with his irascible temperament and religious zeal, this bundle of starkly held political positions ensured that Lang was never satisfied. He was a prominent campaigner for Australian male settlers to be given wider political rights, as well as free access to what were euphemistically termed 'waste lands'. But even when these objectives substantially succeeded, he remained disgruntled. Like so many political texts emerging out of the wider Pacific region, the constitutions issued for New South Wales, South Australia, Victoria and Tasmania over the course of the 1850s were significant and, by some counts, markedly advanced documents. In South Australia, for instance, almost all male residents over the age of twenty-one gained the vote. For the first time on a large scale anywhere in the world, men both here and in other Australian regions also swiftly secured the right to vote by secret ballot.[47]

But these were still *parliamentary* constitutions. That is, in advance of being implemented in Australia, they had to be approved by the Westminster Parliament in London, which might in law subsequently alter or terminate them. 'Like common beggars,' grumbled Lang, 'British colonists must take what is offered by their betters, and be thankful.' This was perhaps not the only reason for his increasingly strident advocacy of a self-governing Australian republic. Contrary to the expectations of many white settlers, these new constitutions resulted in some Aboriginal men exercising the vote. By the 1890s, some Aboriginal women were also voting. Lang himself was dead by this stage, but this was not the future politics he had envisaged when calling so often and so vehemently for 'freedom and independence for the golden lands of Australia'.[48]

### Tahiti and Writing Back

In some of the largest land masses in the Pacific world, the new constitutions functioned, then, to advance the rights and interests of rising numbers of white invaders and settlers, and simultaneously to further the dispossession of local Indigenous peoples. Yet, as events on Pitcairn in 1838 suggest, this was never the whole story. So, what of other Pacific sites of resistance, invention and exception? How far and in what circumstances could the new political technologies also be used by those who were indigenous to this vast oceanic space?

Some of the answers are suggested by events in Tahiti, the largest of what are now styled the Society Islands, which lie roughly equidistant between California and Australia. In 1817, Tahiti's ruling chief, Pomare II, whom incoming Europeans accepted as a king, began the construction of a royal 'chapel' in Pare, in the north of the island. Once completed, this building was huge. At 712 feet in length, it was more than four times as long as the White House in Washington, and probably the largest man-made structure ever created in Oceania up to this point. It was here, in this grand 'chapel' at Pare, that on 13 May 1819 Pomare read out the contents of a new law code, clause by clause, to an assembly of some 6,000 people – that is, almost the entirety of Tahiti's non-white Christian population.[49]

Finishing, Pomare invited the local chiefs present to signal their formal agreement to his eighteen-point code. He then sought a demonstration of approval from the other islanders. 'This was unanimously done,' reported one witness, 'with a remarkable rushing noise, owing to the thousands of arms being lifted at once.' Once ratified in this fashion, the new legal code was 'printed on a large sheet of paper, and not only sent to every chief and magistrate ... but posted up in most of the public places'.[50]

As these events suggest, Pomare was a remarkable individual who merits a higher profile in global history, not least because, far from being an aberrant figure, he was – in some of his ideas and actions – very much a man of his time. Born in the 1770s, he had spent most of his youth and early middle age warring against rival chiefs in Tahiti and its adjacent islands in eastern Polynesia, and at times was driven into exile. Only with his victory at the battle of Te Feipi, in November 1815, five months after Waterloo, did Pomare feel sufficiently secure in his position to focus on constructing a more centralised and expansionist Tahitian state, and on writing it down.[51]

To this extent, Pomare possesses characteristics in common with some far better-known contemporaries, Napoleon

46. Pomare II of Tahiti, a print published in 1821, the year of his death.

Bonaparte in France (whom he read about and admired), Toussaint Louverture in Haiti, and Simón Bolívar in South America. Like these men, Pomare first established himself by means of repeated and relentless warfare, then worked to reinvent his polity and build up his personal authority by issuing new legal and political writings.

In other respects, though, Pomare's situation was manifestly very different, and his career casts light on what was generally necessary for vulnerable Indigenous rulers to have some chance of turning the stuff of the new written politics to their advantage. It helped, to begin with, that Pomare came to view himself and was perceived by others as a king. Right up to the early twentieth century, a disproportionate number of those sparse sectors of the world that managed to retain some level of autonomy in the face of encroaching Western imperial, industrial, economic and military power were monarchies, such as Japan, China, Ottoman Turkey, Siam, Tonga (which issued its own constitution in 1875) and, for a time, Hawaii. Or, as with Haiti, they were territories controlled by a succession of authoritarian leaders.

By contrast, societies and peoples that were perceived as nomadic, with no fixed connections to a specific stretch of land, and with only loose and fluctuating structures of leadership, were far more likely to be swept aside. There are many reasons why New Zealand's Māori were sometimes better treated by the British than Aboriginal Australians, but one of them was that the former were viewed by incoming whites as being in possession of recognised chiefs. As early as 1830, bureaucrats in London were prepared to concede to the Māori a measure of sovereignty, something that imperial officials never did in regard to Aboriginal Australians. It is suggestive, too, that, in the 1850s, some Māori leaders wanted to go further and form a confederacy under a single elected king, arguing that such a strategy offered the best way of keeping hold of their remaining lands.[52]

As well as being a monarchy and too small to attract large numbers of alien settlers and prospectors, Tahiti possessed a further asset, albeit an ambivalent one. It was both aided and changed by incoming Christian missionaries, who spread into Oceania from the 1790s. Such individuals are sometimes viewed as straightforward agents of cultural takeover, complicit in the business of empire. But, more even than in other parts of the

47. A caricatural image of an early nineteenth-century missionary school in southern Africa supervised by a Black female teacher. The print conveys nonetheless the mixed quality of missionary activism and work for literacy at this time.

world, the impact of missionaries in the Pacific region was a mixed one, especially during the first half of the nineteenth century.

It was mixed because many Pacific missionaries were of working-class and impoverished origins. Some were also female, and a few were people of colour. Betsey Stockton was a freed house slave whose surname was a leftover from her former holders in New Jersey. But in the 1820s, she took the Bible to Hawaii and opened a school there.[53] The impact of missionaries was also mixed, in the Pacific world as elsewhere, because these individuals were often more concerned to protect their hard-won local converts than to offer aid to violent white settlers and incoming Western forces. The impact of missionaries was mixed, most of all, though, because of what they regularly did in the course of their work. In the Pacific, as in parts of Asia, Africa and North America, their interventions gave rise to 'an unprecedented number of newly constructed written languages and millions of readers for them'.[54] Missionaries also introduced into multiple, previously virgin territories that important engine of constitutional transformation, the printing press.

In the Tonga archipelago, it was a Protestant missionary who developed the first working alphabet in a local language in the 1820s. Eleven years later, his successors established the first printing press in the islands. This churned out over 17,000 works in its first year of operation, not just bibles and catechisms but readers and grammars, too. A similar timeline is observable in Hawaii. Here, American Calvinist missionaries, along with Indigenous advisers, designed a local alphabet and introduced a printing press in the early 1820s. It was this that laid the basis for the emergence by the end of the nineteenth century of over seventy Hawaiian-language newspapers. As elsewhere in the Pacific world, Hawaii also acquired an abundance of missionary schools, which, by the early 1830s, were educating some 50,000 islanders, many of them adults.[55]

Testimonies to the speed with which the inhabitants of multiple Pacific islands grew 'obsessed with the printed word' became something of a missionary commonplace. So much so, that it is likely that some of these applauding verdicts stemmed from the missionaries' own eagerness to persuade others and themselves of the success of their work. Cherishing the printed word, they were inclined to exaggerate its capacity to overlay pre-existing oral cultures.[56] That said, it is likely that the extreme geographical compactness of small Pacific islands *did* function as an accelerant to the spread of both literacy and ideas. In the wake of the introduction of written languages, print and schools, these small island communities could come to exhibit some of the characteristics of those classic sites of an evolving public sphere: towns.

As in towns, people on small Pacific islands tended to live closely together. This made it easy for them to assemble quickly to discuss ideas, as witnessed by the 6,000 men and women on Tahiti who gathered in the 'chapel' at Pare to ratify Pomare's new legal code in 1819. The physical proximity provided by small islandhood also allowed for the quick transmission of new skills and information, a point remarked on by observers who were *not* missionaries. When a tough naval captain visited Pitcairn in 1841, he judged that the literacy levels and aptitude for writing on show in its single missionary-led school 'could not be surpassed by children of the same age in England'.[57] Islanders here, as elsewhere in the Pacific, seem to have used plantain and palm leaves as a cost-free substitute for paper, carving letters, sums and words on to their tough surfaces with knives.

But while missionaries played major roles in introducing some of the familiar basics of the new political technology – written languages, print, and expanding literacy – they usually possessed only limited and occasional political leverage in the places they serviced. Missionaries in this vast oceanic region were not just overwhelmingly from modest and miscellaneous backgrounds, but also sparse in number. Especially before 1850, there were few nearby Western imperial outposts to be called upon if things went wrong. As a result, Pacific missionaries were dependent for their survival on the Indigenous people around them. They were also dependent on the local rulers, who expected them to serve a useful purpose, and who possessed in addition their own agendas. This was emphatically the case with Pomare II.

Because the journal on which he worked daily so as to develop his writing skills and vocabulary is tragically lost, and because, while he could read some English, Pomare only wrote in Tahitian, our understanding of this man is misted over by the accounts and translations of those Anglophone missionaries who sought to be his allies. Over six feet tall and physically impressive, with long, braided black hair and marked cheek-bones, and gifted with 'a capacious mind', he aroused in these fervent Protestants a mixture of proprietorial pride and alarm. They worried about his drinking and his eclectic sexual practices. Viewing themselves as witnesses of what one of them described as the 'peculiar, plastic forming state' of an emerging Tahitian 'nation', Pomare's missionaries were also troubled by his sometimes arbitrary use of power and his ferocious ambition. But their fortunes in the Tahitian archipelago were tied to him and his dynasty; and he was anyway impressively possessed by the Word and by words in general.[58]

Converting to Christianity in 1812, some ten years after he began learning to write (an ordering suggestive, perhaps, of his priorities), Pomare insisted from the outset that local missionaries 'not teach any of the people till [they]... had fully instructed him in reading and writing', wanting to use these skills to entrench his authority and signal his power. Accordingly, he had a special writing house constructed where he worked at a make-shift table. Increasingly, though, Pomare preferred to lie face down in the open air, with his chest propped up on a cushion, and apply himself to writing and reading this way.[59]

As his proficiency with the written word evolved, Pomare branched into geometry, mathematics and dictionary-compiling. Like another self-conscious maker and writer of a new regime, Toussaint Louverture in Haiti, Pomare also understood the value of composing and sending out letters, both as a means to seek out support, and to shape how his image and policies were projected overseas. 'Friends, send also plenty of muskets and powder; for wars are frequent in our country. Should I be killed, you will have nothing in Tahiti', runs one of his early, blunt messages to London. 'Also,' he adds in this published letter, 'send everything necessary for writing. Paper, ink, and pens in abundance: let no writing utensil be wanting.' When, in 1817, missionaries set up a printing press on a nearby island, Pomare immediately appropriated this word-machine, too, making a point of being present the day it came into operation, and insisting on personally pressing the first sheet of print.[60]

As he seems immediately to have recognised, the printing press gave Pomare an additional means of underlining his authority and advancing his aims. In a letter published on both sides of the Atlantic, he explained how he wanted to draft a new Tahitian legal code on which 'a consultation will take place. The faulty parts will be corrected, and when it is very correct, the people will return to their houses.'[61] The decision to produce this legal code, along with its contents, are sometimes credited to local missionaries, especially to Henry Nott, a one-time bricklayer who arrived in Tahiti in 1797 and had long since settled into a relationship with a Tahitian woman. Nott's fellow missionaries, by contrast, were eager to stress Pomare's role. 'The laws which the king read to the people were written by himself,' insisted one of them, '... and he afterwards wrote out, in a fair, legible, and excellent hand, a copy for the press.'[62]

The truth may lie somewhere in the middle. Anxious not to be viewed as dabbling in Tahitian politics, the missionaries may have understated their own contribution to the island's legal code. At the same time, however, Pomare was a formidable and dangerous ruler with a strong sense of his own rank and importance. It is unlikely that he ever forgot the gulf in status and power between men such as Nott and himself, or that he was ever willing to be pushed in directions he did not wish to go. The code of laws he read out in his extraordinary 'chapel' in May 1819 is therefore best seen as a joint venture between him and his leading Tahitian supporters, on the one hand, and his missionary backers, on the other. It catered to the interests of both. The document made clear that Tahiti was now officially a Christian polity. It provided for the observance of the Sabbath and prohibited adultery. But it also underlined Pomare's status as king of a unified and expanding Tahitian state, outlining new justice and taxation systems and setting out punishments for rebellion and conspiracy.

As far as Pomare himself was concerned, the promulgation of this code turned out to be the apex of his fortunes. He died two years later, in 1821. His son and successor, Pomare III, died at the age of seven; and *his* successor, Pomare's daughter, found it hard to establish herself. It was these successive disruptions in Tahiti's royal dynasty that enabled France to declare a protectorate here in 1842.

Yet there is more to be said about Pomare II's initiatives than this, not least because his code survived him, becoming steadily more wide-ranging. In 1824, a revised version provided for a Tahitian legislative assembly 'for the purpose of devising and enacting new laws, and amending those already in existence'.[63] This body was to be made up not just of chiefs, but of Tahitian district governors and elected landowners as well. There were further revisions and in 1842 more elaborate constitutional clauses were added. All of these revamped codes were initially written only in Tahitian, and published in that language as well as in English.

The effects of all this, and the political and legal ideas and language involved, require deeper and more imaginative investigation. But these repeatedly revised Tahitian codes do seem to have fostered political claim-making on the islands and to have modified ideas. 'We,' a low-status Tahitian reputedly declared during debates on the code's revision in 1824, '*just the same as the chiefs* [my italics], are to throw all our thoughts together, that out of the whole heap the meeting may make those to stand upright which are best whencesoever they come.'[64] The spur provided by these successive codes to the currency of written Tahitian and to political debate and knowledge on the island may also help to explain why French imperial penetration here proved a slow process. Although a protectorate was declared in 1842, the primacy of French law was not put into place until the 1860s, while formal annexation was delayed until 1880. As well as prolonging local resistance and altering understandings and modes of politics, Pomare's code and its successors also attracted attention elsewhere.

It is likely, for instance, that some of the inhabitants of Pitcairn, who are known to have spent time in Tahiti in around 1831, acquired knowledge there of the utility and construction of a written law code.[65] So, when Russell Elliott drafted his constitution on the island in 1838, he may have been responding to suggestions on the part of Pitcairners, and not simply imposing his own views. Observers elsewhere in the Pacific world certainly took note of the constitutional innovations in Tahiti, and recognised their significance. 'Taxation by representation is therefore the order of the day at present in Tahiti', snarled John Dunmore Lang in 1834, remarking on the legislative assembly posthumously brought into being by Pomare II's actions. 'In that particular,' continued Lang, his sense of racial and cultural entitlement clearly outraged, 'the Tahitians have now got the start of His Majesty's Australian colonies.'[66]

Tahiti, then, provides some of the answers. It shows how Indigenous leaders, especially if they were monarchs and/or successful military leaders, could sometimes deploy a written text to engineer local cohesion and keep hovering Euro-American predators at bay, at least for a while. What happened on Tahiti illustrates something else that we will see repeated in other geographies: namely, how able and adroit rulers and political actors in threatened polities outside the West could appropriate elements of the new constitutional technology, while intercutting them with local beliefs, languages and practices, and use the resulting document as a means to proclaim and safeguard autonomy and hopefully repel potential invaders.

Pomare II enjoyed and exploited the printed word, but only up to a point, and only as a part of what he did. It is highly suggestive that – in advance of circulating his legal code in print in 1819 – he chose to read it out aloud to as many of his people as could possibly cram into his vast 'chapel'. Acting in this way was not simply a response to what was still predominantly an oral culture. It is also likely that Pomare's grand building at Pare, which has long since disappeared, and of which no images appear to exist, signified more to Tahitians in terms of aura and power than the local missionaries were able to comprehend. This was a sacred and symbolic space, and not only in a Christian sense. Quite deliberately, Pomare seems to have wanted to combine new and imported political and print technology and gestures towards Christianity with Tahitian structures of ritual and belief.

Events here also show, however, some of the insecurities under which Indigenous leaders laboured in a world of surging white aggression and heightened long-distance mobility. Hereditary monarchy is a gamble at the best of times. But for people threatened by imperial and settler invasions and on the edge, the death of a strong ruler without suitable heirs could be calamitous. Pomare II was not given time to entrench the political and legal system on which he had worked so inventively. In part, this was because of the very modernities he sought selectively to exploit. Wanting to expand his revenue, the king had started an export business, shipping livestock to the rising settler populations of New South Wales. A returning ship seems to have brought back germs against which Pomare possessed no immunity. For an example of a Pacific island community where local rulers invested in the new constitutional technology with more protracted success and significance, we need to turn to Hawaii.

## Hawaii and Different Modernities

This archipelago possessed points in common with Tahiti. As there, the ruling order had been substantially forged by war.

But whereas, in Tahiti, Pomare II was still needing to establish his position on the battlefield as late as 1815 – just six years before he died – the formidable Kamehameha I had succeeded in bringing most of Hawaii's eight major islands and fifteen or so islets under his control twenty years earlier. Like Tahiti, too, Hawaii was significantly altered by missionary activity. By the 1850s, over 70 per cent of its inhabitants were reputedly literate. If true, this means that a higher proportion of the population in Hawaii possessed reading skills at this stage than in much of southern Europe.[67]

Hawaii was ten times larger overall than Tahiti, and far richer. Set roughly midway between Mexico and the south China coast, the islands could take advantage of the ever-expanding volume of maritime exchange between the Americas and Asia. Yet in this more gilded and capacious geography lay their biggest challenge. Whereas small islands in the South Pacific were, for a long time, too limited in size and resources and – even with bigger, faster ships – too much under the tyranny of distance to warrant systematic Western attention, Hawaii offered more land and was situated in the North Pacific, less than 2,400 miles from California. Even before this latter region was taken over by the United States in 1848, Americans already made up the bulk of the 800 or so whites based comfortably in Honolulu, Hawaii's capital.[68]

Most missionaries in the Hawaiian islands were also Americans. Since it was one of these men, a William Richards from Massachusetts, who played a role in the making of a Hawaiian declaration of rights in June 1839, and in the issue of a full-scale constitution the following year, these texts have sometimes been viewed as by-products of encroaching American influence. Yet, like Tahiti's legal codes, they were in fact hybrid creations. Drawing on foreign expertise, ideas and techniques, they also catered to the priorities, beliefs and language systems of an Indigenous ruler and his prime local supporters.[69]

48. An engraving based on drawings by Hawaiians and printed
in Hawaii at the time of the islands' first constitution, *c*.1840.

Thus, the preliminary draft of the 1839 declaration was the
work of a Hawaiian student at the local American missionary
seminary. His text was immediately passed on to the local chiefs
and the king:

> The King and several of the chiefs … met and spent
> two or three hours a day for five days in succession, in

the discussion of the laws, and the various subjects of
which they treated. In some particulars the laws were pronounced defective, in others erroneous, and the writer was
directed to rewrite them ... [They] then passed a second
reading at a meeting of the King and all the important
chiefs of the islands ... They then passed their third and
last reading, after which the King inquired of the chiefs
if they approved, and on their saying, yes, he replied, 'I
also approve', and then rose and in their presence affixed
his name.[70]

The Hawaiian title given to both this declaration of rights
and the 1840 constitution, *Kumu Kānāwai*, was likewise carefully
eclectic. *Kumu* means stem or source, while the word *Kānāwai*
denotes the Hawaiian equivalent of the Western concept of the
law, but had earlier been applied to local rights to water. The use
of this title, *Kumu Kānāwai*, thus served by implication to link
these new political documents with beliefs and practices already
established on the islands.[71]

The 1840 constitution recognised Hawaii's current ruler,
Kamehameha III, as king. A handsome, intelligent man who
sometimes wore Western dress, but who was alert to the political and cultural tightrope he needed to walk, he was given
command over the islands' armed forces, treaty-making and the
execution of the law. The constitution also specified the duties
of the king's premier and of the individual island governors, and
provided for a kind of bicameral government, with a House of
Nobles and a Representative Body 'chosen by the people' (at
this early stage with no specification as to gender). These bodies
were to meet annually, with new laws requiring both the assent
of the House of Nobles and the 'approbation of a majority'
of the elected representatives. Nor could any law take effect
'without having been first printed and made public'. Kamehameha III was to be a constitutional monarch: 'It is our design

to regulate our kingdom according to the above principles and thus seek the greatest prosperity both of all the chiefs and all of the people of these Hawaiian Islands.'[72]

Even more than with most new constitutions, the intended audience for this document was foreign as well as domestic. Although the 1839 and 1840 documents retained customary local law and language, they also incorporated provisions and practices that were expected to be recognisable and congenial to a predatory West: a bicameral legislature; a constitutional monarchy; a statement of rights; and an embrace of print. By thus making clear that 'the Hawaiian [island] group has a government prepared to administer laws like other governments', the hope was, as one of its politicians admitted, that Western powers would 'allow Hawaii to remain independent'. Accordingly, this 1840 constitution was followed by a succession of treaties between Hawaii and a range of European states, Russia, the USA and, ultimately and importantly, Japan.[73] All of these agreements rammed home the point that, with its new constitutional apparatus, Hawaii had shown itself to be fully a modern state, and was therefore not an appropriate target for imperial takeover. That this strategy should have succeeded for over fifty years is more remarkable than the United States' ultimate annexation of the islands in 1898.

It was primarily economic and demographic changes in Hawaii itself, plus surging American power in the Pacific, that brought an end to this experiment. But different understandings of constitutionalism and modernity also played a part. Hailing from a republic where no titular aristocracy existed, Americans, who formed the majority of Hawaii's increasingly large foreign population, naturally possessed little sympathy with either the country's monarchy or its hereditary chiefs. One can see this republican recoil at work in an early twentieth-century constitutional history of Hawaii. Its American author drew attention to what he clearly viewed as the eccentric presence of women in Hawaii's House of Nobles during the early years of the 1840 constitution, representing this as a further malign expression of the influence on the islands of 'rank', an influence which had now been satisfactorily erased by their absorption into the United States. The ideal of *this* writer was instead, of course, republicanism and a wide male democracy.[74]

To some Indigenous interest groups, however, things appeared differently. Widening the franchise in Hawaii seems in practice often to have increased the electoral leverage and bribery levels of its sugar plantation owners, cattle ranchers and merchants, growing numbers of whom were American or European. By the same token, eroding the influence of the country's monarchy and traditional chiefs also weakened distinctive Hawaiian practices and cultural norms. Like many later Asian, African and Arab nationalists, supporters of Hawaiian autonomy were thus increasingly forced to confront the question of what kinds of modernities they wanted for their society, and – in an unequal world – what kinds of modernity were safe and prudent.

Each new Hawaiian constitution became a flashpoint for these rival visions. The second, issued in 1852, introduced universal male suffrage, while restricting the king's authority to declare war, make treaties or convene the legislature. But in 1864, a new monarch, Kamehameha V, pushed through a constitution that was deliberately a design for a more distinctive Hawaii. It imposed literacy and property qualifications for voters, thereby potentially denting Anglo-American employers' capacity to influence low-level and vulnerable workers. In place of a bicameral system, it provided for a single legislative assembly, thereby ensuring, at least in theory, that the islands' hereditary chiefs would be able to sit alongside and monitor the elected representatives, some of whom by now – like some of the government ministers – were white. This constitution also restated the centrality of royal power: 'The king is sovereign of all the chiefs and of all the people: The kingdom is his.'[75]

This arrangement endured until 1887, when a predominantly Anglophone lobby and a white militia group forced upon the monarchy an aptly named 'Bayonet Constitution'. It was an attempt in 1893 by the last Hawaiian monarch, Queen Lili'uokalani, to abolish this and revert to a version of the 1864 constitution – a move backed by a mass petition – that led to her overthrow and precipitated the subsequent American annexation of the islands.[76]

Another Indigenous regime defeated by advancing empire, then; another land mass in the Pacific world taken over. Yet to compare the last decades of an independent Hawaiian kingdom with the rapid demise of Pomare II's political experiment in Tahiti is to be alerted to how options – as well as dangers – were shifting by the last third of the nineteenth century. It was not simply that Hawaii's Indigenous constitutions, unlike Pomare's earlier experimental efforts, managed to endure in various guises for over fifty years. From the 1860s, Hawaiian rulers were also increasingly in a position to cultivate links with non-Western powers in ways that Pomare, for all his intelligence and enterprise, could never have imagined.

With the number of ocean-going steamships multiplying fast, Hawaii's rulers were able to take greater advantage of the Pacific's potential as a highway between different economies, powers and cultures. At one level, this meant that they reached out more consistently to other small Pacific islands, such as Tonga and Sāmoa, even sketching out plans for some kind of loose political federation with them.[77] At another, more portentous level, Hawaii's rulers looked eastwards, towards pan-Asian networks.

Chinese immigrants had been moving into the islands since the 1860s, either to settle there, or in transit to the United States. By 1870, there was a Chinese consulate in Honolulu. Nine years later, the first steamship owned by a Shanghai company docked at Hawaii. After 1874, a new, elected Hawaiian monarch,

49. A glass negative of King Kalākaua.

Kalākaua, also began discussions for a Chinese loan towards the construction of a trans-Pacific cable for which Hawaii would serve as a mid-Pacific substation. A remarkable and perceptive man, over six foot tall, multilingual, a student of law, and deeply interested both in science and in cultivating Hawaiian art and music, Kalākaua also paid close attention to Japan. In 1881, he incorporated that country into the itinerary of his world tour, the first such ambitious journey ever embarked on by a reigning monarch.[78]

The king's tour took in parts of Europe and the United States. But, in addition, he also paid visits to an array of countries that were threatened by and/or planning how to compete with Western advances. These included Burma, Siam, Egypt, parts of India and the Malay Peninsula, China and Japan, in each of which he sought out and discussed ideas with local leaders. 'The European countries make it their policy to think only of themselves', Kalākaua told the Meiji emperor at a meeting in Tokyo in 1881:

> They never consider what harm they may cause other countries or what difficulties they may cause other people. Their countries tend to work together and cooperate when it comes to strategy in dealing with the countries of the East. The countries of the Orient, on the other hand, are mutually isolated and do not help one another. They have no strategy for dealing with the European countries. This is one reason why the rights and benefits of the countries of the East are today in the hands of the European countries. Consequently, it is imperative for the countries of the East to form a league to maintain the status quo in the East, in this way opposing the European countries. The time for action has come.

There should, Kalākaua proposed to the Japanese emperor, be a 'Union and Federation of Asiatic Nations and Sovereigns'.[79]

The king's eagerness for a pan-Asian alliance was at one level a sign of the growing pressures Hawaii was confronting by this stage: pressure from within, from the rising number of

Euro-American businesses, landowners and settlers moving into the islands; and pressure from without, from Washington's ever more elastic ambitions for influence and naval control in the Pacific. Pressure, too, from the dramatic drop, by the 1880s, in the size of Hawaii's own Indigenous population, not just on account of disease and Western appropriation of its cultivatable lands, but also because many of the islands' young males were themselves making use of the Pacific's wide connections and long-distance steamships, and leaving home to seek work and a future elsewhere.

At another level, though, Kalākaua's plans for a pan-Asian alliance and his eagerness and ability to communicate them directly to the emperor of Japan – a country that would soon generate its own seminal constitution – are further illustrations of the marked political creativity that distinguished regions of the Pacific. As regards the spread of constitutions, the degree to which this vast space was characterised by 'so much ocean, too many islands' proved in practice to be an advantage. Some small Pacific islands were able to operate as laboratories for political experiments that would scarcely have been feasible in larger, more conventionally powerful territories. The pioneering enfranchisement of women on Pitcairn in 1838, along with Pomare II's earlier deployment of a mega-building on Tahiti in order to communicate new laws to virtually all his people, are only among the more extreme examples of this.

Aided by faster ships and the introduction of printing presses and new written languages, the sheer expanse of the Pacific provided, too, for interchanges of ideas, skills and activities between a wide array of locations and peoples, in politics and law as in much else. To be sure, Euro-American migrants brought with them extreme armed violence as well as their own systems of overwhelmingly white, male, but otherwise increasingly unabashed, democracy. But the threat posed by these incomers also encouraged some Indigenous societies to experiment with their own defensive forms of modernisation in response, as Hawaii's successive political constitutions illustrate.

Moreover, to focus only on the repercussions of *Western* inroads into the Pacific world would be inappropriate, because this zone also embraced a wealth of Asian frontiers and societies. In the end, it is perhaps the career of Sun Yat-sen, first president of the republic of China, and a man whose ideas inflect Taiwan's constitution even now, which best demonstrates this point – and more.

The experiences and perspectives of Sun Yat-sen, who was born to an artisan family in a coastal province of south China in 1866, were forged throughout by the manifold possibilities made available by a wide but now more interlinked Pacific.[80] There were uncles who had migrated to San Francisco. There was a brother who lived in Honolulu, and who sponsored his education there. Sun himself learned about Christianity and revolutionary ideas during a stay in Hong Kong. He also spent productive time in exile in Japan, and planned at one stage to use the Philippines as a staging post for his political ambitions. In addition, he took steamships to Europe, the United States and Singapore, absorbing yet more ideas and making further contacts there. But always, even after he helped to stage-manage the 1911 Revolution in China, Sun Yat-sen paid tribute to his education in Hawaii. 'It was here', he recalled, 'that I came to know what modern civilized governments are and what they mean.'[81] The wording is significant.

Sectors of the Pacific world were already witnessing radical experiments in written political change in the early 1800s. But, by the end of the nineteenth century, as Sun Yat-sen's life and career trajectory demonstrate, the range and locations of these experiments were expanding. So, too – and not merely in the Pacific world – were expectations and assumptions about which sorts of peoples might benefit from and design projects of constitutional transformation, and which sorts of the world's peoples might get to define what modernity involved.

SEVEN

# THE LIGHT, THE DARK AND
# THE LONG 1860s

## Tunisia

General Husayn Ibn ʿAbdallāh wrote his letter in October 1863, three months after a Union army of over 90,000 men defeated Robert E. Lee's Confederate forces at the battle of Gettysburg in Pennsylvania. Like many long letters, it was revealing about its writer, not just its subject matter. Ostensibly, Husayn was responding to a request from the United States consul in Tunis, Amos Perry. Now that the tide seemed possibly to be turning in America's Civil War, and an ending to human bondage in the Southern states appeared more imaginable, Perry wanted to know how Tunisia had dealt with the emancipation of its own, mainly west African slave population in 1846. Whether this had been 'met by Tunisians, with sorrow, or with joy'? The question provoked Husayn into an outburst of eloquent and calculated exposition. He himself had once been a slave. Perhaps in his own mind and at some level still was.[1]

More precisely, Husayn had been a *mamlūk*, 'one who is owned'. Like others of his sort, he had been snatched as a child from one of the Ottoman empire's partially Christian territories, in his case Circassia, a region in the north Caucasus. Sold as a slave, he was given a new name and trained up in Islam and on how to operate at a high level in Ottoman military and civil administration. For Husayn, from the 1830s, this meant serving the Bey (or governor) of Tunis, a substantially autonomous

Ottoman province on the Mediterranean coast of north Africa. Although he had risen by now to become a general in Tunisia's army and an affluent man of affairs, and although most of the evidence suggests that he had long since been manumitted, some of the passion evident in this letter may have stemmed from a residual resentment on his part at having once been accounted property. But Husayn's prime concern was with present politics, and with the future. He wanted to make clear to Perry – and to the consul's masters in Washington – his conviction that liberty, constitutionalism and modernity might all be accommodated within an Islamic state.

These ideas rested on Husayn's understanding of his adopted faith, but also on other things. Forced to cross cultural and territorial boundaries as a child, he had continued to do so as an adult. Fluent in Arabic, he also spoke Italian, along with French, some English and Ottoman Turkish. Like many other nineteenth-century Ottoman reformers – Hassuna D'Ghies of Tripoli, for instance – Husayn was also a committed traveller. Along with his mentor, Khayr al-Dīn, another, older *mamlūk* of Circassian origins, a fellow Tunisian army officer and a major political thinker and player, Husayn spent the years between 1853 and 1856 on a mission in Paris. Plump, mustachioed and lacking the physical charisma and intellectual power of his companion, he had nonetheless seized the opportunity to mingle with an array of politicians, diplomats and intellectuals in the French capital, and familiarise himself with its cultural institutions and bookshops. Later on, he would visit other European countries, as well as Istanbul, Egypt and the east coast of the United States.

Husayn's ideas were also honed inside his adopted country. He had completed his army training at the Bardo military school in Tunis, a recently established institution that was a forum for modernising ideas, and which taught the art of writing as well as the arts of war.[2] Like so many individuals drawn towards pioneering constitutionalism, Husayn combined a professional military career with an interest in words and multiple literary genres. At different stages of his life, he wrote travelogues, political essays, children's stories, journalism and legal pamphlets.

So, when in 1857 the Tunisian ruler, Muhammad Bey, committed himself to a more sustained programme of political reform and remodelling, Husayn was well positioned to play a creative role in its formation. Initially, he was made chairman of the municipal council of Tunis, the only major city in this country of some million and a quarter people. In 1859, he also became founding editor of the country's first Arabic language newspaper, *al-Rā'id al-Tūnisī* (*The Tunisian Pioneer*), using type-setting blocks ordered in from western Europe. Husayn filled the pages of this official journal with scientific and literary information, international and commercial news, and booster-ish accounts of the changes underway in Tunisia. The most dramatic of these was the introduction of a written constitution, the first to be implemented in a predominantly Muslim country.

Issued in April 1861, and styled the *qânûn al-Dawla al-tunisyya* (the laws of the Tunisian state or dynasty), it was at once an ambivalent document and profoundly and durably significant.[3] It made no provision for elections, voting rights or freedom of expression and association. Like the vast majority of non-Muslim constitutions at this time, it also contained no specific clauses devoted to women. But the constitution did character-ise all Tunisian residents, irrespective of religion and status, as 'creatures of God', and therefore equal before the law. All native-born Tunisian males, except those with a criminal record, were declared eligible for 'the privileges of the state including service to it'. Moreover, article 87 of the *qânûn* gestured towards a Tunisian future in which political knowledge would be universal: 'All our subjects, without exception, have the right to see to the maintenance of the fundamental pact ... [and] become acquainted with the above-mentioned laws.' Efforts were made to bring different ethno-religious groupings together and to familiarise them with the contents of the constitution. Copies were printed in Judeo-Arabic, for instance, the language of Tunisia's Jewish community.[4]

There were other innovations. The constitution described the Bey of Tunis as 'a prince' who ruled, not at the will of the Ottoman sultan, but by hereditary right. It confirmed him in his command over the country's armed forces, and in his power to appoint and dismiss ministers and officials and to pardon offenders. But the *qânûn* also edged the bey in the direction of a constitutional monarchy. It required him to act through his ministers and through a newly created grand council of sixty members. Presided over initially by Khayr al-Dīn, this council was an appointed, not an elected body. But it resembled a parliament in embryo to the extent that its role was to scrutinise and make recommendations on legislation, and to oversee and vote on budgets. On succeeding to the throne, Tunisian rulers were required to take an oath to abide by these constitutional arrangements. If they subsequently violated this oath, their subjects' duty of allegiance was cancelled out.

Amos Perry, the American consul, would later dismiss the *qânûn* as essentially derivative and inauthentic. Privately convinced – like many Westerners – that Arab states were irremediably and intrinsically arbitrary, he found it impossible to take this new Tunisian constitution seriously. It was as if 'an unfortunate Bedouin' were 'forced to adopt a European costume', he wrote, gaining nothing from this masquerade 'except a constraint in his gait and movement, as painful as [it was] ridiculous to look at'.[5] Plainly orientalist, this verdict contained a nugget of accuracy. Since the mid 1850s, Tunisian rulers *had* come under European pressures to implement legal, political and commercial changes, especially from France and Britain. The local French and British consuls are known to have played a part in the drafting of this 1861 constitution.

But so, during the three years of its planning and writing, did a range of Tunisian officials, clerics and military men, including General Husayn and Khayr al-Dīn. The decision to entitle this 1861 legislation *qânûn* – meaning 'laws' – as distinct from seeking out a closer equivalent to the Western term 'constitution', was itself a sign of Tunisian concern to preserve an element of local distinctiveness. The constitution's provision that all Tunisian males over the age of eighteen were liable for military service likewise made clear a determination to push back against any undue foreign interference. In terms of its fundamental rationale, indeed, this Tunisian constitution is best understood not in western European contexts, but rather in the light of developments in a different part of the globe. Like the constitutions issued in Hawaii after 1840, the *quânûn* was an act of calculated repositioning and defensive modernisation.

There may indeed have been some direct Hawaiian influences. In 1843, Hawaii had dispatched delegates to Paris to secure French recognition of its continued independence. In the wake of this visit, translations of the 1840 Hawaiian constitution are known to have circulated in the French capital.[6] It is possible that General Husayn and Khayr al-Dīn came across one of these during their stay in Paris in the mid 1850s, or learned about Hawaii's political experiments in conversations with French officials.

Whether this was so or not, recalling how Hawaiian rulers deployed successive written and printed constitutions in part so as to demonstrate that their kingdom was 'modern, developed, [and] civilized', and therefore deserving of respect and a decent distance on the part of foreign powers, is useful when getting to grips with the 1861 enterprise in Tunisia. Leading activists in *this* country also hoped to use constitutional tools in order to reinforce its political independence in the face of an ever more aggressive and unbalanced world system.

Accordingly, and as Hawaiian monarchs had done, Tunisia's elite used their new constitution to shape relations with the multiple powers that challenged them. Making clear on paper that Tunisia's bey was a monarch, whose position rested on a written contract with his subjects, was at one level a qualified push against the overlordship of the Ottoman sultan. At another level, Muhammad Bey's successor, Muhammad al-Sādiq, was careful to secure advance approval for the Tunisian constitution from Napoleon III of France. The colonial ruler of neighbouring Algeria, with both army garrisons and warships at his disposal, the French emperor was too close and too dangerous to be ignored. Nonetheless, while Sādiq made sure to consult him in the course of a formal visit to Algiers in 1860, he also ensured that this encounter was choreographed in such a way as to proclaim the two rulers' essential parity.[7] Moreover, just as Hawaiian monarchs combined dealings with the Western powers with approaches to Asia and the rising empire of Japan, Tunisian state actors sought to offset their dealings with the Ottoman and European empires by engaging as well with a different, newer empire. They looked to the United States.

After the assassination of Abraham Lincoln in 1865, Sādiq Bey promptly dispatched one of his army generals to Washington to present a personal letter of condolence to the new American president, Andrew Johnson. Along with this, Sādiq sent a gift of a full-length state portrait of himself. Painted by the French artist Louis-Augustin Simil in 1859, when the bey was still working on his country's constitution, this portrait remains on view today in the splendid diplomatic reception rooms of the US State Department.[8] It presents a careful mix of political and cultural messages and allusions.

As President Johnson was expected to recognise, Simil's portrait echoed in its design what by now was the best-known representation of George Washington. This was Gilbert Stuart's 'Lansdowne' portrait of America's first president, painted in 1796, an image which had since been repeatedly copied, and which circulated widely in the form of prints and book illustrations. Simil's

50. *Sadok Bey* [*sic*] by Louis-
Augustin Simil, 1859.

51. *George Washington* by
Gilbert Stuart, 1796.

painting of Sādiq Bey deliberately borrows from Stuart's grand state portrait of Washington, while also being tellingly different.

Stuart had painted Washington with his left hand grasping the hilt of a dress sword. In Simil's portrait, Sādiq's left hand also grasps the handle of a ceremonial weapon, but in his case it is a scimitar. Stuart had shown Washington standing against a background of heavy scarlet drapes, which are pushed to one side to reveal the storm clouds of the American Revolutionary War giving way to a rainbow, a symbol of peace and new beginnings. As painted by Simil, Sādiq also poses grandly against a background of heavy drapes, but they are green, the colour of Islam; and *these* drapes are pushed to one side to reveal a bright, clean and renovated city of Tunis, a demonstration of the bey's solicitous and modernising rule. And whereas, in Stuart's vision, Washington wears black velvet and gestures with his right hand towards a gilded table on which lie copies of the *Federalist Papers* and other founding American texts, Simil's image of Sādiq is again both similar and crucially different. The Tunisian ruler also wears black, but *his* garment is a military frock coat orna-mented with the stars and emblems of Ottoman and Tunisian chivalric orders, while on his head is a fez. Like Washington, Sādiq gestures with his right hand towards a piece of gilded furniture and a text of national and constitutional significance. Only this document is plainly written in Arabic.

Gifting this portrait to the American president was intended to convey multiple messages: that Sādiq Bey of Tunis was an enlightened and reforming ruler in the tradition of other enlight-ened and reforming rulers; that, like George Washington, he was both an armed defender of his country's independence and a creative and benevolent legislator; and that he was capable, moreover, of straddling different worlds. Like other portraits commissioned by Sādiq, including one commemorating his issuing of a written constitution, this 1859 canvas proclaims something else: that Tunisia is not just a Muslim state, but a *modern* Muslim state. This was also the central theme of the letter General Husayn penned to Amos Perry in 1863.[9]

'Like all other Islamic states', he told the American consul, Tunisia possessed 'a theocratic government ... its laws combine religion and politics'. Yet, Husayn went on, as shown by Tunisia's abolition of slavery in 1846, being an Islamic state in no way meant being at odds with freedom and progress. True, he conceded, 'Islamic law', like that of many other religions, had traditionally 'accepted the ownership of a human being'. But, he reminded the American, 'the *shari'a* had never stopped enjoining the care of slaves'; while 'among the most important legal rules' was the Prophet's 'aspiration to liberty'.

As a modern man – and therefore naturally familiar with the classics of political economy – Husayn recognised, he went on, that 'countries where full liberty exists and no enslavement is permitted are more prosperous than other countries'. But his personal commitment to freedom and emancipation rested on more than just material considerations. 'I myself believe', he told Perry, 'that universal liberty and the non-existence of slavery have a deep effect on refining a man's manners as well as on the development of culture.' Liberty, proposed Husayn, consciously or not echoing Thomas Jefferson, has a natural tendency to draw men 'away from evil manners such as roughness, pride, [and] arrogance'.

To illustrate what could happen to human beings in places where liberty did *not* flourish, Husayn fixed calculatingly on an American example. While based in Paris, in 1856, he told Perry:

> I was at the Grand Opera ... accompanied by a black boy. I was really surprised when an American jumped at the boy as a cat jumps at a mouse and was about to seize him by his clothes saying ... 'What does this black slave do in a Hall? What house are we in? And since when have slaves been allowed to sit with masters?' The black boy was utterly amazed he did not understand what the man was saying and did not know why that man was fuming with rage. I came close and said to the white man, 'Take it easy, my friend; we are in Paris and not in Richmond [Virginia].'[10]

Superficially, this may seem like an anecdote that Husayn has inserted in order to needle the self-satisfied and occasionally supercilious Perry, who was in every sense a Harvard man. Only when looked at in the context of the letter as a whole does it become clear that the point the general is seeking to make here goes far beyond that, and is essentially to do with the human capacity to change – for ill, but also for good.

Whereas Perry remained convinced, as he made clear in a subsequent book, that Tunisia's 'backwardness' was the result of its Indigenous population's 'inherent character' – something that was ingrained, and therefore irremediable – Husayn wanted to argue that a human being everywhere was 'the product of his habits, not of his nature'.[11] Hence his inclusion of this apparently genuine episode in 1856. Husayn uses the story to point out that, for all their strident identification with liberty, Americans, too, can be corrupted into 'nastiness, vanity, [and] fanaticism' through contact with unfreedom. Like everyone else, they can become illiberal and oppressive through long exposure to malign habits and institutions, in this case Southern slavery.

By the same token, Husayn clearly implies, the ideas and behaviour of Tunisians – *and of Muslims in general* – are neither static nor pre-ordained. They can change in accordance with prevailing habits and shifting patterns of thought, and with the conditions created for them by enlightened rulers. Tunisians had already demonstrated their adaptability and capacity for improvement by accepting a total ban on slavery years in advance of the United States. Now, Tunisians were changing their habits again, and embracing a political constitution.

The strong sense conveyed by this letter of the possibilities for change, and for freedom and unfreedom among different peoples, gives it a wider relevance than the particular circumstances of its writing. To many observers, in multiple regions of the world, conditions during what can be styled the long 1860s – the years between the mid 1850s and the mid 1870s – appeared to be becoming more open and plastic, the potential for fruitful advances more evident.

These perceptions and hopes affected debates and actions to do with political constitutions. Constitutions, it now came to be more confidently maintained, would not merely continue to evolve in the customary ways in the customary places. As events in Tunisia, and the issue of its *qânûn* in 1861 appeared to confirm, these devices might well now emerge in other geographies and cultures; and they might cater to different aspirations and groupings. To those who were not white. To those who were not Christian.

## War Without Boundaries

This enhanced sense of possibility and volatility had many causes. But vitally contributing to it was an extraordinary synchronicity of wars. As a result of this further wave of often interwoven conflicts, which erupted over the course of the long 1860s in every continent, some regimes were destabilised or badly damaged, while others were overwhelmed entirely. Prolific warfare forged new states. It also altered the boundaries of older ones.[12] Like other crowded periods of conflict since 1750, these violent disruptions provoked and enabled an array of new political constitutions.

There were, however, important respects in which these wars differed from those that had gone before. In the Seven Years' War and the French Revolutionary and Napoleonic Wars, runaway conflict had also fanned out into multiple parts of the world. But, in *those* huge and elastic contests, it had been the prime Western powers that had been the most persistent protagonists. This was not the case to the same degree with the wars erupting between the 1850s and the early 1870s.

To be sure, in some of them, European states still played a dominant or exclusive role. This was true of the Crimean War of 1853–56, in which Britain and France led the way in taking on Russia, in part so as to prop up the Ottoman empire. It was even more true of the struggles that took place between 1859 and 1870 to forge a united Italy, in which the kingdom of Piedmont-Sardinia warred against both Austrian and rival Italian forces, sometimes with the aid of France. And it was true of what developed into a parallel unification project: Prussia's successive wars against Denmark (1864), Austria (1866) and France (1870–71), which culminated in the proclamation in 1871 of a united Germany and in the issuing of a new, written Constitution of the German Empire.

Yet, for all this continuing European violence, most major wars between the mid 1850s and the mid 1870s involved at least one non-European protagonist. In some of the biggest, European forces operated only as auxiliaries, while the three largest and most lethal conflicts of this period occurred outside the boundaries of Europe.

South America offers one example. In 1864, the Brazilian empire, along with Argentina and Uruguay, embarked on an assault against the Paraguayan republic, a conflict that came to be known as the War of the Triple Alliance. By its close in 1870, this war had led to the death of the Paraguayan president, an ambitious army man named Francisco Solano López, whose military addictions had been stoked by his earlier witnessing of battles in the Crimea. This same South American war also killed much of Paraguay's male population.

The scale of the slaughter here becomes more apparent if compared with that of the American Civil War. In terms of numbers of deaths *in battle*, the latter was the second most destructive struggle of this era. Even so, it is estimated that fewer than twenty-one out of every 1,000 Americans in uniform perished as a result of active combat. By contrast, in Paraguay, the number of battle dead *alone* between 1864 and 1870 may have been as high as 400 out of every 1,000 inhabitants. The end of this war was followed by the crafting of a new Paraguayan constitution. It was implemented in a country that was still under foreign occupation, and where women now outnumbered men by four to one.[13]

In terms of total casualty levels and sheer horror, both the War of the Triple Alliance and the American Civil War were eclipsed many times over by this period's most vicious conflict, the so-called Taiping Rebellion in China. This was in fact a civil war between the armies of the Qing empire and rebellious forces in the south of its dominions. By its end in 1864, after more than a decade of fighting, at least 20 million people were dead as a result of battle, starvation and genocide, and – in the final stages of this struggle – mass suicides, especially on the part of women. Some estimates of the total number of Chinese fatalities have been as high as 60 million plus.[14]

The Taiping Rebellion points to a further respect in which the wars of the long 1860s differed from earlier eras of conflict. Both Western and non-Western empires had always been addicted to warfare. But what was striking about this period was the degree to which *all* of the world's major empires, without exception, came under military pressures and ideological challenge.

This was the case with the three traditional maritime empires, Britain, France and Spain. In the spring of 1857, the first of these was hit by revolts in its northern and central Indian territories. These persisted until 1859, and involved much more than mutinies within Britain's huge, largely South Asian Indian army. This insurrection, moreover, was only the biggest of several British imperial setbacks during this period. France, too, experienced mixed fortunes over the course of the long 1860s. Successful in war against the Austrians in Italy in 1859, and in some of its imperial campaigns – in Cambodia, for instance – France's military proved less effective elsewhere. An attempt to exploit American distraction on account of the Civil War, and dispatch a force of 30,000 troops to Mexico to establish a monarchy there and a zone of French influence, had failed embarrassingly by 1867. Three years later, the Second Empire of Napoleon III itself collapsed in the wake of invading Prussian armies. This led to the creation of the Third French Republic and, in 1875, to the issuing of new constitutional laws.[15]

Spain, too, was both convulsed within and challenged without. A revolution in 1854, which witnessed levels of street fighting in Madrid that would not be surpassed in fierceness in Spain until the civil war of the 1930s, was followed in 1856 by the introduction of a new constitution. Then, in 1868, another revolution toppled Spain's long-reigning monarch, Queen Isabel II – 'a stout, weary woman with a shiny, flabby face', in the words of an unfriendly if accurate contemporary. This resulted in the crafting of a further Spanish constitution and the introduction of universal male suffrage. This same year, 1868, also saw a renewal of armed independence struggles in Cuba, one of Spain's few remaining overseas colonies. This unrest dragged at the economy of Spain's prime commercial hub, Barcelona, and further eroded Spaniards' residual sense of being part of a transcontinental empire.[16]

As shown by the Qing dynasty's struggles with the Taiping, predominantly land-based empires also faced deep crises at this time. Defeated in the Crimean War, Russia had to contend as well with a major revolt in 1863 in Poland. The Ottoman empire faced big wars with Russia in the 1850s and again in 1877–8, as well as unrest in some of its European provinces. As for the Austrian empire, a composite of multiple territories, ethnicities and religions, the traumas of the long 1860s confirmed what the disruptions of the 1848 revolutions had already fostered. Defeated first by France in northern Italy in 1859, then by Prussia in 1866, the Habsburg Austrian emperor was forced to concede territory, and give up his traditionally prime position in the German lands.

As had repeatedly been the case since the mid eighteenth century, contagious warfare worked to drive up the rate and range of constitutional writing and ideas. 'The pen', in the words of the Italian nationalist Giuseppe Mazzini, went on being 'sword-shaped'.[17] As so often since 1750, the economic and human costs of war persuaded some governments over the course of the long 1860s to seek to refurbish their authority by means of issuing new political contracts. Tunisia was a case in point. One reason why its bey was willing to risk reform and experiment with a written constitution after 1857 was that his predecessor had dispatched 14,000 troops to support the Ottoman empire in the Crimean War, losing a third of them in the process, and compromising the country's finances.[18]

As had happened previously – and would continue to happen into the twenty-first century – the experience of military victory also sometimes prompted the making and remodelling of constitutions. Winning the Civil War in 1865 allowed the Republican party in the US Congress, as we shall see, both significantly to amend the American constitution and to force a defeated South into issuing new and, it was hoped, durably transformative state constitutions. There were other examples in this era, too, of the constitutional dividends of military triumph. Victor Emmanuel II, king of Sardinia, was a large, brave and undistinguished man. But his forces' successes in Italy's wars of unification made possible the imposition in 1871 of Sardinia's written constitution, the *Statuto Albertino*, over all Italians.[19]

Experiencing shattering military defeat also continued to concentrate minds and precipitate constitution-writing. As so often in the past, some losers sought to appease their resentful populations, reconstruct their territories and draw a line under past failures by issuing new, compensatory paper contracts. This was the case with post-war Paraguay. It was also the case with some of Europe's losers – Denmark and France, for example, but especially the Austrian empire. There had been attempts at creating written constitutions in the latter region in the wake of the 1848 revolutions, and new constitutional laws were tried out here in 1860 and 1861. But it was the combination of the Austrian empire's losses in the Italian peninsula and its military defeats to Prussia that prompted a more thoroughgoing effort at political restructuring, the *Ausgleich*, or Austro-Hungarian Compromise, of 1867.

This new legislation remodelled the Austrian empire into two independent, co-equal states, closely linked – at least in theory – by their allegiance to the same Habsburg emperor. On one side of the Leitha river, there would now be 'Austria' and on the other 'Hungary', though each of these entities contained multiple national, religious and linguistic groupings. In addition, the Austrian segment was given a written constitution intended to calm and unite its different, restive peoples. Issued in December 1867, this proclaimed both the equality of all of Austria's ethnic groupings and their inviolable right to cultivate and express their own languages and nationality.[20]

Much of this will seem reminiscent of earlier developments, and it was. Issuing new constitutions to compensate a country's inhabitants for their rulers' involvement in costly wars and the burdens put upon them in terms of taxation and conscription; seizing the opportunities and leverage conferred by military success to draft or amend constitutions and retool states; or, alternatively, being driven to do so as a result of shattering military defeat: all of these responses on the part of states and empires had become increasingly evident after 1750. But the sheer blur of wars in the long 1860s also gave rise to some more distinctive developments.

To begin with, the degree to which so many of the world's empires came under violent pressure in this period – China, Britain, Austria, Russia, France, Spain, the Ottoman world and the slave and cotton empire of the American South, among others – convinced some observers that power relations across the globe were now perceptibly shifting in exciting ways. Secondly, these optimistic visions of a world opening up and in an unprecedented state of possibly beneficial flux were fostered by seismic changes at this time in technology and communications.

By now, railroads, steamships, ambitious canal projects and cheap, mass-produced newspapers and books were proliferating faster and in more locations than during the first half of the nineteenth century. New modes of transmitting information were also taking hold. Photography, a blurred, expensive and painfully slow process when it first emerged in the 1830s, had become a far cheaper medium, and more reliable and versatile. Even before the grim black and white images of the killing fields of Fredericksburg and Shiloh and other American Civil War battle sites began circulating in the United States, photography was being professionally applied to scenes of conflict, communicating the work of death in the Crimean War.[21] There was also by now a spreading web of electric telegraph lines – one spanning the Atlantic became available in 1866 – which allowed news to be exchanged almost instantaneously between different countries and continents. 'Before the telegraph', as one scholar puts it, information travelled no faster than 'a horse or sailing ship; afterwards it moved at the speed of light'.[22]

All of these transport, communication and commercial developments had an impact on the quality and effects of warfare. They also made it possible for men and women – and not just in the West – to become better and more regularly informed about events and political personalities and projects in different parts of the world. It became easier for people to compare and contrast conditions, including political conditions, in different countries and continents. It became easier, as well, to travel long distances, physically as well as in the mind.

Jules Verne, a descendant of navigators and shipowners, who at the age of eleven had tried to stow away on a vessel in his native Nantes bound for the Indies, drew on these trends for his runaway bestseller, *Around the World in Eighty Days*. This was first serialised in French in 1872, and quickly passed into multiple translations. Verne makes his enigmatic hero Phileas Fogg, 'a polished man of the world', take conspicuous advantage of the new communications. Thus, Fogg embarks on a series of long-distance steamships, like that linking Yokohama in Japan to San Francisco on the west coast of the USA. He rides epic train routes, too, including the Great Indian Peninsula Railway, which by this stage linked Bombay and Allahabad in the north

52. Steam and speed: illustration from an early French
edition of Jules Verne's *Around the World in Eighty Days*.

of the subcontinent and Madras in the south, and America's own Union Pacific Railroad, completed in 1869. Fogg is also shown in the novel making regular use of the electric telegraph, which 'runs ... along his route', all so that he can circle the globe within the appointed eighty days and thus win a substantial bet.

Wanting drama – and readers – Verne exaggerated the spectacular scale and ubiquity of technological and transport changes achieved by this stage. Nonetheless, there *was* a widening and legitimate recognition at this time that a faster rate of technological innovation was in process, and this served further to foster a sense of peculiar, accelerated flux. It nourished the conviction, on which Verne so brilliantly capitalised, that the world's boundaries were up for surveying, crossing and surmounting as never before.

Some historians have suggested that this rising capacity by the long 1860s to traverse, communicate with and acquire knowledge about different sectors of the world had a tendency to close, rather than open, minds.[23] That, instead of challenging preconceptions about gulfs and inequalities between the world's different peoples, the new mobilities could actually work to reinforce them. There is anecdotal evidence that this did sometimes happen. Take the reactions of a real-life circumnavigator of the globe, William Seward, whose unfairly neglected *Travels around the World* was published posthumously a year after Verne's novel, in 1873.

Seward had been Abraham Lincoln's formidable and invaluable Secretary of State during the American Civil War, and had participated in the constitutional restructuring of the USA that followed. He was almost seventy years old and retired from politics when he took the First Transcontinental Railroad westwards to San Francisco in 1870, before embarking on a world tour through Japan, China and parts of India into the Near East by way of the brand new Suez Canal, and into sections of the Ottoman empire and western Europe.[24] Badly wounded in the same spate of assassination attempts that killed Lincoln in 1865, his angular face disfigured by a stab wound, Seward was sometimes obliged to use a wheelchair. His willingness nonetheless to venture on this global circuit is revealing therefore about the improvements by this stage in the quality and ease of communications and transport.

No one as elderly and physically fragile as Seward would probably, in earlier times, have *chosen* to travel such extensive distances, unless they had deep religious, economic or family reasons to do so. That Seward took this trip was in part a testament to his personal toughness and determination not to 'rust' in retirement. But his decision to embark on a world tour also illustrates how markedly the new transport networks and technologies were spreading, making long-distance travel more comfortable, as well as faster and more reliable. Seward's first question on arriving at a new port anywhere along his route was reputedly to enquire whether it was connected to the telegraph.

Seward's world tour is revealing in a further respect. As he travelled, the American seems to have become more and more convinced that the different peoples he encountered were developing at inexorably different rates. He had never been a thoroughgoing radical. Nonetheless, some of Seward's early statements show a nuanced, open and relatively unprejudiced position on racial differences. 'Philosophy', he had told his fellow US senators in 1850, 'meekly expresses her distrust of the asserted natural superiority of the white race.'[25] Not invariably anti-British, he had nevertheless also displayed a suspicion of that country's vast empire. These positions had already shifted by the time of his world tour, but appear to have shifted even more in the course of it.

Visiting India, he noted that 'in due course' it was likely to become independent. But he was nonetheless generally approving of what the British were doing here, viewing them now as fellow Anglo-Saxon expansionists. Neither Britain nor the United

States would 'lose anything of power or prestige', he wrote contentedly, 'while their colonies are increasing, multiplying, and replenishing the waste places of the globe'. As Seward travelled, looking 'the whole human family in the face', he also increasingly analysed the peoples he encountered by reference to an imagined scale of 'civilization' on which some appeared demonstrably to be falling behind. 'How strangely', he remarked as his steamship approached Egypt, 'this divergence of the white and the dark races perplexes the problem of the ultimate civilization and unity of mankind!'[26]

William Seward's *Travels around the World*, the work of a clever, thoughtful man who played a major role in the defeat of the American South and its slave system, seems, then, to confirm that – already – the global colour bar was hardening, increasing along with the rate of white settlement and pseudo-scientific publishing on racial inequalities.[27] Yet, in broad reality, it was never that straightforward.

I come back to the point that this was an era of multiple wars, many of which inflicted major damage on the world's largest empires. In these circumstances – an embarrassment of wars visibly embarrassing virtually all of the world's empires – the sharp rise in communications occurring at this time was as likely to foster questioning and reassessments of divisions between societies and peoples as it was to confirm preconceptions about them. This was especially the case since it was not merely Euro-Americans who exploited the changing volume and speed of communications and the diminishing of distance at this time. By the long 1860s, increasing numbers of non-Europeans were also undertaking long journeys across land and sea boundaries, observing closely as they went.

We have already seen how enthusiastically the Tunisian General Husayn travelled. This was no less true of his friend and fellow *mamlūk*, Khayr al-Dīn. There had been a 'folding-in of the globe', celebrated the latter in *The Surest Path to Knowledge*

53. Louis-Augustin Simil's famous painting of Khayr
al-Dīn as a cavalry commander, 1852.

*Concerning the Condition of Countries*, a book he and others wrote
in Arabic and published in Tunis in 1867. Not only, argued Khayr
al-Dīn, was the world's 'furthest distance' ever more 'connected
with its nearest', by means of railways, steamships and telegraph

systems, there had also been a rise in global interdependence at a deeper level. It was now essential, the Tunisian reformer insisted, to view the world as 'a single, united country peopled by various nations who surely need each other'.[28] It followed that there could – and should – be no irremediable divides between societies in terms of political organisation and aspirations.

Like Husayn, but with a more considered intellectual and political purpose, Khayr al-Dīn himself travelled widely. A tall, physically impressive man, always immaculately dressed and often in splendid uniform, he visited over twenty European states, as well as other parts of the world, 'studying ...[their] civilization and the institutions of the great powers'. As a result of these journeys, he wrote in *The Surest Path*, the most original Islamic treatise on constitutionalism produced in the nineteenth century, he had come to recognise that 'Europe' itself was not a monolith. There was no clear, fixed and absolute gulf between the Dar al-Islam – the domains of Islam – and a rigidly differentiated West that needed to be reacted against and opposed. The various countries of Europe were themselves different from each other.

European political systems also varied, and had evolved in erratic ways. The career of Napoleon Bonaparte, for instance, 'a conquering, irresponsible and heedless person', demonstrated that, just like other peoples, Europeans were capable at intervals of abandoning their constitutional rights and succumbing to overmighty rulers. To be sure, those Western societies which had managed to attain 'the highest ranks of prosperity' were also those which had successfully 'established the roots of liberty and the constitution'. This Khayr al-Dīn was fully prepared to concede. But there was no reason why parliamentary systems and 'liberty for the masses secured by the guarantee of their rights' should be a Western monopoly. Things were fluid. Things could change. There should be nothing, he argued, to stop peoples from other regions, cultures and religions borrowing discriminatingly from these modes of doing politics. Why 'reject or ignore something which is correct ... simply because it comes from others'?[29]

Part of what is striking about these arguments is the timing of their appearance. *The Surest Path* was published in 1867, when Khayr al-Dīn was in exile and his political career apparently over. In addition, by now, the Tunisian constitution of 1861, for which he had painstakingly worked and lobbied, had foundered. Yet, despite these setbacks, his book exudes both hope and confidence. In it, Khayr al-Dīn and his fellow contributors insist that Tunisians, along with other peoples from the Muslim world, can profitably gather 'from the lofty tree of Liberty', and do so moreover without sacrificing what they are. 'Arabs', he writes, have 'naturally mingled with others without becoming absorbed by them or changing their own nature in the process'.[30]

Contributing to this sort of optimism and extended sense of possibility on the part, not just of Khayr al-Dīn and his collaborators, but also of many other political reformers active in the 1860s and early 1870s, was a third distinctive and momentous component of armed conflict at this time, the American Civil War.

## Out of an American Civil War

Not the biggest, or the most lethal, or anything like the most protracted of the wars of this period, the American Civil War was remarkable and widely influential in other ways. It was bound up from the outset with debates over written constitutions. It was also progressively connected with the growing question of how far those who were not white might actively participate in constitutional systems.

The very origins of this conflict arguably lay in the silences of the constitution of 1787. The men of Philadelphia had not ignored slavery in their long, secretive debates. Some of the delegates, such as the otherwise conservative Gouverneur Morris, spoke forcefully and intelligently against it. But when it came to the actual writing of this constitution, the words 'slave' and 'slavery' were carefully left out. Human bondage in the new American republic was tacitly allowed to become a matter for the determination of individual states; it was not explicitly made a subject for the intervention of the federal government. Slavery, lamented John Adams, the former US president, towards the end of his long life, was like a 'black cloud' hanging over his country. This itself, of course, was a racially inflected analogy. It also carried with it the suggestion that American slavery was at once beyond easy redress and profoundly threatening. 'I might probably say', continued Adams in this same 1821 letter to Thomas Jefferson, himself a Southern slave owner, 'I had seen armies of negroes marching and countermarching in the air, shining in armour.'[31]

Well before the outbreak of civil war, indeed, the situation was shifting and sharpening, albeit in divergent ways. At one level, rising global demand and the increasing availability of steamships and railways ensured that raw cotton was easily the United States' biggest export commodity in terms of value. As a result, demand for Black slave labour increased exponentially. The first American census in 1790 had acknowledged the existence of fewer than 700,000 slaves. By 1850, the official total was 3.2 million. Ten years later, their numbers were approaching 4 million, the majority of these enslaved people working in plantations in the Southern states. With its vital raw material, cotton, in demand in every continent, and its politicians overrepresented in Washington, the American South was not sleepy or in retreat from the modern. It was at the heart of one of the world's most buoyant and extrovert capitalist enterprises.[32]

Yet, for all that, the Southern plantocracy was coming under enhanced pressures. By 1850, the number of American states banning slavery in their local constitutions (California, as we have seen, for one) exceeded for the first time the number of states in which it was still legal. Abolitionist activism among both American Blacks and whites was on the rise. Outside the United States, moreover, the mid nineteenth century saw a still insufficiently explored resurgence in official moves against slavery, and not just on the part of the customary great powers.

Tunisia, as General Husayn celebrated, abolished slavery in 1846. During the 1850s, so did Ecuador, Argentina, Peru, Venezuela, Hawaii, and the leaders of the Taiping 'rebels' in China. In some countries, slave emancipation was accompanied by the granting of partial access to political rights for Black people. Thus, in 1853, Colombia's constitution was reformed both so as to eliminate slavery and to admit *all* males over the age of twenty-one to the vote. These transregional changes help to explain why Abraham Lincoln came to view American slavery not just as an evil, but as a political and national embarrassment. As he complained, the fact that high levels of slavery still persisted in regions of the United States offered easy ammunition to foreign critics of its entire mode of government, including its written constitutions.[33]

Lincoln's election as president in November 1860, a known opponent of slavery taking charge of the White House for the first time, famously precipitated the secession of eleven Southern states from the Union. South Carolina, Mississippi, Florida, Alabama, Georgia, Louisiana and Texas had left by January 1861. Virginia, Arkansas, North Carolina and Tennessee followed. Well before the last of these threw in their lot with the Confederacy, its leaders had ordered the drafting of a new constitution that came into effect in early 1862.[34]

Much of this Southern constitution duplicated provisions in the constitution drafted in Philadelphia in 1787. The new, independent South was to be a republic. Titles of nobility were banned. There would be a president and a vice-president. Candidates aspiring to be senators and representatives here had to abide by the self-same age limits as in the North. Yet these and other genuflections to the familiar scarcely concealed the essential iconoclasm involved. The once United States was now to end. As an approving commentator remarked, it was to become 'among the number of those things that have passed away'. Instead, its territory was to be split between two competing republics. Of necessity, therefore, the former, celebrated American constitution would cease to apply so widely. 'We see a disrupted Union', a Louisiana infantryman named William Clegg scribbled in his diary as he trudged off to fight, 'and feel sensibly that after all no written constitutions and laws ... is proof against a separation.' Clegg, who survived the war, was a committed Southerner. Yet he still found it hard to come to terms with the logic of the events in which he was participating. 'Our once ... best of all human governments', he made himself admit, 'is a failure and was but an experiment.'[35]

*But an experiment*: within the United States, but also outside it, this was one of the aspects of this civil war that most grabbed attention. For the last time in global history, it is possible to find in the early stages of this conflict predictions being made in print, speeches and private writings that the advance of written constitutionalism might – just – be beginning to falter. By 1861, the American constitution was easily the oldest example of the genre in existence. Given the limited lifespans of many South American and European constitutions, the prospect of the United States constitution now also being perhaps on the verge of implosion persuaded some observers that this method of doing and inscribing politics was nearing its end. That the game might be over. It was the American Civil War's implications for Black slavery, however, that progressively monopolised attention.

One way in which the twelve men who drafted the Southern Confederate States Constitution of 1862 deviated from the 1787 Philadelphia model was to place more stress in some respects on state rights. 'We the people of the United States' gave way in their preamble to 'We the people of the Confederate states, each state acting in its sovereign and independent character'. However, there was to be a crucial limit to state rights. No single Confederate state, under this constitution, was to be allowed to liberalise its position on slavery: 'No bill of attainder, ex post facto law, or law denying or impairing the right of property in negro slaves shall be passed.' Successful Southern secession was to be unequivocally accompanied by a perpetuation throughout this vast region of the slave system.[36]

Recognition of this point sucked in attention across geographies. It aroused fierce and conflicting debates on humanitarian and religious grounds, on economic grounds, but also on account of its possible repercussions outside the United States. 'All who are interested in the welfare of India', wrote a reforming Calcutta journalist at the end of 1861, 'must, for obvious reasons, watch with anxious attention the great struggle which is advancing so slowly in America.' Reviewing a copy of the draft Confederate constitution (and it is striking that one had already reached northern India), he worried about what this text revealed about white arrogance and oppression more generally. 'Is there any intention or the faintest wish on the part of the [British] rulers of India, to train her people to self-government, and then ... resign their power?' this man agonised: 'Is there any genuine desire to elevate the native to a higher level?' His only comfort was in what the Black republics of Liberia and Haiti were demonstrating of 'the political capacities of slaves thrown ... upon their own resources'. Surely these two countries, each equipped with its own constitution, he suggested, proved 'the capacity for self-government in slaves and those for the most part "born" slaves'?[37]

Yet, while the outbreak of the American Civil War quickly became absorbed into wider debates about the claims and aspirations of non-white peoples, most Americans going to war against the Confederacy in 1861 did not themselves anticipate that victory would involve improved *political* rights for either free or unfree Blacks. What changed this was the evolving nature of the war itself. It was fought out using a greater concentration of deadly technology than had previously been available anywhere.

Pre-war, both Southerners – who dominated the office of US Secretary of War for much of the 1840s and 1850s – and politicians from the North had devoted considerable amounts of effort and tax dollars to modernising America's armed forces. Quick-loading rifles using high-calibre bullets that were potentially lethal at 600 yards or more replaced older, far less accurate muskets. Wrought iron artillery carriages were introduced, along with six-shot Colt revolvers that could kill at a hundred yards. Industrial innovation transformed matters in a further respect. Railways had been used in the Crimean War of 1853–6 and the Indian rebellion of 1857–9. But both the availability and the military potential of railroads in the United States were greater, in the South as well as in the North. True, the Confederate states were less industrialised than their northern neighbours. But the need to transport raw cotton in bulk over long distances to port cities had ensured that, in the South, too, big money had been sunk into railroad expansion. By 1861, rail networks here stretched for 10,000 miles.[38]

In America, as increasingly elsewhere, the availability of extensive railroads altered the pattern and the human costs of warfare. So long as they remained intact, attacking forces could use them to make rapid inroads into enemy territory. Conversely, railroads also allowed defenders to rush reinforcements into vulnerable areas. This was what Confederate forces did at the battle of Bull Run in Virginia in July 1861. They brought in fresh supplies of men by train, thereby changing the dynamics of the battle and winning it. Railroads made it possible for troops to be assembled in large numbers and at speed, in vital zones of combat; and – just as crucially – to be kept regularly supplied with arms, food, horses, and fresh human cannon fodder for the duration of extended campaigns. So long as rail supply lines remained open, and fresh reinforcements were available, armies could now keep fighting for very much longer. As a result, especially if they were equipped with the new, more accurate and rapid-firing guns and cannon, they could kill far more people, far more rapidly and more persistently than had ever been possible before.

In large part because of these technological changes, the American Civil War consumed men at a furious rate. Before it broke out in 1861, the regular US army had contained fewer than 17,000 troops. By the war's end in 1865, the Confederate states alone had been compelled to enlist and equip a million or so soldiers – this out of a total white population of 6 million. In the North, the number of fighting men also surged. The Union total already stood at 570,000 by January 1862. This had risen to nearly 960,000 three years later.[39] The two sides in this war faced, however, rather different manpower challenges. The South made use of unfree Black labour throughout, as army servants and porters, and to maintain its agricultural economy and railroads. But not until the final stages of the war were its leaders willing to disregard racial ideologies and consider the recruitment of Black fighting troops.

For Northern politicians and generals, the challenges were different. The Confederate states needed only to survive intact and thus win time to consolidate their autonomy. But to claw back the Union and – as the avowed aim gradually came to be – to extirpate slavery, the North needed to do much more than survive. Its troops had to invade, subdue and occupy the huge geographical expanse represented by the seceded Southern states. To achieve this, given the rate at which their soldiery was being killed and wounded, the North's leaders were increasingly obliged to raise men ambitiously across racial lines.

54. Dead African American and white Union soldiers lie side
by side on the battlefield, a sketch published in 1865.

This proved a gradual, often grudging process. In July 1862, after a series of costly battles in Virginia and Tennessee, and in advance of what proved to be greater losses in Maryland and Kentucky, Congress passed a new militia act opening up military participation to Black men. But not on equal terms. A Black militiaman opting to fight for the North was paid ten dollars a month; his white counterpart received thirteen dollars, plus a clothing allowance.[40] Compromise was evident even in Lincoln's stirring Emancipation Proclamation of 1 January 1863, initially composed by him on four scrounged pieces of paper the previous summer. This declared an end to slavery in the Confederate states, committed Northern armies to its dismantling, and called on Blacks to enlist in the Union's armed forces:

> That on the first day of January, in the year of our Lord
> one thousand eight hundred and sixty-three, all persons
> held as slaves within any state, or designated part of a state,

the people whereof shall then be in rebellion against the United States, shall be then, thenceforward, and forever free ... And I further declare and make known, that such persons of suitable condition, will be received into the armed service of the United States to garrison forts, positions, stations, and other places, and to man vessels of all sorts in said service ...[41]

Cautious and pragmatic as ever, and needing to keep his allies close, Lincoln still left uncertain the fate of those Blacks living in bondage in the four slave states that had stayed loyal to the Union – Delaware, Maryland, Missouri and his own birth state of Kentucky. Not until 1864 was substantial Black recruitment authorised in these regions. By that stage, though, Blacks were flooding into the Union army and navy, manning the machinery of hybrid warfare. In all, some 200,000 served as soldiers and sailors, of which 140,000 may once have been slaves. Even larger numbers of Blacks may have worked for the North in the Civil War as army labourers.[42]

It would be wrong to place too exclusive a stress on these high levels of Black participation in the North's military effort in regard to the constitutional changes and freedoms that were secured for a time post-war. Well before 1861, Black activists and abolitionists had shown rising interest in using martial language and initiatives as a means of self-defence and masculine self-definition, and as a way of reinforcing arguments for equal Black (male) citizenship. In some American towns, Blacks had set up extralegal militia groups and practised drilling. Others developed cults of Black patriot heroes, such as Crispus Attucks, a man of African and Native American descent killed by British troops in the Boston 'massacre' of 1770.[43] When Blacks started attaching themselves to Union forces in large numbers in the 1860s, a set of languages and ideas was already therefore in existence to link these actions with the demand for Black citizenship and Black male enfranchisement. As the lettering on a triumphal arch for a procession of Black army veterans in Pennsylvania put it: 'He who defends freedom is worthy of all its franchises.'[44]

Yet, for all this, the outbreak of the American Civil War was of critical importance. Without it, the Southern plantocracy would not have been so rapidly destroyed. Nor, for all the rise in pre-war abolitionist radicalism, would its slave system. Moreover, and as had happened in the independence struggles in South America half a century earlier, the need to draw extensively on the military service of Blacks served to focus minds. It forced some previously diffident but politically powerful white Americans to make concessions and alterations they might not otherwise have contemplated so soon. Though it was not until the evening of 11 April 1865, two days after General Robert E. Lee surrendered to General Ulysses S. Grant at Appomattox, that Abraham Lincoln himself *publicly*, from a White House balcony, announced his qualified support for the idea of Black armed service bringing with it improved Black access to constitutional rights:

> It is also unsatisfactory to some that the elective franchise is not given to the colored man. I would myself prefer that [the vote] were now conferred on the very intelligent, *and on those who serve our cause as soldiers* [my italics].[45]

Three days later, at 10 p.m. on 14 April, at Ford's Theatre in Washington DC, a Confederate supporter named John Wilkes Booth, who had been standing listening to this speech in the damp grounds of the White House, shot Lincoln in the head.

This is one of the set pieces of American history, and one of the great what-might-have-beens of history generally. The same is true of the political reconstruction that followed the Civil War. Months before Lincoln's assassination, in January 1865, Congress had passed what became the 13th Amendment to the American constitution, formally abolishing slavery. The silence of the original constitution was now broken, and the word 'slavery' was inserted so as to make clear that this institution was not to 'exist within the United States'. Three years later, in July 1868, there was a 14th Amendment to the constitution. This provided for all Americans to enjoy citizens' rights both federally and in their respective states, while preventing – on paper, at least – the latter from diluting or blocking these rights. No American state was 'to deny to any person within its jurisdiction the equal protection of the laws'. In 1870, there was a further 15th Amendment. The right to vote *among males*, it proclaimed, was not to 'be denied or abridged ... on account of race, color, or previous condition of servitude'.[46]

The effect of these successive changes was potentially to weaponise the American constitution in new ways. From 1800 to the outbreak of the Civil War, it had been amended only once. Now, in the course of just five years, three new amendments were added. Moreover, these amendments were not centrally to do with the workings of American high politics. Nor were they about constraining the executive – rather the reverse. The American constitution was substantially redesigned by the victors in the Civil War, both so as to allow Washington to intervene in the states more aggressively and to alter the compass of citizenship and the nature of political rights. These actions were combined, moreover, with the imposition on a defeated South of new, more capacious state constitutions. Thus, in 1869, Virginia, still under stern occupation by federal troops, had to commit to enfranchising all of its male citizens over the age of twenty-one, and to providing public education for all, Black and white, 'to prevent children growing up in ignorance'.[47]

Within the United States, the consequences of these reconstruction measures proved a riven and partial thing. Abroad, however, the impact was more wide-ranging and creative than is often recognised. The North's success in the Civil War, the demolition of slavery, and seemingly the removal of some of the structures of racism by way of a dramatic redesign of the American constitution: all of these contributed to the already powerful sense of accelerating change and evolving possibilities. The reactions in some regions of the world were immediate.

The year 1867 in which Congress passed the Reconstruction Act which led directly to Black voting rights in the American South, and to Blacks being elected to state and national offices, also saw groundbreaking constitutional changes being implemented, for instance, in New Zealand. Legislation passed here that same year, 1867, gave the Indigenous Māori population the right to four seats in the country's House of Representatives. And whereas white New Zealanders were required until 1879 to meet a property qualification, *all* Māori males over the age of twenty-one now gained the vote irrespective of wealth. To be sure, had proportional representation in terms of population been applied, the Māori would have secured fifteen seats in the New Zealand legislature at this time, not four. Nonetheless, here was another sign of flux. Men viewed as Black had gained the vote. For twelve years, indeed, they enjoyed superior voting rights in New Zealand to modestly incomed men who were accounted white.[48]

There is little doubt that these measures were connected at some level with developments in the United States. The New Zealand colonial governor responsible, Sir George Grey, was both an autocrat and a self-confessed admirer of the American constitution. He had followed events in the American Civil War closely; and he was deeply affected by the actions, words and murder of Abraham Lincoln, composing eulogies on him and writing obituaries. Grey's reactions in this respect are an example of a wider phenomenon. Although Lincoln was killed before the serious reconstruction of the American constitution had begun, the cult that quickly developed around the martyred president helped to focus international attention on the political transformations occurring in the United States after his assassination.[49] Perhaps the most poignant example of how minds in different continents were influenced by these events are the constitutional projects for Africa worked out by a man named James Africanus Beale Horton.

## Into Africa, with Hope

Horton is a difficult man to place. Attempting to position him too precisely is indeed time wasted, because, more than most people, he was obliged and chose to combine different identities. Born in 1835, he was the only surviving child of Igbo parents from what is now south-east Nigeria. The couple had been seized by transatlantic slavers, but their sea passage to bondage was halted by British anti-slavery cruisers, and they were homed instead in a village outside Freetown, the capital of Sierra Leone. Since the early 1800s, this settlement had served as the headquarters for Britain's naval campaign against the slave trade. It also functioned as a base for uncertain British incursions into west Africa, and as a source of cheap – but, crucially, not enslaved – Black labour.[50]

This background partly accounts for Horton's complexity. To a degree that may now seem hard to understand, he grew up with a sense of feeling beholden to Britain as his and his family's liberators and protectors, and this was part of who he was. His father seems to have adopted the family surname from that of an English missionary in Sierra Leone. But it was Horton himself who inserted 'Beale' among his forenames, as a tribute to the British principal of the Freetown mission school where he became a star pupil.

Yet when he arrived in Britain to study medicine, first at King's College London and then at the University of Edinburgh, Horton immediately knew himself to be African, adopting another forename, 'Africanus'. There were more adjustments

55. James Africanus Beale Horton as a surgeon-major.

after he graduated and became a medical officer in the British army, ultimately a surgeon-major, the equivalent in rank to a lieutenant colonel. The best-known photograph of him shows a slender, evidently fit man, with grizzled hair and a slight beard, who is buttoned tightly into his army uniform. On occasions, it is clear, wearing it required Horton to suppress some of what he thought and felt. 'I should not be too hasty in whatever I am about to undertake,' he wrote to an ally, but in reality also to himself, '[nor] give in to the dictate of passion, or take rash measures.'[51] At times, however, this is exactly what he chose to do. Yet, for all its tensions and the prejudice he sometimes encountered, Horton's British army medical career had the great advantage of allowing him to spend most of his adult life working and travelling in west Africa, 'amongst my own countrymen', as he put it, supported by a regular salary that also funded his private research and his adventurous, attacking writings.[52]

Horton's, though, was not simply a double African and British consciousness. Always reading and writing, he was constantly expanding his range of references. At times, he thought in terms of a wide Atlantic world that seemed to him, as to many others, to be in a state of accelerating flux. He wrote excitedly of how the American Civil War had transformed 'the position of the coloured population of … the great Republic of America', and his knowledge of events here was enhanced by visits to Liberia, which lay directly to the east of Sierra Leone.[53]

Liberia had been created in 1822 as a refuge for free Black emigrants from the United States by the American Colonization Society. It was this body which initially prescribed the settlement's form of government, supplying it with constitutions. But, in 1847, local Black and mixed-race settlers declared Liberia to be an independent republic, and staged their own constitutional convention. 'The people of Liberia', insisted one of its delegates, 'do not require the assistance of "white people" to enable them to make a Constitution for the government of

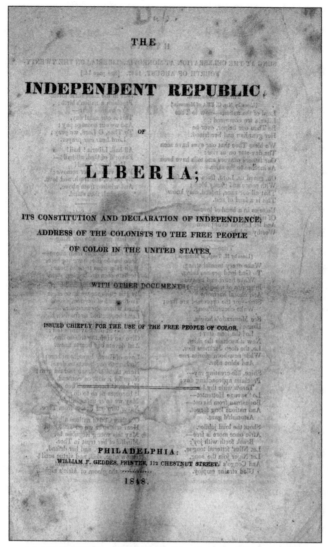

THE

INDEPENDENT REPUBLIC,

OF

LIBERIA;

ITS CONSTITUTION AND DECLARATION OF INDEPENDENCE;

ADDRESS OF THE COLONISTS TO THE FREE PEOPLE

OF COLOR IN THE UNITED STATES,

WITH OTHER DOCUMENTS;

ISSUED CHIEFLY FOR THE USE OF THE FREE PEOPLE OF COLOR.

PHILADELPHIA:

WILLIAM F. GEDDES, PRINTER, 112 CHESTNUT STREET.

1848.

56. A Philadelphia printing of Liberia's constitution of
1847: 'for the use of the free people of color'.

themselves.' 'All power is inherent in the people', proclaimed the
document that these men eventually drafted: 'all free governments are instituted by their authority, and for their benefit, and
they have a right to alter and reform the same when their safety

and happiness require it.' In 1862, struggling with the demands and distractions of the Civil War, Washington finally acquiesced in these arrangements.[54]

Horton was critical of some features of Liberia's organisation and government. As a native Igbo, he disliked how its African American leaders excluded indigenous Black Africans (as distinct from Black settlers) from the terms of the 1847 constitution. Nonetheless, Liberia was important for the evolution of his ideas and arguments. It offered a demonstration that Blacks of African heritage were 'perfectly competent to carry on their own government'.[55] It showed, too, that they could draft a constitution for themselves without white intervention, and without lapsing – or so it seemed – into the sort of authoritarianism that had often characterised that other Black republic, Haiti.

In time, Horton came to position his views on Black and African potentiality within a wider framework even than the Atlantic. 'The history of a country forms a part of the history of the world', he wrote in 1866.[56] As he came to see it, those wanting to understand and improve the conditions of people in Africa needed to pay attention both to the global past and to the global present. This was what he sought to do in the books he wrote and published, and in letters to individuals of influence and in frequent newspaper articles. In the ancient world, Horton reasoned, Rome had conquered the 'savage tribes' of Europe, thereby forcing them along pathways of development that had 'led in eleven hundred years to the gigantic discoveries and improvements which ... [now] startle the denizens of less favoured climes'. But, since the rate and scale of global change were speeding up so impressively, he argued, Africa's own progress to modernity and the full achievement of its potential was bound to be far more rapid than Europe's experience in the distant past. Like Khayr al-Dīn in Tunisia, Horton drew overwhelmingly optimistic conclusions from the technological and industrial transformations of the long 1860s:

Modern inventions, such as printing, steam agency (both as regards railways and navigation), and the electric telegraph, which facilitate rapid communication in a most wonderful degree, leave not a shadow of doubt in my mind that, although it took eleven hundred years to bring France and England to the high standard of civilization which they now occupy, it will take far less time to bring a portion at least of Western Africa to vie with Europe in progressive development.[57]

Some of this confidence in the liberating force of modernisation stayed with Horton to the end. One of his final ventures before his early death in 1883 was to found the Commercial Bank of West Africa, with the intention of establishing branches in Freetown and Lagos, and making credit more easily available to African traders and businessmen.

This interest in economic growth dovetailed with his constitutional reformism. Neither European incomers, nor west Africa's own existing ruling chiefs, Horton believed, were likely to invest in the road networks, railways, schools, banking houses, businesses and more that the region so badly needed. For this to happen, what was required was systematic political restructuring. West Africa must be reconfigured into self-governing nations. Initially, he publicised these ideas in his 1868 book *West African Countries and Peoples* and in articles in the *African Times*, an evangelical newspaper printed in London that boasted of circulating in 'every settlement on the African coast where an educated African is to be found'.[58]

What was needed, Horton urged, was the emergence of 'a number of political communities' in west Africa (and potentially elsewhere in the continent), 'each ruled by a national government'. His own homeland of Sierra Leone could, he thought, be converted quickly into an elected monarchy with a bicameral legislature. Gambia, too, should have an elected monarchy, he suggested, and might be made ready for self-government within a quarter of a century. The coastal Gold Coast region, he proposed, should split into a Fante kingdom and a republic of Accra, where an elected president would serve at most an eight-year term. As for Lagos and the areas dominated by his own Igbo people, these too should evolve into 'independent, united, Christian and civilized' states.[59]

As is often the way with Horton, all this was more radical than it appeared. Unlike his fellow Black activist, the West Indian turned Liberian Edward Wilmot Blyden, Horton was not looking to transform Africa and its politics by means of shipping in people of African descent from the United States, the Caribbean and elsewhere.[60] As far as Horton was concerned, it was indigenous Black Africans who needed to do the work of their own continent's political renaissance, albeit, as far as leadership roles were concerned, drawing on men from Black Africa's tiny educated elites and middle class. Moreover, while his plans called for the creation of strong African monarchies alongside strong African republics, Horton envisaged that all of these new states would adopt 'universal suffrage'.

His use of the phrase 'universal suffrage', as distinct from 'manhood suffrage', is interesting. Horton was a voracious reader and a clever, almost over-assiduous man, so it is unlikely that he was using language sloppily here. He may well indeed have been influenced by reading John Stuart Mill's *Considerations on Representative Government*, which had been published in London in 1861. In this, Mill had denounced 'the silly title of manhood suffrage' on the grounds that it gave male voters 'a class interest as distinguished from women'.[61] An Anglo-Scottish intellectual and politician who went on openly to support the enfranchisement of women, Mill much preferred a careful use of the term 'universal suffrage', and so – possibly for similar reasons – did Horton. His vision of a range of self-governing west African nations, each equipped with its own written constitution, appears to have involved voting by women, not just by men. 'Their position in society should be well defined,' he wrote in regard to improving female education in the new west Africa, 'and no arbitrary infringement on their rights should be tolerated.'[62]

Why did a self-made Black doctor, with no inherited wealth or high social or political position, who was employed by the British army, feel able in the 1860s and early 1870s to formulate and advance detailed projects of this sort in writing and in print? Even more to the point, why did some individuals of higher status and political power, both Africans and Europeans, study Horton's writings and, in the short term, take notice?

Some of the answers should already be clear. Incontestably a remarkable individual, in many ways James Africanus Beale Horton also ran true to form. He operated against the background of the long 1860s, with its heightened sense of political flux and possibilities. He was one more in the long line of ambitious men at arms – from Pasquale Paoli, through Napoleon Bonaparte, to Simón Bolívar, Russell Elliott and others – who drew on the physical mobility of their trade and the confidence that comes from command over others to advance plans for altering a chosen location's constitutional ordering. And, as with so many constitution-writers over time, Horton's schemes took fire in part from warfare.

In 1863–4, he accompanied a British West Indian regiment that was involved in a distinctly unimpressive campaign against the powerful Ashanti kingdom in present-day Ghana. Witnessing these imperial embarrassments seems to have left a lasting impression on Horton. 'Great difficulty was experienced in obtaining transports for the guns, ammunition, and other stores', he wrote of this episode. Instead, the British imperial troops were swallowed up:

The army had to pass through dense and thickly-wooded forests; at times they had to plunge into ravines of great depth, where the pestiferous exhalations of a humid soil steamed up amidst the incense of sweet-scented flowers, which shone through the deep gloom in every conceivable variety of colour. Here in some parts were extensive pools of water, which they had to wade knee and sometimes neck deep, to the great prejudice of discipline and good order; there a rapid and deep stream without a bridge over it, to be crossed in the best way each one could ... Above their heads were chattering monkeys making grimaces ... and there were hideous reptiles of every shape, hue, and kind, from the gigantic boa ... down to the alligators, which basked leisurely in the sun.[63]

Over the course of military manoeuvres lasting six months, Horton claimed later, the British failed even to catch sight of their Ashanti opponents, who were so much more familiar with this landscape, and more resistant to the region's heat, humidity and diseases.

Drawing on his medical training to monitor and highlight the fragilities of white bodies was a tactic that Horton often employed to buttress his own confidence and to counter theories of innate Black inferiority. But the imperial failures he witnessed in this campaign against the Ashanti, and the degree to which the British army units involved 'were laid prostrate by climatic diseases, principally dysentery and fever', signified more to him than this. They help to account for the assurance with which he later pushed his constitutional projects. Once again, Horton thought in global historical terms. In earlier centuries, he reminded his readers, Europeans had invaded the Americas and Australia, bringing with them germs and diseases that had decimated the local Indigenous peoples. But his own home continent was different. Africa killed its invaders. A European or other foreign incomer here had legitimately 'a melancholy foreboding of a speedy termination of his existence'.[64]

'Why are we there?' Horton quoted Britons in west Africa as complaining: 'Why not give it up?' Moreover, it was not simply bedraggled soldiers becoming ever more lost and bewildered in a dangerous and enervating heart of darkness who reacted in this fashion. In 1865, in the wake of the failed military campaign against the Ashanti and other expensive imperial fiascos and indulgences, the House of Commons in London had itself resolved to retreat. British policy in west Africa, a parliamentary committee proposed, should now be 'to encourage in the natives the exercise of those qualities which may render it possible more and more to transfer to them the administration of all the governments, with a view to our ultimate withdrawal'.[65] The empire, it appeared, was going home.

In these circumstances, sketching out constitutional plans for future independent, Black-dominated west African governments could seem a plausible enterprise, and not just to Horton himself. One of the official rationales for Britain's erratic forays into west Africa was that its forces were there to defend the Fante peoples of the Gold Coast against possible inroads by their powerful Ashanti enemies. British lack of success in the Ashanti wars of the 1860s seemed to call this strategy into question. Together with Parliament's resolution of 1865, which was widely reported in parts of west Africa, these and other British imperial failures contributed three years later to the emergence of the Fante Confederation. A loose grouping of Fante chiefs, local kings, Western-educated bureaucrats and mercantile activists, along with representatives of other nearby peoples, this confederation quickly established contact with Horton. Its members also began to draft experimental constitutions.[66]

'In the constitution', declared one of the Fante Confederation's manifestos drawn up in 1871:

it will be observed that we contemplate means for the social improvement of our subjects and people, the growth of education and industrial pursuits, and, in short, every good which British philanthropy *may* have designed for the good of the Gold Coast, but which we think it is impossible for it at present to do for the country at large.[67]

The confederation had therefore resolved to work out its own plans for self-government and to put them into practice. There were to be elected officials, it proposed. There was to be a new national assembly, a supreme court and a common defence policy. The confederation was careful to pay tribute to local political and religious traditions. Mankessim, where its 1871 constitution was drafted, in what is now central Ghana, was a customary sacred heartland of Fante-speaking peoples.

But confederation activists also took some of their ideas from James Africanus Beale Horton, not least his proposals for African economic development. A new independent Fante government would provide for 'good and substantial roads throughout all the interior districts', the draft constitution promised. It would 'establish schools for the education' of all local children. It would work to promote agriculture and industry, introduce new crop plants and develop mineral exploitation. In addition, as Horton himself celebrated, this new, constitutionally ordered Black-ruled Fante state would, as a 'fundamental law', guarantee 'to every citizen equal rights and protection, and direct or indirect participation in the Government'. Detailing these projects in an excited letter to the British Secretary of State for the Colonies, he scribbled at its end: '*Ce n'est que le premier pas qui coûte*' – only the beginning is difficult.[68]

## Losses and Legacies

Beginnings matter, but they are still only beginnings. Examining these different projects for constitutional transformation in tandem has been important. Doing so makes clear how diversely and richly creative in constitutional terms the long, acutely warlike 1860s were across different continents, and across racial and religious and cultural divides. Yet, by the 1880s, many – although not all – of these changes had proved abortive, or been overwhelmed, or were in the process of being eroded.

The Tunisian constitution foundered first. It was withdrawn in April 1864, partly as a result of Indigenous peasant revolts and clerical resistance, but also because of French anxieties that changes in a modernising Tunisia might bleed into their adjacent colony of Algeria. Although some reforms continued, the rulers of the Tunisian state became increasingly entangled in foreign loans; and, in 1881, the French annexed the country, occupying it until the 1950s.[69] General Husayn died in exile in Italy, where he had busied himself funding Arabic publications attacking French imperialism in north Africa and looking after his two daughters. As for Khayr al-Dīn, he eventually took refuge in Istanbul, working on plans for the modernisation of the Ottoman empire until the end.

Post-Civil War transformations in the United States also stuttered into substantial failure. After the 1867 Reconstruction Act, and the passing of the 15th Amendment, African American males became a majority or near majority of voters throughout the former Confederate South, and they voted in large numbers. But these advances were quickly rolled back state by state. In 1876 the Democrats cut a deal, agreeing to accept a Republican president in the White House, Rutherford B. Hayes, in return for the withdrawal of federal troops from the South, plus the granting of home rule there – by which was meant a reversion to white supremacy. Southern whites were left free to use violence, along with tactics such as imposing stiff literacy requirements, in order to restrict Black access to the vote and civic life, and thereby reassert their own dominance. By 1914, the level of Black voter turn-out in Southern elections had fallen to under 2 per cent.[70]

The fate of James Africanus Beale Horton and his plans seems – and in many ways was – just as bleak, and even bleaker. Official British responses to Horton's proposals and to the Fante Confederation were initially mixed. But, by 1874, this organisation had been closed down. Another, this time successful British military expedition was launched against the Ashanti, and the Gold Coast was formally annexed.

This fresh British land grab was only part of a much broader imperial scramble. In the long 1860s, epidemic warfare had put multiple empires under pressure. Some had been forced to retreat; and – as far as Africa was concerned – the scale of imperial penetration by that stage had anyway been modest. When Horton and the Fante Confederation set out their constitutional plans in 1871, less than 10 per cent of Africa was under colonial rule. By 1900, the situation was utterly different. Making ruthless use of the new technologies, European powers had seized control over most of the continent's land mass.[71] Horton himself quickly retreated into economic, not political projects, again with minimal success. Even the £20,000 he managed to accumulate through adroit speculation on the London stock exchange in the hope of founding a Black college in Sierra Leone (well over £2 million in today's values) was frittered away in lawsuits by his descendants.

Yet to focus *only* on these sad, separate endings would be misleading. The fact remains that the long 1860s witnessed a quantum broadening in the range of peoples exploring and potentially benefiting from constitutional projects. More adventurously than ever before, in northern and western Africa, in South America, in the United States and in sectors of the Pacific world, constitutions were extended to, and utilised by, those who were not white, and in some cases not Christian. That many of these projects failed is not as conclusive as it may appear. One of the standard criticisms frequently advanced against written constitutions everywhere has been that they frequently do not last. True enough. But it is also the case that, once this device – a written constitution – has been introduced into a region, then, even if it subsequently fails, so long as it has resulted in some kind of official document, the effects tend to linger and can become cumulative, and can sometimes revive.

Tunisia's 1861 constitution is a case in point. Rapidly terminated, it nonetheless breached a dam. Its appearance signalled more emphatically than any previous event that an Islamic state could experiment with a written, printed constitutional text that constrained the local executive and extended rights. Other Muslim regimes and activists promptly took note. At one level, the Ottoman sultan was persuaded to accept a short-lived but influential written constitution in 1876.[72] At another, *The Surest Path*, Khayr al-Dīn's treatise on the importance of Islamic societies exploring the new politics, rapidly reached audiences outside his own country. Translated into Persian, as well as Ottoman Turkish, French and English, it was studied, for instance, by Muslim political reformers in India.[73]

In Tunisia itself, the failure of the 1861 constitution was also transmuted into a kind of success. After the French occupied the country, Tunisian activists began cultivating a legend that it was these incoming Europeans – and not the local bey – who had been primarily responsible for closing down the constitution. Constitutionalism thus became a plank of anti-colonial Tunisian nationalism. The first nationalist party founded here in 1920 adopted the name *Dustûr*, a Persian equivalent for the word 'constitution'. These trends still continue to reverberate. Tunisia's relative success in the so-called Arab Spring can be overstated. But the fact that this recent political explosion resulted in a new Tunisian constitution in 2014 which thus far still endures may be regarded as a further legacy of what happened in 1861.

In the United States, too, the grim failures of Reconstruction are not the whole story. To be sure, once the original energy behind this movement had ebbed, and for long after – and in some ways even now – American Blacks were not treated as full and equal citizens. Nonetheless, the Civil War indisputably altered, if not conclusively shattered, the mould. The liberating amendments passed in the wake of this war remained intact in the text of the American constitution. To adapt the famous remark of the radical Republican senator for Massachusetts, Charles Sumner, these amendments resembled a 'sleeping giant'. In the future, they could be made to wake and to stir again.[74]

It was the case, too, that, as had happened so speedily in New Zealand, the memory and legend of Abraham Lincoln and his war helped to fuel and influence other, later emancipatory projects. It is significant that B. R. Ambedkar, the jurist chiefly responsible for designing India's independence constitution of 1949–50, regularly referred in his writings and speeches to Abraham Lincoln, even quoting him on the eve of his country's adoption of its constitution.

Ambedkar was a *dalit*, one of India's caste-based 'untouchables'. This was one reason why Lincoln and the reforming results of the American Civil War were compelling points of reference for him, to a degree that they were not for more affluent and patrician Indian nationalists such as Mohandas Gandhi and Jawaharlal Nehru. Ambedkar wanted a constitution that would make the new India fairer and more egalitarian, not simply independent and politically democratic. The examples of Lincoln, America's Civil War and the subsequent constitutional shifts which for a while had promised to transform the lives of excluded Blacks, possessed for him therefore a particular resonance.[75]

And what of the efforts of James Africanus Beale Horton and the Fante Confederation? Manifestly, their situation was utterly different and far weaker. They were not operating out of existing, independent states and governments. With very limited resources and numbers at their disposal, they were seeking rather to create these things. So they were in no position to leave behind a large official archive that later African nationalists could ransack and reinvent. It was not until the heady days of African decolonisation in the 1960s and 1970s that activists and scholars began seriously to examine Horton's life and work. Since then, interest in this man and his work has waned again. I suspect that there are still unexploited sources on him, and echoes of his ideas in later African writings that could be excavated and more closely analysed.[76]

What is already clear is that the so-called 'Scramble for Africa', which wiped out any chance of rapid success for Horton's political projects, had mixed and ambivalent consequences for the spread of written constitutions. This manic European competition for new colonies that in many cases provided little economic and strategic profit, took place in part because the nature of imperial rivalry – like so much else – had changed and become more volatile over the course of the long 1860s.

As a result of this period's rash of armed conflicts, some elderly empires, such as Spain's, were further weakened, while others – such as the Habsburg monarchy – were exposed to more serious strains. At the same time, new and reinvigorated empires had emerged. After 1870, a united Germany called itself an empire, and its leaders claimed the right to behave accordingly, overseas as well as overland. The United States, too, had become more fully an empire. It had not splintered into two competing republics as a result of the American Civil War, as some had anticipated. It had succeeded in remaining intact and, by the 1870s, was at once increasingly rich and more self-consciously imperial.

The long, warlike 1860s also witnessed another portentous change in the cast of assertive empires, the emergence of a remade Japan. After 1868, and yet another war, the political elite of this country were explicitly set on a version of modernisation, and at the core of this project was an ambition to craft a written Japanese constitution. The establishment and persistence of this document – and what followed – would come to change everything.

EIGHT

# BREAK OUT

## Tokyo

The year is 1889, and it is the eleventh of February. Traditionally, this is the feast day for commemorating the enthronement
of Jinmu, the legendary first emperor of Japan. But the press
of people in Tokyo this Monday is far beyond what is customary. Adding to its own million and more inhabitants are not only
incomers from surrounding villages, but also visitors who have
come by train from other cities, many of them in their best
clothes, and some clutching flasks of saké and canisters of special
rice to sustain them through the celebrations. Roads close to the
city centre are unpassable, filled with marching musicians, groups
of *geisha* shrugging off the cold and outraging the proprieties in
fancy dress, ordered lines of schoolchildren, and *dashi*, wooden
floats dragged by men and oxen, which are loaded with miniature
gilded pagodas and painted mythological figures, and have to push
their way through a succession of triumphal arches. But the men
and women inside the palace complex are removed from all this,
shielded by gardens and wooden walls interfaced with stone, and
distracted by a sequence of carefully choreographed ceremonies.[1]
    For the thirty-six-year-old Meiji emperor, the day's rituals
begin early. Well before 9 a.m., he is robed in his heavy brocade
court costume and already en route to the main shrine in the
palace. There, he swears to abide by the new constitution and
seeks approval for it from his ancestress, the sun goddess. After
further obeisances at yet more shrines, it is time to change into

57. *Issuing of the State Constitution in the State Chamber of the New Imperial Palace*, as imagined by Adachi Ginkō in 1889.

his braided military uniform; and, at 10.30 a.m., played in by the newly instituted national anthem, 'Kimigayo', the emperor makes his entrance into the palace's grandest and largest space, the Hall for State Ceremonial.

A woodblock print based on a drawing by Adachi Ginkō offers a version of what happened at this point. It shows the emperor standing on a raised dais under a black and gold fringed canopy, with the chrysanthemum emblem of his monarchy emblazoned behind him and a red carpet snaking out from under his feet towards the hall. Around and in front of him are rows of courtiers, diplomats and uniformed officials. Arms rigidly at their sides, they watch as the emperor presents a scroll inscribed with Japan's new constitution to his bowing prime minister, Kuroda Kiyotaka. Only the Empress Haruko – one of very few women present in the scene – remains seated, albeit enthroned at a lower level than her celestial consort. Later that day, as the imperial couple process through the cleared streets of Tokyo, an inquisitive boy child will have his head pushed down in case he happens to catch the emperor's gaze, and this brief contact with the divine proves too much for his young, mortal eyes. 'I saw cavalrymen with Imperial standards held erect,' his adult self will write in a poem:

And in the carriage that followed
I saw two persons.
At that moment my head was shoved down hard
By someone's hand.
I smelled pebbles wet with snow.
'You'll go blind'.[2]

Properly seeing what happened on this particular day in 1889 in Tokyo still remains challenging. Ostensibly, as a foreign journalist reported at the time, the ceremony at the imperial palace was essentially to do with 'a free and generous gift of Sovereign to People ...[but] nothing to which the latter are in any degree entitled'. The issue of this new constitution had not converted Japan's inhabitants formally into citizens. They remained subjects of an ancient, uniquely powerful dynasty. In the words of an official commentary on the new order, the Japanese emperor was 'Heaven-descended, divine and sacred'. He had inherited the 'sovereign power of reigning over and of governing the State' from his ancestors, 'an unbroken line of one and the same dynasty', and 'all the different legislative as well as executive powers of State' remained as ever united in him.³ Yet, for all this stress on ancient continuities, appearances were misleading, and sometimes intentionally so. Take Ginkō's brilliant representation of the promulgation of this new Japanese constitution. It is not what it seems.

Although ten spaces were set aside at the ceremony for newspaper men, no artists are known to have been admitted to the imperial palace that day. Accordingly, and like other Japanese prints produced to commemorate the occasion, Ginkō's depiction is substantially an imaginary one. The Hall for State Ceremonial was fire-bombed into oblivion in 1945, but it seems unlikely, for instance, that there were wall clocks mounted on each side of its imperial throne. Ginkō includes them in this image in part so as to commemorate the emperor's formal entrance at 10.30 a.m. Witnesses present that day testified that the hall itself was dark and decorated overwhelmingly in red. So, the vivid yellows, greens and purples that roar out of this print are not accurate representations, either. They are examples, rather, of one of many changes occurring in Japan by this stage. The subtle vegetable dyes that had long been favoured by its printmakers were fast giving way to cheaper and cruder aniline dyes, imported mainly from Germany. Like the imperial palace itself, only completed the previous year, like the electric lighting in the Hall for State Ceremonial, and like the Empress Haruko's rose-pink tiered and bustled silk couture outfit, little in Ginkō's scene was fully traditional or all that long established in fact.⁴

But the artist's most significant sleight of hand is an invisible one. He shows the Meiji emperor supreme on his dais in the act of *giving* the constitution to the prime minister: a new Japanese political order being established and bestowed, quite literally, from above. Yet, just before this handover, the emperor had himself received the scroll of the constitution from another minister, Itō Hirobumi, president of the Privy Council. In the words of the historian Carol Gluck: 'in ritual fact, the emperor had merely transferred the document from the hands of one oligarch to another', a point which Ginkō – in this print at least – is careful to pass over.[5] None of this meant that the role of the emperor was unimportant. In all sorts of ways, it remained vital. But, by 1889, he was less the dominant actor in Japan than an indispensable one who was acted upon by others. As his ministers would occasionally confide to paper, Japan's emperor resembled the king on a chessboard. Without him, the game would end. But, while the game was in process, he was susceptible to the moves of more active players. Moreover, for him, as for many others inside and beyond his territories, this new constitution involved and accelerated significant changes.

As far as Japan itself was concerned, that it had come about at all represented a remarkable transformation. As one of the country's liberal politicians remarked, given the prevailing circumstances, this 1889 constitution 'was never going to be one determined by the people'. However, he went on, '[O]ne must not lose sight of the fact that the Japanese people are now a people possessed of a Constitution.'[6] They had made the leap into possessing a set of fundamental laws contained within a single document.

Written constitutions had been spreading into regions outside the Americas and Europe at a faster rate since the 1830s. But some of these non-Western constitutions had quickly failed or been withdrawn; and many had emerged in small locations with limited or no global clout, such as Tunisia, Hawaii and Pitcairn. The case of Japan was manifestly different. Its 1889 constitution was the first to be implemented in east Asia, one more confirmation that this political device was becoming a worldwide phenomenon. At almost 146,000 square miles, Japan was also not a small country. It was larger in extent than the recently unified Germany. Moreover, its constitution would not prove ephemeral. It lasted well into the twentieth century, only shattering – as it was precipitated – on account of war. In addition, the economic, military, technological and cultural power that Japan was fast assembling by 1889 ensured that *this* constitution attracted wide attention across continents. Events in Tokyo illustrate continuing trends, therefore, but they also mark out new beginnings. What happened here in 1889 signalled and furthered a shifting world order.

## The Violence of Change

In some respects, the emergence of this Japanese constitution ran true to form. Its making was influenced by the fear and actuality of armed force, and it was linked to external pressures as well as domestic events and ideas. Since the early seventeenth century, dominant power in Japan had been exercised by successive heads of the Tokugawa samurai clan, who took the title *shōgun*, while the reigning emperor of the day remained revered, but secluded away in his palace at Kyoto. The *shōgun's* influence over domestic affairs was, however, fluctuating and circumscribed. By the 1850s, Japan remained divided into over 250 separate administrative units, each with its own bureaucracy, military force and taxation system, and each headed by a *daimyo*, a quasi-feudal lord who owed obedience to the *shōgun* but was in practice substantially autonomous. This high level of decentralisation, together with the country's long island coastlines, made Japan progressively vulnerable to the ambitions and rising naval reach of competing foreign empires.[7]

For all the efforts and aspirations of some of its rulers, Tokugawa Japan had never been entirely cut off from wider developments. It was integrated in regional markets, and had long had connections with other continents by way of China and generations of Dutch merchants. But, by the mid nineteenth century, the scale and the potential danger of foreign interventions was expanding. There were the British who, in the course of two Opium Wars (1839–42 and 1856–60) attacked coastal China, a fellow East Asian empire and monarchy with which Japan possessed long-standing connections. There was the United States, increasingly flexing its naval and commercial muscles in the Pacific. In July 1853, Commodore Matthew Perry of the US Navy, a veteran both of the War of 1812 and the Mexican–American war, arrived at the entrance of Edo (the future Tokyo) Bay, with his steam-driven naval frigates, his cannon, sailors, marines and military bands, demanding with menaces American access to Japanese ports and markets.

Shortly after, another foreign frigate arrived. This time, it was the *Pallada* of the Russian Imperial Navy, by now, second only to Britain's Royal Navy in terms of size, and markedly active in the North Pacific. With Ivan Goncharov, future author of the novel *Oblomov*, on board, busy scribbling another bestseller out of this voyage, the *Pallada* moored off Nagasaki in western Japan before sailing on to survey other coastal sites. Its mission, like that of Perry's flotilla of black ships – which paid a further visit in February 1854 – was to open up Japan to the influences and traders of its empire of origin, in this case Russia. There were newer predators, too. In September 1860, four Prussian warships arrived off the coast of Japan, on the look-out for commercial treaties, but also primed by what was already a growing German interest in acquiring extra-European naval bases and colonies.[8]

Although Japan's defences were strengthened in response to these maritime incursions, their rising occurrence, and the concessions they were able to extort, sapped the legitimacy of the Tokugawa regime and fostered and emboldened opposition. Largely as a result of this, from early 1868 to the summer of 1869, Japan was convulsed by what became known as the Boshin War. This involved court nobles and low-ranking samurai families, mainly from the west of the country, taking up arms against the Tokugawa *shōgun* and his forces, but doing so in the name of the emperor and with the avowed aim of reasserting his authority and Japanese autonomy and prestige. The resulting fighting on land and sea drew in 120,000 troops; and the different combatants made extensive use of modern weaponry. The struggle ended, at least officially, with the defeat of the Tokugawa. The young and gangly Emperor Mutsuhito was brought from Kyoto by the victors and installed in the former Tokugawa headquarters at Edo, now renamed Tokyo. A new reign name was created for him, 'Meiji', meaning 'enlightened rule'.[9]

In March 1868, this Meiji emperor lent his name to a five-point Charter Oath, which had been drafted for him by others. 'Deliberative assemblies', it was promised, were to be 'widely established and all matters decided by public discussion'. In the future, all classes in Japan, 'high and low', were to 'unite in vigorously carrying out the administration of affairs of state'. All 'the common people, no less than the civil and military officials' would now be free to pursue their 'own calling'. Evil customs from the past were to give way beneficially to 'the just laws of nations'. Finally, knowledge was to be 'sought throughout the world so as to strengthen the foundations of imperial rule'.[10]

As the vagueness of these ambitious undertakings suggests, Japan's newly dominant elite actors were not united among themselves. Nor were they secure or immediately confident in their power. The full scale of what was nonetheless rapidly accomplished is still partly obscured by Japanese historians' relative neglect of the decade following the Boshin civil war, the 1870s. Moreover, at the time, members of the Meiji elite were sometimes more anxious to stress conservatism and continuities, than to admit to the full range of changes that their actions were letting loose. By the start of the twentieth century, indeed, the events of 1868–69 and their aftermath had come officially to be termed the *Meiji Ishin*, or Meiji Restoration. *Ishin*, a word that derives from the Chinese classics, possesses connotations of renewal and regeneration.[11] Even so, making use of this term was hardly the same as admitting to a revolution. Yet, in at least three respects, what happened in Japan between the end of the Boshin war and the issuing of the new constitution in 1889 was both radical and transformative.

To begin with, the new Meiji regime rapidly effected changes in Japan's governing order and in its economic, social and techno-logical organisation. Taxation was centralised, and some of the proceeds were ploughed back into the country's economy and infrastructure. As early as 1869, telegraph lines were beginning to sprout up around the country. Two years later, a new postal system was introduced. Railroad construction was prioritised, so that, by 1872, Tokyo was already connected to Yokohama, the major port for foreign trade. There were new banking and industrial initiatives, too. By the 1880s, Japan possessed more than twenty cotton-spinning factories, while its coal mines were edging out British, American and Australian competitors in the big and important Shanghai coal market.[12]

A second substantial set of changes came from below. Although Meiji governments quickly worked at increasing their control over Japan's population by way of replacing a semi-autonomous samurai soldiery with military conscription, and by introducing compulsory mass education, there was a marked rise after 1869 in popular and informal political activism and rights-talk. This was assisted by a quantum growth in the availability and variety of print. Print here was nothing new, of course. Already, in the eighteenth century, Japan had possessed hundreds of booksellers, as well as a range of lending libraries, and a tradition of cheap, one-page broadsheets. What under-went alterations in the wake of the Boshin War was the range, volume and content of what was being published.

In 1864, there had been only one commercial Japanese-lan-guage newspaper. By the 1880s, however, more newspaper and periodical titles were reputedly being issued in Tokyo than in London; though, until the early 1900s, even the biggest Japanese newspapers had smaller circulations than their counterparts in Britain, the USA or India. Levels of book publication also soared. By 1914, they were running at a higher rate in Japan than anywhere else on the globe, except Germany. Translations of foreign political texts, already on the rise before 1868, also became more numerous. John Stuart Mill's philosophical essay *On Liberty* passed into Japanese for the first time in 1872. Ten years later, so did Jean-Jacques Rousseau's *Social Contract*.[13]

The impact that this ferment of print, along with wider changes, could have on individuals even at a modest level in Japanese society is suggested by the experiences and awakenings of one Chiba Takusaburō (1852–83). From a samurai background, Chiba lost his birth parents when he was very young, and his early life was further catastrophically disrupted by the Boshin War. At just seventeen, he 'answered the call for men to enlist and became a foot soldier', seeing action twice over while fighting for the Tokugawa. Emerging on the losing side, he became a 'wanderer seeking truth', a perennial student, essentially adrift. He explored mathematics, medicine, Buddhism and variants of Christianity. Then, in 1880, and for most of the last three years of his brief life, Chiba settled as a teacher in Itsukaichi, a market and lumber town to the west of Tokyo, finding some peace there and also a measure of sociability and achievement.[14]

For all that Itsukaichi was primarily a commercial and agrarian centre, by this stage the town had acquired its own Arts Lecture Society, a study and debating group where local men interested in political theories and modern political practice could meet and argue with others of their kind. As in many other local study and debating groups mushrooming in Japan at this time, the thirty-odd members of this society devoted their meetings to discussing translations of Western texts, in this case, works by Mill, Blackstone, Locke and Montesquieu, and to examining the political lessons to be drawn from episodes in Japan's real and mythic history and the Confucian classics. Participating in these regular meetings seems to have eased Chiba's loneliness and focused his mind. Along with other members of the society, he quickly set to work on a draft constitution for his country. He also penned an essay entitled 'The Way of the King', an enthusiastic argument for the introduction into Japan of a constitutional monarchy.

'What do we need in these days of Meiji?' he enquired at its start: 'Constitutional government – yes, that is what we need.' There must be a written constitution and a Japanese parliament, he insisted; not least because – as the Charter Oath of 1868 had demonstrated – the emperor himself 'openly' favoured such changes. But the Japanese people, too, Chiba argued, had an important role to play. They also had rights, and there needed to be collaboration between them and their emperor. 'Is this not the time,' he urged, aglow with the seeming possibilities of a new era, 'when we, the people, in response to the imperial wishes, should set up a constitutional government which guarantees the people's liberties?' His essay, he hoped, would 'serve as a ship to carry them to the shores of understanding'.[15]

Along with its frail author, who quickly succumbed to tuberculosis, 'The Way of the King' was swiftly forgotten, the manuscript only resurfacing when it was discovered in a garden shed in the 1960s. Its importance lies less in its specific content than in the circumstances of its making, and in what these demonstrate: namely that, by the 1870s and 1880s, *diverse* forms of constitutional activism and argument were fast evolving in Japan.

As the confidence with which Chiba sets out his arguments suggests, by issuing the Charter Oath in 1868 – and thereby promulgating what appeared to be imperial endorsement of deliberative assemblies, wide political discussion and mass involvement in projects of government – the leading men of Meiji provided a level of sanction for a range of unofficial constitutional activism. Intentionally or no, they lent some legitimacy to the subsequent spread of political and debating societies, petitioning campaigns, newspapers, pamphleteering and translations. As had happened earlier in other parts of the world, there was also a turn at this time towards informal constitution-writing. Over ninety such texts are known to have been produced in Japan between 1867 and 1887, and there must have been many more that have not survived.[16] Some of these informal Japanese constitutions were radical in their demands, and produced by men far more resilient than Chiba Takusaburō.

The writings of Ueki Emori are an extreme case in point. From a middle-ranking samurai family, he studied works by Mill, Bentham, Rousseau and Tocqueville in their recent Japanese translations, along with a range of different countries' constitutions. His own *A Private Draft of the Japanese Constitution* was published in 1881. Ueki wanted a federal structure of government to be introduced in Japan, and possibly in the long run the creation, too, of a global federation. He championed the right of armed resistance to unjust and oppressive governments; and he advocated the extension of the franchise to all Japanese taxpayers, including women. In this pamphlet, as in some of his other writings, Ueki also made it clear that his intended audience was the population at large:

> With your permission, honorable farmers of Japan, and honorable merchants of Japan, and honorable workmen and artisans of Japan, and beyond them honorable warriors of Japan, and honorable physicians and boatmen, and coachmen, and huntsmen, and candy peddlers, and wet nurses, and new commoners – I humbly address all of you, together. You, each and all of you, are equally in possession of a great treasure ... that which we call the right to freedom.[17]

Yet, for all the energy and creativity of this evolving Freedom and People's Rights Movement, as it came to be styled, such aspirations and demands from below were blunted by the third major revolutionary change assisted by the Boshin War, the emergence and consolidation of a substantially new and tougher Japanese governing class.

Intimations of this change were already in evidence *before* 1868. One demonstration of this is a London bank note dating from 1864. It bears the signatures of five Japanese men in their early twenties, all of them from low-level samurai backgrounds, and all hailing from the traditionally anti-Tokugawa Chōshū domain in the extreme south-west of the country. In May 1863, in defiance of Tokugawa rulings against travel abroad, these five men had smuggled themselves in disguise on to a merchant ship moored at Yokohama. Eventually, by way of Shanghai and by means of working their passage, they managed to reach London, incontestably still the world's richest and most tentacular metropolis.

The Chōshū Five, as they came to be known, attached themselves to University College London, where they studied engineering. They also began exploring some of the local sources of Western power, wealth, innovation and reach, one of which was the Bank of England. Impressed by the men's chutzpah, and in all probability, too, by their being the first Japanese individuals they had ever closely encountered, the bank's officials allowed the five men to sign their names on a thousand pound note. It is worth glancing at who these signatories were, and at what happened to them in the wake of the Boshin War.[18]

One of the five, Inoue Masuru, would become Japan's first director of railways in 1871, and would later establish its earliest manufacturer of steam locomotives. Another, Endō Kinsuke, would become head of the new Japanese National Mint, set up in 1871, and help to establish a unified currency. Then there was Yamao Yōzō. Post-1868, having studied further in Glasgow, he quickly turned his energies to expanding shipbuilding and iron works in Japan, before founding its first college of engineering. There was also Inoue Kaoru. By 1871, he was Japan's vice minister of finance, and went on to become the country's first minister of foreign affairs. The fifth shabbily dressed but assertive young man signing this Bank of England note in 1864 was Itō Hirobumi. A future prime minister four times over, it was he who would become the most prominent facilitator of the Japanese constitution.

Here, memorialised in signatures on a single foreign bank note, are extreme examples of the sort of ambitious, often self-made men who powered the Meiji Restoration after 1868, frequently benefited from it personally, and in some cases sought both to direct and to contain its revolutionary potential. The background of the Chōshū Five illuminates something else. It helps to qualify the claim that is sometimes too easily made about the transformations implemented in Japan after the Boshin War: namely, that these were exercises in thoroughgoing westernisation.

When they embarked on their dangerous voyage to London in 1863, these five men of Chōshū were certainly in search of knowledge, advancement and new experiences, but they were not driven by a spirit of generous cosmopolitanism. Three of them had earlier helped to burn down a new British legation being constructed in the outskirts of Edo, viewing the building as further malign evidence of creeping foreign interference in Japan. Itō Hirobumi himself, one of the arsonists involved, went further. Born in 1841, the son of a man who worked as a gardener before the family was adopted into the lowest ranks of a samurai clan, Itō, like his companions, was trained in violence. He was also willing to resort to it off the battlefield, personally carrying out the successful assassination of a Japanese scholar wrongly accused of disrespect to the emperor.[19]

As he aged and became ever more powerful, Itō acquired a more courtly and urbane exterior, regularly exploiting the

English he had learned in London in 1863–64, and had polished in five subsequent visits to the United States, to give smooth interviews to American and European journalists.[20] But it is possible that Itō's attitudes to Western societies did not change entirely over time. These regions of the world were to be scrutinised and gutted for useful ideas, systems and inventions, yes. But borrowing from abroad was not to be allowed to contaminate Japan unduly, or to dilute its most important traditions and characteristics.

As was true of that other soldier constitutionalist, Khayr al-Dīn of Tunisia, there was a degree, indeed, to which frequent visits to Western countries allowed Itō and his closest colleagues not simply to observe and learn, but also to evolve a sharper critique of aspects of the Euro-American world. One sees this honing of ideas at work during the Iwakura embassy, of which Itō was a senior member. This was an epic diplomatic mission designed to gather information about the West, its technologies, industries, medicine and science, as well as its political organisations and laws.[21] The embassy lasted from late 1871 to the autumn of 1873, and took in frequent stops between San Francisco and Washington DC in the United States, along with major cities and industrial sites in Britain, Russia and continental Europe.

Being able to visit Washington meant that Itō and other members of this extensive embassy were able to study American constitutional documents archived there, visit the Capitol and the Supreme Court and meet with US politicians and lawyers. But, as the embassy's chronicler, the thirty-year-old Kume Kunitake, noted, touring the United States and visiting its capital city in the midst of the Reconstruction era also allowed these high-level Japanese operators to form opinions about other things.

Kume recorded accurately how – despite the extreme prejudices still confronting them – some American Blacks had succeeded by now in being elected to the US House of

Auf der Culturreise.

Die Japanesen, getreu ihrer Mission, die europäische Civilisation
kennen zu lernen, gewinnen in Essen einen Einblick in dieselbe.

58. German caricature of a visit by members of Japan's
Iwakura embassy in March 1873 to the Krupp's factory
in Essen, major suppliers of armaments.

Representatives, while 'still others have accumulated great wealth'. 'Clearly,' Kume went on:

> the colour of one's skin has nothing to do with intelligence. People with insight have recognized that education is the key to improvement, and … it is not far-fetched to believe that, in a decade or two, talented black people will rise *and white people who do not study and work hard will fall by the wayside* [my italics].[22]

As far as the United States itself was concerned, this was manifestly a premature judgement. But this is also one of several meditations contained within Kume's huge account of the Iwakura embassy on the possible transience of 'white' advantages and power. 'The contemporary phenomenon of wealth and population in European states', he recorded erroneously but with satisfaction when the embassy moved on to London, '… has become pronounced only in the last forty years.' Things could change. Power relations between different regions and different peoples in the world could shift.[23]

As a result of this mix of ideas, impressions and imperatives – a rooted suspicion of Western interference, wide-ranging exposure to parts of the United States and Europe, a sense that the locations of power across the globe were mutable, and growing apprehension that the Freedom and People's Rights Movement within Japan itself might burgeon out of control – Itō Hirobumi and his associates were more than usually drawn to a policy of pick and mix as regards constitutional design.[24]

At times, Itō encouraged individual Westerners to believe that their particular nation and system of government were the prime influences on him and on a rising Japan. Thus, an American admirer proudly confided to print in the late nineteenth century how the great man had carefully studied both the United States constitution and the *Federalist Papers*, and this may well have been true. Certainly Itō, who purchased books as eagerly as he collected swords, is known to have read and discussed with others an English translation of Alexis de Tocqueville's *Democracy in America*.[25] But the value of the United States as a *constitutional* model was always limited in his eyes by its republican form of government; and, for him, as for other Meiji dynasts, there were more important overseas points of reference.

Dispatched on another mission to Europe in 1882, this time specifically so as to examine its various constitutional systems, Itō went first to Berlin, where he and his colleagues spent six months studying with the leading German jurist, Rudolf von Gneist. They then spent a further eleven weeks in Vienna, working with constitutional scholars there, including Lorenz von Stein, a jurist and economist whose career spanned Denmark and France as well as Germany and Austria.[26] The impact on the future Japanese constitution of these sustained contacts with central European systems and experts would be considerable. But, again, Itō was careful to combine these particular influences with others. On this same trip in 1882, he also paid a visit to London. There, he had several meetings with a multilingual lawyer and academic named W. E. Grigsby. Almost entirely forgotten now, Grigsby was a highly mobile expert on comparative law who had earlier taught the subject in Tokyo, where he helped to educate Hozumi Nobushige, the man who would go on to draft Japan's civil code.[27]

And along with these mixed transcontinental journeys, consultations and readings, Itō also retained throughout a keen attachment to certain Japanese practices and positions. This studied hybridity on his part is nicely mirrored in his choice of dress. Historians and anthropologists have remarked how, over the course of the nineteenth century, ambitious and enterprising individuals outside Euro-America, especially males, increasingly adopted Western costume, choosing to wear shirts, ties, sombre-coloured jackets, waistcoats, trousers, top hats and the like, as useful signifiers of their modernity. In Japan itself, Western attire was made compulsory for government officials in 1872.[28] But Itō's own bodily and sartorial practices are a reminder that it continued to be possible to preserve and project multiple identities in terms of dress as in other things. Over the course of his long career, he adopted an array of civilian and military Western costumes and hairstyles. But, as photographs reveal, in private and with friends, Itō reverted easily to the kimono, a white or pale one in summer and a black one in winter, just as he combined reading English-language newspapers with writing poetry in Japanese and classical Chinese.

In the same way, while Itō drew on various Western states, texts and experts for constitutional knowledge and examples, he combined this with a determination to hold on to certain Japanese institutions, languages and beliefs, and not simply out of patriotic sentiment. 'A constitution is not a legal document', von Gneist had argued; it was rather and essentially the embodiment of 'the spirit and capacities of the nation' – and Itō agreed.[29] Any attempt to design and implement a Japanese political constitution that was merely or mainly imitative would be inappropriate. It would also be bound to fail.

So, as Itō worked intensively over the course of the 1880s on an official Japanese constitution, sometimes travelling abroad in the process, he took care to be aided at home by his chief protégé, Inoue Kowashi. Another military veteran of the Boshin War, Inoue had matured into an impressive state bureaucrat who possessed his own Western connections and sets of knowledge. He had visited Germany and France and had personally translated into Japanese both the Belgian constitution of 1831 and the Prussian constitution of 1850. But he was also deeply interested in Chinese and Confucian thought, and in Japan's own legal traditions, and the linkages he believed he had detected between its religious beliefs and its political practices.[30]

59. Photograph of an elderly Itō Hirobumi in his kimono.

60. Photograph of an elderly Itō Hirobumi in Western dress.

In addition, and like his mentor and master Itō, Inoue was convinced that an official constitution must be forged and implemented at speed before dissident and rival groupings in Japan gained momentum and became unstoppable. 'If we lose this opportunity and vacillate,' Inoue wrote:

> within two or three years the people will become confident that they can succeed and no matter how much oratory we may use, it will be difficult to win them back ... Public opinion will cast aside the draft of a constitution presented by the government, and the private drafts of the constitution will win out in the end.

A political constitution set down on paper, he and Itō were agreed, was indispensable for the successful modernisation of Japan. But there must be limits, and there would need to be calculation and caution. 'In Japan modernization is just at the beginning', remarked Inoue.[31] To be successful here – and to be safe – a written constitution must exhibit continuities with what had gone before.

## The Emperors' New Constitutions

The Japanese constitution of 1889, then, was very much a composite: a quality that partly accounts for its survival and wider significance. At one level, it was plainly *sui generis,* the first such political document ever to be implemented in east Asia. At another level, aspects of its evolution and writing conformed to patterns set earlier in other sectors of the world.

Like most pioneering constitutions, this Japanese text was hastened by war and continuing threats of violence. Rising constitutional activism in this society was also aided – as often elsewhere – by an expanded availability and mix of print. Like earlier writers of constitutions, too, those primarily responsible for shaping this particular text borrowed from other countries and empires. Indeed, they were able to do so more systematically than previous constitution-writers, because of the much greater availability by now of transoceanic steamships and long-distance railway links. At the same time, and like earlier non-Western polities adopting constitutions, such as Tunisia and Hawaii, the men of Meiji were eager to use their text both to assert local distinctiveness and to lay claim to a greater share of the world's attention.

The official *Commentaries on the Constitution of the Empire of Japan,* issued alongside the 1889 constitution, was itself designed to broadcast Japan's particular achievements and firm grasp on modernity. The foreword to the booklet made clear that this was 'a handbook for all', a guide for other peoples and polities on how state-making and constitutional design might profitably be done.[32] Over 160 pages in length, published under Itō Hirobumi's name, and subsequently translated into English and French, it was in fact substantially the work of Inoue Kowashi. Formidable, even scholarly, it bristles with allusions to different Western polities and their constitutional practices, and with erudite references to Japan's own history, laws and archives: 'such is in short what appears from the study of ancient documents and of the customs of the land'.[33]

From the outset, and quite deliberately, the *Commentaries* emphasises the centrality of Japan's emperor and the significance of what he represents: 'a lineal succession unbroken for ages eternal'. The sanctity and longevity of the Chrysanthemum Throne is at the heart of the book's wider strategic argument: namely, that this new Japanese constitution embodies patriotic and national essences and durability as well as innovation. 'The original national polity is by no means changed' by the constitution, it insists, 'but is more strongly confirmed than ever'.[34]

Their desire to stress the significance of Japan's emperor, and to use him to root and legitimise this new constitution, was one reason why Itō and his fellow oligarchs had chosen to look substantially towards Germany. There is no doubt that they drew heavily both on the Prussian constitution of 1850, which Inoue had translated into Japanese, and on the German imperial constitution that had come into effect in April 1871.[35]

Parts of this latter document had also made much of the unifying power of an emperor, in this case, the former king of Prussia, Wilhelm I, now advanced to the title and position of 'German Emperor'. The 1871 constitution had confirmed him in the right to represent the German Reich internationally, to declare war and conclude peace, to summon, open and prorogue the Reichstag, the German parliament, and – critically – to be commander-in-chief of Germany's fast expanding armed forces.

'The organization and composition thereof is the business of the Emperor', declared this 1871 constitution: 'all German troops are bound to obey the commands of the Emperor unconditionally. This duty is to be specified in the banner-oath.'[36]

Many of these German provisions also found echoes in the 1889 Japanese constitution. It, too, was insistent on the close relationship between the emperor and the armed forces, stating (incorrectly) that all Japanese emperors had 'taken the field in person in command of their armies'. This new Japanese constitution also confirmed earlier moves towards conscription, something which had been embedded, too, in the Prussian constitution of 1850 and in the German constitution of 1871. In addition, registering for service in the militia was now made obligatory for all Japanese men between the ages of seventeen and forty:

> Every male adult in the whole country shall be compelled, without distinction of class or family, to fulfill, in accordance with the provisions of law, his duty of serving in the army; that he may be incited to valor while his body undergoes physical training; and that in this way the martial spirit of the country shall be maintained and secured from decline.[37]

The most isolated of rural peasants were to be turned into modern Japanese by way of a common exposure to military service.

These and other German borrowings on the part of the Meiji elite were widely recognised at the time, which helps to explain why some foreign commentators likened Itō Hirobumi to Otto von Bismarck, the formidable politician who became chancellor of a united Germany in 1871, the year of its imperial constitution. In the wake of the Second World War, which saw Japan allying with Nazi Germany, these earlier political and constitutional linkages between the two countries came, however, under more critical scrutiny. An argument grew up – which lingers vestigially to this day – that the constitutional similarities between these two powers, Meiji Japan on the one hand, and Prussia and Germany on the other, were evidence of a common inclination towards authoritarianism and military aggression.[38] Valid in part, this suggestion needs qualifying.

For some Meiji oligarchs, the most compelling attraction of the German imperial constitution was in fact that a united Germany was very much a *recent* political construct, a polity put together out of a collection of ancient domains, that now exhibited high levels of innovation and success. As men like Itō saw it, Meiji Japan, too, was a place of tradition and ancient forms. But – like Germany – it was also a remade and evolving construct, something new in the world that was on the rise. The title page of the official English translation of the *Commentaries* on the Japanese constitution pointedly gives its publication date as '22nd year of Meiji', with the Western calendar year 1889 added only in brackets. There was a degree to which, like French revolutionaries a century before, believers in the Meiji project wanted to lay claim to their own distinctive ordering of time. Japan's future was to begin triumphantly with them.

Accordingly, and alongside their genuflections to custom and to the central importance of the imperial throne, Japan's leaders were careful to identify their country – and themselves – with progress and modes of modernity. This aspiration, too, attracted them powerfully to a fast-changing Germany. By the 1880s, the German economy was booming in areas such as steel production, shipbuilding and railways, which had been made the subject of a special section of the imperial constitution of 1871. German science, too, was in the ascendant, in astronomy, pharmacology, chemistry, geology, physics and more; while the German educational system at all levels was arguably the best in the world. This reputation for cutting-edge expertise and innovation helps to explain why, in 1888, the year before the adoption of its constitution, Japan was employing some seventy German special advisers, a bigger contingent of foreign experts than from any other country.[39]

So, while elements of authoritarianism, military assertiveness and conservatism are certainly to be found in the Japanese constitution of 1889, these characteristics do not adequately sum up its contents or overall direction, any more than they do those of the German imperial constitution of 1871. Both texts demonstrate an appetite for, and a commitment to, change.

Read the *Commentaries* on the Japanese constitution carefully, and you immediately notice the mixed messages. The Meiji emperor and his wisdom are applauded throughout, yes. But it is nonetheless made clear that this constitution will only come into force with the opening of a new, bicameral Japanese diet, which happened in November 1890. It was to be the inception of this parliament – the first in Asia – that was to activate Japan's constitution, not its formal promulgation by the emperor. Yes, the *Commentaries* spells out, the latter has the power to amend this new constitution, but the diet will have to vote on such amendments. The emperor can also issue imperial ordinances. But these – as, in general, Japan's annual budgets – will be invalid if the diet does not approve them; and while the emperor possesses legislative power, 'this power shall always be exercised with the consent of the Diet'. Japan's emperor, in other words, was to be sovereign as well as divine, but only – at least in writing and in print – 'according to the provisions of the present Constitution'.[40]

Moreover, as Itō made clear to ministerial colleagues in advance, this 1889 constitution was to provide for some popular rights. As far as elections to the lower house of the Japanese diet were concerned, there was to be voting by secret ballot, though only by men over twenty-five, and only by those paying a restrictive level of direct taxation. In practice, and in the short term, this worked out as an electorate of some 450,000 out of a population of over 40 million – just over 1 per cent. The proportion of Japanese able to vote subsequently and slowly expanded. But universal male suffrage would not arrive in Japan until 1925, while women would not receive the vote until after another war, in 1947.[41]

But everyone in Japan, by the terms of this 1889 constitution, was now to enjoy freedom from arbitrary arrest and to have access to a trial by a judge, who could not be dismissed during good behaviour. There was to be a right to property, a right to petition, freedom of movement and speech, and liberty of writing and association 'within the limits of law'. There was also – for men – to be a measure of meritocracy, something with which many Meiji politicians, themselves often from relatively obscure backgrounds, felt a measure of sympathy. Neither 'order of nobility nor degree of rank', declares this constitution, are 'any longer [to] be allowed to militate against the equality of all men in regard to appointment to office'. In addition, it was confirmed, there would now officially be freedom of religious belief: 'one of the most beautiful fruits of modern civilization'.[42]

The choice of words here was calculated, and the makers of this constitution and their supporters employed similar language in public and in print. 'By adopting a constitutional form of government,' wrote one of Itō's allies in an American magazine, 'we have given the whole world the strongest evidence that it is our earnest desire to follow closely in the footsteps of civilized nations.'[43] The new Japan was explicitly to form an integral part of the civilised world: that civilisation which Westerners so often invoked as a means of justifying their pre-eminence across the globe. These claims to 'civilisation' formed only part of the challenges and attractions that this constitution came to pose for those operating outside Japan.

## Japan and an Altered World

The emergence of the Japanese constitution worked to alter ideas and power relations in the world irrevocably, in part because so many other changes were now underway. As far as written constitutions were concerned, the years between 1889 and the outbreak of the First World War in 1914 witnessed new versions being adopted at a frantic rate.

Some of these were created in regions already characterised by a tradition of this mode of doing and writing politics. In central and South America, which had been engines and arenas of constitutional creativity since the 1810s, new constitutions sprang up during this era in Brazil (1890), Cuba (1895 and 1901), the Dominican Republic (1896, 1907 and 1908), Ecuador (1897 and 1906), Honduras (1894 and 1904), Nicaragua (1905) and Panama (1904). As for Venezuela, it passed through four different constitutions between 1889 and 1914.

These years were also a busy time for new constitutions in the Pacific world and in Europe, though in both regions, new countries joined the ranks for the first time, while others became noticeably more active. Montenegro, a small country on the Adriatic coast which had long been exposed to Ottoman pressures, secured its first constitution in 1905; while Serbia, a tinderbox of ethnic and political strife, and itself under Ottoman suzerainty until the 1860s, secured a new, more radical constitution in 1888, which allowed most of its male inhabitants to vote. Toppled in 1901, this was restored in 1903, and lasted on paper until the creation of Yugoslavia in 1918.

Most striking of all in this period – and Japan was only one example of this – was the degree to which Asian powers were now experimenting with written constitutionalism. This was true of Persia, which issued its first constitution in 1906. It was true of the Ottoman empire, where – as we have seen – a revolution in 1908 forced a revival of its earlier short-lived constitution of 1876. It was true, as well, of Russia, where, since 1820, successive tsars had consistently stonewalled proposals for constitutional reform. The revolution of 1905, however, gave rise in the following year to a new Russian Fundamental Law and an elected parliament, the Duma. Neither of these prospered, but both had a durable impact on ideas, political vocabulary and expectations.[44]

An even larger and older Asian empire, China, also shifted direction, though not enough. In 1905, the Empress Dowager Cixi, a dominant figure in Beijing since the 1860s, acknowledged the importance of constitutional developments in Japan in two critical respects. As the Meiji elite had done in the 1870s and 1880s, she dispatched a series of commissioners to make a study of political systems in the major Western states. But, in addition, and tellingly, she also sent Chinese officials to investigate constitutional practices in Japan. These exploratory missions, it was given out, were to be a prelude to the implementation of a written constitution in China itself; and, in 1906, edicts were issued formally appointing fourteen bureaucrats to embark on this task. The failure to follow through on these promises of structural reform and wider rights was one reason why the Qing dynasty was overthrown in China's revolution of 1911.[45]

There was yet another massive Asian empire in constitutional flux at this time – British India. Unlike the others, it did not erupt into revolution in the decades immediately before 1914. But levels of activism and resistance increased, and so did the production of innovative constitutional texts. Pressure for change and reform had been growing here since the repression of the Indian Revolt of 1857. Some of the military rebels that year had themselves produced a twelve-point political document, the *Dastur-ul Amal*, an embryonic constitution.[46] There were also attempts from the 1860s onwards in some of the Indian princely states to draft local written constitutions. But the first major, though unofficial, attempt at writing a full-scale political constitution for the Indian subcontinent as a whole was the Swaraj (or Self-rule) Bill of 1895.

This text seems to have been mainly the work of Bal Gangadhar Tilak, an educationalist and journalist from western India, who was deeply conservative on the matter of women's rights but influential in his early nationalism, and from 1890 a member of the Indian National Congress. Tilak planned that – were his Swaraj Bill to pass – the resulting act would be called the 'Constitution of India Act'. Moreover, as the draft introduction to the bill made clear, this legislation was to extend 'to the whole of India'. Its 110 articles included broad provisions for rights. There was to be freedom of speech and written expression in India. There was to be a right to petition, equality before the law and free state education. And, as in the Meiji constitution, all citizens (which in practice meant men) were to enjoy equal access to public employments, and to have a duty to bear arms if need be.[47]

Indian historians have yet to investigate the echoes between these and other provisions in the Swaraj Bill of 1895 and the Meiji constitution six years earlier. Yet that these should have existed was hardly surprising. The detailed commentary published on Japan's constitution in 1889 had been issued in an English translation, while the text itself was widely reported on and extracted in the British and Indian press. A highly educated man like Tilak would have found it easy, and, given his interests and ambitions, irresistible, to familiarise himself with a pioneering east Asian example of engineered constitutional reconfiguration, along with British and American political and legal writings.

Recognising this helps to explain why the Swaraj Bill strives for some of the compromises between modernity, conservatism and tradition that also appealed to the Meiji elite. In Tilak's plan there was to be a bicameral parliament for the 'Indian nation', just as Itō Hirobumi and his allies had sought a bicameral parliament to give expression to a remodelled and reinvigorated Japanese nation. But, as in Meiji Japan, formal sovereign power in Tilak's reformed India was to be invested in a monarch, in this case, the Empress of India, Britain's Queen Victoria. Like the emperor in Japan, she was to function in India as a still point in a fast evolving realm.

This wider Japanese impress on political ideas and written projects – and on the sense of what was possible – can be traced throughout greater Asia and beyond. Events in Japan in the aftermath of the Meiji Restoration and the 1889 constitution contributed in different ways to the outbreak of the revolution in Russia in 1905, and to the issue of a constitution there. They also contributed to the making of the Persian constitutional revolution of 1906, and to the Young Turk revolution in the Ottoman empire, and the restoration of constitutionalism in that region in 1908. The Japanese impact on reform attempts and ideas in China was greater still. The wider contagion of Japan's self-transformation did not stop there. Nor did it cease with the First World War.[48] Why was this?

Part of the answer lies in the continuing advances in flows of knowledge and information. Accelerating technological, transport and media changes meant that information on what was happening in Japan spread over long distances very rapidly. Only think of the degree to which, by the end of the nineteenth century, Japanese prints had become a major influence on multiple Western artists, such as Vincent van Gogh, Paul Gauguin, the American James McNeill Whistler, and a host of lesser figures besides. This scale of artistic transfer was made easier by the fact that industrially produced photographic images of east Asian art works were now circulating more widely than had been possible before. But, in addition, and crucially, many foreigners were now more interested in and attentive to things Japanese.

The same was also true in regard to Japanese constitutional information and propaganda. From the day of its promulgation, accounts of Japan's 1889 constitution were publicised across long distances, by way of the electric telegraph as well as print. The Meiji authorities were themselves proactive in distributing constitutional and other information about the new Japan, so as to boost the country's profile across continents and to outface its power rivals. By 1907, for instance, the Japanese government was subsidising both Malay and Arabic newspapers in Singapore, in return for favourable coverage and appropriate insertions.[49]

As suggested by Tilak's Swaraj Bill, Japan's new politics also attracted notice abroad because they could be viewed as embodying a kind of halfway house, vibrant change embedded within a persistence of certain stabilities. The constitution of 1889 had combined a sovereign monarch with a parliament. It made gestures towards male suffrage, but not many. It borrowed provisions and ideas from Western states, but also insisted on the sanctity of Indigenous traditions. It offered rights for ordinary Japanese people, but it also shored up ministerial power, while providing for conscription and for enlarged armed forces that were tied to the Crown.

These studied compromises, and Japan's rising success, proved particularly attractive to non-Western monarchs who were eager to experiment themselves with modes of modernisation, while still maintaining hierarchy and their own positions. King Kalākaua of Hawaii, who incorporated Japan in the itinerary of his world tour of 1881 and sought out the Meiji emperor's advice and sponsorship, was an early example of this kind of keen royal interest in Japan. Sultan Abu Bakar of Johor, in the Malay peninsula, was another. Having to grapple with rising British penetration in his region of the world, the sultan was careful to pay a six-month visit to Japan in 1883 in advance of ultimately developing plans for his own constitution, the first to emerge in south-east Asia.[50]

Japan's allure for extra-European monarchs persisted after the First World War. In July 1931, a year after his accession to the throne, Emperor Haile Selassie of Ethiopia, an ancient kingdom situated in the horn of Africa, implemented a constitution that was explicitly modelled – like some of his educational and economic policies – on Meiji precedents. Like the 1889 original, this Ethiopian text was emphatic that 'the person of the Emperor is sacred, his dignity is inviolable and his power indisputable'. It also provided for a bicameral parliament like its Japanese model; and it shared some of the strategic thinking behind the latter. Just as the makers of the 1889 constitution had aimed to strengthen Japan's capacity both to withstand and to impress the West, Selassie's text was designed in the (partly legitimate) hope that it would help buttress his country's distinct identity in the face of a likely imperial takeover by Italy.[51]

Japan's constitution and its aftermath also exerted a more transgressive and disruptive influence overseas. There was a degree, indeed, to which what happened in this country after the Boshin War was almost bound to be subversive. Among many (though never all) Western commentators, it had long been a cliché that 'Eastern' societies were wired for arbitrary despotic government. When the Ottoman sultan had introduced a written constitution in 1876, for example, the response of some Western politicians and media outlets had been notably dismissive. This was less, as one scholar puts it, out of a conviction that this Ottoman initiative would fail, than 'because they feared it might succeed'.[52] The fact that this constitution was withdrawn in 1878 only reinforced prejudices, and lent convenient ballast to another set of preconceptions. The Ottoman sultan's row-back could seem to corroborate those who argued that Asian cultures were fundamentally uninterested in change.

The many transformations of Meiji Japan inescapably challenged such positions, and progressively so. Consider what was involved: a large polity which was *not* situated in the Western world, which was *not* Christian, and which was *not* inhabited by people who viewed themselves as white had implemented a constitution which put down roots, a document that provided for a severely restricted franchise, to be sure, but which also embedded certain popular rights and established a functioning parliament. Moreover, Japan achieved all this in tandem with effecting spectacular and well-reported economic, industrial, educational and technological changes. Reactions to these developments were rapid, taking different forms in different geographical spaces.

Among Western commentators, there was recognition and applause, though this could be mixed with apprehension and a measure of condescension. 'Until quite recently,' wrote one British essayist in 1894, 'the Japanese were best known … as the makers of artistic bric-à-brac. They excited a sort of sentimental interest, as a quaint people.' But now, this writer went on, this 'oriental nation has made a sudden forward spring and that is a very remarkable event'.[53] 'Remarkable' here still possessed distinct connotations of surprise. Other foreign observers, though, viewed the changes underway in Japan more single-mindedly and excitedly. Especially among reformers and officials in Qing China and among aspiring Indian nationalists, there was a strong and growing sense after 1889 that Japan's political creativity, like its economic, educational and industrial advances, was at once game-changing and to be eagerly scrutinised and learned from.

Meiji missions dispatched abroad in the 1870s and 1880s to investigate modes of technological, economic and political modernity had gone overwhelmingly to Western locations. After 1889, however, such assumptions about where exactly to look in the world for sites of modernity began to shift. In 1904–5, when the governor of Guangdong in south-east China was in search for foreign countries where the brightest students from his province might ideally go to study politics and law, he took it for granted that the range of options available to him had by now broadened. He dispatched thirty-one Guangdong students to the United States, Britain, France and Germany. But, in addition, he also sent off another fifty-six local students to Japan. This initiative was part of a wider trend. As one historian remarks, the scale of the exodus of bright young men from

China to Japan during the first decade of the twentieth century – there were 8,000 of them by 1906 – represented 'probably the largest mass movement of students overseas in world history up to that point'.[54]

China, of course, at its nearest point, was only some 500 miles away from Japan by sea. For most of those living further away, personally visiting Japan remained out of the question. But limits on outsiders' direct exposure to the country proved in practice no obstacle to Japan's widening global impress and influence. Unable in the main to see Japan for themselves, many reformers and revolutionaries living outside the West simply chose to idealise this east Asian empire anyway, projecting upon it whatever they wanted to see accomplished within their own countries. 'The Japanese have been able to take the Western civilization without losing their religion and national identity: they have been able to reach the levels of Europeans in every respect', wrote one early twentieth-century Turkish intellectual and reformer yearningly. 'Why, then, should we hesitate?' he went on: 'Can we not accept Western civilization definitely and still be Turks and Muslims?'[55]

This kind of idealisation of Japan – this perception of it both as a model of change to be copied and as a successful riposte and alternative to Western power – was further fostered by the country's dramatic success in war. There had repeatedly been connections between the willingness of states to issue con-stitutions, on the one hand, and their appetite, on the other, for increased supplies of men at arms and enhanced levels of taxation so as to fund warfare, and Japan was no exception to this general rule. Its 1889 constitution confirmed its system of conscription and made military service an obligation for all Japa-nese males between the ages of seventeen and forty. In addition, in the aftermath of this constitution, the Japanese government's extractive capacity rose sharply. Itō Hirobumi claimed that from 1889 to 1899 alone the per capita tax burden doubled.[56]

61. Japanese woodcut celebrating Japan's success in the war against China 1894–95. Note the watching western media.

Some of these enhanced fiscal resources went to fund Japan's armed services, especially its burgeoning navy. One example of this arms build-up makes the point. Between 1868 and 1893, Meiji governments purchased five warships from a major British shipbuilder, Armstrong's, as well as additional ships from arms dealers in France, Germany and the United States. Japanese orders for battleships from Armstrong's expanded further between 1894 and 1904. Japan purchased eight, even bigger vessels from the company during these ten years, a more substantial order than that put in by any other power at this time except for Britain itself.[57]

Japan thus equipped itself to be a major participant in long-distance hybrid warfare. These enhanced investments in guns, ships and men helped it to win its 1894–95 war against China, which possessed a larger, but technologically less advanced navy, especially in terms of gunnery. Japan's expensive and expanding navy also played a substantial part in its victory in the Russo-Japanese War of 1904–5. By the end of this conflict, two out of Russia's three major naval fleets had been put out of action and substantially destroyed.[58]

These sequential Japanese victories had immediate constitutional as well as other consequences for the losers. The pace of economic and military change in the Qing empire had been quickening since the 1860s. But, in the wake of defeat by Japan, Chinese bureaucrats, reformers and intellectuals devoted more attention to political, legal and institutional changes, as well as to military reinforcements. In Russia, too, defeat by Japan brought speedy political repercussions. The severe loss of face involved was a factor in rising domestic discontent and in the Russian tsar's decision in October 1905 to concede constitutional reforms. The war forced his hand in another respect. The fact that so many Russian troops had been dispatched to fight Japanese forces away from the heart of the Romanov empire, and towards its eastern-most regions, made it easier for revolutionaries to secure their brief advantage in St Petersburg.

Japanese victories also had cultural and ideological consequences. Perhaps the sharpest evidence of this as far as the war with Russia was concerned is in every sense a graphic one, a shunga print dating from 1905. Shunga is a popular traditional Japanese art form that focuses on the myriad forms of human (and occasionally animal) sensual and sexual pleasures. But, in this particular woodblock print, a piece of Japanese war propaganda, the stress is less on pleasure than on pain and violence. A Japanese infantryman has forced his Russian counterpart into a kneeling position, pulled down his uniform trousers, and is engaged in raping him. In keeping with the stereotypical representation of Westerners in Japanese prints, the Russian soldier is shown as red-haired. The skin of his hands, and on his frozen face and his exposed backside, is very white. That of his Japanese assailant is very clearly not. And, in the background, there is a line of yet more Japanese soldiers, charging forward under a Japanese flag.

Sexual violence is a feature of every war. But that is not the central theme of this shunga print. Recognising what *is* its

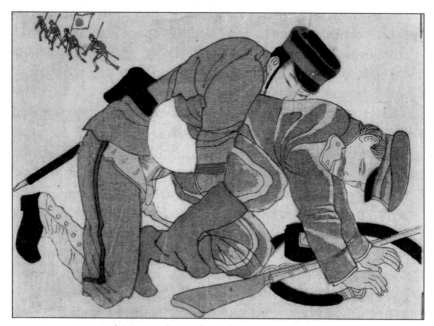

62. Violating and invading the Other: Shunga print
from the Russo-Japanese War, 1904–5.

essential message demands situating it in far wider contexts. It has been estimated that, by 1914, close to 85 per cent of the globe had been colonised and occupied by predominantly 'white' powers, by the western and central European empires, by the United States, and of course by Russia itself. The outcome of the Russo-Japanese War went conspicuously against this global trend. A non-white, non-Western empire had won a major victory on land and sea against what by now was being styled by some critics as the 'white peril'. Hence this shunga print. The world in this particular image is turning upside down. An infantryman of the Russian empire, an increasingly invasive power in Asia since before the days of Catherine the Great, is being subjugated and demeaned by a soldier of another race. Here, the white man is literally and metaphorically being penetrated and invaded by the Other, by a representative of Asia.

Such reactions to the Japanese victory over Russia in 1905 were widespread, albeit generally expressed more decorously. There is a famous anecdote of Alfred Zimmern, a German-born classicist, political scientist and Zionist, and a future founder of UNESCO, changing the introduction to a lecture he was giving at Oxford University at the last minute on receiving news of Japan's success. This was the 'most important event which has happened, or is likely to happen in our lifetime', Zimmern is reputed to have announced to his undergraduate audience: 'the victory of a non-white people over a white people'.[59] More important, though, was the degree to which men and women in societies that had been exposed to Euro-American violence and invasions seized upon this event: Japan's success in the war against the Russian empire.

In India, in the wake of the Russo-Japanese War, there are records of families giving their newborn children the names of successful Japanese generals or admirals. 'Japanese victories stirred up my enthusiasm', the Indian leader Jawaharlal Nehru later recalled, or at least chose to recall: 'I mused of Indian freedom and Asiatic freedom from the thralldom of Europe.'[60] In the Ottoman empire, whose territories had been regularly chipped away by Russia since the seventeenth century, Sultan Abdülhamid II feverishly collected photograph albums devoted to the Russo-Japanese War, depositing them lovingly in his palace library in Istanbul. In Egypt, now under British control, the nationalist lawyer and journalist Mustafā Kāmil devoted extensive newspaper coverage to the war as it happened. Japan's ultimate victory only confirmed his admiration for the country and for the Meiji constitution of 1889. 'We are amazed by Japan,' he wrote, 'because it is the first Eastern government to utilize Western civilization to resist the shield of European imperialism in Asia.'[61]

For some, then, Japanese success against Russia was overwhelmingly welcomed because it seemed to invert crushing racial hierarchies. Others interpreted this conflict (selectively, as we shall see) as a hit against the forces of imperial aggression in general. Among Muslim groupings, especially, there was sometimes a hope, which Meiji political agents encouraged, that the new Japan was emerging as a champion of the oppressed and the colonised against the Christian invader. But, for some observers, what appeared no less significant was that Japan's defeated enemies – the Qing empire, on the one hand, and the Romanov Russian empire, on the other – could both be viewed as ramshackle and ancient regimes that had resisted thoroughgoing governmental and political reform. By contrast, Japan, the victor, was a polity that had embraced change and a written constitution.

'The Japanese are fighting for a country where they are free', wrote one Turkish commentator in late 1904. The conflict between Japan and Russia was in essence a 'war of the constitution', agreed an Egyptian journalist at this time; and whereas Japanese combatants were inspired by the liberties they had secured, their Russian opponents were still held back by tyranny.[62]

In some ways, this was the most momentous argument to be extrapolated from Japan's experience. Its victories over China and Russia could be read – and were read – as a demonstration that constitutional reform, *outside as well as inside the West*, was an indispensable component of being an effective modern state. A journalist in a popular St Petersburg daily paper was commenting tacitly on his own country when, in 1906, he supplied this analysis of the Russo-Japanese War:

> Orientals learned as a result of the Russo-Japanese war that they can keep up with Europe in the fields of civilization and prosperity *just as they know that they cannot keep up except by replacing their oppressive, absolutist governments with constitutional ones* [my italics]. They started attributing

Japan's progress in a short span of time to consultative assembly and constitutional administration and because of that, Chinese, Indians and Philipinos [sic] demand constitutions of their governments.[63]

So, increasingly, did Russians themselves.

Views of this sort represented a serious turning point. A constitution had been established in greater Asia. Within that vast region, and in other non-Western spaces, there had been a rise in efforts to experiment with this same political device. But, in addition, an argument was now being advanced more regularly across different geographies that *only* by having a modern constitution could a state adequately compete with the rest of the world. As a Chinese diplomat and journalist put it: 'That other countries are wealthy and strong is primarily due to the adoption of a constitution.'[64] It was the widening acceptance of such attitudes that confirmed written constitutions as a genuinely global phenomenon.

## Lessons

That events in Japan should have had such a wide and radical impact elsewhere in the world can appear paradoxical. Two decades after the establishment of the Meiji constitution, on 26 October 1909, Itō Hirobumi was shot three times in the chest en route to a secret meeting with a Russian diplomat. His life intertwined with rising modernities to its last moment, the assassination took place at the elegant new railway station at Harbin in north-east China. The killer was Ahn Jung-geun, a Korean nationalist. 'I decided to assassinate Itō', he explained shortly before his own execution, 'to retaliate for the oppression of the Korean people.' For this man, evidently, Japan was not a beacon of hope, a cause for non-Western enthusiasm and emulation. It was just another dominating and repressive empire.[65]

63. *Japan is King of the World*: an advertisement/
hikifuda issued during the Russo-Japanese War.

Japan had already seized control of Taiwan in 1895, in the
wake of its successful war with China. After its victory in
the subsequent Russo-Japanese War, Japan also established a
protectorate in Korea. Once Itō made his fateful decision to
become that country's first Japanese resident-general in 1906,
he immediately began to pursue what he perceived as a civilis-
ing mission there. The following year, Korea was essentially
annexed. To this extent, Meiji Japan did not represent a secure
and satisfactory alternative to an imperialist West. It was rather
joining enthusiastically and successfully in the carve-up of the

398

world. So why did Japan's changes and reforms and, above all, its constitution nonetheless appeal across countries and continents for so long?

They did so in part because, at the time, all this seemed less paradoxical than it probably does now. Western powers had dominated the business of overland and maritime expansion over the course of the long nineteenth century. Before that, however, formidable and elastic empires had also been generated by powers from other regions, not least by Asian powers. The fact that, by the early 1900s, Meiji Japan was establishing its own overseas empire by force could therefore be interpreted – and was interpreted in some quarters – as further evidence that the world was beginning satisfactorily to right itself again, and that the East was emphatically on its way back.

Moreover, many people outside Taiwan and Korea seem not to have known, or not to have cared, about Japan's imperial invasions of these countries. There was a degree to which Japan had so effectively established itself as an emblem of alternative modernities and resistance that this reputation was enough for many to cancel out awkward truths. And there was also, always, Japan's written constitution, backed up as it was after 1889 by further domestic political activism and experiment, and validated, too, by its comparative longevity.

In 1918, in the aftermath of the First World War, a British politician took note of how, by now, even conservative Indian nationalists were being drawn to Japan's example, because 'every attempt in Eastern countries to develop parliamentary government had utterly failed, to wit, in Turkey, Egypt, Persia, China, and now Russia'. By contrast, he went on, Indian spokesmen 'pointed to Japan as a brilliant exception, and said that there was no reason why India should not do equally well'.[66] The allure was still working in some locations in the wake of the Second World War. True, Japanese military campaigns in this conflict killed millions. But they also destabilised the Asian empires of

Britain and other European powers, and thereby gave essential aid to future independence campaigns.

Moreover, the Meiji constitution still exerted an influence, even if only indirectly. The human and economic costs of China's conflict with Japan between 1937 and 1945 were terrible. Yet the preamble of the constitution adopted by the republic of China in December 1946 paid glowing tribute to Sun Yat-sen. In the early twentieth century – like so many other young Chinese reformers – Sun had been a regular visitor to Meiji Japan and a close admirer of its achievements. Bound up repeatedly with armed violence, the audacity and innovativeness of the Meiji experiment continued to have an impact even in the most unexpected places.

# EPILOGUE

The First World War, erupting in July 1914, marked the end of the beginning of the transformation. Like other major conflicts since the mid 1700s, it expanded unpredictably, disrupting and sometimes destroying political orders and quickening the transmission of volatile ideas. In the process, and like so many earlier wars, it also fostered the spread of new constitutions. Only it did so in distinctive ways and on an unprecedented scale.

In part this was because, even more than in the long 1860s, all of the world's major empires were drawn into the fighting. As a result, what remains this war's most celebrated killing field – the Western Front snaking through France, Luxembourg and Belgium – formed only a portion of its overall geography. The involvement of Britain, France and Russia on the one side, and Germany, Austro-Hungary and the Ottoman empire on the other, also brought into the storm their respective colonies and satellites. In practice, this meant all of Africa (except for Ethiopia and Liberia), the Middle East, Canada, most of central and Eastern Europe, and much of Asia and Australasia. The intervention of empires in other continents further magnified the war's scope and repercussions. Japan's entry in August 1914 ensured that hostilities spread into China; while the United States joining the war in 1917 entangled as well its formal and informal colonial spaces, the Philippines, Cuba, Hawaii and much of Central America. Even before this, the war had reached South America and the Pacific, with major battles off the coasts of Chile and the Falkland Islands, and a New Zealand occupation of German Samoa.[1]

As had happened in the Napoleonic Wars, an increasingly transcontinental conflict compelled the prime protagonists at once to raise troops more aggressively than before at home, and to requisition manpower from outside their metropolitan heartlands. But whereas Napoleon had recruited foreign soldiers overwhelmingly from Europe, this struggle saw France grasping for manpower further afield. After 1914, it enlisted over half a million troops from its colonies overseas. The United Kingdom also expanded its recruiting reach. Between 1914 and 1918, India alone supplied it with 1.4 million soldiers and close to half a million labourers. Many of these men served outside their home subcontinent, changing the quality and cultures of warfare in ways that still require more searching and imaginative investigation. Miscellaneous Europeans had been arriving in the Indian peninsula by sea, and fighting there since the late fifteenth century. Now, for the first time in global history, *this* war witnessed large numbers of South Asian troops and indentured servants engaging in combat and field work within continental Europe itself.[2]

There were other signal alterations. As in many of the wars of the long 1860s, technological changes in this conflict resulted in a quantum leap in mortality rates. Only this time, it was not just a matter of quick firing rifles, steam power and the telegraph. After 1914, fighting involved tanks, submarines, planes, automatic machine guns, poison gas and the use of telephones and two-way radio to synchronise troop movements. Together with war-related diseases, famine, accidents and massacres of civilians, this may have resulted in the deaths of at least forty million people, and the maiming, bereavement and forced migrations of millions more.

The English novelist, political activist and futurist, H. G. Wells, burly, formidably clever and even more prolific in his publishing rate than in his womanising, had initially supported the righteousness of a war against Germany. But, even before the formal outbreak of peace, Wells was acknowledging that 'much of the old system' was now 'dead', and that much therefore would require 'to be re-made'. A crucial task, he thought, was to devise ways by 'which people [might] make sense of humankind after the world war'.[3] For him, as for many other intellectuals and politicians at this time, a necessary part of this healing work of reconstruction and reappraisal was the creation of a league of nations, a new, expert body that would monitor and supervise global affairs and thereby anticipate, manage and suppress future armed conflicts.[4]

In May 1918, Wells published an urgent and influential set of essays entitled *In the Fourth Year: Anticipations of a World Peace*. He devoted a section of this to the challenge of writing a constitution for this future league of nations. As an example of what might be achieved, and in order to appeal to readers in the United States – now made so much more powerful on account of the war – Wells invoked the achievements of the Philadelphia Constitutional Convention of 1787: 'a real, deliberate creation of the English-speaking intelligence'.[5] Today, it is the cultural chauvinism of this remark that is likely to strike us. But something else about Wells's assumptions and language also merits attention.

The mortality levels, and extreme economic dislocations of this world war, together with an outbreak of plague – the Spanish flu – which killed fifty million people between 1918 and 1921, provoked more than grief and a protracted moroseness. Across frontiers, it also resulted in a well-documented sense of disorientation, a lingering conviction, as Wells put it, that 'much of the old system' had been extinguished or rendered redundant. But, as his proposals for a league of nations illustrate, this post-war angst and a feeling of enforced severance from the past did not extend to the business of writing constitutions. On the contrary: 'Of the making of constitutions', one China-based commentator noted early in 1919, 'there is no end'. He added a further significant observation: 'in the making of republics, there is now much activity'.[6]

Over a hundred years earlier, French military invasions of the Iberian peninsula had accelerated the disintegration of the Portuguese and Spanish empires, thereby paving the way for the emergence of multiple South American states equipped with experimental written constitutions. A similar pattern of mammoth levels and scales of warfare quickening the dissolution of long-established royal empires, and giving rise in their place to new, mainly republican nations and constitutions occurred after 1914, but on a larger scale and in different continents. It was at this stage, in the wake of the First World War, that it became far more difficult – though still not impossible – for monarchies to coexist comfortably with ambitious written constitutions.

The Ottoman empire had entered the war on Germany's side in 1914 in the hope of reasserting its position in the Middle East and the Balkans. Emerging on the losing side brought an end both to this empire and to its line of ruling sultans. Back in the summer of 1908, the Chinese exile Kang Youwei had watched entranced as crowds in Istanbul celebrated the reinstatement of the Ottoman constitution. By 1924, under the leadership of Mustafa Kemal Atatürk – one more in the long line of professional soldiers turned law-makers – this document had given way to a brand-new constitution. Its first article was stark: 'The Turkish state is a republic'.[7]

The Hohenzollern dynasty and the constitution of the German empire of 1871, along with the Habsburg dynasty and the Austro-Hungarian constitution of 1866 also shattered on the anvil of military defeat. In 1919, both a severely diminished Germany and a much-reduced Austria adopted new, explicitly national constitutions, which provided in each case for the introduction of a republic. The constitutions spun by some of Austria's former imperial provinces did much the same.

Czechoslovakia, for instance, proclaimed its independence late in 1918, and had implemented a republican constitution by 1920.

Even Britain, ostensibly one of the prime victors, and a monarchy that survived, was substantially weakened by this war, with repercussions again for the spread of new constitutions and new republics. Irish nationalist agitation had been rising unevenly since the 1860s. But it was London's distraction by the demands of worldwide warfare that allowed a small and initially bungled Irish nationalist rising in Dublin in 1916 to escalate into a violent and unstoppable revolution. By 1922, all but six northern counties in Ireland had succeeded in splitting away from what was emphatically no longer a United Kingdom. A new Irish Free State was forged, equipped with a written constitution; though it took a further Irish constitution in 1937 to make this independent polity explicitly a republic.[8]

Two years earlier, in 1935, the Westminster Parliament had passed a Government of India Act. Designed in part to appease and contain Indian nationalist resistance, which had broadened conspicuously since and on account of the war, this British imperial legislation satisfied no one and was soon overtaken by events. Nonetheless, its passing is a demonstration of how even those European empires which survived the First World War apparently intact, came thereafter under more sustained pressures. For all its imperfections, imperial bias and pointedly sober language, the Government of India Act is also an example of the fecundity and importance of post-war constitutional design. This legislation would go on to shape two-thirds of the content of the Indian independence constitution of 1949–50, the postcolonial world's longest-surviving constitution, and a document which once again provided for a republic.[9]

But it was the First World War's immediate destruction of yet another long-standing monarchical empire, namely Russia, which did most to give subsequent constitutions a distinctive cast.[10] The Romanov dynasty had survived the failed revolution of 1905, and had circumvented the constitution attempted the following year. After 1914, it was different. Neither the Russian empire in its customary form, nor the Romanovs were able to withstand the shocks of multiple wartime defeats, the damage these inflicted on an already ill-functioning economy, and nagging German incitement of the empire's many oppositionists.

In the case of Vladimir Ilyich Lenin, who had published a leaflet on constitutional systems during the 1905 revolution, such German subversion famously took the form of making available a sealed train, which smuggled him out of exile in Switzerland and back into Russia in 1917. As Lenin aptly remarked, drawing on the imagery of Karl Marx, war had 'given an impetus to history which is now moving with the speed of a locomotive'.[11] In February that year, there was another Russian revolution. The following month, army garrisons in St Petersburg joined striking workers to force Nicholas II from the throne. By October 1917, the Bolsheviks, a revolutionary socialist party, had come violently to power.

Initially, the collapse of the dynastic Russian empire allowed some of its former provinces to clutch eagerly at autonomy and to embody this in written texts. Thus, Georgia, a multi-ethnic territory set between Western Asia and Eastern Europe, first declared itself a republic, and then issued a constitution in February 1921. This made room for well-established reforms such as a parliamentary system and freedom of religion, but it also provided for more innovative measures. Georgian women – at least on paper – now gained equal political rights with men. The constitution also catered to the demands of organised labour, enshrining the right to strike and imposing by law restrictions on working hours. Its promise that there would be 'no distinction of class' in the new Georgia was even reinforced by an undertaking that vulnerable children were now to receive state-subsidised clothing.[12]

As this initiative suggests, post-war written constitutional-ism acquired a busy and activist social colouring, and not just in parts of Europe and Asia. Even before the war's end, in 1917, politicians in Mexico, brought to power by a series of revolu-tions, had crafted one of this era's most striking and durable constitutions. Out went the formula 'In the name of God', a feature of preambles in previous Mexican constitutions, and a relic of the constitution of Cádiz of 1812. In its place, the consti-tution instituted in 1917 gave Mexico's governments the right to divide up the country's large landed estates, and the obligation to aid its smallholders and peasantry.[13]

An emphatic turn to the social and the socialist naturally also characterised the Russian Soviet Republic's Fundamental Law of July 1918, which opened with a 'Declaration of the Rights of the Labouring and Exploited People'. Throughout the inter-war era, and even after 1945, this text would function as a reference point for left-wing radicals and reformers in the West, and for some anti-colonial activists outside the West. A calculated turn to the social was evident too in the Weimar constitution. A product of the German Revolution of 1918–19, which took fire both from the deprivations of war and from revolution in Russia, this doc-ument focused on 'social progress' throughout. Like Georgia's post-war constitution, it gave women equal political rights with men. It also mandated state control of education, a comprehen-sive system of social insurance, and cooperation 'on an equal footing between workers and employers'.[14] An unapologetic turn to the social was manifest too in some Eastern European post-war constitutions, such as Poland's 'March Constitution' of 1921. 'Labour', this proclaimed, was 'the main basis of the wealth of the republic'.[15]

Many of these radical and socialist post-war constitutions did not flourish and many of them did not last. Germany's Weimar constitution, for instance, drafted by the Jewish lawyer, academic and liberal politician Hugo Preuss, and a careful and influential document for all its faults, failed to halt – and predictably did not survive – the rise to power of Adolf Hitler. The autonomous socialist republics that swiftly emerged out of tsarist Russia after 1917 were also rapid casualties, along with their constitutional creativity. The Democratic Republic of Georgia, for one, was almost immediately wiped out by Russian troops.

Yet these and other inter-war failures did not halt the turn towards the social in constitution-making. Nor did these disappointments, and a rise in the number of new authoritarian regimes in Europe, Asia and South America result in fundamental disillusionment with, and a prolonged turning away from, the project of writing constitutions. Indeed, one of this period's most remarkable and ambitious documents was itself the work of a dictator: the constitution for the Soviet Union promulgated by Joseph Stalin in December 1936.

The Fabian socialist Beatrice Webb wrote at the time that this had the potential to create 'the most inclusive and equalised democracy in the world', a verdict which now appears almost unbearably naïve. But such optimism, which could be found across borders in the late 1930s, was partly a reaction to the extraordinary and moving way in which this Soviet constitution was crafted. Stalin himself, to be sure, was heavily involved. But so, too, during the second half of 1936, were over forty million men and women from different parts of the Soviet Union, who took excited part in special meetings and discussions, and wrote submissions on the draft version of this text. Here was the ratification of a constitution – an increasingly widespread political technique since the late eighteenth century – being put into practice with an unprecedented degree of mass involvement.[16]

Again, though, these innovations and endeavours proved abortive. In the 1760s, in the aftermath of the Seven Years' War, Catherine the Great of Russia had been superbly busy in her writing, and highly original in her anticipation of a constitutional convention in regard to the *Nakaz*. But she had quickly

64. Fedor Aleksandrovich Modorov's celebratory painting of
Stalin reporting on his draft constitution to the Extraordinary
Eighth Congress of the Soviets, 25 November 1936.

pushed all this legislative work and organisational creativity
aside to focus on expanding her empire and consolidating her
own position. Much the same happened, though in an infinitely

harsher fashion, with Joseph Stalin's constitution of 1936. Just two years later, this measure, too, had been pushed roughly aside, and programmes of mass repression and extermination of those in the Soviet Union deemed dissident or unhelpful were fully underway.

Yet, once again, for all these catastrophic failures, this proved nothing like a beginning of the end. Belief in the value and possibilities of written constitutions survived the onset of a new age of dictators, just as it had easily survived the carnage and alienation of the First World War.

There was an important sense indeed in which the very scale of this war worked to expand the traction and purview of written constitutions. At one level, the degree to which some imperial powers were obliged after 1914 to draw on extra European manpower helped to empower and validate those anti-colonial activists who were pressing for extensions of rights across the colour bar. 'As coloured people we will be fighting for something more, something inestimable to ourselves', wrote a Black journalist in 1915 about recruitment drives in British-ruled Grenada in the eastern Caribbean: '…We will be fighting to prove that we are no longer merely subjects, but citizens'.[17] By the same token, the degree to which women were officially drawn on and conscripted during this global war worked – though only in certain parts of the world – to reinforce and expand arguments that they, too, should now be brought in law and in writing within the compass of full and active citizenship.

Such claims about the instrumentality of warfare are sometimes resisted on the grounds that they detract from the degree to which ideas and alignments were already in flux *before* 1914. Socialism and socialist-inspired trade-union and welfare reforms were indeed on the rise in different countries and continents well in advance of the First World War.[18] So were feminist campaigns and anti-colonial activism. Nonetheless, the strains, shocks and demands of unprecedented levels of warfare after

1914 were vitally important because they worked to popular-
ise, deepen and advance these and other critiques of existing
political systems. Unparalleled levels of conflict, and the need
for more and wider varieties of combatants and war-workers,
could also concentrate and moderate the minds of influential
actors who had previously defended systems of exclusion on the
grounds of race, income, class, religion or gender.

The scale *and crucially the official status* of women's participation in the war after 1914 – like colonial participation in these same
wartime efforts – supplied some political leaders with an acceptable way to climb down and to move towards validating change.
During the first term of his presidency, from 1913 to March 1917,
Woodrow Wilson was at best lukewarm in his attitudes to female
suffrage. By September 1918 however – eighteen months after
America's entry into the war – his language and position had
markedly altered, at least as far as women were concerned. 'We
have made partners of women in this war', he told the US Senate
firmly. As a result, he went on, it was now unthinkable to admit
women 'only to a partnership of sacrifice and suffering and toil
and not to a partnership of privilege and of right'.[19]

So, for all the collapse of many post-1918 constitutions, and
the subsequent emergence of a new wave of authoritarian
leaders, there was no long-term and pervasive disillusionment
with the wider project of writing states and writing down government and rights in single, emotive texts. When the Second
World War once again shattered states and peoples across
the globe, quickening the collapse of the remaining Western
European maritime empires, the making of constitutions only
proceeded at an even faster pace. This war's formal end in 1945
was followed by a fresh spike in the creation of new nation
states, first in Asia, and then, from the mid-1950s, in Africa. This
led to further explosions of political constitutions.[20]

Nor was this remotely the end of the story. The expense and
effort of keeping up with a prohibitively expensive Cold War

with the United States and its allies played a major part in the fall of the Soviet empire in 1991. Its dissolution resulted in the emergence or re-emergence of fifteen, ostensibly independent countries in Eastern Europe, central Asia and Transcaucasia. Each of these polities promptly created its own new constitution.

There were other sorts of wars, too, in other places. The recurrent transcontinental conflicts that had characterised the period from the 1700s to the mid twentieth century might have ceased – at least for the time being – but the number of civil wars kept on rising. It has been estimated that, at each and every moment since 1989, an average of twenty *intra*-state wars have been in progress somewhere in the world, and especially in parts of the Middle East, Africa and central Asia.[21]

The rising incidence of civil wars has helped to drive up the rate of constitution-writing to unparalleled levels. Already, by 1991, only about twenty of the 167 single document constitutions in existence at that point were more than forty years old, so rapid had been the making of new texts since 1950, and the collapse or replacement of older ones. Since then, the rate of flux and constitution-manufacture has only quickened.[22]

So, why, you may wonder, all this repeated effort? Why, in the light of the limited longevity of so many written constitutions over the centuries, and the limited effectiveness in many cases of these texts as guarantors of responsible rule and durable rights, have multiple societies and peoples kept on investing time, imagination, thought and hope so insistently in this kind of paper and parchment political and legal device?

★

This book has been concerned to chart an extraordinary transformation, which occurred across a matter of a few centuries, in how states, political actors and ordinary men and women across the world came to react, think, behave and sometimes place their trust. In accounting for this alteration – the relentless progress across geographical space of single-document written constitutions – I have highlighted the role played by sequential bouts of large-scale warfare and aggression, and deliberately so. The proliferation of texts of this sort has often been explained *only* by reference to the rise of democracy and the lure of certain (mainly Western) notions of constitutionalism. Focusing on the contribution made by recurrent episodes of armed violence provides for a more comprehensive and variegated view and brings in a wider range of terrains and voices. It also makes for a better awareness that, from the outset, written constitutions have been protean phenomena. They have always taken different forms and served multiple purposes, and this has been an essential reason for their success and persistence.

From the 1750s, constitutions heralded and aided the emergence of revolutionary republics, Corsica, the United States, France, Haiti and more. Nonetheless, in advance of the First World War, some of the most influential political texts of this sort were products not of republican regimes, but rather of different kinds of monarchies. This was the case with Spain's constitution of Cádiz. It was also the case with the Belgian constitution of 1831 and the Japanese constitution of 1889. Then, again, constitutions have regularly been products of revolutions against empire. But, across the long nineteenth century, and arguably and residually even today, important written constitutions have also worked to assist the making and maintenance of empires.

This was the case with some long-established European empires such as Habsburg Austria, which implemented its Ausgleich of 1866 in a bid to calm and contain some of its internal dissensions. It was also the case with newer, more ephemeral European empires, such as that forged by Napoleon; and it was the case too with some empires outside Europe. The United States' expanding web of state constitutions, together with its iconic Federal constitution of 1787, offer a conspicuous example of the essentially protean nature of this political and legal device. At one level, these multiple American constitutions provided for exceptional levels of white, male democracy and opportunity. At another level, however, many of these same documents also helped to further, order and legitimise the appropriation of other peoples' lands on the part of advancing armies of mainly white settlers, thereby acting as building blocks for the construction of a continent-wide American empire.

Even today, constitutions can still function as aids to territorial expansion. Consider the constitution of the People's Republic of China, adopted in 1982. The careful, potted history inserted in its preamble celebrates, while manicuring, this huge terrain's multi-national composition ('The people of all nationalities in China have jointly created a splendid culture and have a glorious revolutionary tradition'), thereby – among other things – glossing over the degree to which many inhabitants of Tibet, Xinjiang and Hong Kong, say, do not wish in fact to view themselves as Chinese. This same document insists that Taiwan, where a majority of voters currently favour continuing independence, 'is part of the sacred territory of the People's Republic of China', and that absorbing it and 'reunifying the motherland' remains a 'lofty duty'.[23] As this powerful and calculated document demonstrates, another persistent attraction of written constitutions has been that they provide political regimes with an exportable and sometimes charismatic manifesto and vindication.

This is one reason why their allure expanded so markedly after 1750. Rising levels of competition and warfare between different states and empires made manifestos of this sort profoundly attractive both to those already possessed of power, and to those in search of power. By means of designing and issuing a constitution, a polity that had been newly cobbled together out of armed conflict could hope to organise its inhabitants, demarcate its boundaries, develop and trademark its emerging identity, and proclaim its arrival as a modern player on the world stage. As for more well-established states, they could – and progressively did – employ constitutions as a means to strengthen themselves against domestic and external threats, to celebrate and order territory acquired by war or imperial expansion and, conversely, to reconstruct and re-validate themselves in the wake of military defeat.

Written constitutions have thus supplied state and rulers with valuable performative and presentational opportunities; although in order to exploit these opportunities to the full, political actors – at least in the past – generally required access to print. A good demonstration of this point, and of the degree to which constitutions rapidly came to be recognised as indispensable assets, is also an indirect one.

As we have seen, after the 1650s, the state that became Great Britain and then, for a while, the United Kingdom of Great Britain and Ireland, possessed nothing resembling a single, codified constitution. An unusual degree of immunity from successful invasions and violent domestic transitions meant that its rulers in London never felt – and still do not feel – an urgent need to concede one. But since written constitutions *were* so intimately bound up with competition between states, and since they also possessed such evident propaganda and manifesto value, an ambitious warlike and imperial British state could not afford to remain entirely aloof from them.

The solution adopted in this society was to develop and expand the genre of constitutional history, a strategy which had the advantage of also exploiting Britain's dense printing industry with its worldwide networks. Between the 1820s and the 1920s, the publication of new constitutional histories of Britain on the part of printing presses in London, Oxford and Cambridge increased almost twenty times over.[24] Unable or unwilling to design and deploy a formal written constitution, British jurists, polemicists and politicians resorted instead and deliberately to another form of print: patriotic and widely distributed and exported histories of their real and imagined political constitution.

This particular British response serves to highlight some general and important points: how written constitutions progressively became a norm and a habit which it was hard for states anywhere to ignore and resist, and how, too, these political devices were often bound up with the printed word. Yet this very relationship with print also helped to ensure that – while written constitutions have always serviced power – they were nonetheless volatile and unpredictable creations. To paraphrase the great political scientist Benedict Anderson, a written constitution 'proved an invention on which it was impossible to secure a patent'. Like other printed works, like many eighteenth- and nineteenth-century novels indeed, this kind of constitution 'became available for pirating by widely different, and sometimes unexpected hands'.[25]

At one level, the relentless reprinting and export of rising numbers of constitutions meant that even the most avowedly nationalistic texts of this sort were usually hybrid creations. Those drafting them were always attracted to the art of pick and mix, taking material, ideas and provisions from analogous published texts originating in different parts of the world. This is one reason why constitutions need approaching and interpreting in more than purely national terms. At another level, the printing, extracting and translation of especially momentous constitutional texts – the American constitution of 1787, the French constitutions of 1791 and 1793, the Cádiz constitution of 1812, the Liberian constitution of 1847, the Japanese constitution of 1889 and more – could work in other spaces in the world to seduce, disrupt and subvert.

Printed material of this sort supplied ideas, hope and inspiration to reformers and radicals in countries and regions that lacked a constitution, or were in need of a new one, or were subject to other states. The widening distribution of constitutions in print also encouraged extraordinary numbers of activists and enthusiasts – usually men, and frequently military men – to attempt their own unofficial, sometimes dissident texts. Moreover, as constitutional texts crossed into other territories and other languages, not only did this help to propagate the brand in general, the texts themselves were also frequently read and interpreted in different, sometimes incendiary ways.

Once translated and reprinted in Calcutta, the Mexican general Agustín de Iturbide's *Plan de Iguala* could become reconfigured into a defence of wider rights for South Asians. And while the Meiji constitution was built around respect for a hereditary Japanese emperor, some of those reading it in translation later on in the Ottoman empire or Iran were in search of arguments for a republic. Documents outlining power, law and rights easily become combustible: and this proved the fate not just of many formal political constitutions, but also of published works on British constitutional history. In the 1930s, and after the Second World War, anti-colonial activists such as the Trinidadian, C. L. R. James, and Kwame Nkrumah in what is now Ghana would carefully mine these learned and reverential tomes for ammunition to use against acts of British imperial hypocrisy and violence, and for arguments and points of law that might reinforce the case they were building for independence.[26]

The significance of print for the global spread of written constitutions, and the overwhelming importance of recurrent bouts of warfare in providing for this spread, unavoidably raise questions about the effectiveness and resonance of this ubiquitous political instrument now, in the early decades of the twenty-first century. In the past, to be sure, and for all their relentless reproduction in pamphlets, newspapers, broadsheets, compendia and school books, constitutions were never as attentively scrutinised by the mass of people as their most ardent champions would ideally have wished.[27] Now, however, far more systemic challenges exist to the political impact and reach of the printed word.

Today, many of us inhabit societies where growing numbers of people get such political information as they see and want not from the printed page, but rather from a screen. The digital age has brought into being, moreover, a balkanisation of political information. In more affluent regions, especially, there is no longer a narrow aperture world where the mass of people rely on simply a few television channels, or just a few major newspapers – *or on a single, iconic written and printed constitutional text*. Instead, the range of unfiltered information and viewpoints on politics and political ideas, as on so much else, is constantly efflorescing in multiple media.

The ways in which written constitutions were able to evolve so rapidly and powerfully in the past should alert us to other challenges which now exist to their continuing and future efficacy and renewal. Especially after 1750, outbreaks of war repeatedly led across continents to periods of dramatic rupture, which then – sometimes – prompted the creation of constructive new political constitutions. War, and the costs and burdens of war, also frequently obliged states and rulers to make gestures and concessions on paper to their respective populations.

It is different now. For those of us fortunate enough to inhabit societies which are not repeatedly afflicted by civil warfare, *this* kind of stimulus to the creation and amendment of constitutions no longer operates. Since the Second World War, the nature of warfare has anyway substantially altered. Most present-day significant states rely on professional, highly specialised armies, navies, air forces and lethal elite units, on nuclear technology, cyber-technicians and more. Consequently, the likelihood of governments now and in the future having to concede new, more enlightened constitutions as a means to ensure mass conscription and to reward and entice sustained wartime loyalty is much diminished.

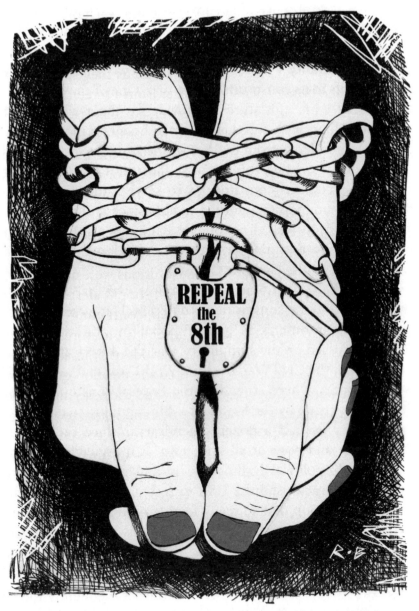

65. Using constitutions now: A contribution by the artist Róisín
Blade to the successful campaign in 2016 to repeal the 8th provision
of the Irish constitution which had effectively banned abortion.

The relative absence of such wartime stimuli matters less in secure democracies where it is relatively easy to amend existing constitutions. In the Republic of Ireland for instance – which practises neutrality – there have been no fewer than thirty-five amendments to its constitution since 1972. One of these, in 2018, allowed the Irish legislature to provide for the availability of abortion. Along with subsequent amendments removing blasphemy as an offence from the text of the Irish constitution and making divorce easier, this initiative illustrates the continuing capacity of codified constitutions to serve a manifesto function. These amendments served to announce and make clear, internationally as well as nationally, that a modern Republic of Ireland was now essentially a secular state, no longer dominated as in the past by the Catholic Church.

But in the United States, for example, the case as regards amendments to the constitution is different. Here, constitution-making and momentous constitutional modifications have repeatedly relied on the stimulus of war, the American Revolutionary War, the Civil War, the First World War and more. This is also a polity where amending the Federal constitution was deliberately made by the founders a difficult thing to do. There have been only half a dozen amendments since the Second World War, and none at all since 1992. It is arguable that one reason for the political dysfunctionality and hampering divisions that have characterised the USA in recent decades is that the iconic constitution that so many former men at arms laboured over in Philadelphia back in 1787 is, by this stage, simply too old and too limited, and in need therefore of sustained and expert amplification and revitalisation. Yet, without the external massive pressures of something like a major war how are such alterations ever to be brought about and agreed upon? Might another kind of overwhelming emergency do the work?

But the broadest and most ubiquitous challenge, you might think, is that in the early twenty-first century – as always – written constitutions by themselves do not and cannot guarantee either good government or the secure possession of basic rights. Texts of this sort now exist in virtually all of the world's states. Yet in its annual surveys of over two hundred countries over the past fourteen years, and on the basis of carefully garnered evidence, the American-based NGO, Freedom House, has reported a steady decline in levels of political rights and civil liberties.[28] Even as I write, populist, authoritarian, would-be authoritarian, repressive and corrupt governments are flourishing and multiplying across continents, for all the wide availability of written constitutions.

Yet despite this – indeed in part because of it – written constitutions continue to matter. These texts matter enormously, as I have sought to show, as a historical phenomenon and as a means by which to investigate the global past and the evolution of different visions of the modern. But they also matter now. For all that we inhabit an increasingly digital world, the intrinsic genius of this paper political device which informs and can inspire and provoke, which is capable of endless reproduction in every language, and which is also cheap and easily portable, has a persistent value. One sees this vividly and often in the case of individuals operating under extreme stress.

Go back for instance to a flashpoint in South Africa in 2017, and to a member of the Economic Freedom Fighters, a far-left, sometimes paramilitary organisation. The man concerned was part of a mass demonstration in Pretoria demanding the resignation of then President Jacob Zuma, who was steeped in corruption. Seeing a photographer approaching, this protester – whose name for good reason we cannot know – quickly concealed his face behind a battered copy of his country's constitution.

This was the famous text signed into law in December 1996 by Nelson Mandela, and drafted so as to signal and advance a post-apartheid South Africa. Tellingly, it was to the cheap paper

66. Pretoria, South Africa, 2017: using a
constitution to conceal and affirm.

edition of the constitution that this demonstrator in Pretoria
resorted. Smaller than your average paperback, it had been deliberately priced and manufactured to reach the widest readership
possible and to fit easily into a pocket. It proved nonetheless big
enough to hide this man's face. Yet, by concealing his identity in
this way, by means of a cheap paperback edition of his country's
constitution, this man in a fashion also went public. By means
of this action, he identified himself intimately with a reformed
South Africa, thereby proclaiming that it was essentially to do
with people like him.

In a deeply uncertain, shifting, unequal and violent world,
these kinds of imperfect but sometimes stirring, diversely useful
and easily available texts may be the best we can hope for. As
Thomas Jefferson put it in 1802: 'tho' written constitutions may

67. Moscow, Russia, 2019: Olga Misik and her constitution.

be violated in moments of passion or delusion, yet they furnish a text to which those who are watchful may again rally & recall the people'.[29] Over 200 years later, much the same point was being acted out by another individual under stress, a young woman named Olga Misik who was protesting in the streets of Moscow.

Under the protracted rule of Vladimir Putin, a one-time lieutenant-general turned first prime minister and then president, the Russian constitution has undoubtedly been undermined as far as some of its provisions for free expression and fundamental liberties are concerned. Even so, this text still sometimes works to moderate acts of excessive power and – in Jefferson's words – to rally and remind. The constitution's provisions for religious freedom in Russia, for instance, have proved under Putin to be markedly resilient.[30] And since this *is* a written constitution, easily and cheaply available in print, it is available to be drawn on, again, by individuals under pressure and in need.

A pro-democracy activist, Misik found herself early in August 2019 encircled by riot police, formidable men in body armour, brandishing shields and batons. Her response was to sit down in the street and to read aloud passages from the pages of a paperback copy of the Russian constitution. Misik was seventeen at this point and still at school. She cannot seriously have imagined that her actions would substantially change the actions and orientation of the Russian government. Nor did they. But she turned to her constitution for support and inspiration anyway. The armed men surrounding her on this occasion knew of course that they were being photographed and that these images were likely to go viral. But they also heard the words that Misik was speaking, and they recognised the text from where she was reading – and they did not move in and attack.

# NOTES

These endnotes constitute what is in effect a running bibliography and also offer suggestions for further reading. References to authors, titles and places of publication are given in full at the start of each chapter. Whenever possible, I include the current on-line details for the particular constitutions I discuss, as well as their original on-paper locations.

## Introduction

1. Giray Fidan, 'The Turk Travelogue: Kang Youwei's Journey to the Ottoman Empire', *Bilig* 76 (2016), 227–43. For the Ottoman background, see Erik Jan Zürcher, 'The Young Turk Revolution: Comparisons and Connections', *Middle Eastern Studies* 55 (2019), 481–98.

2. Aida Yuen Wong, *The Other Kang Youwei: Calligrapher, Art Activist, and Aesthetic Reformer in Modern China* (Leiden, 2016), 86.

3. William Blackstone, *The Great Charter and Charter of the Forest* (Oxford, 1759), i.

4. For a classic exposition of this thesis, see R. R. Palmer, *The Age of the Democratic Revolution: A Political History of Europe and America, 1760–1800* (2 vols., Princeton, NJ, 1959–64). This work's enduring influence can still be traced in the introduction to David Armitage and Sanjay Subrahmanyam (eds.), *The Age of Revolutions in Global Contexts, c.1760–1840* (New York, 2010).

5. Theda Skocpol, *States and Social Revolutions: A Comparative Analysis of France, Russia, and China* (Cambridge, 1979), 186.

6. Max Roser *et al*, 'Global deaths in conflicts since the year 1400', in Max Roser (2020) 'War and Peace'. Published online at OurWorldinData.org. Retrieved from https://ourworldindata.org/war-and-peace, consulted in 2019. I am grateful to Professor Roser for allowing me to reproduce this chart.

7. I owe this concept of an 'umbrella war' to Professor Jeremy Black.

8. Quoted from the book of these lectures: *General Economic History*, trans. Frank H. Knight (London, 1927), 325.
9. Jürgen Osterhammel, *The Transformation of the World: A Global History of the Nineteenth Century* (Princeton, NJ, 2014), 118–19. For the American move into overseas empire and its wider contexts, see A. G. Hopkins, *American Empire: A Global History* (Princeton, NJ, 2018).
10. Sebastian Conrad, 'Enlightenment in Global History: A Historiographical Critique', *American Historical Review* 117 (2012), 999–1027, at 1027.
11. See Wong, *The Other Kang Youwei*.

**Chapter One: The Multiple Trajectories of War**
1. On the cult that evolved around Paoli, see David Bell, *Men on Horseback: The Power of Charisma in the Age of Revolutions* (New York, 2020), 19–52; *Independent Chronicle*, 16 October 1770.
2. The best studies are in French: Antoine-Marie Graziani, *Pascal Paoli: Père de la patrie corse* (Paris, 2002), and Michel Vergé-Franceschi, *Paoli: Un Corse des Lumières* (Paris, 2005); *Correspondance Pascal Paoli: Édition critique établie par Antoine-Marie Graziani* (Ajaccio, 7 vols., 2003–18), I, 84–91.
3. *Correspondance Pascal Paoli*, I, 84–91.
4. An authoritative version of this constitution is in *Correspondance Pascal Paoli*, I, 222–47; for an earlier but still valuable survey, see Dorothy Carrington, 'The Corsican Constitution of Pasquale Paoli (1755–1769)', *English Historical Review* 88 (1973), 481–503.
5. Carrington, 'The Corsican Constitution of Pasquale Paoli', 495–6, 500.
6. See Vergé-Franceschi, *Paoli*, chapter two; Fernand Ettori, 'La formation intellectuelle de Pascal Paoli (1725–1755)', in *Correspondance Pascal Paoli*, I, 11–31.
7. *Correspondance Pascal Paoli*, II, 136–8.
8. Ibid.
9. *Correspondance Pascal Paoli*, I, 239.
10. Graziani, *Pascal Paoli*, 139.
11. Paoli did make attempts at building up a maritime force. See James Boswell, *An Account of Corsica, the Journal of a Tour to That Island,*

*and Memoirs of Pascal Paoli*, James T. Boulton and T. O. McLoughlin (eds.) (Oxford, 2006), 30.

12. As he seems to have realised. See *Correspondance Pascal Paoli*, II, 62–3.

13. Winston Churchill employs this description in the third volume of his *A History of the English-Speaking Peoples*. The Seven Years' War was not a world war in the sense that every region of the globe was drawn into it, but rather in regard to the unprecedented degree to which its violence and repercussions affected multiple continents.

14. See Tonio Andrade, *The Gunpowder Age: China, Military Innovation, and the Rise of the West in World History* (Princeton, NJ, 2016), and Kenneth Chase, *Firearms: A Global History to 1700* (Cambridge, 2003); the classic argument for the state-making potential of warfare is Charles Tilly, *Coercion, Capital, and European States, AD 990–1990* (Oxford, 1990).

15. Robert Orme, *A History of the Military Transactions of the British Nation in Indostan* (London, 1763), 345; M. S. Anderson, *War and Society in Europe of the Old Regime 1618–1789* (Montreal, 1998), 80.

16. Daniel A. Baugh, *The Global Seven Years' War 1754–1763: Britain and France in a Great Power Contest* (London, 2011).

17. Pradeep P. Barua, *The State at War in South Asia* (Lincoln, NE, 2005), 47; for an introduction to Nādir Shāh and his worlds, see Peter Avery's chapter in his edited volume of *The Cambridge History of Iran* (Cambridge, 1991): 'Nādir Shāh and the Ashfarid Legacy', vol. 7, 1–62.

18. Peter C. Perdue, *China Marches West: The Qing Conquest of Central Eurasia* (Cambridge, MA, 2005).

19. I am playing here on the title used by Kenneth Pomeranz: *The Great Divergence: China, Europe, and the Making of the Modern World Economy* (Princeton, NJ, 2000). Joanna Waley-Cohen's 'Commemorating War in Eighteenth-century China', *Modern Asian Studies* 30 (1996), 869–99, offers a fascinating sidelight on this mid-century convergence between different world regions and their wars. She shows how Qianlong's advisers made use of engravers in post-Seven Years' War Paris to memorialise his victories over the Zunghars.

20. For current definitions of hybrid warfare, see the British Ministry of Defence's online publication *Understanding Hybrid Warfare* (2017).
21. I owe this information to my colleague at Princeton, Professor Susan Naquin.
22. See Jaap R. Bruijn, 'States and Their Navies from the Late Sixteenth to the End of the Eighteenth Centuries', in Philippe Contamine (ed.), *War and Competition between States: The Origins of the Modern State in Europe, 13th to 18th Centuries* (New York, 2000).
23. Peter McPhee, 'Rethinking the French Revolution and the "Global Crisis" of the Late-Eighteenth Century', *French History and Civilization* 6 (2015), 57.
24. Bruijn, 'States and Their Navies', 71.
25. John Brewer, *The Sinews of Power: War, Money and the English State, 1688–1783* (Boston, MA, 1989), 29–63.
26. David Bell, *The First Total War: Napoleon's Europe and the Birth of Warfare as We Know It* (Boston, MA, 2007), 17.
27. See my *Captives: Britain, Empire and the World, 1600–1850* (London, 2002), 269–307. For the challenges to other Indian states at this time, see Tirthankar Roy, 'Rethinking the Origins of British India: State Formation and Military-Fiscal Undertakings in an Eighteenth-Century World Region', *Modern Asian Studies* 47 (2013), 1125–56.
28. I have benefited here from a close reading of C. A. Bayly's classic *The Birth of the Modern World, 1780–1914: Global Connections and Comparisons* (London, 2004), especially 86–121. I would want to place more emphasis, however, on the degree to which, by the 1750s, large-scale warfare on the part of big Western powers involved the sea as well as the land, and the many consequences of this. To this extent, Bayly's valuable map in this volume (84–5) of the spread of armed conflicts across the globe is too static and land-focused. Ideally, a map of this topic would include rising numbers of ships in motion in different seas and oceans.
29. The best recent survey of this evolving crisis is Alan Taylor, *American Revolutions: A Continental History, 1750–1804* (New York, 2016).
30. Edward J. Cashin, *Governor Henry Ellis and the Transformation of British North America* (Athens, GA, 1994), 211.

31. See Eric Hinderaker, *Boston's Massacre* (Cambridge, MA, 2017).
32. Peter D. G. Thomas, 'The Cost of the British Army in North America, 1763–1775', *William and Mary Quarterly* 45 (1988), 510–16.
33. Charles Townshend, a future Chancellor of the Exchequer, quoted in Taylor, *American Revolutions*, 98. Townshend's championship of new taxes on the American colonies is well known. It is less well known that he had previously served as a Lord of the Admiralty. He knew exactly what warships cost.
34. John Shy's verdict still applies: 'Armed force, and nothing else, decided the outcome of the American Revolution ... without war to sustain it, the Declaration of Independence would be a forgotten, abortive manifesto', in *A People Numerous and Armed: Reflections on the Military Struggle for American Independence* (New York, 1976), 165. It is also the case that, without the strains imposed by the previous Seven Years' War, this further transatlantic crisis would never have evolved in the manner it did, or as quickly as it did.
35. James C. Riley, *The Seven Years' War and the Old Regime in France: The Economic and Financial Toll* (Princeton, NJ, 1986).
36. Rafe Blaufarb, 'Noble Privilege and Absolutist State Building: French Military Administration after the Seven Years' War', *French Historical Studies* 24 (2001), 223–46; and, for another facet of France's post-1763 *revanche*, Emma Rothschild, 'A Horrible Tragedy in the French Atlantic', *Past and Present* 192 (2006), 67–108.
37. Lynn Hunt, 'The Global Financial Origins of 1789', in Lynn Hunt, Suzanne Desan and William Max Nelson (eds.), *The French Revolution in Global Perspective* (Ithaca, NY, 2013), 32 and *passim*.
38. Pierre Serna, Antonio de Francesco and Judith Miller (eds.), *Republics at War, 1776–1840: Revolutions, Conflicts and Geopolitics in Europe and the Atlantic World* (New York, 2013), 243; for estimates of the size of leading European armies in 1789, see Paul Kennedy, *The Rise and Fall of the Great Powers: Economic Change and Military Conflict from 1500 to 2000* (New York, 1987), 99.
39. The best survey is John Elliott, *Empires of the Atlantic World: Britain and Spain in America 1492–1830* (New Haven, CT, 2006), 292 *et seq.* For a regional example of the post-1763 refurbishment of Spanish imperial control in South America, see Leon G. Campbell, *The*

*Military and Society in Colonial Peru, 1750–1810* (Philadelphia, PA, 1978).

40. Carlos Marichal, *Bankruptcy of Empire: Mexican Silver and the Wars between Spain, Britain, and France, 1760–1810* (New York, 2007).

41. Arjun Appadurai, commenting on Stuart Alexander Rockefeller, 'Flow', *Current Anthropology* 52 (2011), 557–78, at 569.

42. The recent historiography is enormous. Good and differently slanted surveys include: Jeremy D. Popkin, *A Concise History of the Haitian Revolution* (Chichester, 2012); David P. Geggus, *The Impact of the Haitian Revolution in the Atlantic World* (Columbia, SC, 2001); and Laurent Dubois, *Avengers of the New World: The Story of the Haitian Revolution* (Cambridge, MA, 2004).

43. As reported in the *Pennsylvania Gazette* on 12 October 1791. See https://revolution.chnm.org/items/show/317.

44. Julia Gaffield, 'Complexities of Imagining Haiti: A Study of the National Constitutions, 1801–1807', *Journal of Social History* 41 (2007), 81–103. English translations of the 1801, 1804, 1805, 1806 and 1811 Haitian constitutions are available online.

45. James Stephen, *The Opportunity; Or, Reasons for an Immediate Alliance with St Domingo* (London, 1804), 11–12.

46. For this text, see Julia Gaffield (ed.), *The Haitian Declaration of Independence* (Charlottesville, VA, 2016); the comment on Black authorship of constitutional texts is by Prince Saunders, an African American who set up schools in Haiti, in his (ed.) *Haytian Papers: A Collection of the Very Interesting Proclamations and Other Documents ... of the Kingdom of Hayti* (London, 1816), iii.

47. Robert W. Harms, *The Diligent: A Voyage through the Worlds of the Slave Trade* (New York, 2002), xi.

48. David Richardson, 'Slave Exports from West and West-Central Africa, 1700–1810: New Estimates of Volume and Distribution', *Journal of African History* 30 (1989), 1–22.

49. See Richard J. Reid, *Warfare in African History* (Cambridge, 2012).

50. John Thornton, 'African Soldiers in the Haitian Revolution', *Journal of Caribbean History* 25 (1991), 58–80. This thesis has been disputed.

51. I owe this information to Professor David Geggus.

52. For Toussaint, see Bell, *Men on Horseback*, 133–70; and for a selection of his letters, including this account of his war wounds, see

Jean-Bertrand Aristide, *The Haitian Revolution: Toussaint L'Ouverture* (New York, 2008), 112–13 and *passim*. The most authoritative biography is now Sudhir Hazareesingh, *Black Spartacus: The Epic Life of Toussaint Louverture* (New York, 2020).

53. For a revisionist and contested view of this man, see Philippe R. Girard, 'Jean-Jacques Dessalines and the Atlantic System: A Reappraisal', *William and Mary Quarterly* 69 (2012), 549–82.

54. Mimi Sheller, 'Sword-Bearing Citizens: Militarism and Manhood in Nineteenth-Century Haiti', in Alyssa Goldstein Sepinwall (ed.), *Haitian History: New Perspectives* (New York, 2012), 157–79.

55. Saunders (ed.), *Haytian Papers*, 139.

56. Ibid., 97 *et seq.*; Clive Cheesman (ed.), *The Armorial of Haiti: Symbols of Nobility in the Reign of Henry Christophe* (London, 2007).

57. Saunders (ed.), *Haytian Papers*, 126–7.

58. Title page of *The Formation of the New Dynasty of the Kingdom of Hayti* (Philadelphia, 1811).

59. I am indebted here to a 2011 paper delivered by Professor Doris L. Garraway, 'Picturing Haitian Sovereignty: Portraiture and Self-fashioning in the Kingdom of Henry Christophe', at the Shelby Cullom Davis Center for Historical Studies, Princeton University.

60. Laurent Dubois, *Haiti: The Aftershocks of History* (New York, 2012), 61.

61. As Paul Schroeder puts it, progressively after 1750, many politicians 'did not so much fear war because they thought it would bring revolution as because they had learned from bitter experience that war *was* revolution': *The Transformation of European Politics, 1763–1848* (Oxford, 1994), 802.

## Chapter Two: Old Europe, New Ideas

1. William E. Butler and Vladimir A. Tomsinov (eds.), *The Nakaz of Catherine the Great: Collected Texts* (Clark, NJ, 2010), vii–24.

2. Isabel De Madariaga, 'Catherine the Great', in H. M. Scott (ed.), *Enlightened Absolutism: Reform and Reformers in Late Eighteenth-century Europe* (Basingstoke, 1990), 289.

3. Hannah Arendt, *On Revolution* (London, 1963), 157.

4. For these and other post-Seven Years' War British cartographic

projects, see Max Edelson, *The New Map of Empire: How Britain Imagined America before Independence* (Cambridge, MA, 2017).

5. This Sardinian text was an extension of a 1723 code; Allan J. Kuethe and Kenneth J. Andrien, *The Spanish Atlantic World in the Eighteenth Century: War and the Bourbon Reforms, 1713–1796* (New York, 2014), 229–304.

6. See my 'Empires of Writing: Britain, America and Constitutions, 1776–1848', *Law and History Review* 32 (2014), 240 n.

7. Victor Kamendrowsky, 'Catherine II's *Nakaz*: State Finances and the Encyclopédie', *Canadian American Slavic Studies* 13 (1979), 545–55; *The Nakaz of Catherine the Great*, 14.

8. Voltaire, *The Age of Louis XIV*, R. Griffith (trans.) (London, 3 vols., 1779), I, 220.

9. Jean-Jacques Rousseau, *Of the Social Contract and Other Political Writings*, Christopher Bertram (ed.) (London, 2012), 153; see also Christine Jane Carter, *Rousseau and the Problem of War* (New York, 1987).

10. See Rousseau, 'Constitutional Proposal for Corsica', in *Of the Social Contract and Other Political Writings*, Christopher Bertram (ed.), 187–240.

11. Dan Edelstein, *The Enlightenment: A Genealogy* (Chicago, IL, 2010), 94.

12. Dan Edelstein, 'War and Terror: The Law of Nations from Grotius to the French Revolution', *French Historical Studies* 31 (2008), 241 *et seq.*

13. Quoted in Keith Michael Baker, *Inventing the French Revolution: Essays on French Political Culture in the Eighteenth Century* (Cambridge, 1990), 256. Another Enlightenment man, the Englishman Samuel Johnson, made a similar point at roughly this same period. His famous dictionary, published in London in 1755, defines a 'constitution' as an 'established form of government', but only after offering a more dynamic definition: 'the *act* of constituting, enacting ... establishing [my italics]'. See his *A Dictionary of the English Language* (2 vols., London, 1755), I (unpaginated).

14. M. de Montesquieu, *The Spirit of Laws*, Thomas Nugent (trans.) (London, 2 vols., 1752), I, 310–11; for Catherine on Montesquieu, see

Isabella Forbes, *Catherine the Great: Treasures of Imperial Russia from the State Hermitage Museum, Leningrad* (London, 1993), xii.

15. Montesquieu, *The Spirit of Laws, Including D'Alembert's Analysis on the Work* (London, 2015), xxviii.

16. Jean-Jacques Rousseau, *'The Social Contract' and Other Later Political Writings*, Victor Gourevitch (ed. and trans.) (Cambridge, 1997), 41.

17. Edelstein, *The Enlightenment*, 50. This rising cult of the legislator was not confined to continental Europe. The database Eighteenth Century Collections Online (ECCO) indicates that almost six out of seven of the 750 plus references to Alfred the Great, the fabled English lawgiver, in British and Irish books in the eighteenth century occurred *after* 1760.

18. See the English version, Louis-Sébastien Mercier, *Memoirs of the Year Two Thousand Five Hundred*, W. Hooper (trans.) (London, 1772), 214–15, 332–3.

19. Quoted in Derek Beales, *Enlightenment and Reform in Eighteenth-century Europe* (London, 2005), 48.

20. Isabel de Madariaga, *Catherine the Great: A Short History* (London, 2002) and Simon Dixon, *Catherine the Great* (New York, 2001) offer excellent and lucid summaries of her life and political career.

21. For this ruler's calculated image-making – including attempts to present herself as a legislator – see Erin McBurney, 'Art and Power in the Reign of Catherine the Great: The State Portraits' (2014), Columbia University PhD dissertation.

22. See, for instance, *Imperial Lovers behind Closed Doors*, an erotic watercolour from the 1790s reproduced in Cynthia Hyla Whitaker (ed.), *Russia Engages the World, 1453–1825* (Cambridge, MA, 2002), 180.

23. Simon Dixon, 'The Posthumous Reputation of Catherine II in Russia 1797–1837', *Slavonic and East European Review* 77 (1999), 648–9.

24. Anthony Cross, 'Condemned by Correspondence: Horace Walpole and Catherine "Slay-Czar"', *Journal of European Studies* 27 (1997), 129–41.

25. Madariaga, *Catherine the Great*, 40.

26. Nikolai Nekrasov, quoted in *The Rise of Fiscal States: A Global History, 1500–1914*, Bartolomé Yun-Casalilla and Patrick K. O'Brien (eds.) (Cambridge, 2012), 210.

27. *The Nakaz of Catherine the Great*, 446.
28. Ibid., 446–7.
29. Ibid., 463 and 518.
30. Ibid., 489, 503–4.
31. Ibid., 482, 484, 513.
32. Quoted in John T. Alexander, *Catherine the Great: Life and Legend* (Oxford, 1989), 113.
33. 'Observations on the Introduction of the Empress of Russia to the Deputies for the Making of the Laws', in *Denis Diderot: Political Writings*, John Hope Mason and Robert Wokler (eds. and trans.) (Cambridge, 1992), 81.
34. The most comprehensive English-language account is still Robert Vincent Allen, 'The Great Legislative Commission of Catherine II of 1767' (1950), Yale University PhD dissertation, and I draw on this in succeeding paragraphs.
35. Isabel de Madariaga, 'Catherine II and the Serfs: A Reconsideration of Some Problems', *Slavonic and East European Review* 52 (1974), 34–62.
36. Antony Lentin (ed. and trans.),*Voltaire and Catherine the Great: Selected Correspondence* (Cambridge, 1974), 49.
37. *The Nakaz of Catherine the Great*, 22.
38. Ibid., 521–31.
39. *Lloyds Evening Post*, 29/31 October 1770; Lentin, *Voltaire and Catherine the Great*, 111.
40. For Voulgaris, see Paschalis M. Kitromilides, *Enlightenment and Revolution: The Making of Modern Greece* (Cambridge, MA, 2013), 39 *et seq.*
41. Michael Tatischeff, *The Grand Instruction to the Commissioners Appointed to Frame a New Code of Laws for the Russian Empire* (London, 1768), 192. I am indebted to my colleague Professor Ekaterina Pravilova for information on Russian uses of the term 'constitution' and for her advice on this chapter.
42. Quoted in Martin J. Daunton, *State and Market in Victorian Britain: War, Welfare and Capitalism* (Rochester, NY, 2008), 40.
43. For a recent, expert biography, see T. C. W. Blanning, *Frederick the Great: King of Prussia* (London, 2013).

44. T. C. W. Blanning, *The Pursuit of Glory: Europe 1648–1815* (London, 2007), 593.

45. *Correspondance de Catherine Alexéievna, Grande-Duchesse de Russie, et de Sir Charles H. Williams, ambassadeur d'Angleterre, 1756 et 1757* (Moscow, 1909), 241.

46. Even the title in translation was ambitious: *The Frederician Code: Or, a Body of Law for the Dominions of the King of Prussia. Founded on Reason, and the Constitution of the Country* (Edinburgh, 2 vols., 1761), I, 29 and 32.

47. The best political biography of Gustaf is still Erik Lönnroth, *Den stora rollen. Kung Gustaf III spelad av honum själv* (Stockholm, 1986) and I have drawn on it throughout. For the background, see Pasi Ihalainen *et al.* (eds.), *Scandinavia in the Age of Revolution: Nordic Political Cultures, 1740–1820* (Farnham, 2011).

48. Michael Roberts, *The Swedish Imperial Experience, 1560–1718* (Cambridge, 1979).

49. *The Dispute between the King and Senate of Sweden ... to which is prefixed, A short account of the Swedish constitution* (London, 1756), 1.

50. Michael F. Metcalf, *The Riksdag: A History of the Swedish Parliament* (New York, 1987). See also Marie-Christine Skuncke, 'Press Freedom in the Riksdag' in *Press Freedom 250 years: Freedom of the Press and Public Access to Official Documents in Sweden and Finland – A Living Heritage from 1766* (Stockholm, 2018). I thank Professor Skuncke for her invaluable advice on matters Swedish.

51. Gunnar von Proschwitz (ed.), *Gustave III, par ses lettres* (Stockholm, 1987), 156.

52. Lönnroth, *Den stora rollen*, 70–82.

53. Patrik Winton, 'Sweden and the Seven Years' War, 1757–1762: War, Debt and Politics', *War in History* 19 (2012), 5–31. In other words, in Sweden, as in other parts of the globe, this episode of hybrid warfare fed into a signal reconfiguring of the political order.

54. *State Papers Relating the Change of the Constitution of Sweden* (London, 1772), 31 and *passim*.

55. Ibid., 55. On Frederick the Great's use of the term 'citizen', implicitly in regard to himself, see his unpublished 1777 essay 'Forms of Government and the Duties of Rulers', which is available online.

56. *State Papers Relating the Change of the Constitution*, 10. On this speech's diffusion, see Marie-Christine Skuncke, 'Appropriation of Political Rhetoric in Eighteenth-century Sweden', in Otto Fischer and Ann Öhrberg (eds.), *Metamorphoses of Rhetoric: Classical Rhetoric in the Eighteenth Century* (Uppsala, 2011), 133–51.

57. *State Papers Relating the Change of the Constitution*, 11–12, 15.

58. Jack N. Rakove (ed.), *The Annotated U.S. Constitution and Declaration of Independence* (Cambridge, MA, 2009), 104.

59. *The Critical Review* vol. 31 (London, 1771), 65. The author here is borrowing from Rousseau's *Social Contract*.

60. Diderot, *Political Writings*, 111.

61. For the details of this assassination, see https://decorativeartstrust. org under 'Sweden's Culture King'; *Form of Government, Enacted by His Majesty the King and the States of Sweden* (Stockholm, 1772), 29.

62. As Mark Philp points out, we do not even 'know what Paine read'. See his *Reforming Ideas in Britain: Politics and Language in the Shadow of the French Revolution, 1789–1815* (Cambridge, 2014), 194.

63. For an expert guide to the American component of his life, and also an acknowledgement of the British side, see Eric Foner, *Tom Paine and Revolutionary America* (Oxford, 2004).

64. John Brewer, *The Sinews of Power: War, Money and the English State, 1688–1783* (London, 1989), 85–6.

65. Thomas Paine, *Common Sense* (Philadelphia, 1st edn, 1776), 22; Brewer, *The Sinews of Power*, 178.

66. Thomas Paine, *Rights of Man. Part the Second* (London, 1792), 165; Thomas Paine, *Rights of Man, being an answer to Mr Burke's attack on the French Revolution* (London, 1791), 128.

67. Paine, *Common Sense*, 15; and see the second part of his *Rights of Man* for similar arguments, e.g. 'All the monarchical governments are military. War is their trade, plunder and revenue their objects' (4).

68. Paine, *Rights of Man*, 53; Paine, *Common Sense*, 41–2.

69. James Delbourgo, *Collecting the World: The Life and Curiosity of Hans Sloane* (London, 2017), 323.

70. See my 'Empires of Writing', 242–5.

71. I am grateful to Professor Wilfrid Prest for this reference; Daniel J. Hulsebosch, *Constituting Empire: New York and the Transformation of*

*Constitutionalism in the Atlantic World, 1664–1830* (Chapel Hill, NC, 2005), 8.

72. Allan Ramsay, *An Essay on the Constitution of England* (London, 2nd edn, 1766), xiv and 13.

73. Thomas Paine, *Public Good, being an Examination into the Claim of Virginia to the Vacant Western Territory, and of the Right of the United States to the Same* (Philadelphia, 1780), 24.

74. Paine, *Common Sense*, 31–2; for sales of this work, see Trish Loughran, *The Republic in Print: Print Culture in the Age of U.S. Nation Building, 1770–1870* (New York, 2007).

75. Quoted in Eric Slauter, *The State as a Work of Art: The Cultural Origins of the Constitution* (Chicago, IL, 2009), 39.

76. Robert P. Hay, 'George Washington: American Moses', *American Quarterly* 21 (1969), 780–91.

77. Paine, *Common Sense*, 18.

## Chapter Three: The Force of Print

1. *Notes of Debates in the Federal Convention of 1787, Reported by James Madison*, Adrienne Koch (introduction) (New York, 2nd edn, 1987). The prohibition on disclosing information was made on 29 May.

2. For the fluctuations in this manuscript's treatment over time, see Jill Lepore, 'The Commandments: The Constitution and Its Worshippers', *The New Yorker*, 17 January 2011.

3. Pauline Maier, *Ratification: The People Debate the Constitution, 1787–1788* (New York, 2010), 70. Dunlap and Claypoole had earlier printed 500 broadsides of the draft constitution for the Philadelphia delegates' personal distribution. I thank Professor Daniel Hulsebosch for this information and for his advice on this chapter in general.

4. In a conversation in 1835 recorded by Harriet Martineau. See her *Society in America* (New York, 2 vols., 1837), I, 1.

5. Bernard Bailyn, *Ideological Origins of the American Revolution* (Cambridge, MA, 1992 edn), 193.

6. Gordon S. Wood, 'Foreword: State Constitution-making in the American Revolution', *Rutgers Law Journal* 24 (1992–3), 911.

7. See Alan Taylor, *American Revolutions: A Continental History, 1750–1804* (New York, 2016).

8. David Armitage, 'The Declaration of Independence and International Law', *William and Mary Quarterly* 59 (2002), 39–64. Online texts of the Declaration are legion.

9. See https://avalon.law.yale.edu/18th_century/NY01.asp.

10. Daniel J. Hulsebosch, 'The Revolutionary Portfolio: Constitution-making and the Wider World in the American Revolution', *Suffolk University Law Review* 47 (2014), 759–822.

11. See https://avalon.law.yale.edu/18th_century/fed01.asp.

12. Mary Wollstonecraft, *An Historical and Moral View of the Origin and Progress of the French Revolution and the Effect It Has Produced in Europe* (London, 1794), 14. Wollstonecraft is echoing Thomas Jefferson here.

13. Alexander Hamilton in Essay 24. All the *Federalist* essays can be accessed at https://avalon.law.yale.edu/subject_menus/fed.asp.

14. Harold C. Syrett (ed.), *The Papers of Alexander Hamilton* (Charlottesville, VA, 2011), letter to Francis Childs, 14 March 1787.

15. I draw here and in subsequent paragraphs on Michael J. Klarman, *The Framers' Coup: The Making of the United States Constitution* (New York, 2016). Jefferson's famous description of the Philadelphia delegates was made in a letter to John Adams in August 1787.

16. Joanne B. Freeman, 'Will the Real Alexander Hamilton Please Stand Up', *Journal of the Early Republic* 37 (2017), 255–62.

17. Quoted in Jared Sparks, *The Life of Gouverneur Morris* (Boston, MA, 3 vols., 1832), I, 106.

18. See https://avalon.law.yale.edu/18th_century/fed04.asp.

19. Klarman, *The Framers' Coup*, 149.

20. In the debates on 6 June 1787. See https://avalon.law.yale.edu/18th_century/debates_606.asp. On recent revisionism on the constitution, see Max M. Edling, 'A More Perfect Union: The Framing and Ratification of the Constitution', in Jane Kamensky and Edward G. Gray (eds.), *The Oxford Handbook of the American Revolution* (New York, 2013), 388–406.

21. For a close analysis of the wording, see Jack N. Rakove, *Original Meanings: Politics and Ideas in the Making of the Constitution* (New York, 1996).

22. Michael Warner, *The Letters of the Republic: Publication and the Public Sphere in Eighteenth-Century America* (Cambridge, MA, 1990); Hugh

Amory and David D. Hall (eds.), *A History of the Book in America: Volume I: The Colonial Book in the Atlantic World* (Cambridge, 2000), 361.

23. See Franco Moretti (ed.), *The Novel* (Princeton, NJ, 2 vols., 2006).

24. Pauline Maier, *American Scripture: Making the Declaration of Independence* (New York, 1997), 156.

25. Maier, *Ratification, passim*.

26. Hulsebosch, 'Revolutionary Portfolio', and see his and David M. Golove's 'A Civilized Nation: The Early American Constitution, the Law of Nations, and the Pursuit of International Recognition', *New York University Law Review* 85 (2010), 932–1066.

27. This letter by Washington crossed continents a further time, being printed in the *Calcutta Journal* in May 1822.

28. Leon Fraser, *English Opinion of the American Constitution and Government, 1783–1798* (New York, 1915).

29. This verbal shift was further confirmed by French revolutionaries' eager embrace of 'paper' constitutions. See, for instance, John Bowles's angry and much reprinted *Dialogues on the Rights of Britons, Between a Farmer, a Sailor, and a Manufacturer* (London, 1793), 11.

30. This table is based on a website 'Constitutions of the world from the late 18th century to the middle of the 19th century online: Sources on the rise of modern constitutionalism', edited by Horst Dippel. At present, this website, which I accessed in 2019, is offline. But the multi-volume series of the same title, on which this website was based, is partly available in hard copy. See *Constitutions of the World from the late 18th Century to the Middle of the 19th Century: Sources on the Rise of Modern Constitutionalism*, editor in chief Horst Dippel (Munich and Berlin, 2005–).

31. Claude Moïse, *Le projet national de Toussaint Louverture et la constitution de 1801* (Port-au-Prince, Haiti, 2001). I thank my colleague Professor David Bell for this reference.

32. Julia Gaffield (ed.), *The Haitian Declaration of Independence* (Charlottesville, VA, 2016).

33. Comte de Lally-Tollendal, quoted in Elise Marienstras and Naomi Wulf, 'French Translations and Reception of the Declaration of Independence', *Journal of American History* 85 (1999), 1309.

34. Alan Bronfman (ed.), *Documentos constitucionales de Chile 1811–1833* (Munich, 2006); Chile's subsequent 1823 constitution explicitly cited the USA as a model.

35. Francisco Isnardi *et al.*, *Interesting Official Documents Relating to the United Provinces of Venezuela ... Together with the Constitution Framed for the Administration of Their Government: In Spanish and English* (London, 1812). The preface of this was by Andrés Bello.

36. Ibid., 89, 141, 151.

37. Ibid., 307.

38. David Armitage, *The Declaration of Independence: A Global History* (Cambridge, MA, 2007), 145–55.

39. In part because of political imperatives in his native France. In 1848, and in the wake of a further revolution, Tocqueville would serve as a delegate in the making of a new constitution there. Between April and September that year alone, seven different French translations of the United States constitution were published. See Marienstras and Wulf, 'French Translations', 1318 n.

40. A pioneering example is Jacques Vincent Delacroix's widely translated *Constitutions des principaux états de l'Europe et des États-Unis de l'Amérique* (Paris, 2 vols., 1791).

41. *Select Constitutions of the World. Prepared for Presentation to Dáil Eireann by Order of the Irish Provisional Government 1922* (Dublin, 1922).

42. Kåre Tønnesson, 'The Norwegian Constitution of 17 May 1814: International Influences and Models', *Parliaments, Estates and Representation* 21 (2001), 175–86.

43. McNeill is quoted in Franco Moretti, *Atlas of the European Novel, 1800–1900* (New York, 1998), 190.

44. Tønnesson, 'The Norwegian Constitution', 179.

45. See Karen Gammelgaard and Eirik Holmøyvik (eds.), *Writing Democracy: The Norwegian Constitution 1814–2014* (New York, 2015).

46. For this translation of the Plan de Iguala, see https://scholarship.rice.edu website.

47. As re-printed in the *Calcutta Journal*, 9 May 1822.

48. On Calcutta's print culture and its mixed politics, see Miles Ogborn, *Indian Ink: Script and Print in the Making of the English East India Company* (Chicago, IL, 2007) and Daniel E. White, *From Little*

*London to Little Bengal: Religion, Print and Modernity in Early British India, 1793–1835* (Baltimore, MD, 2013).

49. James Silk Buckingham, *America, Historical, Statistic, and Descriptive* (London, 3 vols., 1841), I, 1. On Buckingham's career and ideas, see Kieran Hazzard, 'From Conquest to Consent: British Political Thought and India' (2017), King's College London PhD dissertation.

50. Two excellent introductions to Roy's thought are Bruce Carlisle Robertson (ed.), *The Essential Writings of Raja Rammohan Ray* (Delhi, 1999) and C. A. Bayly, 'Rammohan Roy and the Advent of Constitutional Liberalism in India, 1800–1830', *Modern Intellectual History* 4 (2007), 25–41.

51. See Buckingham's 'Sketch of the Life, Writings and Character of Ram Mohun Roy', *The Biographical Reporter* 4 (1833), 113–20. I am grateful to Dr Kieran Hazzard for this reference.

52. Buckingham, *America, Historical, Statistic, and Descriptive*, I, 261.

53. See, for instance, Henry John Stephen, *New Commentaries on the Laws of England: (Partly Founded on Blackstone)* (London, 3rd edn, 4 vols., 1853), IV, 312.

54. *Calcutta Journal*, 7 September 1821, 6 April, 9 May, 9 November 1822, 14 February 1823.

55. Richard Carlisle in *The Republican* (London, 1820), 229–30.

56. For how networking and long-distance communication – including in regards to politics – could operate without print, see James Robert Pickett, 'The Persianate Sphere during the Age of Empires: Islamic Scholars and Networks of Exchange in Central Asia, 1747–1917' (2015), Princeton University PhD dissertation.

57. Preface of B. Shiva Rao (ed.), *Select Constitutions of the World* (Madras, 1934).

58. *Canton Miscellany* (1831), 32–4.

59. Philip A. Kuhn, 'Ideas behind China's Modern State', *Harvard Journal of Asiatic Studies* 55 (1995), 295–337.

60. William G. McLoughlin, *Cherokee Renascence in the New Republic* (Princeton, NJ, 1986). On Sequoyah and his background, see Robert A. Gross and Mary Kelly (eds.), *A History of the Book in America: Volume 2: An Extensive Republic: Print, Culture, and Society in the New Nation, 1790–1840* (Chapel Hill, NC, 2010), 499–513.

61. *Constitution of the Cherokee Nation, Formed by a Convention of Delegates from the Several Districts at New Echota* (New Echota, 1827).
62. For later Native American constitutions, see David E. Wilkins (ed.), *Documents of Native American Political Development: 1500s to 1933* (Oxford, 2009); and James Oberly, *Nation of Statesmen: The Political Culture of the Stockbridge-Munsee Mohicans, 1815–1972* (Norman, OK, 2005).

## Chapter Four: Armies of Legislators

1. Melanie Randolph Miller, *Envoy to the Terror: Gouverneur Morris and the French Revolution* (Washington DC, 2006); for Morris's diary, see Anne Cary Morris (ed.), *The Diary and Letters of Gouverneur Morris* (New York, 2 vols., 1888), I, 136.
2. Cary Morris, *The Diary and Letters of Gouverneur Morris*, I, 16 and 26.
3. See Keith M. Baker, *Inventing the French Revolution: Essays on French Political Culture in the Eighteenth Century* (Cambridge, 1990), 252–306.
4. William Howard Adams, *Gouverneur Morris: An Independent Life* (New Haven, CT, 2003), 154; for French creativity and radicalism on rights, see Lynn Hunt, *Inventing Human Rights: A History* (New York, 2007), especially 113–75.
5. Cary Morris, *The Diary and Letters of Gouverneur Morris*, I, 360. On the making of this text, see Michael P. Fitzsimmons, 'The Committee of the Constitution and the Remaking of France, 1789–1791', *French History* 4 (1990), 23–47.
6. Cary Morris, *The Diary and Letters of Gouverneur Morris*, I, 486; Miller, *Envoy to the Terror*, 23.
7. Cary Morris, *The Diary and Letters of Gouverneur Morris*, I, 486.
8. Daniel Schönpflug, *Der Weg in die Terreur: Radikalisierung und Konflikte im Strassburger Jakobinerclub (1790–1795)* (Munich, 2002), 62.
9. Miller, *Envoy to the Terror*, 9 and 88.
10. See Aqil Shah, *The Army and Democracy: Military Politics in Pakistan* (Cambridge, MA, 2014).
11. See Chapter Three, note 30 for information on the sources used in this table.
12. Dušan T. Bataković, 'A Balkan-style French Revolution: The 1804 Serbian Uprising in European Perspective', *Balcanica* 36 (2005),

113–29. A comprehensive table covering *attempted* constitutions in this 1790–1820 era would also include Granville Sharp's plans to write a constitution for Sierra Leone in west Africa: see L. E. C. Evans, 'An Early Constitution of Sierra Leone', *Sierra Leone Studies* 11 (1932).

13. For an impressive rendition of this thesis, see David Bell, *The First Total War: Napoleon's Europe and the Birth of Warfare as We Know It* (Boston, MA, 2007). For an expert critique, see Michael Broers, 'The Concept of "Total War" in the Revolutionary-Napoleonic period', *War in History* 15 (2008), 247–68.

14. I owe these references to a 2017 workshop paper at Princeton University by Professor Thomas Dodman: 'When Emile Went to War: Becoming a Citizen-soldier'.

15. The best account in English is now Dominic Lieven, *Russia against Napoleon: The Battle for Europe, 1807 to 1814* (London, 2009).

16. Patrice Gueniffey, *Bonaparte: 1769–1802*, Steven Rendall (trans.) (Cambridge, MA, 2015), 446.

17. Ibid., 55.

18. Philip G. Dwyer, 'Napoleon Bonaparte as Hero and Saviour: Image, Rhetoric and Behaviour in the Construction of a Legend', *French History* 18 (2004), 396; and see Juan Cole, *Napoleon's Egypt: Invading the Middle East* (New York, 2007).

19. Peter McPhee, 'The French Revolution seen from the *Terres Australes*' in Alan Forrest and Matthias Middell (eds.), *The Routledge Companion to the French Revolution* (London, 2016), 274–5.

20. Philippe R. Girard, *The Slaves Who Defeated Napoleon: Toussaint Louverture and the Haitian War of Independence* (Tuscaloosa, AL, 2011); Gueniffey, *Bonaparte*, 702.

21. For Napoleon's persistent interest in the Caribbean region, see Ute Planert (ed.), *Napoleon's Empire: European Politics in Global Perspective* (Basingstoke, 2016), 32 n.

22. For an expert (and sometimes celebratory) account of the British war at sea at this stage, see N. A. M. Rodger, *The Command of the Ocean: A Naval History of Britain, 1649–1815* (London, 2004), especially 380–525.

23. Edmund Burke, *A Letter from the Right Honourable Edmund Burke to a Noble Lord* (London, 1796), 26.

24. Burke made this comparison in a speech in December 1792, accusing revolutionaries of wanting to bring 'all the world in the confraternity of France': see William Cobbett, *Cobbett's Parliamentary History of England* (London, 36 vols., 1806–20), XXX, 71–2.
25. David Bell, *Napoleon: A Concise Biography* (New York, 2015), 41–2.
26. As with other French constitutions of this era, an English translation of this 1804 text is available at Wikisource: https://en.wikisource.org/wiki/Constitution_of_the_Year_XII.
27. Alan Forrest, 'Propaganda and the Legitimation of Power in Napoleonic France', *French History* 18 (2004), 426–45.
28. Bell, *First Total War*, 212. For an Egyptian perspective on Napoleon's invasion, see Robert L. Tignor *et al.*, *Napoleon in Egypt: Al-Jabartî's Chronicle of the French Occupation, 1798* (New York, 1993).
29. Philip G. Dwyer, 'From Corsican Nationalist to French Revolutionary: Problems of Identity in the Writings of the Young Napoleon, 1785–1793', *French History* 16 (2002), 132 and *passim*.
30. Ibid., 140–44.
31. Bruno Colson (ed.), *Napoleon: On War*, Gregory Elliott (trans.) (Oxford, 2015), 344; Dwyer, 'From Corsican Nationalist to French Revolutionary', 146.
32. *Constitution des Républiques Française, Cisalpine et Ligurienne ... dans les quatre langues* (Paris, 1798), second section, 1–133.
33. Ibid.
34. In a review of an exhibition, 'Napoleon: Images of the Legend', Musée des Beaux-Arts, Arras, by Kim Willsher in the London *Observer*, 3 September 2017.
35. Noah Feldman, *What We Owe Iraq: War and the Ethics of Nation Building* (Princeton, NJ, 2004), 7–8. For a wide-ranging, often critical analysis of Napoleonic imperialism, see Michael Broers, Peter Hicks and Agustín Guimerá (eds.), *The Napoleonic Empire and the New European Political Culture* (Basingstoke, 2012).
36. English translation of Cisalpine constitution in *Constitution des Républiques*, 5.
37. Comte de Las Cases, *Mémorial de Sainte-Hélène: Journal of the Private Life and Conversations of the Emperor Napoleon at Saint Helena* (London, 4 vols., 1823), II, 88.

38. Thierry Lentz *et al.* (eds.), *Correspondance générale de Napoléon Bonaparte* (Paris, 15 vols., 2004–18), VIII, 620 and 631.

39. As recorded by a Scottish army colonel, Sir Neil Campbell: see Jonathan North (ed.), *Napoleon on Elba: Diary of an Eyewitness to Exile* (Welwyn Garden City, 2004), 71 and 96. Napoleon also assured Campbell that, had he successfully invaded Britain, he would have gone on to liberate Ireland.

40. I owe this reference to Dr Tom Toelle.

41. Ewald Grothe, 'Model or Myth? The Constitution of Westphalia of 1807 and Early German Constitutionalism', *German Studies Review* 28 (2005), 1–19.

42. Jaroslaw Czubaty, *The Duchy of Warsaw, 1807–1815: A Napoleonic Outpost in Central Europe*, Ursula Phillips (trans.) (London, 2016), 38.

43. Ibid., *passim*.

44. According to Las Cases, *Mémorial de Sainte-Hélène*, I, Part 1, 189.

45. See, for instance, Ambrogio A. Caiani, 'Collaborators, Collaboration, and the Problems of Empire in Napoleonic Italy, the Oppizzoni Affair, 1805–1807', *Historical Journal* 60 (2017), 385–407.

46. For this episode, see Antonio Feros, *Speaking of Spain: The Evolution of Race and Nation in the Hispanic World* (Cambridge, MA, 2017), 233–77.

47. Ignacio Fernández Sarasola, 'La primera constitución española: El Estatuto de Bayona', *Revista de Derecho* 26 (2006), 89–109. The text (in French and Spanish) is available in António Barbas Homem *et al* (eds.), *Constitutional Documents of Portugal and Spain 1808–1845* (Berlin, 2010), 195–236.

48. Lentz *et al.* (eds.), *Correspondance générale de Napoléon Bonaparte*, VIII, 600, 630–1, 675.

49. See Jaime E. Rodríguez O., 'Hispanic Constitutions, 1812 and 1824', in Silke Hensel *et al.* (eds.), *Constitutional Cultures: On the Concept and Representation of Constitutions in the Atlantic World* (Newcastle upon Tyne, 2012).

50. M. C. Mirow, *Latin American Constitutions: The Constitution of Cádiz and Its Legacy in Spanish America* (Cambridge, 2015), 276.

51. Ruth de Llobet, 'Chinese mestizo and natives' disputes in Manila and the 1812 Constitution: Old Privileges and new political realities (1813–15)', *Journal of Southeast Asian Studies* 45 (2014), 220.

52. Rodríguez O., 'Hispanic Constitutions', 77–8.
53. Quoted in C. W. Crawley, 'French and English Influences in the Cortes of Cadiz, 1810–1814', *Cambridge Historical Journal* 6 (1939), 196.
54. See David Hook and Graciela Iglesias-Rogers (eds.), *Translations in Times of Disruption: An Interdisciplinary Study in Transnational Contexts* (London, 2017).
55. Zachary Elkins, 'Diffusion and the Constitutionalization of Europe', *Comparative Political Studies* 43 (2010), 992.
56. See Jefferson's letter to the Spanish liberal, Luis de Onís, 28 April 1814: https://founders.archives.gov/documents/Jefferson/03-07-02-0238.
57. Though clerical advocacy could not be relied on: see Maurizio Isabella, 'Citizens or Faithful? Religion and the Liberal Revolutions of the 1820s in Southern Europe', *Modern Intellectual History* 12 (2015), 555–78.
58. Katrin Dircksen, 'Representations of Competing Political Orders: Constitutional Festivities in Mexico City, 1824–1846', in Hensel *et al.*, *Constitutional Cultures*, 129–62.
59. Leslie Bethell (ed.), *The Independence of Latin America* (Cambridge, 1987), 197.
60. For the life, see Betty T. Bennett, *Mary Wollstonecraft Shelley: An Introduction* (Baltimore, MD, 1998).
61. Mary Shelley, *History of a Six Weeks' Tour through a Part of France, Switzerland, Germany, and Holland* (London, 1817), 17.
62. Mary Shelley, *Frankenstein, or the Modern Prometheus: Annotated for Scientists, Engineers, and Creators of All Kinds*, David H. Guston, Ed Finn and Jason Scott Robert (eds.) (Cambridge, MA, 2017), 37, 89, 107, 175 and 185.
63. In volume I, chapter ten, of the unpaginated Project Gutenberg edition of *The Last Man*, and chapter one of volume II; Shelley, *Frankenstein*, xxvii.
64. Markus J. Prutsch, *Making Sense of Constitutional Monarchism in Post-Napoleonic France and Germany* (Basingstoke, 2013).
65. Eugenio F. Biagini, 'Liberty, Class and Nation-building: Ugo Foscolo's "English" Constitutional Thought, 1816–1827', *European Journal of Political Theory* 5 (2006), 43.

66. Rafe Blaufarb, *Bonapartists in the Borderlands: French Exiles and Refugees on the Gulf Coast, 1815–1835* (Tuscaloosa, AL, 2005). I also draw here on papers delivered at a workshop I convened with Dr Jan Jansen in Berlin in 2018: 'Exile and Emigration in an Age of War and Revolution'.

67. Hook and Iglesias-Rogers (eds.), *Translations in Times of Disruption*, 45–74.

68. On Muravyov and other Russian army veterans turned oppositionists, see Richard Stites, *The Four Horsemen: Riding to Liberty in Post-Napoleonic Europe* (New York, 2014), 240–321.

69. Sophia Raffles, *Memoir of the Life and Public Services of Sir Thomas Stamford Raffles* (London, 2 vols., 1835), I, 304–6.

70. Ibid., II, 242–4, 304.

## Chapter Five: Exception and Engine

1. For this encounter, see Eduard Gans, *Rückblicke auf Personen und Zustände* (Berlin, 1836), 200–14. I am grateful to Professor Jürgen Osterhammel for alerting me to this source.

2. David Armitage, 'Globalizing Jeremy Bentham', *History of Political Thought* 32 (2011), 65; *Codification Proposal, Addressed by Jeremy Bentham to All Nations Professing Liberal Opinions* (London, 1822), 44 (italics in original).

3. Gans, *Rückblicke auf Personen und Zustände*, 207–8.

4. Southwood Smith, *A Lecture Delivered over the Remains of Jeremy Bentham, Esq.* (London, 1832).

5. For an introduction to the life, see Philip Schofield, *Bentham: A Guide for the Perplexed* (New York, 2009). For some of his constitutional projects and ideas, see Frederick Rosen, *Jeremy Bentham and Representative Democracy* (Oxford, 1983) and Philip Schofield and Jonathan Harris (eds.), *The Collected Works of Jeremy Bentham: 'Legislator of the World': Writings on Codification, Law, and Education* (Oxford, 1998). I have drawn on these sources throughout.

6. Miriam Williford, *Jeremy Bentham on Spanish America* (Baton Rouge, LA, 1980), 4 and *passim*. Burr's present of *The Federalist: Or the New Constitution* (New York, 1802), lightly annotated by Bentham, is in the British Library.

7. Theodora L. McKennan, 'Jeremy Bentham and the Colombian Liberators', *The Americas* 34 (1978), 466.

8. Bentham's published correspondence, one of the great editorial projects of recent decades, is a rich source on these multifarious transcontinental contacts: see T. L. S. Sprigge *et al* (ed.), *The Correspondence of Jeremy Bentham* (London, 12 vols., 1968–2006).

9. Ibid., XI, 177–8.

10. L. J. Hume, 'Preparations for Civil War in Tripoli in the 1820s: Ali Karamanli, Hassuna D'Ghies and Jeremy Bentham', *Journal of African History* 21 (1980), 311–22; and Ian Coller, 'African Liberalism in the Age of Empire? Hassuna d'Ghies and Liberal Constitutionalism in North Africa, 1822–1835', *Modern Intellectual History* 12 (2015), 529–53.

11. James Burns, 'Bentham, Brissot and the Challenge of Revolution', *History of European Ideas* 35 (2009), 221.

12. McKennan, 'Bentham and the Colombian Liberators', 473; Jennifer Pitts, 'Legislator of the World? A Rereading of Bentham on Colonies', *Political Theory* 31 (2003), 200–34.

13. The literature is extensive but for an acute summary, see Edmund S. Morgan, *Inventing the People: The Rise of Popular Sovereignty in England and America* (New York, 1988), 72–4.

14. As quoted in Alan Craig Houston, *Algernon Sidney and the Republican Heritage in England and America* (Princeton, NJ, 2014), 191–2.

15. Vicki Hsueh, *Hybrid Constitutions: Challenging Legacies of Law, Privilege, and Culture in Colonial America* (Durham, NC, 2010) 55 *et seq.* As Hsueh argues, constitutionalism in Britain has been 'far from uniform', and it has tended to become even more hybridised in overseas locations.

16. Quoted in Bernadette Meyler, 'Daniel Defoe and the Written Constitution', *Cornell Law Review* 94 (2008), 111.

17. Lois G. Schwoerer, *The Declaration of Rights* (Baltimore, MD, 1981).

18. The Indian histories of this armed force are increasingly well researched. Its impact on the British state itself is less so: see Alan G. Guy and Peter B. Boyden, *Soldiers of the Raj: The Indian Army 1600–1947* (London, 1997).

19. Saxo, *A Hasty Sketch of the Origins, Nature, and Progress of the British*

*Constitution* (York, 1817), 25–6; and see Robert Saunders, 'Parliament and People: The British Constitution in the Long Nineteenth Century', *Journal of Modern European History* 6 (2008), 72–87.

20. H. J. Hanham, *The Nineteenth Century Constitution, 1815–1914* (Cambridge, 1969), 12.

21. *The New Monthly Magazine and Literary Journal* (London, 1832), 79. The notion of fundamental law as being quintessentially and desirably an internal commodity, something set down in the heart, and therefore not dependent on writing, was an ancient one.

22. Google's Ngram Viewer suggests indeed that the description 'unwritten constitution', in regard to the British system, only became widespread after 1860.

23. In his foreword to Henry Elliot Malden (ed.), *Magna Carta Commemoration Essays* (London, 1917).

24. As suggested by the chaos of arguments over the constitutional validity and parliamentary implications of the Brexit referendum in 2016. For the theory, rather than mass beliefs, see Jeffrey Goldsworthy, *Parliamentary Sovereignty: Contemporary Debates* (Cambridge, 2010).

25. Leo Tolstoy, *War and Peace*, Louise and Aylmer Maude (trans.) (Minneapolis, MN, 2016), 884; and see Daria Olivier, *The Burning of Moscow, 1812* (London, 1966).

26. For an evocative and illustrated survey that conveys something of the size and wealth of the city at this stage, see Celina Fox (ed.), *London – World City, 1800–1840* (New Haven, CT, 1992).

27. Rebeca Viguera Ruiz, *El exilio de Ramón Alesón Alonso de Tejada: Experiencia liberal de un emigrado en Londres (1823–1826)* (Lewiston, ID, 2012), 43 and 56.

28. Martin Daunton, 'London and the World', in Fox (ed.), *London – World City*. For British investment in the new South America more broadly, see P. J. Cain and A. G. Hopkins, *British Imperialism: 1688–2015* (London, 3rd edn, 2016) and Frank Griffith Dawson, *The First Latin American Debt Crisis: The City of London and the 1822–25 Loan Bubble* (London, 1990). Historians have been more interested in the economic and informal imperial drives behind these British

investments than in the political and ideological motives sometimes also involved.

29. *The Times* (London), 24 December 1824.

30. As John J. McCusker remarks, London newspapers crossed the globe in part because of the dense commercial and financial reportage they carried: 'The Demise of Distance: The Business Press and the Origins of the Information Revolution in the Early Modern Atlantic World', *American Historical Review* 110 (2005), 295–321. The figures in this paragraph are based on those in the British Newspaper Archive (https://www.britishnewspaperarchive. co.uk/), which is not yet complete.

31. For an important sidelight on Jeddah, see Ulrike Freitag, 'Helpless Representatives of the Great Powers? Western Consuls in Jeddah, 1830s to 1914', *Journal of Imperial and Commonwealth History* 40 (2012), 357–81.

32. Professor John Darwin is at work on a study of Britain's global port network and its extensive impact.

33. Eric Hobsbawm, *The Age of Revolution: Europe 1789–1848* (London, 1962).

34. John Lynch, *Simón Bolívar: A Life* (New Haven, CT, 2006), 122–4; for these men, see Malcolm Brown, *Adventuring through Spanish Colonies: Simón Bolívar, Foreign Mercenaries and the Birth of New Nations* (Liverpool, 2008).

35. *The Times* (London), 27 October 1819.

36. For an example, see Aileen Fyfe, *Steam-powered Knowledge: William Chambers and the Business of Publishing, 1820–1860* (Chicago, IL, 2012).

37. Karen Racine, 'Newsprint Nations: Spanish American Publishing in London, 1808–1827', in Constance Bantman and Ana Cláudia Suriani da Silva (eds.), *The Foreign Political Press in Nineteenth-Century London: Politics from a Distance* (London, 2017).

38. Daniel Alves and Paulo Jorge Fernandes, 'The Press as a Reflection of the Divisions among the Portuguese Political Exiles (1808–1832)', in Bantman and da Silva (eds.), *The Foreign Political Press in Nineteenth-Century London*, 73–90.

39. *Foreign Quarterly Review* (London, 1833), 174, reviewing a memoir by Count Pecchio.

40. Juan Luis Simal, *Emigrados: España y el exilio internacional, 1814–1834* (Madrid, 2012), especially 186, 195, 201, 223–7.

41. Karen Racine, '"This England and This Now": British Cultural and Intellectual Influence in the Spanish American Independence Era', *Hispanic American Historical Review* 90 (2010), 423.

42. *The Literary Examiner: Consisting of The Indicator, a Review of Books, and Miscellaneous Pieces in Prose and Verse* (London, 1823), 351–2.

43. The most recent study is Antonio Ramos Argüelles, *Agustín Argüelles (1776–1844): Padre del constitucionalismo español* (Madrid, 1990). He deserves to be better known in the English language.

44. For another example of a foreign revolutionary in London who relied on the British Museum's library, see Robert Henderson, *Vladimir Burtsev and the Struggle for a Free Russia: A Revolutionary in the Time of Tsarism and Bolshevism* (London, 2017).

45. The most accessible biography is Lynch, *Simón Bolívar*.

46. For this address, see *El Libertador: Writings of Simón Bolívar*, David Bushnell (ed.) (Oxford, 2003), 31–53.

47. Ibid., especially 42–3.

48. Ibid., 43, 45.

49. See, for instance, the impressions of a British agent in 1825 in Harold Temperley, *The Foreign Policy of Canning, 1822–1827* (London, 1966 edn), 557–8.

50. *El Libertador*, 116.

51. For the *Jamaica Letter*, see ibid., 12–30.

52. Lynch, *Simón Bolívar*, 181.

53. For the story, see Hilda Sábato, *Republics of the New World: The Revolutionary Political Experiment in Nineteenth-Century Latin America* (Princeton, NJ, 2018).

54. *El Libertador*, 177; Sábato, *Republics of the New World*.

55. I owe this information to Felice M. Physioc of Princeton University.

56. For a list of constitutions attempted in Mexico in this period and after, see Sebastian Dorsch (ed.), *Constitutional Documents of Mexico, 1814–1849* (Berlin, 3 vols., 2010–13).

57. Richard A. Warren, *Vagrants and Citizens: Politics and the Masses in Mexico City from Colony to Republic* (Lanham, MD, 2007), 59.

58. The texts of these Mexican provincial constitutions are available (in Spanish) in Dorsch, *Constitutional Documents*, vols 2–3.

59. *El Libertador*, 101.
60. For the rising disenchantment of the 1820s, see Rafael Rojas, *Las repúblicas de aire: Utopía y desencanto en la revolución de Hispanoamérica* (Mexico, DF, 2009); and, for Bolívar himself, ibid., 19.
61. *El Libertador*, 47.
62. For Rodríguez and his influence, see Ronald Briggs, *Tropes of Enlightenment: Simón Rodríguez and the American Essay at Revolution* (Nashville, TN, 2010).
63. *El Libertador*, 24.
64. Simon Collier, *Ideas and Politics of Chilean Independence 1808–1833* (Cambridge, 1967), 345–6.
65. Annelien de Dijn, 'A Pragmatic Conservatism: Montesquieu and the Framing of the Belgian Constitution (1830–1831)', *History of European Ideas* 28 (2002), 227–45; *Morning Post* (London), 2 November 1830.
66. Paul Stock, 'Liberty and Independence: The Shelley–Byron Circle and the State(s) of Europe', *Romanticism* 15 (2009), 121–30. There is an image of the poets' two boats racing against each other in the Bodleian Library, MS. Shelley adds. c. 12, fol. 26.
67. Thus, in his bestselling *American Independence, the Interest and Glory of Great Britain* (1775), Cartwright tried to reconcile the demands of imperial reform and placating dissident American whites with providing the requisite protection for Indigenous lands. See Jeffers Lennox, 'Mapping the End of Empire' (2018), in 'Cartography and Empire' (essay series), https://earlycanadianhistory.ca/category/cartography-and-empire-series.
68. See my 'Empires of Writing: Britain, America and Constitutions, 1776–1848', *Law and History Review* 32 (2014), 252–3.
69. John Cartwright, *Diálogo político entre un italiano, un español, un frances, un aleman, y un ingles* (London, 1825).
70. F. D. Cartwright, *The Life and Correspondence of Major Cartwright* (London, 2 vols., 1826), II, 66, 262–3, 283.
71. Classically, in E. P. Thompson, *The Making of the English Working Class* (London, 1963), 666–8.
72. *The Chartist Circular*, 21 December 1839. The Charter has yet to be imaginatively integrated into a transnational history of innovative

constitutional texts. Yet, as Gareth Stedman Jones remarked long
ago, the question 'Why was the Charter considered desirable?' in
this movement is a central one. See Gareth Stedman Jones,
*Languages of Class: Studies in English Working Class History 1832–1982*
(Cambridge, 1984), 108.
73.   *The Chartist*, 9 June 1838, 23 March 1839.
74.   *Northern Star*, 21 April 1838.

**Chapter Six: Those Not Meant to Win, Those Unwilling to Lose**
1.    Recent studies on which I have drawn are Adrian Young, 'Mutiny's
Bounty: Pitcairn Islanders and the Making of a Natural Laboratory
on the Edge of Britain's Pacific Empire' (2016), Princeton
University PhD dissertation; and Nigel Erskine, 'The Historical
Archaeology of Settlement at Pitcairn Island 1790–1856' (2004),
James Cook University PhD dissertation.
2.    The full text is published in Walter Brodie, *Pitcairn's Island, and the
Islanders, in 1850* (London, 1851), 84–91; Elliott's report to his
Admiralty superiors on his voyage to Pitcairn and actions there can
be accessed at the University of Hawaii's digital eVols respository,
at https://evols.library.manoa.hawaii.edu.
3.    Brodie, *Pitcairn's Island*, 84.
4.    Greg Denning, quoted in David Armitage and Alison Bashford
(eds.), *Pacific Histories, Ocean, Land, People* (Basingstoke, 2014), 8; see
also Alison Bashford, 'The Pacific Ocean', in David Armitage,
Alison Bashford and Sujit Sivasundaram (eds.), *Oceanic Histories*
(Cambridge, 2018); and Professor Sivasundaram's recent *Waves
across the South: A New History of Revolution and Empire* (Cambridge,
2020) for the importance of the Pacific world in the Age of
Revolution and after.
5.    Twain uses this description in his 1879 short story 'The Great
Revolution in Pitcairn', in which he imagines an ambitious
American adventurer taking over the island.
6.    For this Corsican constitution, see National Archives, Kew, PC
1/34/90. A manuscript account by Russell Elliott of his journey to
Pitcairn, 'Facts and Impressions Recorded during a Cruise from the
Coast of Chile', was sold at Christie's of London auction house in
1998, but seems to have disappeared into a private collection.

7. Strzelecki acknowledges Russell Elliott's aid in his *Physical Description of New South Wales, and Van Diemen's Land* (London, 1845); for his famine work, see Frank McNally, 'Strzelecki's List', *Irish Times*, 9 May 2019.

8. See *infra* 295–305.

9. J. N. Reynolds, *Pacific and Indian Oceans: or, the South Sea Surveying and Exploring Expedition: Its Inception, Progress, and Objects* (New York, 1841).

10. Good surveys of these developments, on which I draw, are Stuart Banner, *Possessing the Pacific: Land, Settlers, and Indigenous People from Australia to Alaska* (Cambridge, MA, 2007) and James Belich, *Replenishing the Earth: The Settler Revolution and the Rise of the Anglo World, 1783–1939* (Oxford, 2009).

11. Ingrid Lohmann, 'Educating the Citizen: Two Case Studies in Inclusion and Exclusion in Prussia in the Early Nineteenth Century', *Paedagogica Historica* 43 (2007), 17.

12. *The Constitutions of the Ancient and Honourable Fraternity of Free and Accepted Masons* (Worcester, MA, 1792), 275. The song seems to date back to at least the 1750s.

13. See Margaret C. Jacob, *Living the Enlightenment: Freemasonry and Politics in Eighteenth-century Europe* (New York, 1991).

14. For the British case, see my *Britons: Forging the Nation, 1707–1837* (New Haven, CT, 2009 edn), 237–81.

15. Alyssa Goldstein Sepinwall, 'Robespierre, Old Regime Feminist? Gender, the Late Eighteenth Century, and the French Revolution Revisited', *Journal of Modern History* 82 (2010), 1–29.

16. Mary Wollstonecraft, *An Historical and Moral View of the Origin and Progress of the French Revolution* (London, 1794), 404; Mary Wollstonecraft, *A Vindication of the Rights of Woman*, Miriam Brody (ed.) (London, 2004), 5.

17. Jan Ellen Lewis, 'What Happened to the Three-fifths Clause: The Relationship between Women and Slaves in Constitutional Thought, 1787–1866', *Journal of the Early Republic* 37 (2017), 2–3, 15–16 n.

18. The texts of these U.S. state constitutions are available in Horst Dippel (ed.), *Constitutional Documents of the United States of America, 1776–1860*, Parts 1–8 (Munich and Berlin, 2006–11).

19. Antonio Feros, *Speaking of Spain: The Evolution of Race and Nation in the Hispanic World* (Cambridge, MA, 2017), 256.
20. Sally Eagle Merry, *Colonizing Hawai'i: The Cultural Power of Law* (Princeton, NJ, 2000), 95; Robert C. Lydecker, *Roster Legislatures of Hawaii 1841–1918: Constitutions of Monarchy and Republic* (Honolulu, HI, 1918), 23, 32, 35, 44.
21. Mara Patessio, *Women and Public Life in Early Meiji Japan: The Development of the Feminist Movement* (Ann Arbor, MI, 2011), especially 45–8. I am grateful to Professor Watanabe Hiroshi of Tokyo University for information on women and pre-Meiji palace bureaucracies.
22. It is important not to romanticise Pitcairn women's life and opportunities on or off their home island. Not only were there sporadic bouts of violence and incest, in addition, while women here precociously achieved the right to vote, no female magistrate was ever elected: *ex informatio* Dr Adrian M. Young.
23. See Sally Gregory McMillen, *Seneca Falls and the Origins of the Women's Rights Movement* (Oxford, 2008); and Olympe de Gouges, *The Declaration of the Rights of Woman* (1791), on the Liberté, Égalité, Fraternité: Exploring the French Revolution website https://revolution.chnm.org/items/show/557.
24. Virginia Woolf, *A Room of One's Own* (London, 1929; 2002 edn), 77.
25. *Queen Victoria's Journals*, 3 April and 3 May 1848, XXV, 123–4, 175 at qvj.chadwyck.com.
26. Catharine Macaulay, *Loose Remarks … with a Short Sketch of a Democratical Form of Government, in a Letter to Signor Paoli* (London, 1767).
27. This estimate was based on an index search of 'Constitutions of the world from the late 18th century to the middle of the 19th century online: Sources on the rise of modern constitutionalism', edited by Horst Dippel, accessed in 2019. As set out in Chapter Three, note 30, this collection is currently offline, but is also published in print, with some volumes still forthcoming.
28. See Hilda Sábato, *Republics of the New World: The Revolutionary Political Experiment in Nineteenth-century Latin America* (Princeton, NJ, 2018), 89–131. I am grateful to both Professor Sábato and

Professor Rebecca Earle for information on provisions in South American constitutions.

29. A point made much of at the time, e.g. John Adams, the future president of the United States, remarked in his *Defence of the Constitutions of Government of the United States of America* (London, 3 vols., 1787–8), that in 'ancient democratical republics' men who 'refused to take arms for their country, or quit their ranks in the army' were punished by being 'exposed three days in a public square of the city in women's clothes' (I, 350). But such references to the Western classical past covered over a profound, recent shift. Instead of military service being viewed as an obligation of *pre-existing* male citizenship, as in some cultures in the past, by the later eighteenth century, the emphasis was coming to be more on military service of the state as a necessary *qualification* for males achieving a monopoly on active citizenship.

30. Karen Hagemann, Gisela Mettele and Jane Rendall (eds.), *Gender, War and Politics: Transatlantic Perspectives, 1775–1830* (Basingstoke, 2010).

31. See Jonathan Sperber, *The European Revolutions, 1848–1851* (Cambridge, 2005), especially 4, 167, 172 n., 177, 185–90.

32. Stanley B. Alpern, 'On the Origins of the Amazons of Dahomey', *History of Africa* 25 (1998), 9–25. Referring to these female soldiers as 'Amazons' reflected, of course, how atypical and archaic they were perceived as being.

33. See, for instance, some of the paintings of H. B. Willis, held in the National Library of New Zealand, and the drawings of Frederick William Beechey in the 1820s, held in the National Library of Australia.

34. On Russian settler colonialism, see Alexander Morrison, 'Metropole, Colony, and Imperial Citizenship in the Russian Empire', *Kritika* 13 (2012), 327–61.

35. Mark McKenna, 'Transplanted to Savage Shores: Indigenous Australians and British Birthright in the Mid Nineteenth-century Australian Colonies', *Journal of Colonialism and Colonial History* 13 (2012), 10; and see Belich, *Replenishing the Earth*, especially 65, 82 and 261; Ann Curthoys and Jessie Mitchell, *Taking Liberty:*

*Indigenous Rights and Settler Self-government in Colonial Australia, 1830–1890* (Cambridge, 2018).

36. Benjamin Madley, *An American Genocide: The United States and the California Indian Catastrophe, 1846–1873* (New Haven, CT, 2016), *passim*; James Belich, *The Victorian Interpretation of Racial Conflict: The Maori, the British, and the New Zealand Wars* (Kingston, ON, 1989).

37. For the British empire and the international legal order, see Lauren Benton and Lisa Ford, *Rage for Order: The British Empire and the Origins of International Law, 1800–1850* (Cambridge, MA, 2016).

38. For the background, see Madley, *An American Genocide*; the text of the 1849 Californian constitution is available in Dippel, *Constitutional Documents of the United States*, Part I, 149–86.

39. David John Headon and Elizabeth Perkins (ed.), *Our First Republicans: John Dunmore Lang, Charles Harpur, David Henry Deniehy* (Sydney, 1998), 19. For other examples of parallels and links between white settlers in parts of the USA and Australia, see Lisa Ford, *Settler Sovereignty: Jurisdiction and Indigenous People in America and Australia, 1788–1836* (Cambridge, MA, 2010).

40. I draw here on a paper by James Belich, 'Folk Globalization: "Crew Culture" and the Mid Nineteenth-century Gold Rushes', delivered at a conference, 'The Global 1860s', which I co-organised at Princeton University in October 2015.

41. See the tense account of this man in the *Oxford Dictionary of National Biography* https://doi.org.10.1093/ref:odnb/10766, which evokes some of his contradictions and difficulties.

42. National Library of New Zealand, Wellington, NZ, qMS-0842.

43. Ibid. American vindications of white overland expansionism were also drawn on by some colonial enthusiasts in the British Westminster Parliament. See the speeches on the Australian Colonies Government Bill on 19 April 1850 in *Hansard*, vol. 110, columns 554–622.

44. See, for instance, John Dunmore Lang, *Freedom and Independence for the Golden Lands of Australia* (Sydney, 1857), 392–400. Lang's transcontinental as distinct from just Australian political significance needs further exploration. For a sympathetic assessment of his national and radical importance, see Benjamin

Jones and Paul Pickering, 'A New Terror to Death: Public Memory and the Disappearance of John Dunmore Lang', *History Australia* 11 (2014), 24–45.

45. Lang, *Freedom and Independence for the Golden Lands*, 45 and 59.
46. John Dunmore Lang, *Cooksland in North-Eastern Australia ... with a Disquisition on the Origin, Manners, and Customs of the Aborigines* (London, 1847), 268–9, 359; Lang, *Freedom and Independence for the Golden Lands*, 128. Lang had almost certainly read Alexis de Tocqueville's *Democracy in America* (1835), which also represents the erosion of Indigenous peoples as unavoidable.
47. Malcolm Crook and Tom Crook, 'Reforming Voting Practices in a Global Age: The Making and Remaking of the Modern Secret Ballot in Britain, France and the United States, *c.*1600–*c.*1950', *Past & Present* 212 (2011), 218–19; the various Australian Constitution Acts of the 1850s are to be found at https://www.foundingdocs. gov.au.
48. Lang, *Freedom and Independence for the Golden Lands*, 218. A constitution for the Commonwealth of Australia as a whole, drafted by a convention of fifty delegates, would not be introduced until January 1901. Section 127 excluded 'aboriginal natives' from being counted as part of this Commonwealth.
49. Jeffrey Sissons, 'Heroic History and Chiefly Chapels in 19th Century Tahiti', *Oceania* 78 (2008), 320–31.
50. Ibid., 327; William Ellis, *Polynesian Researches during a Residence of Nearly Six Years in the South Sea Islands* (London, 2 vols., 1829), II, 386.
51. For valuable background, see the third volume of Douglas L. Oliver, *Ancient Tahitian Society* (Honolulu, 3 vols., 1974); also, Niels Gunson, 'Pomare II of Tahiti and Polynesian Imperialism', *Journal of Pacific History* 4 (1969), 65–82.
52. See, for instance, 'The Native King and Our New Zealand Constitution', *The Times* (London), 16 November 1860; S. Cheyne, 'Act of Parliament or Royal Prerogative: James Stephen and the First New Zealand Constitution Bill', *New Zealand Journal of History* 21 (1990), 182–9.
53. A garden is now named in Betsey Stockton's honour at Princeton University.

54. Paul Landau, 'Language', in Norman Etherington (ed.), *Missions and Empire* (Oxford, 2009), 213.

55. Jonathan Y. Okamura, 'Aloha Kanaka Me Ke Aloha 'Aina: Local Culture and Society in Hawaii', *Amerasia Journal* 7 (1980), 119–37; Martin Daly, 'Another Agency in This Great Work: The Beginnings of Missionary Printing in Tonga', *Journal of Pacific History* 43 (2008), 367–74.

56. See D. F. McKenzie, *Bibliography and the Sociology of Texts* (Cambridge, 1999), 77–128.

57. *The United Service Magazine* (London, 1842), 611.

58. Ellis, *Polynesian Researches*, II, 10 and 124; Colin Newbury and Adam J. Darling, 'Te Hau Pahu Rahi: Pomare II and the Concept of Inter-island Government in Eastern Polynesia', *Journal of the Polynesian Society* 76 (1967), 498–9.

59. Ellis, *Polynesian Researches*, II, 178, 529.

60. Ibid., II, 393–96; *Select Reviews* (London, 1809), 417.

61. *The Christian Observer* 19 (London, 1820), 134.

62. Ellis, *Polynesian Researches*, II, 386.

63. Ibid., II, 455.

64. James Montgomery (ed.), *Journal of Voyages and Travels by the Rev. Daniel Tyerman and George Bennet, Esq.: Deputed from the London Missionary Society ... between the Years 1821 and 1829* (Boston, MA, 3 vols., 1832), II, 215.

65. Robert B. Nicolson, *The Pitcairners* (Honolulu, HI, 1997).

66. John Dunmore Lang, *View of the Origin and Migrations of the Polynesian Nation* (London, 1834), 100.

67. For an even higher estimate, see J. K. Laimana Jr, 'The Phenomenal Rise to Literacy in Hawaii: Hawaiian Society in the Early Nineteenth Century' (2011), University of Hawaii MA dissertation.

68. Hawaiian history has been re-energised in recent decades, partly because a resurgence in Hawaiian nationalism has promoted the exploration and exploitation of Indigenous sources. Works I have found especially valuable include: Jonathan K. K. Osorio, *Dismembering Lāhui: A History of the Hawaiian Nation to 1887* (Honolulu, HI, 2002); Noenoe K. Silva, *The Power of the Steel-tipped Pen: Reconstructing Native Hawaiian Intellectual History* (Durham,

NC, 2017); and Lorenz Gonschor, *A Power in the World: The Hawaiian Kingdom in Oceania* (Honolulu, HI, 2019).

69. See Merry, *Colonizing Hawai'i*; and, for a modification, Chandos Culleen, 'The Hawaiian Constitution of 1840: Acquiescence to or Defiance of Euro-American Pacific Colonialism' (2013), University of Arizona MA dissertation, which also offers a detailed account of this constitution's making.

70. Ralph Simpson Kuykendall, *The Hawaiian Kingdom* (Honolulu, 3 vols., 1938–67), I, 159–61.

71. I am grateful to Dr Lorenz Gonschor for this information.

72. https://www.hawaii-nation.org/constitution-1840.html.

73. Lorenz Gonschor, 'Law as a Tool of Oppression and Liberation: Institutional Histories and Perspectives on Political Independence' (2008), University of Hawaii at Manoa MA dissertation, 26–7.

74. Lydecker (ed.), *Roster Legislatures of Hawaii*, 6.

75. Jason Kapena, 'Ke Kumukānāwi o Ka Makahiki 1864: The 1864 Constitution', in *Journal of Hawaiian Language Sources* 2 (2003), 16–51; for white, mainly American penetration of Hawaiian government by this stage, see Banner, *Possessing the Pacific*, 139.

76. For this ending, see Ralph S. Kuykendall, *The Hawaiian Kingdom, 1874–1893: The Kalākaua Dynasty* (Honolulu, HI, 1967).

77. Gonschor, *A Power in the World*, 88–153.

78. For a sidelight on the king's Asian interests, see Lorenz Gonschor and Louis Bousquet, 'A Showdown at Honolulu Harbor: Exploring Late 19th Century Hawaiian Politics through a Narrative Biography of Celso Cesare Moreno', *Journal of Narrative Politics* 3 (2017), 131–51. The king's cultural ventures, which had a political purpose, emerge from Stacy L. Kamehiro, *The Arts of Kingship: Hawaiian Art and National Culture of the Kalākaua Era* (Honolulu, HI, 2009).

79. Kalākaua, as quoted in Donald Keene, *Emperor of Japan: Meiji and His World, 1852–1912* (New York, 2002), 347–8.

80. The best biography, which also stresses the maritime and oceanic dimensions of his career, is Marie-Claire Bergère, *Sun Yat-sen*, Janet Lloyd (trans.) (Stanford, CA, 1998).

81. Lorenz Gonschor, 'Revisiting the Hawaiian Influence on the

Political Thought of Sun Yat-sen', *Journal of Pacific History* 52 (2017), 52–67.

**Chapter Seven: The Light, the Dark and the Long 1860s**

1. For Husayn and his mobile career and complex status, see M'hamed Oualdi, *A Slave between Empires: A Transimperial History of North Africa* (New York, 2020).
2. On this institution and the city out of which it emerged, see Kenneth Perkins, *A History of Modern Tunisia* (Cambridge, 2nd edn, 2014), 15–43.
3. Theresa Liane Womble, 'Early Constitutionalism in Tunisia, 1857–1864: Reform and Revolt' (1997), Princeton University PhD dissertation. The text of the constitution (in French) can be found at www.legislation.tn/en/content/constitution-1959-and-previous-constitutions. Concessions to wider political rights in Tunisia had already been made earlier through the *'Ahd al-Aman*, or Security Covenant, implemented in 1857.
4. I owe this information to Joshua Picard of Princeton University.
5. Amos Perry, *Carthage and Tunis, Past and Present: In Two Parts* (Providence, RI, 1869), 207.
6. I thank Dr Lorenz Gonschor for suggesting this.
7. Unpublished paper by M'hamed Oualdi, 'Are We Still Parts of the Same World? North Africans between 1860s Empires'. The careful ritual of this Franco-Tunisian meeting was commemorated in a contemporary painting by Alexandre Debelle, which is now in Tunis.
8. For this and other politically charged images emerging out of a changing Tunisia at this time, see the wonderful catalogue produced by Ridha Moumni, *L'éveil d'une nation: l'art à l'aube de la Tunisie moderne (1837–1881)* (Milan, 2016).
9. An English translation of this letter is available in Ra'īf Khūrī, *Modern Arab Thought: Channels of the French Revolution to the Arab East* (Princeton, NJ, 1983), 152–7. I am grateful to Professor M'hamed Oualdi for referring me to this text, and for his generous advice on this chapter.
10. Ibid., 156. Perry, who passed on a copy of this letter to the then US

Secretary of State, William Seward, was personally convinced of the truth of this story.

11. Ibid., 155; Perry, *Carthage and Tunis*, 207.

12. I have benefited throughout this section from papers delivered at 'The Global 1860s', a conference held at Princeton University in October 2015. For a panoramic survey of just some of the wars of this period, see Michael Geyer and Charles Bright, 'Global Violence and Nationalizing Wars in Eurasia and America: The Geopolitics of War in the Mid-Nineteenth Century', *Comparative Studies in Society and History* 38 (1996), 619–57.

13. Thomas L. Whigham, *The Paraguayan War: Causes and Early Conduct* (Calgary, AB, 2nd edn, 2018); Geyer and Bright, 'Global Violence', 657.

14. Stephen R. Platt, *Autumn in the Heavenly Kingdom: China, the West, and the Epic Story of the Taiping Civil War* (New York, 2012).

15. Geoffrey Wawro, *The Franco-Prussian War: The German Conquest of France in 1870–1871* (Cambridge, 2003). French and monarchical ambitions in Mexico may have come closer to success than was once thought: see Erika Pani, 'Dreaming of a Mexican Empire: The Political Projects of the "Imperialistas"', *Hispanic American Historical Review* 82 (2002), 1–31.

16. Guy Thomson, *The Birth of Modern Politics in Spain: Democracy, Association, and Revolution, 1854–75* (New York, 2010).

17. Giuseppe Mazzini, 'Europe: Its Condition and Prospects', reprinted in Sandi E. Cooper (ed.), *Five Views on European Peace* (New York, 1972), 443.

18. Leon Carl Brown, *The Tunisia of Ahmad Bey, 1837–1855* (Princeton, NJ, 1974), 303–10.

19. On this Sardinian constitution, see Horst Dippel (ed.), *Executive and Legislative Powers in the Constitutions of 1848–49* (Berlin, 1999), 129–62. Enrico Dal Lago's *The Age of Lincoln and Cavour: Comparative Perspectives on Nineteenth-century American and Italian Nation-building* (New York, 2015) illumines some of the linkages between the multiple conflicts of this era.

20. For a recent exploration, see Natasha Wheatley, 'Law, Time, and Sovereignty in Central Europe: Imperial Constitutions, Historical

Rights, and the Afterlives of Empire' (2016), Columbia University PhD dissertation.

21. See Sophie Gordon, *Shadow of War: Roger Fenton's Photographs of the Crimea, 1855* (London, 2017). Photographic images of episodes in the American Civil War are finely discussed in Drew Gilpin Faust, *The Republic of Suffering: Death and the American Civil War* (New York, 2008).

22. David Nye, 'Shaping Communication Networks: Telegraph, Telephone, Computer', *Social Research* 64 (1997), 1073.

23. For example, Vanessa Ogle, *The Global Transformation of Time: 1870–1950* (Cambridge, MA, 2015).

24. Jay Sexton, 'William H. Seward in the World', *Journal of the Civil War Era* 4 (2014), 398–430.

25. I owe this quotation to my colleague at Princeton, Professor Matthew Karp and thank him for his generous help with this chapter.

26. Olive Risley Seward (ed.), *William H. Seward's Travels around the World* (New York, 1873), 464, 481.

27. For how this trend became more pronounced in some regions at the end of the nineteenth century, see Marilyn Lake and Henry Reynolds, *Drawing the Global Colour Line: White Man's Countries and the International Challenge of Racial Equality* (Cambridge, 2008).

28. Khayr al-Dīn Tūnisī, *The Surest Path: The Political Treatise of a Nineteenth-century Muslim Statesman*, Leon Carl Brown (trans. and intro.) (Cambridge, MA, 1967), 72–3; and for Muslim travellers at this time, see Nile Green, 'Spacetime and the Muslim Journey West: Industrial Communications in the Making of the "Muslim World"', *American Historical Review* 118 (2013), 401–29.

29. Khayr al-Dīn Tūnisī, *The Surest Path*, 94, 110, 162–4.

30. Ibid., 110.

31. Lester J. Cappon (ed.), *The Adams–Jefferson Letters: The Complete Correspondence Between Thomas Jefferson and Abigail and John Adams* (Chapel Hill, NC, 1988), 571; for a different interpretation of the original implications of the constitution, see Sean Wilentz, *No Property in Man: Slavery and Antislavery at the Nation's Founding* (Cambridge, MA, 2018).

32. Sven Beckert, *Empire of Cotton: A Global History* (New York, 2015), especially 199–273.

33. See, for instance, Lincoln's speech in 1854 on how slavery was depriving 'our republican example of its just influence in the world': Stig Förster and Jörg Nagler (ed.), *On the Road to Total War: The American Civil War and the German Wars of Unification, 1861–1871* (Washington DC, 1997), 105.

34. Marshall L. DeRosa, *The Confederate Constitution of 1861: An Inquiry into American Constitutionalism* (Columbia, MI, 1991); the text is to be found at www.avalon.law.yale.edu.

35. Robert E. Bonner, *The Soldier's Pen: Firsthand Impressions of the Civil War* (New York, 2006), 46.

36. Matthew Karp, *This Vast Southern Empire: Slaveholders at the Helm of American Foreign Policy* (Cambridge, MA, 2016), 245.

37. *The Calcutta Review* 37 (1861), 161–93.

38. On antebellum Southern power and change, see Karp, *This Vast Southern Empire, passim.*

39. Förster and Nagler, *On the Road to Total War*, 174; Timothy J. Perri, 'The Economics of US Civil War Conscription', *American Law and Economics Review* 10 (2008), 427.

40. See https://www.archives.gov/publications/prologue/2017/winter/summer-of-1862.

41. The text of this proclamation is available on the US National Archives website at https://www.archives.gov/exhibits/featured-documents/emancipation-proclamation/transcript.html.

42. Steven Hahn, *The Political Worlds of Slavery and Freedom* (Cambridge, MA, 2009), 55–114.

43. For these and other antebellum Black initiatives, see chapter five of Peter Wirzbicki's forthcoming *Higher Laws: Black and White Transcendentalism and the Fight against Slavery.*

44. *The Weekly Anglo-African*, 11 November 1865.

45. Eric Foner, *The Fiery Trial: Abraham Lincoln and American Slavery* (New York, 2010), 330–31.

46. The classic account is Eric Foner, *Reconstruction: America's Unfinished Revolution, 1863–1877* (New York, 2014 edn); and see also his *The Second Founding: How the Civil War and Reconstruction Remade the Constitution* (New York, 2019).

47. Though grassroots Black and white activism played a large part in the retooling of these Southern state constitutions, not just diktats from Washington.

48. For the history of the Māori Representation Act of 1867, see https://nzhistory.govt.nz/politics/maori-and-the-vote. It is also significant that it was in the 1860s that the Treaty of Waitangi between the British Crown and about 540 Māori chiefs began to be styled the 'Maori Magna Carta', not just the 'New Zealand Magna Carta', as before. This 1840 treaty remains deeply controversial. But what is striking about the name change is the implication that Māori inhabitants merited and might possess a rights-giving document analogous to Magna Carta. I owe this information to Dr Geoff Kemp.

49. Richard Carwardine and Jay Sexton (eds.), *The Global Lincoln* (Oxford, 2011).

50. For a brief and sympathetic introduction to the life, see Christopher Fyfe, 'Africanus Horton as a Constitution-maker', *Journal of Commonwealth and Comparative Politics* 26 (1988), 173–84; for Horton's place of origin, see Padraic Scanlan, *Freedom's Debtors: British Antislavery in Sierra Leone in the Age of Revolution* (London, 2017).

51. Cited by E. A. Ayandele in his introduction to James Africanus Beale Horton, *Letters on the Political Condition of the Gold Coast* (London, 1866; 1970 edn), 13.

52. Ibid., 5–35.

53. James Africanus B. Horton, *West African Countries and Peoples, British and Native: With the Requirements Necessary for Establishing Self Government ... and a Vindication of the African Race* (London, 1868), 271–2.

54. James Ciment, *Another America: The Story of Liberia and the Former Slaves Who Ruled It* (New York, 2013). The text of the 1847 Liberia constitution is available at http://crc.gov.lr/doc/CONSTITUTIONOF1847final.pdf.

55. Horton, *West African Countries and Peoples*, 16.

56. 'Circular Introduction' in Horton, *Letters on the Political Condition of the Gold Coast*, vii.

57. Ibid., ii.

58. E. A. Ayandele, 'James Africanus Beale Horton, 1835–1883: Prophet of Modernization in West Africa', *African Historical Studies* 4 (1971), 696.

59. Fyfe, 'Africanus Horton as a Constitution-maker', 176–7.

60. On Blyden and Horton as part of a wider African 'renaissance' at this time, see Meghan Vaughan, 'Africa and the Birth of the Modern World', *Transactions of the Royal Historical Society*, sixth series, 16 (2006), 143–62.

61. John Stuart Mill, *Considerations on Representative Government* (London, 1861; Auckland, NZ, 2009 edn), 239.

62. Horton, *West African Countries and Peoples*, 193.

63. Horton, *Letters on the Political Condition of the Gold Coast*, 71; Fyfe, 'Africanus Horton as a Constitution-maker', 179.

64. James Africanus Beale Horton, *Physical and Medical Climate and Meteorology of the West Coast of Africa* (London, 1867).

65. Horton, *West African Countries and People*, 19–20; Fyfe, 'Africanus Horton as a Constitution-maker', 176.

66. See Rebecca Shumway, 'From Atlantic Creoles to African Nationalists: Reflections on the Historiography of Nineteenth-Century Fanteland', *History in Africa* 42 (2015), 139–64; and for one of these Fante constitutions, see https://www.modernghana.com/news/123177/1/constitution-of-the-new-Fante-confederacy.html.

67. See https://www.modernghana.com/news/123177/1/constitution-of-the-new-Fante-confederacy.html.

68. Horton, *Letters on the Political Condition of the Gold Coast*, 167; Fyfe, 'Africanus Horton as a Constitution-maker', 180.

69. Perkins, *A History of Modern Tunisia*, 32–43.

70. For these events, see Foner, *Reconstruction*, and Richard M. Valelly, *The Two Reconstructions: The Struggle for Black Enfranchisement* (Chicago, IL, 2004), especially 121–48.

71. For an expert summary, see Jürgen Osterhammel, *The Transformation of the World: A Global History of the Nineteenth Century* (Princeton, NJ, 2014), 392–468.

72. On this text, and what led up to it, see Aylin Koçunyan, *Negotiating the Ottoman Constitution, 1839–1876* (Leuven, 2018).

73. Julia A. Clancy-Smith, 'Khayr al-Din al-Tunisi and a Mediterranean

Community of Thought', in her *Mediterraneans: North Africa and Europe in an Age of Migration, c.1800–1900* (Berkeley, CA, 2011), 331.

74. Quoted in Larry J. Griffin and Don H. Doyle (eds.), *The South as an American Problem* (Athens, GA, 1995), 115.

75. Vinay Lal cited in 'Interchange: The Global Lincoln', *Journal of American History* 96 (2009), 472–3.

76. Insufficiently exploited manuscript and printed sources on Horton, and by him, are scattered and thinly spread, but they exist. For a recent reassessment through the lens of medicine, see Jessica Howell, *Exploring Victorian Travel Literature: Disease, Race and Climate* (Edinburgh, 2014), 83–108.

## Chapter Eight: Break Out

1. For this ceremony and its organisation, see Hidemasa Kokaze, 'The Political Space of Meiji 22 (1889): The Promulgation of the Constitution and the Birth of the Nation', *Japan Review* 23 (2011), 119–41.

2. Takamura Kōtarō, 'Kowtow (Promulgation of the Constitution)', quoted in Mikiko Hirayama, 'The Emperor's New Clothes: Japanese Visuality and Imperial Portrait Photography', *History of Photography* 33 (2009), 165.

3. *Commentaries on the Constitution of the Empire of Japan*, Miyoji Itō (trans.) (Tokyo, 1889), 2, 6–7; *The Times* (London), 21 February 1889.

4. For these inventions, see Kokaze, 'The Political Space of Meiji 22 (1889)', *passim*.

5. Carol Gluck, *Japan's Modern Myths: Ideology in the Late Meiji Period* (Princeton, NJ, 1985), 43; in a print for the satirical magazine *Tonchi kyōkai zasshi* (*Journal of the Society of Ready Wit*), Ginkō – breaking free from his official depiction of the event – represented the emperor in the promulgation ceremony as a mere skeleton. This cost him a year in prison.

6. Kokaze, 'The Political Space of Meiji 22 (1889)', 129.

7. For an excellent survey of Japan in this era, see Andrew Gordon, *A Modern History of Japan: From Tokugawa Times to the Present* (Oxford, 4th edn, 2020).

8. Edyta M. Bojanowska, *A World of Empires: The Russian Voyage of the Frigate* Pallada (Cambridge, MA, 2018); for Prussian and German

ambitions in Japan, see Erik Grimmer-Solem, *Learning Empire: Globalization and the German Quest for World Status, 1875–1919* (Cambridge, 2019), 79–118.

9.  I have benefited here from an unpublished essay by my Princeton colleague Professor Federico Marcon, 'The Meiji Restoration of 1868: The Contradictory Nature of a Global Event', and I thank him for his advice on this chapter throughout.

10. Gordon, *A Modern History of Japan*, 78–9.

11. Marcon, 'The Meiji Restoration of 1868'.

12. Fauziah Fathil, 'British Diplomatic Perceptions of Modernisation and Change in Early Meiji Japan, 1868–90' (2006), SOAS PhD dissertation, 133–7.

13. See James L. Huffman, *Creating a Public: People and Press in Meiji Japan* (Honolulu, HI, 1997); and Nathan Shockey, *The Typographic Imagination: Reading and Writing in Japan's Age of Modern Print Media* (New York, 2019).

14. Richard Devine, 'The Way of the King: An Early Meiji Essay on Government', *Monumenta Nipponica* 34 (1979), 49–72.

15. Ibid., 67 and 70.

16. Some of the more patrician projects emerging in Japan at this time are discussed in George M. Beckmann, *The Making of the Meiji Constitution: The Oligarchs and the Constitutional Development of Japan, 1868–1891* (Lawrence, KS, 1957).

17. Amin Ghadimi, 'The Federalist Papers of Ueki Emori: Liberalism and Empire in the Japanese Enlightenment', *Global Intellectual History* 2 (2017), 196 and *passim*.

18. Jennifer Adam and Chris Shadforth, 'Curiosities from the Vaults: A Bank Miscellany', *Bank of England Quarterly Bulletin* (2014), 71–2; for a contemporary photograph of these five men in their newly acquired Western suits and haircuts, see Hanako Murata, '"The Choshu Five" in Scotland', *History of Photography* 27 (2003), 284–8.

19. Takii Kazuhiro, *Itō Hirobumi: Japan's First Prime Minister and Father of the Meiji Constitution*, Takechi Manabu (trans.) (London, 2014), 8 and *passim*. An early and evocative account of Itō written by an admirer, but still worth reading, is Kaju Nakamura, *Prince Ito, The Man and Statesman: A Brief History of His Life* (New York, 1910).

20. See Itō's adept exchange with a journalist in New York, reprinted in

the *Milwaukee Journal* on 4 June 1897, in support of higher education for women and in praise of their position in the United States.

21. See the report by the British consul in December 1871 in Fathil, 'British Diplomatic Perceptions of Modernisation and Change in Early Meiji Japan, 1868–90', 56.

22. Kume Kunitake (compiler), *The Iwakura Embassy, 1871–73: A True Account of the Ambassador Extraordinary & Plenipotentiary's Journey of Observation through the United States of America and Europe*, Martin Collcutt *et al.* (trans.) (5 vols., Princeton, NJ, 2002), I, 219.

23. Quoted in Marius B. Jansen (ed.), *The Cambridge History of Japan Vol. 5: Nineteenth Century* (Cambridge, 1989), 464. By the same token, some African–Americans seem to have drawn inspiration from this and earlier Japanese missions to the United States, and from the challenges to racial segregation and invariable white power they seemed to represent: see Natalia Doan, 'The 1860 Japanese Embassy and the Antebellum African American Press', *Historical Journal* 62 (2019), 997–1020.

24. Beckmann, *The Making of the Meiji Constitution* remains useful as a top-down discussion of this constitution's evolution; see also Junji Banno, *The Establishment of the Japanese Constitutional System*, J. A. A. Stockwin (trans.) (London, 1992).

25. Kazuhiro, *Itō Hirobumi*, 218.

26. Ibid., 48–51, 71–3.

27. Peter van den Berg, 'Politics of Codification in Meiji Japan (1868–1912): Comparative Perspective of Position of Composition of Customary Law in Japanese Civil Code', *Osaka University Law Review* 65 (2018), 69–88.

28. On these changes in elite male clothing over the nineteenth century, see C. A. Bayly, *The Birth of the Modern World, 1780–1914* (Oxford, 2004), 12–17.

29. Quoted in Takii Kazuhiro, *The Meiji Constitution: The Japanese Experience of the West and the Shaping of the Modern State*, David Noble (trans.) (Tokyo, 2007), 55.

30. Useful English-language accounts of Inoue and his ideas include Yoshimitsu Khan, 'Inoue Kowashi and the Dual Images of the Emperor of Japan', *Pacific Affairs* 71 (1998), 215–30; and Joseph

Pittau, 'Inoue Kowashi and the Formation of Modern Japan', *Monumenta Nipponica* 20 (1965), 253–82.

31. Devine, 'Way of the King', 53. Compare this with Itō Hirobumi's own reasoning in 1880: 'If we do not decide the aims of the nation, what will stop popular sentiments from drifting': see Beckmann, *The Making of the Meiji Constitution*, 135.

32. *Commentaries on the Constitution*, iii.

33. Ibid., 36.

34. Ibid., xi, 2.

35. For one of the leading German actors active in Japan, see Johannes Siemes, *Hermann Roesler and the Making of the Meiji State* (Tokyo, 1968).

36. The text of this 1871 German constitution is available in English in James Retallack, 'Forging an Empire: Bismarckian Germany (1866–1890)' at https://ghdi.ghi-dc.org/section.cfm?section_id=10.

37. *Commentaries on the Constitution*, 24, 41.

38. For a recent version of this claim, see 'After 150 Years, Why Does the Meiji Restoration Matter?', *The Economist*, 2 February 2018.

39. Grimmer-Solem, *Learning Empire*, 79–118. I am grateful to Professor Grimmer-Solem for his expert advice on German–Japanese connections.

40. *Commentaries on the Constitution*, 7, and for provisions on the diet, see 9, 14, 18, 68 and 119.

41. Junji Banno, *Japan's Modern History, 1857–1937*, J. A. A. Stockwin (trans.) (London, 2016), 106–73; Hidemasa, 'The Political Space of Meiji 22 (1889)', 128.

42. *Commentaries on the Constitution*, 38–9, 54–5.

43. Kaneko Kentarō, a former personal secretary to Itō, and a member of Japan's House of Peers, writing in *The Century Illustrated Monthly Magazine* 46 (1904), 486.

44. For an impressive account, see Abraham Ascher, *The Revolution of 1905* (Stanford, CA, 2 vols., 1988–92).

45. As the historian Murata Yūjirō puts it, 'the central issues in the political world during the last decade of the Qing were constitutions and parliaments'; see Joshua A. Fogel and Peter G. Zarrow (eds.), *Imagining the People: Chinese Intellectuals and the Concept of Citizenship, 1890–1920* (Armonk, NY, 1997), 131; see also

E-Tu Zen Sun, 'The Chinese Constitutional Missions of 1905–1906', *Journal of Modern History* 24 (1952), 251–69.

46. A recent commentary on the *Dastur-ul Amal* is available at 'Constitution: A Tool of Resistance Today as well as in Colonial Era', Newsd.in (4 February 2020), https://newsd.in/constitution-a-tool-of-resistance-today-as-well-as-in-colonial-era.

47. On the Swaraj Bill and its contexts, see Rohit De, 'Constitutional Antecedents', in Sujit Choudhry *et al* (eds.), *The Oxford Handbook of the Indian Constitution* (Oxford, 2016), 17–37.

48. See Cemil Aydin, *The Politics of Anti-Westernism in Asia: Visions of World Order in Pan-Islamic and Pan-Asian Thought* (New York, 2007).

49. Renée Worringer, 'Comparing Perceptions: Japan as Archetype for Ottoman Modernity, 1876–1918' (2001), University of Chicago PhD dissertation, 99.

50. On this Johor constitution, see Iza Hussin, 'Misreading and Mobility in Constitutional Texts: A Nineteenth Century Case', *Indiana Journal of Global Legal Studies* 21 (2014), 145–58.

51. J. Calvitt Clarke III, *Alliance of the Colored Peoples: Ethiopia and Japan before World War II* (Oxford, 2011).

52. Robert Devereux, *The First Ottoman Constitutional Period: A Study of the Midhat Constitution and Parliament* (Baltimore, MD, 1963), 90. Only two major London newspapers came out in favour of the introduction of this 1876 Ottoman constitution.

53. C. B. Roylance-Kent, 'The New Japanese Constitution', *MacMillan's Magazine* 10 (1894), 420.

54. Denis Twitchett *et al* (eds.), *The Cambridge History of China. Volume 11: Late Ch'ing, 1800–1911, Part Two* (Cambridge, 1980), 348, and see also 339–74 *passim*.

55. Worringer, 'Comparing Perceptions', 289.

56. Kazuhiro, *Itō Hirobumi*, 88.

57. J. E. C. Hymans, 'Why Recognize? Explaining Victorian Britain's Decision to Recognize the Sovereignty of Imperial Japan', *Korean Journal of International Studies* 12 (2014), 49–78.

58. On this conflict, see John W. Steinberg *et al* (eds.), *The Russo-Japanese War in Global Perspective: World War Zero* (Leiden, 2 vols., 2005–7). The Qing dynasty's need to compete militarily with Asian and not just Western aggressors, and consequently to hike up its

taxation levels, was one factor in its belated turn towards constitutionalism. See Stephen R. Halsey, 'Money, Power, and the State: The Origins of the Military-Fiscal State in Modern China', *Journal of the Economic and Social History of the Orient* 56 (2013), 392–432.

59. Aydin, *The Politics of Anti-Westernism in Asia*, 73.
60. Steinberg *et al* (eds.), *The Russo-Japanese War in Global Perspective*, I, 612–13.
61. Worringer, 'Comparing Perceptions', 34, 95 n., 184.
62. Ibid., 290, 324, 369; see also Steinberg *et al* (eds.), *The Russo-Japanese War in Global Perspective*, I, 368–9.
63. Quoted in Worringer, 'Comparing Perceptions', 37.
64. Tiao Min-Ch'ien, *China's New Constitution and International Problems* (Shanghai, 1918), 9.
65. Y. S. Kim, 'Russian and Japanese Diplomatic Responses on Interrogations Records of Ahn Jung-geun', *Korea Journal* 55 (2015), 113–38.
66. Lord Selborne to the Secretary of State, 17 December 1918, British Library IOR Q/27/1, fols. 180–82.

## Epilogue

1. The literature on this conflict is enormous, but for excellent surveys of the global dimensions, see Robert Gerwarth and Erez Manela (eds.), *Empires at War: 1911–1923* (Oxford, 2014); and Hew Strachan, 'The First World War as a Global War', *First World War Studies*, I (2010), 3–14.
2. See David Omissi's *Indian Voices of the Great War: Soldiers' Letters, 1914–18* (New York, 1999); and Santanu Das, *India, Empire, and First World War Culture* (Cambridge, 2018).
3. This is a current scholar's summary of Wells's position at this time: Fupeng Li, 'Becoming Policy: Cultural Translation of the Weimar Constitution in China (1919–1949)', *Journal of the Max Planck Institute of European Legal History* 27 (2019), 211. For the broad significance of Wells, a figure under busy reinterpretation at present, see Sarah Cole, *Inventing Tomorrow: H. G. Wells and the Twentieth Century* (New York, 2019).
4. On the lure and some of the limits of this project, see Susan

Pedersen, *The Guardians: The League of Nations and the Crisis of Empire* (Oxford, 2015).

5. H. G. Wells's essay in this volume, 'The League of Free Nations: Its Possible Constitution' was also published in Canada's *Maclean's Magazine*, I April 1918, and, edited by Walter Lippmann, in *The New Republic* in the United States.

6. H. B. Morse, 'The New Constitution of China', *Journal of Comparative Legislation and International Law*, I (1919), 183–95.

7. For a recent survey, see Yesim Bayar, 'Constitution-writing, Nationalism and the Turkish Experience', *Nations and Nationalism* 22 (2016), 725–43. For all its makers' concern to design and proclaim a new and modern 'Turkishness', like so many constitutions, this 1924 text was something of a pastiche, drawing inspiration especially from the French constitution of 1875 and the Polish 'March' constitution of 1921.

8. On these events, see Charles Townshend, *Easter 1916: The Irish Rebellion* (London, 2015); and, for wider repercussions and connections, Enrico Dal Lago, Róisin Healy and Gearóid Barry (eds.), *1916 in Global Context: An Anti-Imperial Moment* (Abingdon, 2018) and Donal K.Coffey, *Constitutionalism in Ireland, 1932–1938: National, Commonwealth, and International Perspectives* (Cham, Switzerland, 2018).

9. Rohit De, 'Constitutional antecedents', in Sujit Choudry, Madhav Khosla and Pratap Bhanu Mehta (eds.), *The Oxford Handbook of the Indian Constitution* (Oxford, 2016), 17–37.

10. See Rachel G. Hoffman's survey 'The Red Revolutionary Moment: Russia's Revolution and the World', in David Motadel (ed.), *Global Revolution: A History* (forthcoming).

11. Quoted in Geoff Eley, *Forging Democracy: The History of the Left in Europe, 1850-2000* (New York, 2002), 149. Lenin's 1905 leaflet 'Three Constitutions or Three Systems of Government' is available online.

12. George Papuashvili, 'The 1921 constitution of the Democratic Republic of Georgia: Looking Back after Ninety Years', *European Public Law*, 18 (2012), 323–50.

13. E. V. Niemeyer, *Revolution at Querétaro: The Mexican Constitutional Convention of 1916–17* (Austin, Texas, 1974).

14. German History in Documents and Images (GHDI) offers a good translation of the Weimar constitution online.
15. This text, along with other post-war creations, can be found in Howard Lee McBain and Lindsay Rogers, *The New Constitutions of Europe* (Garden City, New York, 1922).
16. Samantha Lomb, *Stalin's Constitution: Soviet Participatory Politics and the Discussion of the 1936 Constitution* (London, 2018).
17. *Grenada Federalist*, 27 October 1915.
18. See, for instance, Daniel T. Rodger, *Atlantic Crossings: Social Politics in a Progressive Age* (Cambridge, MA, 1998).
19. Quoted in Neil S. Siegel, 'Why the Nineteenth Amendment Matters Today: A Guide for the Centennial', *Duke Journal of Gender Law & Policy* 27 (2020), 10.
20. For an illuminating graph showing successive twentieth-century spikes in nation-state creations, see Andreas Wimmer and Brian Min, 'From Empire to Nation State: Explaining Wars in the Modern World, 1816–2001', *American Sociological Review*, 71 (2006), 872.
21. David Armitage, *Civil Wars: A History in Ideas* (New York, 2017), 5.
22. Lawrence W. Beer (ed.), *Constitutional Systems in Late Twentieth Century Asia* (Seattle, 1992), 4.
23. English translations of the text of this Chinese constitution are widely available online.
24. I owe this information to research carried out by Dr Iain Watts.
25. Benedict Anderson, *Imagined Communities: Reflections on the Origin and Spread of Nationalism* (London, revised edn, 1991), 67.
26. See, for instance, the opening lament of Arthur J. Stansbury's *Elementary Catechism on the Constitution of the United States for the Use of Schools* (Boston, MA, 1828).
27. Harshan Kumarasingham, 'Written Differently: A Survey of Commonwealth Constitutional History in the Age of Decolonization', *Journal of Imperial and Commonwealth History* 46 (2018), 874–908.
28. These reports can be accessed at https://freedomhouse.org/countries/freedom-world/scores.
29. Quoted in David N. Mayer, *The Constitutional Thought of Thomas Jefferson* (Charlottesville, VA, 1994), 128.

30. On Putin and the Russian constitution, see the introduction to Adam Chilton and Mila Versteeg, *How Constitutional Rights Matter* (Oxford, 2020).

# ACKNOWLEDGEMENTS

Anyone who embarks on a work of global history necessarily accumulates a particularly wide variety of debts. Throughout the ten years of planning and writing this book, I was sustained throughout by colleagues at Princeton University. Particular thanks go to David Bell, Michael Blaakman, Fara Dabhoiwala, Jacob Dlamini, Yaacob Dweck, Sheldon Garon, Hendrik Hartog, Michael Laffan, Yair Mintzker, Susan Naquin, Philip Nord, Gyan Prakesh, Kim Lane Scheppele and Wendy Warren, each of whom answered questions about different sectors of the world and passed on valuable insights. In addition, Jeremy Adelman, Matthew Karp, Federico Marcon, M'hamed Oualdi, Ekaterina Pravilova, Daniel Rodgers, Robert Tignor and Sean Wilentz were kind enough to read and critique sections of this book in manuscript. So, abundantly and generously, did Eric Foner of Columbia University. The Shelby Cullom Davis Center for Historical Studies, along with Princeton's Law and Public Affairs Program, have been inspirations and treasuries of information throughout.

So, too, have a range of practitioners of global history. I was first introduced to this diverse method of thinking and writing about the past by Paul Kennedy and Jonathan Spence at Yale University, and by conversations on both sides of the Atlantic with John Elliott. Since then, I have benefitted enormously from exchanges with David Armitage, James Belich, the late Chris Bayly, Sebastian Conrad, John Darwin, Natalie Zemon Davis, Andreas Eckert, Masashi Haneda, Tony Hopkins, Maya Jasanoff (who generously read a draft of this book), Rana Mitter, Patrick O'Brien, Jürgen Osterhammel, Emma Rothschild and Sanjay Subrahmanyam, as well as from feedback in too many conferences and workshops to list, but for which I am grateful.

One of the joys and challenges of writing history in this fashion is that you have no choice but to trespass into other peoples' specialist fields. Bruce Ackerman, John Allison, Richard Gordon, Dan Hulsebosch, Harshan Kumarasingham, and the late Anthony Lester helped me to think harder about law, constitutions and power. I also wish especially to thank Jeremy Black, Michael Broers, Rohit De, Rebecca Earle, Antonio Feros, Kieran Hazzard, Peter Holquist, Carol Gluck, Lorenz Gonschor, Jan Jansen, Svante Lindqvist, Aryo Makko, Eduardo Posada-Carbó, Marie-Christine Skuncke, the University of London Bentham Project, and the many people at the University of Tokyo with whom I discussed the Meiji constitution, for their kindness and expertise.

At different stages in the writing of this book, I benefitted from fellowships and stays at the Huntington Library, Pasadena, the Cullman Center for Scholars and Writers at the New York Public Library, the University of Auckland in New Zealand, and from Björn Wittrock's invitation to spend a year at the wonderful Swedish Collegium for Advanced Study in Uppsala. I also benefitted immensely from the award of a Guggenheim Fellowship in constitutional studies made possible by the generosity and enthusiasm of Dorothy Goldman.

The list goes on, because books have to pass through many phases. Numerous undergraduates and graduate students have helped me to develop and sharpen my ideas over the years. Particular mention goes to Charlie Argon, Martha Groppo, Jezzica Israelsson, Samuel Lazerwitz, Matthew McDonald, Felice Physioc, Tom Toelle and Iain Watts who at different times aided my research and translations. Paris Spies-Gans of the Society of Fellows at Harvard University proved, once again, a superb researcher of visual images; while Joseph Puchner, Jeremy Teow and Guy Waller have corrected my proofs with skill and close attention.

As always, my literary agents, Michael Carlisle in New York and Natasha Fairweather in London, have proved wise, supportive and expert in their advice. I have also been immensely lucky in my publishers. Andrew Franklin at Profile and Robert Weil at W. W. Norton/ Liveright are dream editors, who know when to intervene and when to leave alone. In the case of this book, they have also both exhibited a rare and necessary capacity for patience. My deep gratitude to them, as to Cordelia Calvert, Penny Daniel, Sally Holloway, Gabriel Kachuck, Peter Miller, Valentina Zanca and the many others who invested time, work, skill and imagination in this volume.

Last, but emphatically not least, David Cannadine has been an unfailing source of cheer, insight and support. But, then, he has had practice.

LJC

*Princeton, New Jersey, 2020*

# LIST OF ILLUSTRATIONS

1. 'Global deaths in conflicts since the year 1400', Max Roser (2020) 'War and Peace'. Published online at OurWorldInData.org. Retrieved from https://ourworldindata.org/war-and-peace [online resource]
2. Hendrik Kobell after S. Cruys, *Pasqal Paoli* [sic], etching, 1768. © Trustees of the British Museum
3. Jean-Denis Attiret, *Victory at Heluo Heshi*. Etching from *Battle Scenes of the Quelling of Rebellions in the Western Regions, with Imperial Poems*, c.1765–74. John L. Severance Fund 1998.103.4. Image courtesy of the Cleveland Museum of Art
4. 'The form of landing, our troops on the island of Cuba: for the besieging of the Havana, 1762', copper engraving in *London Magazine*, vol. 32 (1763). Courtesy Special Collections, The University of Texas at Arlington Libraries
5. Unknown artist, *Le 1er. Juillet 1801, Toussaint-L'Ouverture, chargés des pouvoirs du peuple d'Haïty et auspices du Tout-puissante, proclame la Gouverneur général, assisté des mandataires légalement convoqués, en présence et sous les Constitution de la république d'Haïty*, lithograph, 1801. Prints and Photographs Division, Library of Congress, LC-DIG-ppmsca-31021
6. Richard Evans, *King Henry Christophe*, oil on canvas, c.1816. Josefina del Toro Fulladosa Collection, Alfred Nemours Collection, University of Puerto Rico, Río Piedras Campus
7. Unknown artist, *The ghost of Christophe ex-King of Hayti, appearing to the Un-Holy Alliance!!*, hand-coloured etching, 1821, published by John Fairburn, London, 1821. © Trustees of the British Museum
8. Unknown artist, *Catherine II Holding her 'Instruction'*, enamel on copperplate, third quarter of the eighteenth century. The State Hermitage Museum, St Petersburg. Photograph © The State Hermitage Museum/photo by Vladimir Terebenin, Natalia Antonova, Inna Regentova

*independence, proclamation, manifesto to the world of the causes which have impelled the said provinces to separate from the mother country; together with the constitution framed for the administration of their government. In Spanish and English*, London, 1812. Rare Book Division, Special Collections, Princeton University Library

21. Oscar Wergeland, *Riksforsamlingen på Eidsvoll 1814 / The National Assembly at Eidsvoll passing the Norwegian Constitution in 1814*, oil on canvas, 1884–85. Teigens Fotoatelier a/s/Stortinget

22. Henry William Pickersgill, *James Silk Buckingham and his wife Elizabeth Jennings in Arab costume of Baghdad 1816*, oil on canvas, 1825. Royal Geographical Society via Getty Images

23. Samuel De Wilde, *The Rajah Rammohan Roy*, drawing, pen and coloured inks and wash, 1826. Photo credit: © Royal Academy of Arts, London

24. Henry Inman, copy after Charles Bird King, *Sequoyah*, oil on canvas, c.1830. National Portrait Gallery, Smithsonian Institution

25. Cherokee nation, *Constitution of the Cherokee nation formed by a convention of delegates from the several districts at New Echota, July 1827*, New Echota, GA, 1827. Courtesy of the Newberry Library, Chicago, VAULT Ayer 251 .C211 1828 Special Collections

26. James Gillray, *The French-Consular-Triumverate settl'ing the New Constitution: with a peep at the constitutional-pigeon-holes of the Abbe Seiyes* [sic] *in the back ground*, hand-coloured etching published by Hannah Humphrey, London, 1800. Courtesy of The Lewis Walpole Library, Yale University

27. Jacques-Louis David, *The Emperor Napoleon in his Study at the Tuileries*, oil on canvas, 1812. National Gallery of Art, Washington DC

28. Title page, *Constitucion Politica de La Monarquía Española, promulgada en Cádiz á 19 de Marzo de 1812 / grabada y dedicada a las Cortes por Dn. José María de Santiago*, Madrid, 1822, engraved by José María de Santiago. Rare Book Collection, Lillian Goldman Law Library, Yale Law School

29. Title page, *Proyecto de constitucion política de la Monarquía Española presentado a las Córtes generales y extraordinarias por su Comisión de constitucion*, Cádiz and Mexico, 1811. Rare Book Collection, Lillian Goldman Law Library, Yale Law School

*original drawings by Lieut.-Colonel Batty*, London, 1831. Rare Book Division, Special Collections, Princeton University Library

42. Nanine Vallain, *La Liberté (Liberty)*, oil on canvas, 1794. Inv. MRF D1986-4. © Coll. Musée de la Révolution française / Domaine de Vizille / Dépôt du Musée du Louvre

43. Jonathan Spilsbury after Katharine Read, *Catharine Macaulay*, mezzotint, 1764. British Prints Collection (GC106); Graphic Arts Collection, Special Collections, Princeton University Library

44. Francisco de Goya y Lucientes, 'Que valor! / What courage!', Plate 7 from *The Disasters of War*, etching, aquatint and drypoint, 1810, published in 1863. The Metropolitan Museum of Art

45. Thomas Crawford, *The Indian: The Dying Chief Contemplating the Progress of Civilisation*, white marble and wood, 1856. Photography © New-York Historical Society

46. Samuel Freeman, *His Majesty Pomarrè, King of Taheite*, stipple print, London, 1821. © Trustees of the British Museum

47. Charles Davidson Bell, *Education in the Early Days at The Cape*, watercolour, n.d. © National Maritime Museum, Greenwich, London

48. Rev. Lorrin Andrews (but in fact produced by some of his Hawaiian pupils), *Hawaiian Costume*, engraving, printed in Hawaii, c.1837–40. © Trustees of the British Museum

49. Unknown photographer, *King Kalākaua*, glass negative, n.d. Prints and Photographs Division, Library of Congress, LC-DIG-ggbain-06548

50. Louis-Augustin Simil, *Portrait of His Highness The Mushir Mohammed Essadek, Bey of Tunis* [Sadok Bey], oil on canvas, 1859. The Diplomatic Reception Rooms, US Department of State, Washington DC

51. Gilbert Stuart, *George Washington (Lansdowne Portrait)*, oil on canvas, 1796. National Portrait Gallery, Smithsonian Institution; acquired as a gift to the nation through the generosity of the Donald W. Reynolds Foundation

52. 'Suspéndu d'une main entre le wagon de bagages ...,' Jules Verne, *Le tour du monde en quatre-vingts jours*, Paris, n.d., illustrations by Alphonse-Marie-Adolphe de Neuville and Léon Benett. General Research Division, The New York Public Library

*flag*, colour woodblock print, koban format, *c*.1904–5. © Trustees of the British Museum

63. Unknown artist, *Sekai no o wa Nippon nari/Japan is King of the World*, colour woodblock print, 1904–5. Advertisement (hikifuda) probably issued at the time of the Russo-Japanese War. The inscription reads: 'Japan is king of the world, The king of flower is cherry blossom, The king of animals is lion, The king of study is this shop'. © Trustees of the British Museum

64. F. A. Modorov, 'Stalin's Report on the Project for a Constitution at the Extraordinary Eighth Congress of the Soviets, 25 November, 1936'/Doklad Stalina na Chrezvychainom VIII s"ezde Sovetov o proekte Konstitutsii, SSSR, oil on canvas, 1937–1938. Digital Library of Staliniana, Archives & Special Collections, University of Pittsburgh Library System

65. Róisín Blade, *Repeal the 8th*, pen and ink, 2016. As the artist puts it: the hands bound in chains represent the struggle for reproductive rights, the ethical dilemma faced by our medical professionals and the threat of a fourteen-year prison sentence. Image courtesy of Róisín Blade

66. Kim Ludbrook, *Mass protests against South Africa President Zuma, Pretoria, 12 April, 2017*, photograph. Kim Ludbrook/EPA/Shutterstock

67. Olga Misik reads from the Constitution of Russia to law enforcement officers during a rally in support of the registration of independent candidates for elections to the Moscow City Duma, on Tverskaya Street, in Moscow. Photograph by Eugene Odinokov, 27 July 2019. Eugene Odinokov/Sputnik via AP Images

# INDEX

Page references for illustrations are in *italics*